Introduction to the Boost C++ Libraries

Volume II – Advanced Libraries

Robert Demming
Daniel J. Duffy

Datasim Education BV

Published by Datasim Education BV, 't Veer 1, 1832 AK Koedijk, The Netherlands

Phone +31 (0)72 2204802

The publisher offers discounts on this book when ordered in quantity. For more information, please contact:
Datasim Education BV
't Veer 1
1832 AK Koedijk
Phone: +31 (0)72 2204802
info@datasim.nl

Visit our home page **www.datasimfinancial.com**

Dutch library
A copy of this book is available from the Dutch Library

ISBN/EAN 978-94-91028-02-1

History:
February 2012:   First printing
July 2012:   Second printing

Table of Contents

Preface

Goals of this Book

The main goal of this book is to discuss approximately twenty C++ libraries in Boost. The libraries deal with topics that should appeal to a wide range of developers. As with Volume I, the approach is hands-on and is based on concrete examples. Furthermore, we have attempted to document the libraries in such a way that the reader can learn each one in a step-by-step manner. This feature in combination with code examples and the additional relationship with Volume I will hopefully ensure that the developer can use the library as building blocks or *glue* in applications.

Structure of the Book

We can group the libraries into categories that are associated with a number of important application areas:

- Special functions in mathematics and orthogonal polynomials.
- Classes for univariate statistical distributions.
- Date and time classes.
- uBLAS: classes for vectors and matrices that have applications in numerical linear algebra.
- asio: synchronous and asynchronous network communication using the socket interface.
- classes for interprocessor communication (IPC) using heavyweight software processes.
- A library for Interval Arithmetic and an interval library (ICL) that can be used in many kinds of management information systems.
- Three chapters explaining the Boost Graph Library (BGL), including numerous examples and applications.
- Several utility libraries for pool memory, circular queues, dynamic bit sets and UUDs.

Each library is described in detail and each chapter contains working code and the full code is provided when you purchase this book.

For whom is this Book?

This book is for C++ developers and programmers who have several years experience with small, medium and large applications. We assume that the reader knows how the object-oriented model is supported in C++ (encapsulation, inheritance, polymorphic functions) and knows STL containers, algorithms and iterators. Working experience with these techniques is assumed. Advanced generics – such as traits and policy based design – will be reviewed in appendices A and B for those readers for whom these topics are new.

In our experience an incremental approach to learning the libraries is best. In particular, concentrating on the most important functionality in each library in the short term is an approach that we recommend. When you have succeeded in compiling and running the code you can then concentrate on optimising it in addition to resolving exceptional and pathological use cases. It is also useful to take examples that relate to your own application area or area of interest.

Ideally, you should be familiar with the libraries that we discuss in Volume I.

Using the Boost Libraries

How can we use these libraries? In general, it is better to use them rather than implementing the same functionality yourself in our opinion. For example, instead of writing code to do string manipulation we prefer to use the String Algo library. Likewise, we use Boost.MultiArray instead of creating our own n-dimensional data structures. Furthermore, the Pareto rule will probably be applicable; a number of libraries will be important in a given software project and for each of these libraries you will see that some classes are more often used than other ones. Finally, we can use the Boost libraries directly in new projects. A second scenario is to replace code by similar Boost code in legacy applications.

The chapters in this book should hopefully appeal to a wide audience. We have resisted discussing more advanced and domain-specific libraries, for example networking, graph and mathematical libraries as well as libraries for advanced data structures, interoperability and advanced parsers. We discuss these libraries in Volume II and their applications to engineering, optimisation, mixed language development (C#, C++/CLI), computer graphics and computational finance.

You can study the chapters in this book in any order because there are few dependencies between them. In order to learn a library we suggest one possible approach. First, you can read the Introduction and Summary sections to get an overview of what a given library has to offer, then you can compile and run the 'Hello World/101' examples to make sure that compiler settings are correct and then you can read the sections in the book that discuss advanced functionality in the library.

Practical Hints and Guidelines

In order to help the reader become acquainted with Boost as quickly as possible we recommend that you download the Boost libraries for Windows/Visual Studio distribution. We also recommend using Microsoft's Visual Studio. Of course, other compilers and development environments can be used but we emphasise that our code was written and tested using Visual Studio 2008 and Visual Studio 2010. Finally, reading Appendices A and B before commencing with chapter 1 will provide you with relevant background knowledge of C++ templates and generic programming concepts.

The full source code becomes available to the owner of this book by completing the (original) Book Registration Form and sending it to Datasim Education. We shall then send you the code. The code is runnable and we have provided Visual Studio projects.

We wish to thank Ilona Hooft Graafland of Datasim Education who produced this book and made it production-ready.

What's Next?

We have documented approximately fifty Boost C++ libraries in Volumes I and II. There is a wealth of functionality in these libraries that developers can deploy in their applications. In order to help accelerate process we will deliver a third volume in this series devoting our attention to using Boost in the design process (in particular, GOF, POSA and parallel design patterns) and to a detailed discussion of creating applications in areas such as engineering, science, computational finance, computer graphics, for example. We adopt a multi-paradigm approach by integrating the object-oriented, generic and functional programming models with the Boost C++ libraries.

We also have produced online audio courses to support Volumes I and II. For more information, please see the latest news and related courses on www.datasim-press.com and www.datasimfinancial.com.

Robert Demming
Daniel J. Duffy

1 The Boost C++ Libraries Overview

1.1 Library Classification

There are approximately one hundred Boost libraries. Each library realises some concern in software development. These concerns are related to a number of software categories as shown in Figures 1.1 and 1.2. In general, a given library addresses one or more concerns and hence can be classified in one or more categories. For convenience, we place each library in one category. We further partition the categories into context-dependent groups that are (in our opinion) useful for applications (the libraries in Figure 1.1) and those libraries that are nonetheless important but which developers may not use on a regular basis (the libraries in Figure 1.2).

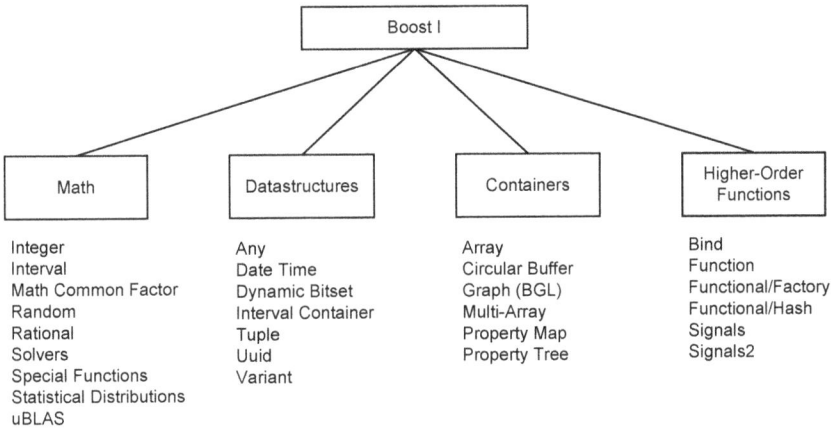

```
                              Boost I

      Math        Datastructures      Containers     Higher-Order
                                                       Functions

Integer          Any                Array            Bind
Interval         Date Time          Circular Buffer  Function
Math Common Factor Dynamic Bitset   Graph (BGL)      Functional/Factory
Random           Interval Container Multi-Array      Functional/Hash
Rational         Tuple              Property Map     Signals
Solvers          Uuid               Property Tree    Signals2
Special Functions Variant
Statistical Distributions
uBLAS
```

Figure 1.1 Essential Libraries

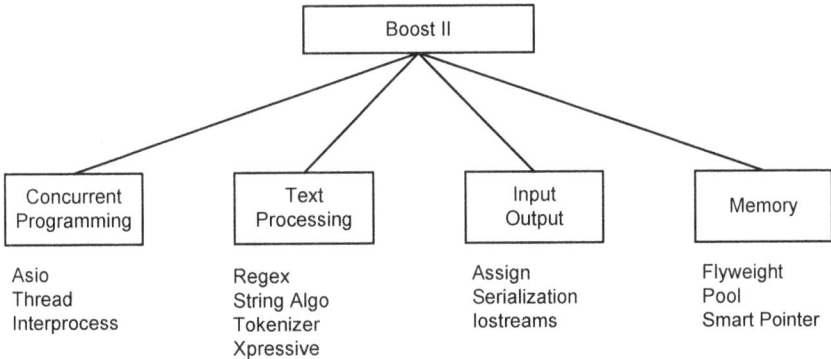

```
                              Boost II

  Concurrent        Text           Input          Memory
  Programming     Processing       Output

Asio             Regex          Assign          Flyweight
Thread           String Algo    Serialization   Pool
Interprocess     Tokenizer      Iostreams       Smart Pointer
                 Xpressive
```

Figure 1.2 Supporting Libraries

We now give a high-level overview of each library in Figures 1.1 and 1.2 and we describe each one in such a way that the reader can determine if the library is useful for the job at hand. Having determined that the library is useful the developer can then examine prototypical examples of use and discussions on the general applicability of the library. For more details on how to use these libraries, see Demming 2010, the current book and the online documentation at www.boost.org.

We stress that the list of libraries in Figures 1.1 and 1.2 does not include all the libraries in Boost. For a complete and up-to-date list we refer the reader to the Boost site www.boost.org.

1.2 Essential Libraries

We now refer to Figure 1.1. The *Math category* contains libraries for a number of topics in applied and numerical mathematics, including:
- Special Functions, for example Bessel, gamma, factorial and error functions.
- Orthogonal polynomials.
- Approximately thirty univariate statistical distributions.
- Matrix library for a range of matrix and vector structures and associated operations.
- Random number generators.
- Support for Interval Analysis.
- Classes to represent integers and rational numbers.
- Functions to compute greatest common divisor and least common multiple of two numbers.
- Non-linear solvers (for example, the Newton-Raphson method).

The libraries in the *Data Structures* category extend the range of capabilities in C++ and they help us to directly use advanced data structures in C++ code. Some of these data structures are fundamental improvements to and replacements for existing structures in C and C++ while others are more advanced and have many applications:
- Any: this class models heterogeneous data; it is a type-safe generalisation of `void*` in C.
- Date and Time: contains a set of generic modules that support a wide range of operations on date and time classes. This library is useful in applications that need dates and time.
- Dynamic BitSet: this class represents a set of bits. The number of bits in instances of this class is dynamic and this number can be set in the constructor. This is in contrast to `std::bitset<N>` for which the number of bits is fixed at compile-time.
- Interval Container: this library has functionality for defining interval sets and maps. It has many applications to scheduling problems.
- Tuple: this class groups a fixed number of objects of different types into one logical whole. It is a sequence of values and it can be seen as a generalisation of `std::pair`.
- Uuid: this is a class that models a universally unique identifier and it can be used in applications in which we wish to assign unique 'tag' numbers to certain objects.
- Variant: a type-safe class that can hold objects of different types and sizes at different times. It is similar to the (unsafe) C *union* but is type-safe.

These data structures are of general applicability and their use promotes code robustness and readability.

The libraries in the *Containers* category are suitable for advanced mathematical applications in which structured data needs to be processed. In the past developers tended to create these data structures themselves or they used proprietary libraries:
- Array: this is an STL-compliant container for fixed-sized (that is, at compile-time) vectors.
- Circular buffer: an STL-compliant container that never overflows. It is used in *producer-consumer* applications.

- Graph (BGL): this library contains a massive amount of functionality for graphs, graph operations and graph algorithms. It has many applications.
- Multi-Array: this library offers functionality for modelling N-dimensional arrays. It can be used in applications in which the concept of n-dimensional geometry plays a role.
- Property Map: Concepts that define interfaces that map key objects to value objects. This library plays an important and supporting role when developing BGL applications.
- Property Tree: this is a tree data structure that is suitable for storing configuration data.

Finally, the libraries in the *Higher-Order Functions* category represent major improvements and extensions to how functions are defined and used in C++ and STL. Furthermore, their use allows us to apply modern design methods to create flexible and extendible software systems:
- Bind: this is a generalisation of bind in STL. It supports arbitrary function objects, function pointers and member function pointers. It also supports function composition and the binding of function arguments.
- Function: this important library implements function object wrappers for deferred calls or callbacks. In general, it is possible to define *delayed functions.*
- Functional/Factory: this library contains function object templates for dynamic and static object creation. It is the Boost equivalent of the Gamma (GOF) Factory Method pattern. One of the disadvantages of OOP patterns is the amount of boilerplate code that needs to be written. Using Functional/Factory we can achieve the same ends with less code and without having to define extra classes.
- Functional/Hash: a hash function that can be extended to hash user-defined types.
- Signals: this is a library that implements *event-notification patterns*, such as the GOF *Observer*, *Mediator* and *Chain of Responsibility*. The difference however, is that Signals is based on a *delegates mechanism* (as we see in C#) rather than using inheritance as is the case with GOF patterns.
- Signals2: This is the thread-safe version of Signals and it implements signals and slot callback mechanisms.

There are many ways to use these libraries in applications, both on a standalone basis and in combination with each other and with libraries for data types and containers.

1.3   Supporting Libraries

The libraries that we discussed in the previous section are of direct relevance to developers in particular libraries for mathematical and higher-order functions are useful. Most of the productivity gains will be realised by using these libraries.

In this section we discuss a number of libraries which certainly do have applications but may be needed on an incidental basis only. We refer to Figure 1.2 and we classify the libraries into four main categories for concurrent and network programming, text and string processing, input-output and memory management.

The libraries that deal with multi-threading and network programming allow developers to create efficient and scalable software systems. The most important libraries are:
- Asio: a portable library for network programming (including sockets) with support for TCP/UDP protocols, IP addressing and name resolution.
- Thread: a library that enables the creation of efficient applications on multi-processor shared memory computers. This library allows the creation of *lightweight processes* or *threads.*

- Interprocess: a library that supports shared memory, memory mapped files, process-shared mutexes, condition variables, containers and allocators. This library enables communication between *heavyweight processes*.

In some cases developers may need to create applications that process text and string data in some way. There are many situations in which text needs to be created, processed and exported to different formats. The libraries in the *Text Processing* category have similarities with activities in compiler theory, lexical analysis and parsing:

- Regex: a library that supports the creation of regular expressions, regular expression matching, searching for strings in a regular expression and replacing matches of a regular expression in a character sequence. In general, this library is used for static (that is, defined at compile-time) regular expressions.
- String Algo: STL has little support for string manipulation. The String Algorithm library fills this gap. It has support for a wide range of text and string manipulation functions.
- Tokenizer: this library allows developers to break a string or other sequence of characters into so-called *tokens*. Examples of tokens are keywords, identifiers and punctuation symbols.
- Xpressive: a library that supports lexical analysis and the creation of regular expression objects. Both static (compile-time) and dynamic (run-time) regular expressions can be created. Nested expressions and semantic actions are also supported. A *semantic action* is a C++ function that is called whenever the parser successfully recognises a portion of the input.

For completeness, we should mention the Boost Spirit library that is an object-oriented, recursive-descent parser and output generation library for C++. It allows developers to write grammars and format descriptions using a format similar to Extended Backus Naur Form (EBNF) directly in C++. This looks like a promising library for new applications.

There are a number of useful libraries to realise input-output:

- Assign: the ability to initialise data in STL containers using comma-separated lists of data. We see this as a *convenience library* and it speeds up development when testing and debugging code. It also makes the code more readable in general.
- Serialization: this library has functionality to save objects and data to *persistent storage* and to reconstruct the original objects from a persistent representation. It supports the serialisation of STL containers and other complex objects. Furthermore, the library supports XML and binary formats.
- Iostreams: this library provides a framework for defining streams, stream buffers and I/O filters.

Finally, Boost has several libraries (the first two of which are rather specialised) that allow developers to control how memory is created and managed, for example:

- Flyweight: this library is an implementation of the GOF *Flyweight* design pattern that manages large numbers of highly redundant objects.
- Pool: pool allocation is a memory allocation scheme that is very fast, but limited in its usage. Using pools gives you more control over how memory is used in a program.
- Smart Pointer: smart pointers are objects that store pointers to dynamically allocated (heap) objects. They behave much like built-in C++ pointers except that they automatically delete the object pointed to at the appropriate time. There are six smart pointer class templates in this library.

We have now completed our short overview of a number of major libraries in Boost. We need to determine if we can use them in applications and if so how to align them to current developer work practices and what the consequences are.

2 Math Toolkit: Special Functions

2.1 Introduction and Objectives

In this chapter we discuss a number of functions that arise in mathematical, physical, financial and engineering applications. These are the *Special Functions* in the Boost Math Toolkit. The functions have a complicated structure and are in many cases expressed as an integral, recurrence relation or possibly as the solution of a differential equation, for example. We use these functions in mathematical and numerical applications and in particular we need to calculate the values of these functions at given points. They are difficult to compute and special algorithms and numerical methods have been created to provide accurate and efficient approximations to them. A number of proprietary libraries exist that support these functions but we choose the Boost version. The Boost Math Toolkit online documentation is extensive and it describes these special functions in great detail and with care.

Our contribution in this chapter is to describe each special function from a number of perspectives:
- The mathematical definition of the function.
- The applicability of the function.
- Implementing the functions and their variations in C++.
- Some examples on using the function.
- Special concerns, for example performance, reliability and accuracy of the implementation of the special function.

The main goal of this chapter is to explain each function in so much detail that the chapter can be used as a compact and detailed reference guide for developers.

In general, the amount of text we need in order to document special functions is minimal because the corresponding mathematical formulae and C++ 'tell it all'. One formulae is worth a thousand words as it were.

2.2 An Overview of the Math Toolkit Special Functions

In this chapter we introduce a number of software modules from the Boost Math Toolkit, for example:
- Gamma and beta functions.
- Beta and Error function.
- Factorials and binomical coefficients.
- Bessel functions.
- Elliptic integrals.
- Other functions, such as the zeta function, exponential integrals and inverse hyperbolic functions.

These functions have many applications in mathematical physics, statistics and engineering. Other applications include the solution of ordinary and partial differential equations, signal processing and eigenvalue analysis. The library supports many of the functionality that these applications need. Using the library in your applications is easy and an advantage is that the code is portable and that you do not have to write your own library. The main goal of this chapter is to get you up to speed with the Math Toolkit as quickly as possible.

We declare following namespace in code:

```
using namespace boost::math;
```

Furthermore, we use the following convenience file. The advantage is that it contains the headers of all special functions in the Toolkit:

```
#include <boost/math/special_functions.hpp>
```

Alternatively, if we are only interested in specific functions (for example, the gamma function) we can be more selective in what we include, for example:

```
#include <boost/math/special_functions/gamma.hpp>
```

2.3   Gamma Functions

The *(true) gamma function* is a generalisation of the well-known *factorial function* and it is undoubtedly one of the most important and widely used functions in probability, statistics and combinatorics. The function involves an integral on the positive half-line and there are several variations.

2.3.1   Gamma Function

The gamma function (sometimes called the *'true' gamma function*) is defined by the integral:

$$\Gamma(z) = \int_0^\infty t^{z-1} e^{-t} dt. \tag{2.1}$$

There are two implementations of this function; the first version (`tgamma`) is generic, slow and reasonably accurate. There is a more efficient implementation (`tgamma1pm1`) that is based on a Lanczos approximation. Examples of use are:

```
// The famous gamma function gamma(n) = (n-1)! for n an integer.
// Slow and accurate.
double d = tgamma(5);
cout << "t gamma: " << d << endl;

double d2 = tgamma(5.01);
cout << "t gamma: " << d2 << endl;

// More accurate, due to Lanczos.
// tgamma1pm1(z) = tgamma(z+1) - 1
double d3 = tgamma1pm1(4);
cout << "t gamma: " << d3 << endl;
```

A special case is when the argument z is an integer (call it n); in that case the gamma function evaluates to a factorial:

$$\Gamma(n) = (n-1)!$$

Regarding implementation, `tgamma` is implemented by combining series and continued fraction representations for the incomplete gamma function that we soon discuss in section 2.3.2. Furthermore, the function `tgamm1pm1(z)` is implemented by a rational function when the variable `z` is in the range (0.5, 2.5).

The *log gamma* function is defined by:

$$l\text{gamma} = \log |\Gamma(z)|. \tag{2.2}$$

There are two implementations of this function; the first form is generic, slow and accurate. There is also a more efficient approximation:

```
// Log gamma function.
double d4 = lgamma(5.0);
cout << "log gamma: " << d4 << endl;
```

It is also possible to calculate the log gamma function that takes an extra integer pointer as argument; if non-null it is set on output to the sign of the gamma function `tgamma`:

```
int sgn;
double d5 = lgamma(5.0, &sgn);
cout << "log gamma with sign: " << d5 << ", " << sgn << endl;
```

The *digamma* (or psi *function*) is the logarithmic derivative of the gamma function and it is defined by:

$$\psi(x) = \tfrac{d}{dx} \log \Gamma(x) = \tfrac{\Gamma'(x)}{\Gamma(x)}. \tag{2.3}$$

There is no generic C++ version of this function and implementations are tuned to accuracy levels; the most precise version has 34 digits of precision. An example of use is:

```
// Digamma.
cout << "Digamma, z = 10: " << digamma(10.0) << endl;
cout << "Digamma, z = 0.01: " << digamma(0.01) << endl;
```

It is possible to define the ratio of gamma functions, for example:

$$\text{tgamma-ratio}(a, b) = \tfrac{\Gamma(a)}{\Gamma(b)}. \tag{2.4}$$

An example of use is:

```
// Ratios of gamma functions.
double a = 1.0; double b = 2.0;
cout << "Gamma ratio: " << tgamma_ratio(a,b) << endl;
```

It is also possible to calculate the ratio of gamma functions based on small perturbations using the following formula:

$$\text{gamma-delta-ratio } \gamma(a, \delta) = \Gamma(a)/\Gamma(a + \delta).$$

The corresponding code is:

```
double delta = -0.5;
a = 40.0;
cout << "Gamma ratio, delta: " << tgamma_delta_ratio(a,delta) << endl;
```

2.3.2   Incomplete Gamma Functions and their Inverses

There are four incomplete gamma functions, two of which are *normalised* (that is, they have values in the closed range [0,1]) and two of which are *unnormalised*. The *normalised lower incomplete gamma function* depending on the parameters a and z is defined by:

$$\text{gamma\_}p(a, z) = P(a, z) = \tfrac{\gamma(a,z)}{\Gamma(a)} = \tfrac{1}{\Gamma(a)} \int_0^z t^{a-1} e^{-t} dt. \tag{2.5}$$

This function changes rapidly from 0 to 1 at the point $z = a$. The gradient is steep.

The *normalised upper incomplete gamma function* of a and z is defined by:

$$\text{gamma\_}q(z) = Q(a, z) = \tfrac{\Gamma(a,z)}{\Gamma(a)} = \tfrac{1}{\Gamma(a)} \int_z^\infty t^{a-1} e^{-t} dt. \tag{2.6}$$

This function changes rapidly from 1 to 0 at the point $z = a$. The gradient is steep.

Some examples on using these functions are:

```
// Normalised incomplete gamma function.
double a1 = 5.0;
double a2 = 10.0;

cout << "Normalised lower incomplete: " << gamma_p(a1, 5.0) << endl;
cout << "Normalised lower incomplete: " << gamma_p(a2, 10.0) << endl;

cout << "Normalised upper incomplete: " << gamma_q(a1, 2.0) << endl;
cout << "Normalised upper incomplete: " << gamma_q(a2, 10.0) << endl;
```

Finally, we remark that these functions require that $a > 0$ and $z >= 0$; if not, a domain_error exception will be returned.

We discuss the *non-normalised lower* and *upper incomplete gamma* functions defined by:

$$\text{tgamma\_lower}(a, z) = \gamma(a, z) = \int_0^z t^{a-1} e^{-t} dt \tag{2.7}$$

and

$$\text{tgamma}(a, z) = \Gamma(a, z) = \int_z^\infty t^{a-1} e^{-t} dt, \tag{2.8}$$

respectively. An example of use is:

```
// Non-normalised incomplete gamma function.
a1 = 5.0;
a2 = 7.5;

cout << "Non-normalised lower incomplete: " << tgamma_lower(a1,5.0);
cout << "Non-normalised upper incomplete: " << tgamma(a2,10.0);
```

We come to the important topic of calculating the *inverses* of the incomplete gamma functions. In other words, we wish to find the abscissa value that corresponds to a given value of an incomplete gamma function. There are two cases (referring to equations (2.5) and (2.6)):

- Given the parameter a and the function value y then compute the abscissa value z; the constraints are that $a > 0$, and that y is in the closed interval $[0,1]$.
- Given the function value y and the abscissa value z then compute the parameter a; the constraints are that $x > 0$ and that y is in the closed interval $[0,1]$.

We take an example of each of these options:

```
// Incomplete gamma function inverses.

// 1. Given y and a, find x.
double y = 0.4;
double a4 = 2.0;
cout << "Inverse, lower gamma I: " << gamma_p_inv(a4, y) << endl;
cout << "Inverse, upper gamma I: " << gamma_q_inv(a4, y) << endl;

// 2. Given y and x, find a.
y = 0.4;
a4 = 2.0;
cout << "Inverse, lower gamma II: " << gamma_p_inva(a4, y) << endl;
cout << "Inverse, upper gamma II: " << gamma_q_inva(a4, y) << endl;
```

These functions are computed internally using iterative methods, for example the Newton-Raphson, Brent or fixed-point algorithms.

Finally, we discuss the *derivative with respect to* z of the normalised incomplete gamma function as given by equation (2.5):

$$\text{gamma\_p\_derivative}\,(a, x) = \tfrac{\partial}{\partial x} P(a, x) = \tfrac{x^{a-1}e^{-x}}{\Gamma(a)}.$$

An example of use is:

```
// Derivative of incomplete gamma function.
a1 = 5.0;
cout << "Derivative normalised lower incomplete: "
     << gamma_p_derivative(a1, 5.0) << endl;
```

The gamma function is of fundamental importance and it is used extensively in many applications.

2.4 Beta and Error Functions

The *beta function* (also known as the *Euler integral*) has applications in probability theory. It is defined in terms of the gamma function:

$$\text{beta}\,(a, b) = B(a, b) = \tfrac{\Gamma(a)\Gamma(b)}{\Gamma(a+b)}. \tag{2.9}$$

The *normalised incomplete beta function* of a, b and x is defined by:

$$\text{ibeta}\,(a, b, x) = I_x(a, b) = \tfrac{1}{B(a,b)} \int_0^x t^{a-1}(1-t)^{b-1} dt. \tag{2.10}$$

The *normalised complement* of the incomplete beta function is defined by:

$$\text{ibetac}(a, b, x) = 1 - I_x(a, b) = I_{1-x}(b, a). \tag{2.11}$$

The full *(non-normalised) incomplete beta function* is defined by:

$$\text{beta}(a, b, x) = B_x(a, b) = \int_0^x t^{a-1}(1-t)^{b-1} dt. \tag{2.12}$$

The equations (2.9) to (2.12) constitute the essential functionality of the Beta functions in Boost. The corresponding C++ functionality is similar in style to that for the gamma function. To this end, we summarise the C++ functions that correspond to each of the above formulae:

```
beta(a,b)
ibeta(a,b,x)
ibetac(a,b,x)
beta(a,b,x)
```

We show some C++ code examples. We note the constraints on the parameters a and b and the value x; the parameters a and b must be positive and the value x must be contained in the closed interval [0,1]. We thus see the need for a *try/catch* block in the following code:

```
// Beta function (a > 0, b > 0).
double a = 10.0; double b = 2.0;
cout << "beta: " << beta(a,b) << endl;
```

```
// Normalised incomplete beta function, x in closed interval [0,1].
double x = 0.3;
cout << "Normalised incomplete beta: " << ibeta(a,b,x) << endl;
cout << "Normalised ibeta,complement: " << ibetac(a,b,x) << endl;

// Non-normalised incomplete beta function, x in closed interval [0,1].
x = 10.25; // !! input outside allowed range.
try
{
    cout << "Non-normalised incomplete beta: " << beta(a,b,x);
    cout << "Non-normalised ibeta, complement: " << betac(a,b,x);
}
catch (std::exception& e)
{
    cout << e.what() << endl;
}
```

Finally, the derivative of the incomplete beta function is given by:

$$\text{ibeta-derivative}\,(a,b,x) = \frac{\partial}{\partial x}I_x(a,b) = \frac{x^{a-1}(1-x)^{b-1}}{B(a,b)}.$$

An example of use in C++ is:

```
// Derivative of incomplete beta function.
double a1 = 2.0; double b1 = 2.0;
double x1 = 0.5;
cout << "Derivative incomplete beta: " << ibeta_derivative(a1,b1,x1);
```

2.5   Incomplete Beta Functions and their Inverses

There are Boost functions to compute the inverse of beta functions. We can compute the inverses of the incomplete beta function and its complement and then one of the variables in the set $\{a, b, x\}$ is output while two of the other variables are input. An example of using these functions is:

```
// Incomplete beta fumction inverses.

// 1. Given y and a, b, find x.
double y = 0.4;
double a4 = 2.0; double b4 = 3.0;
cout << "Inverse, incomplete beta: " << ibeta_inv(a4,b4,y) << endl;
cout << "Inverse, incomplete complement beta:" << ibetac_inv(a4,b4,y);

// 2. Given y and x and 1 parameter, find the other parameter (a or b).
double x = 0.2; y = 0.4;
a4 = 2.0; b4 = 6.0;
cout << "Inverse, incomplete beta: " << ibeta_inva(b4,x,y) << endl;
cout << "Inverse, incomplete complement beta: " << betac_inva(b4,x,y);

cout << "Inverse, incomplete beta: " << ibeta_invb(a4,x,y) << endl;
cout << "Inverse, incomplete complement beta: " << ibetac_invb(a4,x,y);
```

2.6   Factorials and Binomial Coefficients

These functions are of fundamental importance and are used in many areas of mathematics. The most basic formula is the well-known *factorial*:

$$n! = n(n-1)(n-2)\ldots3.2.1.$$

For n < `max_factorial<T>::value` the factorial function is implemented by table look-up; for larger values of n it is implemented using the gamma function `tgamma`. If the parameter n cannot be represented by type `T` an `overflow_error` exception will be raised.

The *double factorial* is defined by :

$$n!! = \begin{cases} n(n-2)\dots 5.3.1, n \text{ odd}, n > 0 \\ n(n-2)\dots 6.4.2, n \text{ even}, n > 0 \\ 1, n = -1, n = 0. \end{cases}$$

The *rising* and *falling factorials* are defined by:

$$\text{rising-factorial}(x,i) = \Gamma(x+i)/\Gamma(x) \qquad (2.13)$$

and

$$\text{falling-factorial}(x,i) = x(x-1)(x-2)(x-3)\dots(x-i+1), \qquad (2.14)$$

respectively. Finally, *binomial coefficients* are defined by the formula:

$$_nC_k = \binom{n}{k} = \frac{n!}{k!(n-k)!}. \qquad (2.15)$$

A code example is:

```
// Factorials.
int n = 3;

try
{
    cout << "Factorial: " << factorial<double>(n) << endl;
    cout << "Unchecked factorial: "
        << unchecked_factorial<double>(n) << endl;
}
catch (exception& e)
{
    cout << e.what() << endl;
}

// Double factorial n!!
try
{
    cout << "Double factorial: " << double_factorial<double>(n);
}
catch (exception& e)
{
    cout << e.what() << endl;
}

// Rising and falling factorials.
try
{
    int i = 2; double x = 8;
    cout << "Rising factorial: " << rising_factorial(x,i) << endl;
    cout << "Falling factorial: " << falling_factorial(x,i) << endl;
}
catch (exception& e)
{
    cout << e.what() << endl;
```

```
    }

    // Binomial coefficients.
    try
    {
        unsigned n = 10; unsigned k = 2;

        cout << "Binomial coefficient: "
            << binomial_coefficient<double>(n,k);
    }
    catch (exception& e)
    {
        cout << e.what() << endl;
    }
```

2.7   The Error Function and its Inverse

The *error function* is another important function. It has numerous applications in probability, statistics and partial differential equations.

The error function is defined by:

$$\mathrm{erf}\,(z) = \tfrac{2}{\sqrt{\pi}} \int_0^z e^{-t^2}\,dt.$$

(2.16) (a)

The complement of the error function is defined by:

$$\mathrm{erfc}(z) = 1 - \mathrm{erf}\,(z).$$

(2.16) (b)

A code snippet is:

```
// Error function.
double z = 2.75;
cout << "Error function: " << erf(z) << endl;
z = -3.0;
cout << "Error function: " << erf(z) << endl;

// Complement of error function.
z = 2.75;
cout << "Error function, complement: " << erfc(z) << endl;
z = -3.0;
cout << "Error function, complement: " << erfc(z) << endl;
```

We can compute the inverse of the error function and the inverse of its complement. In other words, we find the value z in the two equations (2.16)(a) and (2.16)(b) above given the value of the function. The following code gives a typical example of use:

```
double u = 0.5;
try
{
    // The variable 'u' must be in range (-1,1) CHECK ERROR MESSAGE.
    cout << "erf inverse: " << erf_inv(u) << endl;
    cout << "erf inverse: " << erf_inv(u - 1.0) << endl;

    // The variable 'u' must be in range (0,2) CHECK ERROR MESSAGE.
    cout << "erfc inverse: " << erfc_inv(u) << endl;
    cout << "erfc inverse: " << erfc_inv(1.99999) << endl;
}
catch (const std::exception& e)
{
    cout << e.what() << endl;
}
```

2.8   Bessel Functions

The *Bessel function* is a solution to *Bessel's ordinary differential* equation:

$$z^2 \frac{d^2u}{dz^2} + z\frac{du}{dz} + (z^2 - \nu^2)u = 0 \tag{2.17}$$

where ν is called the *order* of the differential equation. Since this is a second order equation it has two solutions, one of which is given by the *Bessel function of the first kind*:

$$J_\nu(z) = \left(\frac{z}{2}\right)^\nu \sum_{k=0}^\infty \frac{\left(-\frac{z^2}{4}\right)^k}{k!\Gamma(\nu + k + 1)}. \tag{2.18}$$

The Bessel functions are valid for any complex number z. A special case is when this number z is purely imaginary and then the solution satisfies the ordinary differential equation:

$$z^2 \frac{d^2u}{dz^2} + z\frac{du}{dz} - (z^2 + \nu^2)\, u = 0. \tag{2.19}$$

The solutions to this equation are known as the *modified Bessel functions of the first and second kind* and are given by:

$$I_\nu(z) = \left(\frac{z}{2}\right)^\nu \sum_{k=0}^\infty \frac{\left(\frac{z^2}{4}\right)^k}{k!\Gamma(\nu + k + 1)} \tag{2.20}$$

and by

$$K_\nu(z) = \frac{\pi}{2}\left(\frac{I_{-\nu}(z) - I_\nu(z)}{\sin(\nu\pi)}\right), \tag{2.21}$$

respectively.

The *spherical Bessel function* satisfies the ordinary differential equation:

$$z^2 \frac{d^2u}{dz^2} + 2z\frac{du}{dz} + \left[(z^2 - n(n + 1)\right] u = 0. \tag{2.22}$$

The two linearly independent solutions of equation (2.22) are given by:

$$j_n(z) = \sqrt{\frac{\pi}{2z}} J_{n+1/2}(z) \tag{2.23}$$

and

$$y_n(z) = \sqrt{\frac{\pi}{2z}} Y_{n+1/2}(z), \tag{2.24}$$

respectively.

Finally, the *Bessel function of the second kind* is given by:

$$Y_\nu(z) = \frac{J_\nu(z)\cos(\nu\pi) - J_{-\nu}(z)}{\sin(\nu\pi)}.$$

(2.25)

We now give code examples on how the Math Toolkit implements the above functions. The code is straightforward and easy to understand. For completeness, we include error-catching code for the cases of overflow/underflow and when using incorrect input arguments:

```
int main()
{
    double x = 1.0; double v = 1.1; int n = 2;

    // Bessel function of first kind.
    try
    {
        cout << "Bessel, first kind: " << cyl_bessel_j(x,v) << endl;
        cout << "Bessel, first kind: " << cyl_bessel_j(x,n) << endl;
    }
    catch (const std::exception& e)
    {
        cout << e.what() << endl;
    }

    // Bessel function of second kind.
    try
    {
        cout << "Bessel, second kind: " << cyl_neumann(x,v) << endl;
        cout << "Bessel, second kind: " << cyl_neumann(x,n) << endl;
    }
    catch (const std::exception& e)
    {
        cout << e.what() << endl;
    }

    // Modified Bessel function of first kind.
    try
    {
        cout << "Modified Bessel, first kind: "
            << cyl_bessel_i(v,x) << endl;       // i because I form.
        cout << "Modified Bessel, first kind: "
            << cyl_bessel_i(n,x) << endl;
    }
    catch (const std::exception& e)
    {
        cout << e.what() << endl;
    }

    // Modified Bessel function of second kind.
    try
    {
        cout << "Modified Bessel, second kind: "
            << cyl_bessel_k(v,x) << endl;
        cout << "Modified Bessel, second kind: "
            << cyl_bessel_k(n,x) << endl;
    }
    catch (const std::exception& e)
    {
        cout << e.what() << endl;
    }

    try
    {
        // Spherical Bessel function of first kind.
        cout << "Spherical Bessel, first kind: "
            << sph_bessel(n,x) << endl;
```

```
        // Spherical Bessel function of second kind.
        cout << "Spherical Bessel, second kind: "
            << sph_neumann(n,x) << endl;
    }
    catch (const std::exception& e)
    {
        cout << e.what() << endl;
    }

    return 0;
}
```

2.9 Elliptic Integral Functions

In this section we discuss elliptic integral functions which have many applications.

2.9.1 Elliptic Integrals of the First, Second and Third Kinds

The definition of an *elliptic integral* is as follows: let $R(x, y)$ be a *rational function* of x and y (that is, it is a quotient of two polynomials in x and y). Then the integral:

$$\int R(x, y) dx$$

is called an *elliptic integral*.

The *incomplete elliptic integral of the first kind (Legendre form)* is defined by:

$$F(\varphi, k) = \int_0^\varphi \frac{d\theta}{\sqrt{1 - k^2 \sin^2 \theta}} \tag{2.26}$$

while the *incomplete elliptic integral of the second kind (Legendre form)* is defined by:

$$E(\varphi, k) = \int_0^\varphi \sqrt{1 - k^2 \sin^2 \theta} d\theta. \tag{2.27}$$

The *incomplete elliptic integral of the third kind (Legendre form)* is defined by:

$$\prod(n, \varphi, k) = \int_0^\varphi \frac{d\theta}{(1 - n \sin^2 \theta) \sqrt{1 - k^2 \sin^2 \theta}}, \quad k = \sin \alpha, \quad |k| \leq 1. \tag{2.28}$$

2.9.2 Complete Elliptic Integrals

The *complete elliptic integrals of the first, second and thirds forms (all Legendre forms)* are defined by:

$$K(k) = F(\pi/2, k) = \int_0^{\pi/2} \frac{d\theta}{\sqrt{1 - k^2 \sin^2 \theta}} \tag{2.29},$$

$$E(k) = E(\pi/2, k) = \int_0^{\pi/2} \sqrt{1 - k^2 \sin} d\theta \tag{2.30}$$

and

$$\prod(n, k) = \prod(n, \pi/2, k) = \int_0^{\pi/2} \frac{d\theta}{(1 - n \sin^2 \theta) \sqrt{1 - k^2 \sin^2 \theta}}. \tag{2.31}$$

We now give some test code to show how to use these functions:

```
int main()
{
    // (Carlson) Elliptic Integral function of first kind.
    double x = 1.0; double y = 1.1; double z = 3.0;
    try
    {
        cout << "Elliptic Integral, first kind: "
            << ellint_rf(x,y,z) << endl;
    }
    catch (const std::exception& e)
    {
        cout << e.what() << endl;
    }

    // Elliptic Integral function of second kind.
    try
    {
        cout << "Elliptic Integral, second kind: "
            << ellint_rd(x,y,z) << endl;
    }
    catch (const std::exception& e)
    {
        cout << e.what() << endl;
    }

    // Elliptic Integral function of third kind.
    double p = 4.7;
    try
    {
        cout << "Elliptic Integral, third kind: "
            << ellint_rj(x,y,z,p) << endl;
    }
    catch (const std::exception& e)
    {
        cout << e.what() << endl;
    }

    // Elliptic integral of first kind, Legendre form.
    try
    {
        cout << "Elliptic Integral, first kind: "
            << ellint_1(x,y) << endl;
    }
    catch (const std::exception& e)
    {
        cout << e.what() << endl;
    }

    x = 0.95; // Must be in (-1,1)
    try
    {
        cout << "Elliptic Integral, first kind: " << ellint_1(x) << endl;
    }
    catch (const std::exception& e)
    {
        cout << e.what() << endl;
    }

    // Elliptic integral of second kind, Legendre form.
    try
    {
        cout << "Elliptic Integral, second kind: "
```

```
                            << ellint_2(x,y) << endl;
    }
    catch (const std::exception& e)
    {
        cout << e.what() << endl;
    }

    x = 0.95; // Must be in (-1,1)
    try
    {
        cout << "Elliptic Integral, second kind: "
             << ellint_2(x) << endl;
    }
    catch (const std::exception& e)
    {
        cout << e.what() << endl;
    }

    return 0;
}
```

2.10 Other Functions

We now give a short introduction to other functions in the Math Toolkit.

2.10.1 Zeta Function

The Riemann *zeta function* of z is defined by the infinite series:

$$\varphi(z) = \sum_{k=1}^{\infty} \frac{1}{k^z}. \tag{2.32}$$

A code example is given by:

```
double z = 2.0;
cout << "Value: " << zeta<double>(z) << endl;
```

2.10.2 Exponential Integrals

The *exponential integral* is defined by:

$$E_n(x) = \int_1^{\infty} \frac{e^{-xt} dt}{t^n} \tag{2.33}$$

and a specialisation is defined by:

$$Ei(x) = \int_{-x}^{\infty} \frac{e^{-t} dt}{t}. \tag{2.34}$$

2.10.3 Inverse Hyperbolic Functions

The *hyperbolic cosine* and *sine* functions are defined by:

$$\cosh(x) = \frac{e^x + e^{-x}}{2} \tag{2.35}$$

and

$$\sinh(x) = \frac{e^x - e^{-x}}{2}, \tag{2.36}$$

respectively.

Their inverses are defined by:

$$\mathrm{acosh}(x) = \log(x + \sqrt{x^2 - 1}) \qquad (2.37)$$

and

$$\mathrm{asinh}(x) = \log(x + \sqrt{x^2 + 1}), \qquad (2.38)$$

respectively.

A code example is:

```
// Inverse hyperbolic cosine, sine, tan functions.
double x = 3.0;
try
{
    cout << "Inverse hyperbolic cosine function: "
         << acosh(x) << endl;
}
catch (const std::exception& e)
{
    cout << e.what() << endl;
}

// etc. similar for asinh & atanh.
```

2.11 Sinus Cardinal and Hyperbolic Sinus Cardinal Functions

The *Sinus Cardinal family of functions* based on the parameter $a > 0$ is defined by:

$$\mathrm{sinc}_a(x) = \frac{\sin(\pi x/a)}{\pi x/a}. \qquad (2.39)$$

The *Hyperbolic Sinus Cardinal family of functions* based on the parameter $a > 0$ is defined by:

$$\mathrm{sinhc}_a(x) = \frac{\sinh(\pi x/a)}{\pi x/a}. \qquad (2.40)$$

The corresponding C++ code is:

```
// Sinus Cardinal Integral.
double x = 3.0;
try
{
    cout << "Sinus Cardinal: " << sinc_pi(x) << endl;
}
catch (const std::exception& e)
{
    cout << e.what() << endl;
}

// Hyperbolic Sinus Cardinal Integral.
try
{
    cout << "Hyperbolic Sinus Cardinal: " << sinhc_pi(x) << endl;
}
catch (const std::exception& e)
{
    cout << e.what() << endl;
}
```

2.12 Rounding, Truncation and Integer Conversions

We discuss a number of issues whose introduction into code will improve its robustness and general accuracy:

- Rounding, truncation and integer conversion.
- Floating-point classification: infinities and NaNs (Not a Number).
- Floating-point representation distance (ULP).

We now discuss each of these topics in turn. Our objective is to give a global overview of the functionality that the Math Toolkit offers.

Rounding functions return the closest integer to a given argument. If the input argument is non-finite or outside the range of the return type an exception of type `boost::math::rounding_error` will be thrown. An example of use is:

```
double d = -2.344;
TestRounding(d);  // Output is -2,-2,-2,-2.

double d2 = 2.5;
TestRounding(d2); // Output 3,3,3,3.

// Exceptional case; an exception will be thrown.
double d3 = 1e20;
try
{
    TestRounding(d3);  // CANNOT CAST TO int.
}
catch (const std::exception& e)
{
    cout << e.what() << endl;
}
```

where we have defined the function:

```
#include <boost/math/special_functions/round.hpp>

template <typename T>
void TestRounding(const T& t)
{
    cout << "round: " << round(t) << endl;
    cout << "iround: " << iround(t) << endl;
    cout << "lround: " << lround(t) << endl;
    cout << "llround: " << llround(t) << endl;
}
```

The truncation functions round an argument to that integer value nearest to it but no larger in magnitude than the argument. If the input argument is non-finite or outside the range of the return type an exception of type `boost::math::rounding_error` will be thrown. For convenience, we use `std::exception` in the following code. An example of use is:

```
#include <boost/math/special_functions/trunc.hpp>

template <typename T>
void TestTruncation(const T& t)
{
    cout << "trunc: " << trunc(t) << endl;
    cout << "itrunc: " << itrunc(t) << endl;
    cout << "ltrunc: " << ltrunc(t) << endl;
    cout << "lltrunc: " << lltrunc(t) << endl;
}
```

```
int main()
{
    double d = -2.344;
    TestTruncation(d);  // Output is -2,-2,-2,-2.

    double d2 = 2.5;
    TestTruncation(d2); // Output 2,2,2,2.

    // Exceptional case.
    double d3 = 1e20;
    try
    {
        TestTruncation(d3);  // CANNOT CAST TO int.
    }
    catch (const std::exception& e)
    {
        cout << e.what() << endl;
    }

    return 0;
}
```

The *modf* functions store the integer part of the function argument and they return the fractional part of the argument. There are several overloaded versions that operate on int and long, for example. We give a representative example:

```
#include <boost/math/special_functions/modf.hpp>

template <typename T>
void TestSplitting(const T& t)
{
    // Integer and fractional parts.
    int i_part = 0; double fi_part;
    long l_part = 0; double fl_part;

    fi_part = modf(t, &i_part);
    cout << "Integer part: " << i_part << ", fractional part: "
        << fi_part << endl;

    fl_part = modf(t, &l_part);
    cout << "Long part: " << l_part << ", fractional part: "
        << fl_part << endl;
}

int main()
{
    double d = -2.344;
    TestSplitting(d);  // Output: (-2, 0.344)

    double d2 = 2.5;
    TestSplitting(d2); // Output: (2, 0.5)

    return 0;
}
```

We now discuss a number of functions that classify a numerical quantity, for example if it is infinite/non-infinite, not a number or whether it is denormalised. These provide the same functionality as the macros (with the same name) in the C99 standard. We encapsulate this functionality in a function:

```
#include <boost/math/special_functions/fpclassify.hpp>

template <typename T>
void Classify(const T& t)
```

```
{
    cout << "\nClassify the number: " << t << endl;
    cout << boolalpha << "Is finite (not +- infinity): "
        << isfinite(t) << endl;
    cout << boolalpha << "Is NaN: " << isnan(t) << endl;
    cout << boolalpha << "Is normalsed: " << isnan(t) << endl;
}
```

A test program which you can run and whose output you can test:

```
double d = -2.344;
Classify(d);

double d2 = std::numeric_limits<double>::infinity();
Classify(d2);

double d3 = std::numeric_limits<double>::max();
Classify(d3);

double d4 = std::numeric_limits<double>::quiet_NaN();
Classify(d4);
```

The final topic is concerned with the representation and comparison of numeric quantities. The *Unit of Least Precision (ULP)* (also known as the *Unit in the Last Place*) is the gap between two different – but as close as possible – floating point numbers. In general, we are interested in finding adjacent greater and lesser floating-point values as well as estimating the number of gaps between two given floating-point values. To this end, we discuss the function nextafter(x, y) that returns the next representable value after x in the direction y. The functions float_next(x) and float_prior(x) give the next representable value that is greater than x and less than x, respectively. The function float_distance(x,y) gives the number of ULP gaps between the floating-point numbers x and y. Finally, the function float_advance(x, i) advances the floating-point number x by a specific number of gaps i.

The following code shows the use of these functions:

```
#include <boost/math/special_functions/next.hpp>

using namespace boost::math;

int main()
{
    cout.precision(20);

    // The nextafter function.
    double x = 2.344; double y = 2.2;
    cout << "Next after " << x << " in direction "
        << y << " is " << nextafter(x,y) << endl;

    y = std::numeric_limits<double>::max();
    cout << "Next after " << x << " in direction "
        << y << " is " << nextafter(x,y) << endl;

    y = std::numeric_limits<double>::min();
    cout << "Next after " << x << " in direction "
        << y << " is " << nextafter(x,y) << endl;

    // Next representable value greater than x.
    cout << "Next value: " << float_next(x) << endl;

    // Previous representable value greater than x.
    cout << "Previous value: " << float_prior(x) << endl;
```

```
// Stress test.
x = std::numeric_limits<double>::max();
cout << "Max: " << x << endl;

cout << "Previous value: " << float_prior(x) << endl;


double val = 1.98;
double upper = 4.0;

// Number of ULP gaps (distance) between 2 floating point numbers.
cout << "Float distance, prior -1: "
    << float_distance(float_prior(val), val) << endl;
cout << "Float distance, next +1: "
    << float_distance(float_next(val), val) << endl;
cout << "Float distance, next +1: "
    << float_distance(val, val) << endl; // +1

cout << "Distance with advance 1: "
    << float_distance(float_advance(val,2),upper) << endl;
cout << "Distance with advance 2: "
    << float_distance(float_advance(val,-2),upper) << endl;

double xA = 3.1415;
cout << "Advance -100 gaps from "<<xA<<": " <<
        float_advance(xA, -100) << endl;

try
{
    // Gives overflow error.
    cout << "Next value: " << float_next(x) << endl;
}
catch (exception& e)
{
    cout << e.what() << endl;
}

return 0;
}
```

The output from this code is:

```
Next after 2.3439999999999999 in direction 2.2000000000000002 is
2.3439999999999994
Next after 2.3439999999999999 in direction 1.7976931348623157e+308 is
2.3440000000000003
Next after 2.3439999999999999 in direction 2.2250738585072014e-308 is
2.3439999999999994
Next value: 2.3440000000000003
Previous value: 2.3439999999999994
Max: 1.7976931348623157e+308
Previous value: 1.7976931348623155e+308
Float distance, prior -1: 1
Float distance, next +1: -1
Float distance: 0
Distance with advance 1: 4593671619917904
Distance with advance 2: 4593671619917908
Distance with advance 3: 3.1414999999999558
Error in function float_next<double>(double): Overflow Error
```

Policies are compile-time mechanisms for customising the behaviour of special functions and statistical distributions. In this chapter we did not discuss these issues and instead we accept the default settings:

- *Domain errors*: throws a `domain_error` exception.
- *Pole error*: occurs when a function that we evaluate at a pole throws a `domain_error` exception.
- *Overflow error*: throws an `std::overflow_error` exception.
- *Underflow error*: ignore the underflow and return zero.
- *Denormalised result*: ignores the fact that the result is denormalised.
- *Rounding error*: throws a `boost::rounding_error` exception.
- *Internal Evaluation Error*: throws a `boost::math::evauation_error` exception.

In general, these defaults are probably sufficient for most applications but you may wish to customise them under certain circumstances.

2.13 Applications and Relationships with STL and Boost

The main goal of this chapter was to introduce the special functions in the Math Toolkit and to show how to call the corresponding functions in C++. Developers can use the functionality in applications and to this end we can brainstorm about integrating the functionality with other Boost, STL and user-defined libraries. The rationale for doing this could be for functionality, suitability or efficiency reasons. Some scenarios are:

- Creating data structures containing data that has been generated from Math Toolkit function calls, for example multi-arrays, vectors and matrices from uBLAS.
- Improving performance by using parallel design patterns (Mattson 2005) in combination with the Boost Thread library (or OpenMP).
- Serialisation of generated data.

We shall discuss some of these issues in this book and in future work.

2.14 Summary and Conclusions

We have given an introduction to the special functions in the Boost Math Toolkit, in particular the family of gamma functions, factorials and binomial coefficients, beta functions, error functions, Bessel functions, elliptic integrals and some other classes of functions.

3 Math Toolkit: Orthogonal Functions

3.1 Introduction and Objectives

In this relatively short chapter we continue our discussion of Special Functions in the Math Toolkit by introducing the class of Orthogonal Polynomials. Most of the names of these polynomials stem from their creators and the list reads like a who's-who of mathematical physics: Jacobi, Legendre, Hermite, Chebychev and Laguerre, to name a few. There are various ways to define and represent these polynomials and we shall discuss these representations for a number of orthogonal polynomials. We also show how these polynomials are implemented in Boost.

Orthogonal polynomials have many applications in mathematical physics, numerical analysis, atomic and quantum physics. The main goal is to develop enough of theory and its realisation in Boost and to serve as a foundation for more extended applications.

We employ a simple visualisation package for Excel that we use to display groups. For an example, see Figure 3.1. The source code is made available to you.

3.2 An Introduction to Orthogonal Polynomials

In this chapter we give an introduction to the theory of *orthogonal polynomials* and we discuss how a number of them are supported in the Boost Math Toolkit. We give some simple examples of use in order to motivate further investigations.

The main polynomial types are:
- *Legendre* (and *associated Legendre*) *polynomials*: these occur when solving the *Laplace equation* in spherical coordinates and they have applications in potential theory.
- *Hermite polynomials*: these have applications to probability theory, physics and quantum mechanics.
- *Laguerre polynomials*: these have applications to quantum mechanics, for example solving the radial part of the *Schrödinger equation*.
- *Spherical Harmonics*: these represent the angular part of the solution to the Laplace equation. They also have many applications to atomic physics and three-dimensional computer graphics.

These polynomials are supported in the Math Toolkit and we shall give some C++ code examples later in this chapter. For completeness, we summarise some of the other kinds of orthogonal polynomials:
- *Chebychev polynomials*: these have applications to *approximation theory* because the roots of Chebychev polynomials of the first kind are used as nodes in polynomial interpolation and applications to the Clenshaw-Curtis quadrature formula, for example.
- *Jacobi polynomials*: these are used in numerical integration.
- *Gegenbauer polynomials*: these are also known as ultraspherical polynomials. They are generalisations of Legendre and Chebychev polynomials and at the same time are a special case of Jacobi polynomials. They have applications to potential theory and harmonic analysis.

For more information on orthogonal polynomials, see Davis 1975 and Press 2002.

3.3 Common Properties

All the orthogonal polynomials can be characterised by certain properties which are in fact equivalent representations of these polynomials. The most general type is the Jacobi orthogonal polynomials and the others can be defined in terms of it by parameter specialisation. In general, we can describe all orthogonal polynomials as follows:

a) The name of the polynomial.
b) The symbol we use to represent the polynomial.
c) The interval in which the polynomial's independent variable is defined (in most cases it is the closed interval [-1,1]).
d) The polynomial's weight function w(x).
e) The normalisation of the polynomial.
f) The Euclidean norm of the polynomial and orthogonality property.
g) An explicit expression for the polynomial.
h) The recurrence relationship to define the polynomial.
i) The differential equation that describes the behaviour of the polynomial.
j) *Rodrigues' formula* that gives an explicit representation for the polynomial in terms of higher-order derivatives of a polynomial.
k) The generating function (a formal power series representation based on the polynomial).
l) Bounds on the absolute value of the polynomial.

Each kind of polynomial has its own entries for the properties (a) to (l). Due to the scope of this book we are unable to discuss these entries for all orthogonal polynomials and instead we restrict our attention to the Legendre orthogonal polynomials. We discuss each of the above properties although not in the same order as above.

The *Legendre functions* of the first kind are solutions to the *Legendre's differential equation*:

$$\frac{d}{dx}\left[(1-x^2)\frac{d}{dx}P_n(x)\right] + n(n+1)P_n(x) = 0. \tag{3.1}$$

We can solve this differential equation using the standard power series method and in general it has regular singular points at $x = -1$ and at $x = 1$. We define the normalisation factor $P_n(1) = 1$. The weight function is identically equal to 1.

Each Legendre polynomial is an nth-order polynomial defined by *Rodrigues' formula*:

$$P_n(x) = \frac{(-1)^n}{2^n n!}\frac{d^n}{dx^n}\left[(1-x^2)^n\right]. \tag{3.2}$$

The differential equation that is satisfied by the polynomial is given by:

$$(1-x^2)\frac{d^2y}{dx^2} - 2x\frac{dy}{dx} + n(n+1)y = 0$$

$$y = P_n(x). \tag{3.3}$$

This is in fact the differential equation (3.1) in *non-conservative form*. The *recurrence relationship* that defines Legendre polynomials is given by:

$$(n+1)P_{n+1}(x) = (2n+1)xP_n(x) - nP_{n-1}(x), \quad n \geq 1$$

$$P_0(x) = 1, \quad P_1(x) = x. \tag{3.4}$$

Some terms are:

$$P_2(x) = \tfrac{1}{2}(3x^2 - 1)$$

$$P_3(x) = \tfrac{1}{2}(5x^3 - 3x).$$

(3.5)

The Legendre polynomials are *orthogonal* on the interval $[-1, +1]$ by which we mean:

$$\int_{-1}^{+1} P_m(x)P_n(x)dx = \left\{ \begin{array}{l} 0 \text{ if } m \neq n \\ \frac{2}{2n+1} \text{ if } m = n. \end{array} \right.$$

(3.6)

The *generating function* is given by:

$$\sum_{n=0}^{\infty} P_n(x)t^n = \frac{1}{\sqrt{1 - 2xt + t^2}}.$$

(3.7)

This function is useful in potential theory when computing multipole expansions. Finally, we see that the absolute value of the Legendre polynomial is bounded by 1 in absolute value:

$$|P_n(x)| \leq 1 \,\forall x \in [-1, 1].$$

(2.8)

Boost distinguishes between Legendre polynomials of the first and second kinds. The latter are also solutions of the differential equation (3.1). We give the first three terms:

$$\text{Legendre: } q(0, x) = Q_0(x) = \tfrac{1}{2} \log \left(\tfrac{1+x}{1-x} \right)$$

$$Q_1(x) = \tfrac{x}{2} \log \left(\tfrac{1+x}{1-x} \right) - 1$$

$$Q_2(x) = \tfrac{3x^2-1}{4} \log \left(\tfrac{1+x}{1-x} \right) - \tfrac{3x}{2}.$$

(3.9)

Finally, the *associated Legendre polynomials* are the solutions of the general Legendre equation:

$$(1 - x^2)\frac{d^2y}{dx^2} - 2x\frac{dy}{dx} + \left(l(l+1) - \frac{m^2}{1 - x^2} \right) y = 0.$$

(3.10)

and the most direct representation is given as:

$$P_l^m(x) = (-1)^m(1 - x^2)^{m/2}\frac{d^m P_l(x)}{dx^m}.$$

(3.11)

The differential equation (3.10) has applications in physics, for example when solving the Laplace equation in spherical coordinates.

We have now completed the mathematical discussion. Next we discuss the implementation of the three Legendre polynomial types in C++. The first step is to include the files containing code for Legendre, Laguerre and Hermite polynomials:

```
#include <boost/math/special_functions/legendre.hpp>
#include <boost/math/special_functions/laguerre.hpp>
#include <boost/math/special_functions/hermite.hpp>
#include <boost/function.hpp>
```

Since we compute polynomial values, we place them in vectors and display these vectors in Excel. We also need to include the following files containing code developed by the authors of this book:

```
#include "Vector.cpp"
#include "ExcelMechanisms.hpp"
#include "DatasimException.hpp"
```

The first code example shows how to compute Legendre polynomials of the first, second and associated types:

```
cout << "Degree n of Legendre polynomial: "; int n; cin >> n;
cout << "Degree m for associated Legendre polynomial: ";
int m; cin >> m;

// '101' test.
double x = 0.5;
try
{
    cout << legendre_p<double>(n, x) << endl;      // Legendre first kind.
    cout << legendre_q<double>(n, x) << endl;      // Legendre second kind.

    // Associated Legendre polynomials
    cout << legendre_p<double>(n, m, x) << endl;
}
catch (exception& e) // x in closed range [-1,1]
{
    cout << e.what();
}
```

The next example defines a function that creates a vector of polynomial values:

```
// Create a discrete set of values of Legendre polynomial of first kind.
Vector<double, long> LegendreArray(long n,
                                   const Vector<double, long>& xarr)
{ // Compute discrete values of Legendre array; n == degree of polynomial.

    Vector<double, long> functionArray(xarr);
    try
    {
        for (int j = functionArray.MinIndex();
             j <= functionArray.MaxIndex(); ++j)
        {
            functionArray[j] = legendre_p<double>(n, xarr[j]);
        }
    }
    catch (exception& e)    // x in closed range [-1,1]
    {
        cout << e.what();
    }

    return functionArray;
}
```

Then the above function is used to create vectors with Legendre polynomial values and then displayed in Excel:

```
// Create array with x-values.
Range<double> interval(-0.99, 0.99);
Vector<double, long> xarr = interval.mesh(12);

// Now print a set of values of the Legendre polynomial.
list<string> labels;                              // Names of each vector.
list<Vector<double, long > > functionResult;  // The list of Y values.
```

```
labels.push_back("Legendre 1");
labels.push_back("Legendre 3");
labels.push_back("Legendre 5");
labels.push_back("Legendre 8");
labels.push_back("Legendre 99");

functionResult.push_back(LegendreArray(1, xarr));
functionResult.push_back(LegendreArray(3, xarr));
functionResult.push_back(LegendreArray(5, xarr));
functionResult.push_back(LegendreArray(8, xarr));
functionResult.push_back(LegendreArray(99, xarr));

try
{
    printInExcel(xarr,labels, functionResult, "Combined",
                "Abscissa", "Value");
}
catch(DatasimException& e)
{
    e.print();
}
```

The generated output from this program is shown in Figure 3.1.

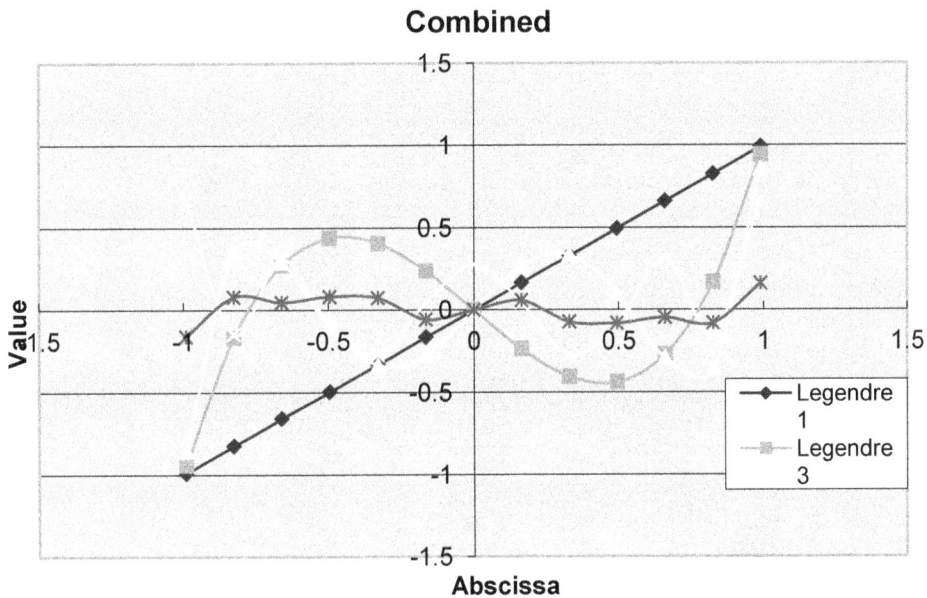

Figure 3.1 Displaying Legendre polynomials

3.4   Laguerre and Hermite Polynomials

The *Laguerre polynomials* are defined by the Rodrigues' formula:

$$L_n(x) = \frac{e^x}{n!} \frac{d^n}{dx^n}(x^n e^{-x}).$$ (3.12)

They are also the canonical solutions of Laguerre polynomials:

$$x\frac{d^2y}{dx^2} + (1 - x)\frac{dy}{dx} + ny = 0.$$ (3.13)

This second-order differential equation has non-singular solutions only if n is a non-negative integer. The first two Laguerre polynomials and the general recurrence relationship is:

$$L_0(x) = 1, \quad L_1(x) = 1 - x,$$

$$(n+1)L_{n+1}(x) = (2n + 1 - x)L_n(x) - nL_{n-1}(x), \quad n \geq 1. \tag{3.14}$$

Laguerre polynomials have applications in quantum mechanics.

We now discuss Hermite polynomials. They have applications to probability, combinatorics and quantum mechanics. The Rodrigues' formula is:

$$H_n(x) = (-1)^n e^{x^2} \frac{d^n}{dx^n} e^{-x^2}. \tag{3.15}$$

The interval on which the polynomial is defined is the real line. The *Hermite differential equation* is given by:

$$\frac{d^2 y}{dx^2} - 2x\frac{dy}{dx} + 2ny = 0$$

$$y = H_n(x) \tag{3.16}$$

and the recurrence relationship for Hermite polynomials is:

$$H_{n+1}(x) = 2xH_n(x) - 2nH_{n-1}(x), \quad n \geq 0. \tag{3.17}$$

Some examples of implementing Laguerre and Hermite polynomials are:

```
int N=12;
cout << "Degree of Laguerre polynomial: "; int L; cin >> L;
cout << "Degree of Hermite polynomial: "; int H; cin >> H;

// Display Laguerre and Hermite polynomials in a given range using
// generic function.
Range<double> intervalL(-5.0, 10.0);
Vector<double, long> xarrL = intervalL.mesh(N);
Range<double> intervalH(-2.0, 2.0);
Vector<double, long> xarrH = intervalH.mesh(N);

Vector<double, long> LaguerreArray(xarrL);
Vector<double, long> HermiteArray(xarrH);

try
{
    for (int j = LaguerreArray.MinIndex();
        j <= LaguerreArray.MaxIndex(); ++j)
    {
        LaguerreArray[j] = laguerre<double>(L, xarrL[j]);
    }
    for (int j = HermiteArray.MinIndex();
        j <= HermiteArray.MaxIndex(); ++j)
    {
        HermiteArray[j] = hermite<double>(H, xarrH[j]);
    }
}
catch (exception& e) // x in closed range [-1,1].
{
    cout << e.what();
}

try
```

```
{
    printOneExcel(xarrL, LaguerreArray, string("Laguerre"), string("x"),
                string("Abscissa"), string("Value"));

    printOneExcel(xarrH, HermiteArray, string("Hermite"), string("x"),
                string("Abscissa"), string("Value"));

}
catch (DatasimException& e)
{
    e.print();
}
```

Output from this code is given in Figures 3.2 and 3.3 when the polynomian degree value is 3.

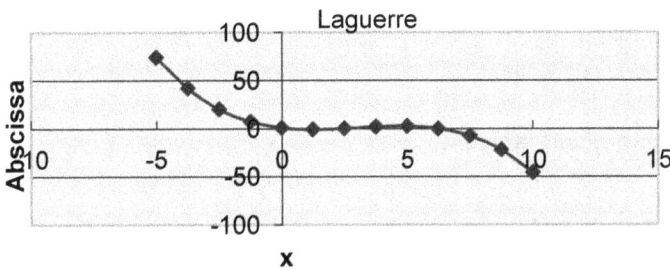

Figure 3.2 Displaying Laguerre polynomials

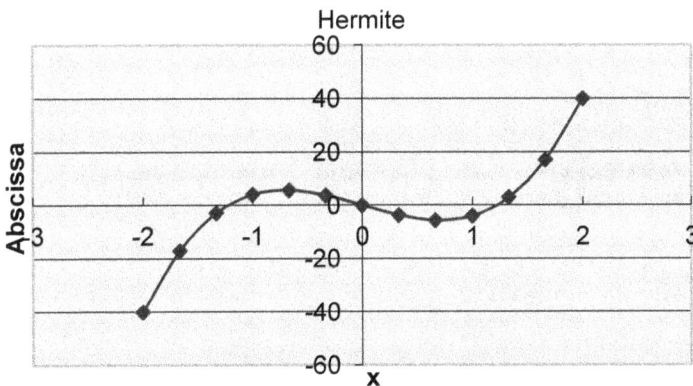

Figure 3.3 Displaying Hermite polynomials

3.5   Spherical Harmonics

These functions have applications in physics, seismology, signal processing and magnetism, for example. They typically occur when solving the Laplace equation in spherical coordinates and they can be seen as a generalisation of Fourier series but now we take expansions in terms of spherical harmonics instead of trigonometric functions.

There are several forms for the *Laplace spherical harmonics* and we choose the form that is used in physics and seismology, namely:

$$Y_n^m(\theta, \varphi) = \sqrt{\frac{(2n+1)(n-m)!}{4\pi(n+m)!}} P_n^m(\cos\theta)e^{im\varphi}. \qquad (3.18)$$

In this formula $P_n^m(\cos\theta)$ is the associated Legendre polynomial.

An example on how to code spherical harmonics in Boost is:

```
// Spherical Harmonic polynomial Y(n,m,theta, psi).
try
{
    int n = 20; int m = 4;
    double theta = 3.1415/4.0; double psi = 3.1415/2.0;
    cout << "Spherical Harmonic polynomial: "
        << spherical_harmonic(n, m, theta, psi) << endl;
}
catch (const std::exception& e)
{
    cout << e.what() << endl;
}


// Real part of Spherical Harmonic polynomial Y(n,m,theta, psi).
try
{
    int n = 20; int m = 3;
    double theta = 45.0; double psi = 90.0;
    cout << "Spherical Harmonic polynomial, real part: "
        << spherical_harmonic_r(n, m, theta, psi) << endl;
}
catch (const std::exception& e)
{
    cout << e.what() << endl;
}


// Imaginary part of Spherical Harmonic polynomial Y(n,m,theta, psi).
try
{
    int n = 20; int m = 13;
    double theta = 45.0; double psi = 90.0;
    cout << "Spherical Harmonic polynomial, imaginary part: "
        << spherical_harmonic_i(n, m, theta, psi) << endl;
}
catch (const std::exception& e)
{
    cout << e.what() << endl;
}
```

3.6   Chebychev Polynomials

Although not implemented in Boost, we give an introduction to Chebychev orthogonal polynomials because of their pervasiveness in numerical analysis. In particular, they are important in approximation theory because the roots (the so-called *Chebychev nodes*) of the Chebychev polynomials of the first kind are used as nodes in polynomial interpolation. The *Chebychev differential equation* for the polynomial of the first kind is given by:

$$(1-x^2)\frac{d^2y}{dx^2} - x\frac{dy}{dx} + n^2y = 0. \qquad (3.19)$$

These polynomials satisfy the recurrence relationship:

$$T_0(x) = 1, T_1(x) = x$$

$$T_{n+1}(x) = 2xT_n(x) - T_{n-1}(x)$$

(3.20)

or more explicitly as a trigonometric definition:

$$T_n(x) = \cos(\arccos x) = \cosh(n \arccos x).$$

(3.21)

The *Chebychev polynomial of the first kind* of degree n has n different roots in the interval [-1,1]. The roots can be deduced using the trigonometric definition:

$$x_j = \cos\left(\frac{\pi}{2} \frac{2j-1}{n}\right), \quad j = 1, \ldots, n.$$

(3.22)

A discussion of applications of Chebychev orthogonal polynomials to numerical integration is given in Krylov 2005.

3.7 Computing the Roots of Bessel Functions

In chapter two we discussed the various kinds of Bessel functions. In this section we discuss the problem of computing the roots of Bessel functions of the first kind:

$$J_n(x) = 0, \quad n \geq 0.$$

(3.23)

There are different ways to compute these roots. We choose for a combination of some properties of Bessel functions and the Newton-Raphson iterative method. First, we note some properties of these functions:

$$J_n(-x) = (-1)^n J_n(x)$$

$$(x^n J_n(x))' = x^n J_{n-1}(x) \left(J_n' \equiv \frac{dJ_n}{dx}\right)$$

$$(x^{-n} J_n(x))' = -x^{-n} J_{n+1}(x)$$

$$xJ_n'(x) = nJ_n(x) - xJ_{n+1}(x)$$

$$xJ_n'(x) = -nJ_n(x) + xJ_{n-1}(x)$$

$$\int_0^x t^n J_{n-1}(t)dt = x^n J_n(x).$$

(3.24)

From these equations it is possible to describe the first-order derivative of a Bessel function of order n in terms of Bessel functions of order $n-1$ and $n+1$:

$$xJ_{n+1} - 2nJ_n + xJ_{n-1} = 0$$

$$J_{n+1} + 2J_n' - J_{n-1} = 0.$$

(3.25)

The next step is to apply the Newton-Raphson method and we use equation (3.25) to avoid our having to compute derivatives:

$$x_{m+1} = x_m - \frac{J_n(x_m)}{J_n'(x_m)}$$

$$= x_m - \frac{J_n(x_m)}{\frac{1}{2}(J_{n-1}(x_m) - J_{n+1}(x_m))}, \quad n \geq 1 \text{ and } x_0 \text{ given.}$$

(3.26)

The case of the zero-order Bessel function is given by:

$$x_{m+1} = x_m - J_0(x_m)/J_0'(x_m) =$$

$$= x_m + J_0(x_m)/J_1(x_m) \text{ and } x_0 \text{ given.}$$

(3.27)

We have created a routine that implements the algorithm in equation (3.26):

```
// Compute the first M roots of J(n).
vector<double> GetRoots(int n, int M, double startValue)
{
    double xOld = startValue;
    double xNew = 999.0;
    int counter = 0;
    double tmp;

    vector<double> result;
    result.push_back(xOld);

    for (int j = 1; j <= M; ++j)
    {
        xOld += 3.1415;
        while (fabs(xNew - xOld) > 0.00001)
        {
            counter++;
            tmp = 0.5*(cyl_bessel_j(n-1,xOld) - cyl_bessel_j(n+1,xOld));
            xNew = xOld - (cyl_bessel_j(n,xOld) /tmp);

            result.push_back(xNew);
            xOld = xNew;
        }
    }

    return result;
}
```

Some test code is:

```
// Compute roots of J(1).
int n = 1;
int M = 23;
double kickOff = 3.83171;
vector<double> result = GetRoots(n, M, kickOff);

// Print roots.
cout.precision(8);     // Increase output precision.
for (size_t i = 0; i < result.size(); ++i)
{
    cout << "[" << i+1 << "," << result[i] << "] ";
}
```

The output from this code produces the desired roots:

```
[1,3.83171] [2,7.0154831] [3,10.173456] [4, 13.323689] [5,16.470629]
[6,19.615858] [7,22.760084] [8,25.903672] [9,29.046828] [10,32.18968]
[11,35.332308] [12,38.474766] [13,41.617094] [14,44.759319] [15,47.901461]
[16,51.043535] [17,54.185554] [18,57.327525] [19,60.469458] [20,63.611357]
[21,66.753227] [22,69.895072] [23,73.036895] [24,76.1787]
```

Why would we need to compute the roots of Bessel functions? One application is when solving partial differential equations by the Separation of Variables method. For a discussion, see MacCluer 2004.

3.8   Statistics Distributions

We give an overview of the univariate statistical distributions and functions in the Math Toolkit. The emphasis is on discussing the functionality in the Toolkit, in particular:
- Discrete and continuous distributions, their member functions and defining properties.
- Other non-member functions, for example the probability function and cumulative density functions, kurtosis and skewness.
- Some examples to motivate how to use the classes in the Toolkit.

All distributions use random variables which are mappings of a probability space into some other space, typically a real number. A *discrete probability distribution* is one in which the distribution of the random variable is discrete while a *continuous probability* distribution is one whose cumulative distribution is continuous.

The discrete probability distributions are:
- Bernoulli (a single trial whose outcome is 0 (failure) or 1 (success)).
- Binomial (used to obtain the probability of observing k successes in N trials).
- Negative Binomial (used to obtain the probability of k failures and r successes in k + r trials).
- Hypergeometric (describes the number of events k from a sample n drawn from a total population N without replacement).
- Poisson (expresses the probability of a number of events occurring in a fixed period of time).

The continuous probability distributions are:
- Beta (used in Bayesian statistics applications).
- Cauchy-Lorentz (used in physics, spectroscopy and to solve differential equations).
- Chi-Squared (used in statistical tests).
- Exponential (models the time between independent events).
- Extreme Value (models rare events).
- F (The Fisher F-distribution that tests if two samples have the same variance).
- Gamma (and Erlang) (used to model waiting times).
- Laplace (the distribution of differences between two independent variates with identical exponential distributions).
- Logistic (used in logistic regression and feedforward neural network applications).
- Log Normal (used when the logarithm of the random variable is normally distributed).
- Noncentral Beta (a generalisation of the Beta Distribution).
- Noncentral Chi-Squared (a generalisation of the Chi-Squared Distribution).
- Noncentral F (a generalisation of the Fisher F-distribution).
- Noncentral T (generalisation of Student's t-Distribution).
- Normal (Gaussian) (probably the best known distribution).
- Pareto (compare large and small numbers).
- Rayleigh (combine two orthogonal components having an absolute value).
- Student's t (the 'best' approximate distribution to an unknown distribution).
- Triangular (used when a distribution is only vaguely known, for example in software projects).
- Weibull (used in failure analysis models).

- Uniform (also known as the rectangular distribution and it models a probability distribution with a constant probability).

Each of the above distributions is implemented by a corresponding template class with two template parameters. The first parameter is the underlying data type used by the distribution (the default type is `double`) and the second parameter is the *policy*. In general, a policy is a fine-grained compile-time mechanism that we can use to customise the behaviour of a library. It allows us to change error-handling mechanisms or calculation precision at both program level and at the client site.

The global functions for the distributions are:
- Cdf (cumulative distribution function).
- Cdf complement (this is 1 – cdf).
- Hazard (the event rate at time t conditional on survival until time t or later; useful when modelling failure in mechanical systems).
- Chf (cumulative hazard function that measures the accumulation of hazard over time).
- Kurtosis (a measure of the 'peakedness' of a probability distribution).
- Kurtosis_excess (does a distribution have fatter tails than a normal distribution?).
- Mean (the expected value).
- Median (the value separating the lower and higher halves of a distribution).
- Mode (the point at which the probability mass or density function takes its maximum).
- Pdf (probability density function).
- Range (the length of the smallest interval which contains all the data).
- Quantile (points taken at regular intervals from the cdf).
- Skewness (a measure of the asymmetry of a probability distribution).
- Support (the smallest closed interval/set whose complement has probability zero).
- Variance (how far do values differ from the mean).

We discuss a well-known case. The *normal (or Gaussian) distribution* is one of the most important statistical distributions because of its ability to model many kinds of phenomena in diverse areas such as economics, computational finance, physics and the social sciences. In general, the normal distribution is used to describe variables that tend to cluster around a mean value. We now show how to implement the normal distribution in Boost and we show how to call the member and non-member functions:

```cpp
#include <boost/math/distributions/normal.hpp>
#include <boost/math/distributions.hpp>        // Non-member functions.

#include <iostream>
using namespace std;

int main()
{
    // Don't forget to tell compiler which namespace.
    using namespace boost::math;

    normal_distribution<> myNormal(1.0, 10.0); // Default is 'double'.
    cout << "Mean: " << myNormal.mean() << ", standard deviation: "
        << myNormal.standard_deviation() << endl;

    // Distributional properties.
    double x = 10.25;

    cout << "pdf: " << pdf(myNormal, x) << endl;
    cout << "cdf: " << cdf(myNormal, x) << endl;
```

```
// Choose another data type and now a N(0,1) variate.
normal_distribution<float> myNormal2;
cout << "Mean: " << myNormal2.mean() << ", standard deviation: "
     << myNormal2.standard_deviation() << endl;

cout << "pdf: " << pdf(myNormal2, x) << endl;
cout << "cdf: " << cdf(myNormal2, x) << endl;

// Choose precision.
cout.precision(10); // Number of values behind the comma.

// Other properties.
cout << "\n***normal distribution:\n";
cout << "mean: " << mean(myNormal) << endl;
cout << "variance: " << variance(myNormal) << endl;
cout << "median: " << median(myNormal) << endl;
cout << "mode: " << mode(myNormal) << endl;
cout << "kurtosis excess: " << kurtosis_excess(myNormal) << endl;
cout << "kurtosis: " << kurtosis(myNormal) << endl;
cout << "characteristic function: " << chf(myNormal, x) << endl;
cout << "hazard: " << hazard(myNormal, x) << endl;

return 0;
}
```

We conclude this section with some remarks on using the current functionality in combination with Excel. The primary motive was to call Boost functionality from C#. The Microsoft .NET supports the creation of interoperable applications consisting of both C++ and C# code. To this end, we use the C++/CLI language to create *wrapper classes* that embed native C++ code and that can be called from C#. An example is the case of the non-central Chi-squared distribution. We need to use its functions by calling them from C#. The corresponding C++/CLI wrapper class is:

```
#include <boost/math/distributions.hpp>

using namespace System;

// Wrapper for the boost::math::non_central_chi_squared_ditribution class.
// We use the .NET naming conventions instead of the original C++ name.
public ref class NonCentralChiSquaredDistribution
{
private:
    // The wrapped native class.
    boost::math::non_central_chi_squared_distribution<>* m_distribution;

public:
    // Default constructor.
    NonCentralChiSquaredDistribution();

    // Constructor with lower and upper value.
    NonCentralChiSquaredDistribution(double df, double lambda);

    // Finaliser (called by garbage collector or destructor).
    !NonCentralChiSquaredDistribution();

    // Destructor (Dispose).
    ~NonCentralChiSquaredDistribution();

    // Get the native object.
    boost::math::non_central_chi_squared_distribution<>* GetNative();

    double Pdf(double x);
    double Cdf(double x);
};
```

We are primarily interested in the probability density and cumulative probability density functions that we have implemented as follows:

```
double NonCentralChiSquaredDistribution::Pdf(double x)
{
    return boost::math::pdf(*GetNative(), x);
}

double NonCentralChiSquaredDistribution::Cdf(double x)
{
    return boost::math::cdf(*GetNative(), x);
}
```

Now we give an example of C# client code:

```
class Program
{
    static void Main(string[] args)
    {
        double x = 10;

        NonCentralChiSquaredDistribution dist =
            new NonCentralChiSquaredDistribution();
        Console.WriteLine("Pdf: {0}", dist.Pdf(x));
        Console.WriteLine("Cdf: {0}", dist.Cdf(x));
    }
}
```

We see how easy it is to reuse Boost code from C#. This is a general pattern that can also be used in other situations.

The Math Toolkit is well-documented (see www.boost.org) and it contains full descriptions of the classes, the corresponding global functions and numerous applications.

3.9   Summary and Conclusions

In this chapter we have given an overview of how the Boost Math Toolkit implements Legendre, Laguerre, Hermite and spherical harmonic orthogonal polynomials. We gave a short mathematical introduction to these functions as well as giving some code examples. Finally, we discussed how to find the roots of the Bessel functions of the first kind.

4 Date and Time

4.1 Introduction and Objectives

In this chapter we introduce the Boost library that supports date and time entities. It is an understatement to say that having access to datastructures and C++ classes that model *temporal entities* is important in many kinds of scheduling, management information (MIS) and calendar-driven applications. To this end, the Boost date-time library has extensive support for many use cases, for example:

- Creating dates and times based on Gregorian, Posix and local time regimes.
- Date iterators; for example, iterating over the days in a week.
- Date generators and algorithms.
- Local and UTC (*Coordinated Universal Time*) support.
- Date and Time input/output and serialisation.

The approach that we take in this book is to discuss the main features in the library and to give a number of '101' examples. We then continue by examining several extended examples and applications in which dates and times are used. For example, one project is to migrate and extend legacy code for computational finance applications to the current library (see Duffy 2004).

This chapter takes a hands-on approach and we discuss numerous examples to show the usefulness of the Boost date-time library. It is a large library.

4.2 Overview of Concepts and Functionality

Date and time abstractions are of fundamental importance in many kinds of applications. In particular, systems that incorporate *temporal logic* are numerous. Instead of defining our own libraries and functions to process dates and times (which the authors did) we now prefer to use the Boost date-time library and extend it to suit the needs of specific application areas. To this end, we discuss the most important classes and functionality in the library. We can view time as a one-dimensional line or continuum.

There are three basic *temporal types*:

- *Time Point*: this is a specifier for a location in the time continuum.
- *Time Duration*: this is a length of time that is unattached to any point in the time continuum. It is a 'floating' quantity with a magnitude.
- *Time Interval* (*Time Period*): this is a duration of time that is attached to a specific point in the time continuum.

Corresponding to each of these concepts is a so-called *resolution* that is defined as the smallest representable duration. We define a *Time System* as a set of temporal types in combination with rules and operations to label and to compute with these temporal types. A *Calendar System* is a time system with a resolution of one day. In this chapter we focus on the *Gregorian Calendar System* because it is the most widely used system. We also discuss *UTC* (*Coordinated Universal Time*) calendar system that is used in civil time applications. *Local time systems* are based on UTC and are adjusted for the rotation of the earth so that daylight hours are similar everywhere. Finally, a *Clock Device* is a software component that is tied to hardware and that provides the current date or time in a time system.

4.3   Gregorian Time

The Boost implementation of the Gregorian system consists of the following types:

- date: this is the primary interface when working with dates.
- date_duration: this is a day count class which we use when calculating with Gregorian dates.
- date_period: this is a class that represents a range or interval between two dates.

Furthermore, the library has support for iterating in different ways over a date period. It also has a number of functions for generating dates and schedules of dates.

In order to use the library, we recommend that you use the following namespace and include files in your code:

```
using namespace boost::gregorian;

#include <boost/date_time/gregorian/gregorian.hpp>        // Types and I/O.
#include <boost/date_time/gregorian/gregorian_types.hpp>  // Types only.
```

We now discuss the Gregorian types in some detail.

4.3.1   Date

The date class has functionality for:

- Creating dates from date parts (day, month and year), from strings and from the system clock.
- Date accessors, for example retrieving date parts; queries on dates.
- Converting dates to strings.
- Operators, for example adding a duration to a date to produce another date.

We first consider date constructors. We note that the default constructor produces an invalid date. If we wish to create a date based on today's date we should call a constructor using the hardware clock. We can also create dates based on the Gregorian day, month and year. Finally, in some cases it can be advantageous to create dates having 'special' values such as:

- Negative and positive infinity.
- Maximum and minimum dates.

We now give some examples to show how to create instances of date:

```
// Some basic constructors.
try
{
    date d1; Print(d1);         // Produces not_a_date_time.
}
catch (bad_year& e)
{
    cout << e.what() << endl;  // Year not valid range [1400, 10000].
}

// Create date from Gregorian year, month and day.
date myDate2(2011, May, 16); Print(myDate2);  // Print is author-defined.

// Copy constructor.
date myDate3(myDate2); Print(myDate3);

// Constructor at the 'extremes'.
try
{
    date myDate4(pos_infin); Print(myDate4, "Positive infinity");
```

```
    }
catch (bad_year& e)
{
    cout << e.what() << endl;
}

try
{
    date myDate5(neg_infin); Print(myDate5, "Negative infinity");
}
catch (bad_year& e)
{
    cout << e.what() << endl;
}

try
{
    date myDate6(max_date_time); Print(myDate6, "Max Date Time");
}
catch (bad_year& e)
{
    cout << e.what() << endl;
}

try
{
    date myDate7(min_date_time); Print(myDate7, "Min Date Time");
}
catch (bad_year& e)
{
    cout << e.what() << endl;
}
```

The output from this code is:

```
Date Information...
not-a-date-time
Year is out of valid range: 1400..10000

Date Information...
2011-May-16
Year: 2011, Month: May, Day: 16
Day of week: Mon, Day of year: 136
End of month: 2011-May-31
ISO 8601 week number: 20, Day of year: 2455698

Date Information...
2011-May-16
Year: 2011, Month: May, Day: 16
Day of week: Mon, Day of year: 136
End of month: 2011-May-31
ISO 8601 week number: 20, Day of year: 2455698

Date Information...Positive infinity
+infinity
Year is out of valid range: 1400..10000

Date Information...Negative infinity
-infinity
Year is out of valid range: 1400..10000

Date Information...Max Date Time
9999-Dec-31
Year: 9999, Month: Dec, Day: 31
Day of week: Fri, Day of year: 365
```

```
End of month: 9999-Dec-31
ISO 8601 week number: 52, Day of year: 5373484

Date Information...Min Date Time
1400-Jan-01
Year: 1400, Month: Jan, Day: 1
Day of week: Wed, Day of year: 1
End of month: 1400-Jan-31
ISO 8601 week number: 1, Day of year: 2232400
```

Please note that we have created a function to print dates:

```cpp
void Print(const date& myDate, const string& type = "")
{
    cout << "\nDate Information..." << type << endl;
    cout << myDate << endl;
    cout << "Year: " << myDate.year() << ", Month: "
        << myDate.month() << ", Day: " << myDate.day() << endl;

    // Extra stuff.
    cout << "Day of week: " << myDate.day_of_week()
        << ", Day of year: " << myDate.day_of_year() << endl;
    cout << "End of month: " << myDate.end_of_month() << endl;
    cout << "ISO 8601 week number: " << myDate.week_number()
        << ", Day of year: " << myDate.julian_day() << endl;
}
```

Continuing, we note that it is possible to create dates both from strings and from information based on the hardware clock, as the following example shows:

```cpp
// Constructing dates from strings.
string s("2009/1/9");                        // 9 January 2009.
date myDate8(from_simple_string(s));
Print(myDate8,"from simple string");

// ISO 8601 extended format CCYY-MM-DD.
string s2("2009-10-9");                       // 9 October 2009.
date myDate9(from_simple_string(s2));
Print(myDate9,"from delimited string");

// Now convert to a string
string converted = to_simple_string(myDate9);
cout << "String: " << converted << endl;      // OUTPUT is 2009-Oct-09.

string s3("2009109");                         // 10 October 2009.
date myDate10(from_undelimited_string(s3));
Print(myDate10,"from UNdelimited string");

// Create dates from the clock.
date myDate11(day_clock::local_day());
Print(myDate11,"Local day based on time zone settings of computer");
date myDate12(day_clock::universal_day());
Print(myDate12,"Coordinated UniversalTime (UTC)");
```

The output from this code is (it depends on the current time):

```
Date Information...from simple string
2009-Jan-09
Year: 2009, Month: Jan, Day: 9
Day of week: Fri, Day of year: 9
End of month: 2009-Jan-31
ISO 8601 week number: 2, Day of year: 2454841

Date Information...from delimited string
2009-Oct-09
```

```
Year: 2009, Month: Oct, Day: 9
Day of week: Fri, Day of year: 282
End of month: 2009-Oct-31
ISO 8601 week number: 41, Day of year: 2455114
String: 2009-Oct-09

Date Information...from UNdelimited string
2009-Oct-09
Year: 2009, Month: Oct, Day: 9
Day of week: Fri, Day of year: 282
End of month: 2009-Oct-31
ISO 8601 week number: 41, Day of year: 2455114

Date Information...Local day based on time zone settings of computer
2011-May-18
Year: 2011, Month: May, Day: 18
Day of week: Wed, Day of year: 138
End of month: 2011-May-31
ISO 8601 week number: 20, Day of year: 2455700

Date Information...Coordinated Universal Time (UTC)
2011-May-18
Year: 2011, Month: May, Day: 18
Day of week: Wed, Day of year: 138
End of month: 2011-May-31
ISO 8601 week number: 20, Day of year: 2455700
```

We have now completed our discussion of the main functionality in class date.

4.3.2   Date Duration

The class date_duration implements a simple *day count* whose value may be positive or negative.
Here is code to show how to create some instances:

```
// Some basic constructors.
date_duration dd(10);                    // 10 days.

// Constructor at the 'extremes'.
try
{
    date_duration myDateDuration(pos_infin);
    Print(myDateDuration, "Positive infinity"); // Print() is a
                                                 // author-defined function
}
catch (bad_year& e)
{
    cout << e.what() << endl;
}

try
{
    date_duration myDateDuration2(neg_infin);
    Print(myDateDuration2, "Negative infinity");
}
catch (bad_year& e)
{
    cout << e.what() << endl;
}

try
{
    date_duration myDateDuration3(max_date_time);
    Print(myDateDuration3, "Max Date Time");
}
```

```
catch (bad_year& e)
{
    cout << e.what() << endl;
}

try
{
    date_duration myDateDuration4(min_date_time);
    Print(myDateDuration4, "Min Date Time");
}
catch (bad_year& e)
{
    cout << e.what() << endl;
}
```

The output from this code is:

```
Date Duration Information...Positive infinity
+infinity
Day count: 2147483647, is negative: 0
Smallest unit of duration type: 1, is special value: true

Date Duration Information...Negative infinity
-infinity
Day count: -2147483648, is negative: true
Smallest unit of duration type: 1, is special value: true

Date Duration Information...Max Date Time
2147483645
Day count: 2147483645, is negative: false
Smallest unit of duration type: 1, is special value: false

Date Duration Information...Min Date Time
-2147483647
Day count: -2147483647, is negative: true
Smallest unit of duration type: 1, is special value: false
Operating overloading...
```

Finally, operator overloading is supported and it is possible to add durations to and substract durations from dates, for example:

```
// Comparison of operators.
cout << "Operating overloading...\n";
date d1(day_clock::local_day()); Print(d1);
date_duration myDuration(10);                    // 10 days duration.
date d2 = d1 + myDuration; Print(d2);
date d3 = d1 - myDuration; Print(d3);

cout<<endl;

if (d1 != d2)
{
    cout << d1 << ", not equal to " << d2 << endl;
}

if (d1 < d2)
{
    cout << d1 << ", less than " << d2 << endl;
}

if (d1 >= d3)
{
    cout << d3 << ", less than " << d1 << endl;
}
```

The output from this code is (note that it depends on the current time):

```
Date Information...d1
2011-May-18
Year: 2011, Month: May, Day: 18
Day of week: Wed, Day of year: 138
End of month: 2011-May-31
ISO 8601 week number: 20, Day of year: 2455700

Date Information...d2
2011-May-28
Year: 2011, Month: May, Day: 28
Day of week: Sat, Day of year: 148
End of month: 2011-May-31
ISO 8601 week number: 21, Day of year: 2455710

Date Information...d3
2011-May-08
Year: 2011, Month: May, Day: 8
Day of week: Sun, Day of year: 128
End of month: 2011-May-31
ISO 8601 week number: 18, Day of year: 2455690

2011-May-18, not equal to 2011-May-28
2011-May-18, less than 2011-May-28
2011-May-08, less than 2011-May-18
```

The user-defined function to print a `date_duration` instance is given by:

```cpp
void Print(const date_duration& myDateDuration, const string& type = "")
{
    cout << "\nDate Duration Information..." << type << endl;
    cout << myDateDuration << endl;
    cout << "Day count: " << myDateDuration.days() << ", is negative: "
        << myDateDuration.is_negative() << endl;

    // Extra stuff.
    cout << "Smallest unit of duration type: " << myDateDuration.unit()
        << ", is special value: " << boolalpha
        << myDateDuration.is_special() << endl;
}
```

4.3.3   Date Period

We discuss the class `date_period` that implements a range of two dates. This is a useful class and it simplifies conditional logic in a program. Some of the functionality in this class consists of the following:

- Constructors, for example creating a period from two dates.
- Accessor functions, for example the first and last days of a period, the last day plus one and the length of the period.
- Does a period contain a date? Is a period contained in another period?
- Intersection of periods; are periods adjacent to one another?
- Various relationships between periods and dates, for example determine if a period is before a given date.
- Merge periods; in other words, find the union of two periods.
- Convert a period to a string.

The first code sample is concerned with `date_period` constructors:

```cpp
// Date period constructors.
date d1(day_clock::local_day());
```

```
date_duration myDuration(10); // 10 days duration.
date d2 = d1 + myDuration;
date d3 = d1 - myDuration;

date_period dp1(d1, d2); Print(dp1);
date_period dp2(d3, d1); Print(dp2);

// Copy constructor.
date_period dp3(dp1); Print(dp3);

// Date period with days offset.
days myDays(10);
date_period dp4(date(day_clock::local_day()), myDays); Print(dp4);
```

The output from this code is:

```
Date Information for date_period...[2011-May-18/2011-May-27]
First date of period: 2011-May-18
Last date: 2011-May-27, One past last: 2011-May-28
Length of date period: 10, Period is null?: false

Date Information for date_period...[2011-May-08/2011-May-17]
First date of period: 2011-May-08
Last date: 2011-May-17, One past last: 2011-May-18
Length of date period: 10, Period is null?: false

Date Information for date_period...[2011-May-18/2011-May-27]
First date of period: 2011-May-18
Last date: 2011-May-27, One past last: 2011-May-28
Length of date period: 10, Period is null?: false

Date Information for date_period...[2011-May-18/2011-May-27]
First date of period: 2011-May-18
Last date: 2011-May-27, One past last: 2011-May-28
Length of date period: 10, Period is null?: false
```

The code that realises this output is given by the function (created by the authors):

```
void Print(const date_period& myDatePeriod, const string& type = "")
{
    cout << "\nDate Information for date_period..."
        << myDatePeriod << " " << type << endl;
    cout << "First date of period: " << myDatePeriod.begin()
        << endl << "Last date: " << myDatePeriod.last()
        << ", One past last: " << myDatePeriod.end() << endl;

    // Extra stuff.
    cout << "Length of date period: " << myDatePeriod.length()
        << ", Period is null?: " << boolalpha
        << myDatePeriod.is_null() << endl;
}
```

We now discuss some accessor functions. The code has been documented as follows:

```
// Interaction between date periods and other entities.
date myDateMiddle(day_clock::local_day());

date_duration duration(5);        // 5 days duration.
date myDateLower = myDateMiddle - duration;
date myDateUpper = myDateMiddle + duration;

date_period dpFirst(myDateLower, myDateUpper);

// Does one period contain another period.
cout << dpFirst << " contains " << myDateMiddle
```

```
                    << boolalpha << " " << dpFirst.contains(myDateMiddle) << endl;

// Merging periods (unions). Results in a NULL set if the periods
// do not intersect.
date_period dpA(date(2011,Jan,1), date(2011,Jan,10));
date_period dpB(date(2011,Jan,9), date(2100,Jan,31));
date_period dpUnion = dpA.merge(dpB); Print(dpUnion, "union");

// Combine two periods and any gaps between them.
date_period dpC(date(2011,Jan,1), date(2011,Jan,5));
date_period dpD(date(2011,Jan,19), date(2100,Jan,31));
date_period dpSpan = dpC.span(dpD); Print(dpSpan, "span");

// Add a given number of days to begin and end of period.
days daysShift(7);                        // Next week.
dpSpan.shift(daysShift); Print(dpSpan, "shifted period");

// Relationship between a period and a date.
date_period dpE(date(2011,Jan,1), date(2011,Jan,31));
date dateA(2010, Dec, 31); date dateB(2011, Feb, 1);
cout << "Period before date: " << dpE.is_before(dateA) << endl;
cout << "Period before date: " << dpE.is_before(dateB) << endl;
```

The output from this code is:

```
[2011-May-13/2011-May-22] contains 2011-May-18 true

Date Information for date_period...[2011-Jan-01/2100-Jan-30] union
First date of period: 2011-Jan-01
Last date: 2100-Jan-30, One past last: 2100-Jan-31
Length of date period: 32537, Period is null?: false

Date Information for date_period...[2011-Jan-01/2100-Jan-30] span
First date of period: 2011-Jan-01
Last date: 2100-Jan-30, One past last: 2100-Jan-31
Length of date period: 32537, Period is null?: false

Date Information for date_period...[2011-Jan-08/2100-Feb-06] shifted period
First date of period: 2011-Jan-08
Last date: 2100-Feb-06, One past last: 2100-Feb-07
Length of date period: 32537, Period is null?: false
Period before date: false
Period before date: true
```

Finally, it is possible to compare periods and convert them to strings, as the following code shows:

```
// Comparing periods.
date_duration duration2(2);                        // 2 days duration.
date myDateLower2 = myDateMiddle - duration2;
date myDateUpper2 = myDateMiddle + duration2;

date_period dpSecond(myDateLower2, myDateUpper2);

ComparePeriods(dpFirst, dpSecond);

// Convert to a string.
string s = to_simple_string(dpFirst);
cout << "String form of date period: " << s << endl;
```

The output from this code is:

```
[2011-May-13/2011-May-22] contains [2011-May-16/2011-May-19] true
[2011-May-16/2011-May-19] contains [2011-May-13/2011-May-22] false
[2011-May-13/2011-May-22] intersects [2011-May-16/2011-May-19] true
```

```
[2011-May-16/2011-May-19] intersects [2011-May-13/2011-May-22] true
Intersection of [2011-May-13/2011-May-22], and [2011-May-16/2011-May-19]
==> [2011-May-16/2011-May-19]
String form of date period: [2011-May-13/2011-May-22]
```

We created the following function in order to compare time periods:

```
// Comparing date periods.
void ComparePeriods(const date_period& dp1, const date_period& dp2)
{
    cout << endl;
    cout << dp1 << " contains " << dp2 << boolalpha
         << " " << dp1.contains(dp2) << endl;
    cout << dp2 << " contains " << dp1 << boolalpha
         << " " << dp2.contains(dp1) << endl;

    cout << dp1 << " intersects " << dp2 << boolalpha
         << " " << dp1.intersects(dp2) << endl;
    cout << dp2 << " intersects " << dp1 << boolalpha
         << " " << dp2.intersects(dp1) << endl;

    cout << "Intersection of " << dp1 << ", and "
         << dp2 << " ==> " << dp1.intersection(dp2) << endl;
}
```

There are many applications of set-like operations for date and time. It is possible to use these operations in your applications. In chapter 18 we introduce the Interval Container Library (ICL) that can be used in the current context.

4.3.4   Date Iterators

Date (bidirectional) iterators provide a standard mechanism for iteration through dates. The 'granularity' can be at the level of day, week, month or year. Normally, we create an iterator of a given type and we use it to navigate between two dates. The following code shows how to create instances of the four major iterator types and to generate the corresponding set of dates:

```
// Create date from Gregorian year, month and day.
date myDateL(2011, May, 16); Print(myDateL);
date myDateU(2011, Jun, 16);

// Day iterators.
cout << "\n*** DAYS ***\n";
day_iterator di(myDateL);
for (; di < myDateU; ++di)
{
    cout << *di << ", ";
}

// Week iterators.
cout << "\n\n*** WEEKS ***\n";
week_iterator wi(myDateL);
for (; wi < myDateU; ++wi)
{
    cout << *wi << ", ";
}

// Month iterators.
cout << "\n\n*** MONTHS ***\n";
month_iterator mi(myDateL);
for (; mi < myDateU; ++mi)
{
    cout << *mi << ", ";
}
```

```
// Year iterators.
cout << "\n\n*** YEARS ***\n";
date myDateFarAway(2020, May, 17); // Up to but not including end date.
year_iterator yi(myDateL);
for (; yi < myDateFarAway; ++yi)
{
    cout << *yi << ", ";
}
```

The output of this code is:

```
Date Information...
2011-May-16
Year: 2011, Month: May, Day: 16
Day of week: Mon, Day of year: 136
End of month: 2011-May-31
ISO 8601 week number: 20, Day of year: 2455698

*** DAYS ***
2011-May-16, 2011-May-17, 2011-May-18, 2011-May-19, 2011-May-20, 2011-May-
21, 2011-May-22, 2011-May-23, 2011-May-24, 2011-May-25, 2011-May-26, 2011-
May-27, 2011-May-28, 2011-May-29, 2011-May-30, 2011-May-31, 2011-Jun-01,
2011-Jun-02, 2011-Jun-03, 2011-Jun-04, 2011-Jun-05, 2011-Jun-06, 2011-Jun-
07, 2011-Jun-08, 2011-Jun-09, 2011-Jun-10, 2011-Jun-11, 2011-Jun-12, 2011-
Jun-13, 2011-Jun-14, 2011-Jun-15,

*** WEEKS ***
2011-May-16, 2011-May-23, 2011-May-30, 2011-Jun-06, 2011-Jun-13,

*** MONTHS ***
2011-May-16,

*** YEARS ***
2011-May-16, 2012-May-16, 2013-May-16, 2014-May-16, 2015-May-16, 2016-May-
16, 2017-May-16, 2018-May-16, 2019-May-16, 2020-May-16,
```

4.4   Creating User-defined Utilities

We give some examples of using and extending date classes to produce new functionality. The code has been written by the authors.

4.4.1   A generic Date Iterator using Boost Variant

We create a generic module to iterate in an interval bounded by two dates. In particular, we can iterate over the days, weeks, months and years in the interval. To this end, we shall use Boost variant and we define:

```
typedef variant<day_iterator, week_iterator, month_iterator, year_iterator>
    PeriodIterator;
```

As we saw in Volume I (see Demming 2010) we create a *visitor* to effect the functionality:

```
// Base class; functionality for all periods.
class PeriodVisitor : public boost::static_visitor<vector<date> >
{
private:
    date upper;              // 'To' date.

    // Private generic function to create arrays of dates
    // based on an iterator.
    template <typename Iter> vector<date> CreateDates(Iter it) const
    {
        vector<date> result;
        for (;it < upper; ++it)
```

```
            {
                result.push_back(*it);
            }

            return result;
        }

    public:
        PeriodVisitor(const date& end) { upper = end;}

        vector<date> operator () (day_iterator di) const
        {
            return CreateDates<day_iterator>(di);
        }

        vector<date> operator () (week_iterator wi) const
        {
            return CreateDates<week_iterator>(wi);
        }

        vector<date> operator () (month_iterator mi) const
        {
            return CreateDates<month_iterator>(mi);
        }

        vector<date> operator () (year_iterator yi) const
        {
            return CreateDates<year_iterator>(yi);
        }
};
```

A test case is:

```
// Using variant in combination with date iterators.
cout << "\nOffset value in the iterator: "; int offset; cin >> offset;

date dateA(2001, Jan, 1); date dateB(2002, Jan, 1);
month_iterator monthIterator(dateA, offset);

// Assign a month iterator to the variant.
PeriodIterator myIterator = monthIterator;

PeriodVisitor periodVisitor(dateB);

// V1: using Visitor.
vector<date> result = boost::apply_visitor(periodVisitor, myIterator);
cout << "\nResult of visitor: " << endl;
for (size_t j = 0; j < result.size(); ++j)
{
    cout << result[j] << ", ";
}
```

The output from this code is (when the offset input is 1):

```
Result of visitor:
2001-Jan-01, 2001-Feb-01, 2001-Mar-01, 2001-Apr-01, 2001-May-01, 2001-Jun-
01, 2001-Jul-01, 2001-Aug-01, 2001-Sep-01, 2001-Oct-01, 2001-Nov-01, 2001-
Dec-01,
```

Instead of having to use low-level visitor code we can encapsulate the above code in a wrapper function:

```
// Modular wrapper function for generating dates.
vector<date> createDates(PeriodIterator it, const date& dateUpper)
{
```

```
        PeriodVisitor periodVisitor(dateUpper);
        return boost::apply_visitor(periodVisitor, it);
}
```

The resulting code now becomes:

```
// V2: Using friendlier wrapper function.
vector<date> result2 = CreateDates(monthIterator, dateB);
cout << "\n\nWrapper for visitor: " << endl;
for (size_t j = 0; j < result2.size(); ++j)
{
    cout << result2[j] << ", ";
}
```

The output is the same as before and we give it for completeness (offset=1):

```
Wrapper for visitor:
2001-Jan-01, 2001-Feb-01, 2001-Mar-01, 2001-Apr-01, 2001-May-01, 2001-Jun-
01, 2001-Jul-01, 2001-Aug-01, 2001-Sep-01, 2001-Oct-01, 2001-Nov-01, 2001-
Dec-01,
```

Finally, here is code (and resulting output) to compute and display the days of October in the year 2835:

```
// Special tests.
cout << "\n\nSpecial dates:\n";
date myDateA(2835, Oct, 1);
date myDateB(2835, Nov, 1);
day_iterator diA(myDateA);
for (; diA < myDateB; ++diA)
{
    cout << (*diA).day_of_week() << ", " << (*diA) << endl;
}


Special dates:
Mon, 2835-Oct-01 Tue, 2835-Oct-02 Wed, 2835-Oct-03 Thu, 2835-Oct-04
Fri, 2835-Oct-05 Sat, 2835-Oct-06 Sun, 2835-Oct-07 Mon, 2835-Oct-08
Tue, 2835-Oct-09 Wed, 2835-Oct-10 Thu, 2835-Oct-11 Fri, 2835-Oct-12
Sat, 2835-Oct-13 Sun, 2835-Oct-14 Mon, 2835-Oct-15 Tue, 2835-Oct-16
Wed, 2835-Oct-17 Thu, 2835-Oct-18 Fri, 2835-Oct-19 Sat, 2835-Oct-20
Sun, 2835-Oct-21 Mon, 2835-Oct-22 Tue, 2835-Oct-23 Wed, 2835-Oct-24
Thu, 2835-Oct-25 Fri, 2835-Oct-26 Sat, 2835-Oct-27 Sun, 2835-Oct-28
Mon, 2835-Oct-29 Tue, 2835-Oct-30 Wed, 2835-Oct-31
```

4.4.2   General Schedules of Date Period

The following function creates a collection of date_period instances based on a start date and a collection of durations:

```
// Create contiguous date periods of given durations.
vector<date_period> CreatePeriods(const date& dateBegin,
                                  const vector<long>& durations)
{
    vector<date_period> result;

    date dL = dateBegin;
    date dU; date_duration duration;
    for (size_t n = 0; n < durations.size(); ++n)
    {
        duration = date_duration(durations[n]);
        dU = dL + duration;
        result.push_back(date_period(dL, dU));
        dL = dU;
    }
```

```
    return result;
}
```

An example of use is:

```
date d1(day_clock::local_day());

// Use Boost Assign library here.
vector<long> durations;
durations += 7, 7, 7, 40;

vector<date_period> result = CreatePeriods(d1, durations);

cout << "*** Created periods ***\n";
for (size_t n = 0; n < result.size(); ++n)
{
    Print(result[n]);
}
```

The output from this code is (output depends on the current date):

```
Date Information for date_period...[2011-Jun-25/2011-Jul-04]
First date of period: 2011-Jun-25
Last date: 2011-Jul-04, One past last: 2011-Jul-05
Length of date period: 7, Period is null?: false

Date Information for date_period...[2011-Jun-15/2011-Jun-24]
First date of period: 2011-Jun-15
Last date: 2011-Jun-24, One past last: 2011-Jun-25
Length of date period: 7, Period is null?: false

Date Information for date_period...[2011-Jun-25/2011-Jul-04]
First date of period: 2011-Jun-25
Last date: 2011-Jul-04, One past last: 2011-Jul-05
Length of date period: 7, Period is null?: false

Date Information for date_period...[2011-Jun-25/2011-Jul-04]
First date of period: 2011-Jun-25
Last date: 2011-Jul-04, One past last: 2011-Jul-05
Length of date period: 40, Period is null?: false
```

4.4.3   International Money Market (IMM) Dates in Trading Systems

Certain financial applications work with predefined dates. In the case of *futures contracts* for example, traders use the third Wednesday of the months March, June, September and December. The code for computing these dates is:

```
// Generate IMM date
typedef nth_day_of_the_week_in_month NthDow;

NthDow ndm(NthDow::third, Wednesday, Jun);
date dIMM = ndm.get_date(2011);
Print(dIMM, "IMM date: "); // June 15 2011.

int NYears = 2;
int year = 2011;

// Generate IMM dates over a period of two years.
for (int n = 0; n < NYears; ++n)
{
    for (int m = Mar; m <= Dec; m += 3)
    {
        NthDow ndm2 = NthDow(NthDow::third, Wednesday, m);
        dIMM = ndm2.get_date(year);
```

```
            cout << dIMM << endl;
    }
    year++;
}
```

The output from this code is:

```
Date Information...IMM date:
2011-Jun-15
Year: 2011, Month: Jun, Day: 15
Day of week: Wed, Day of year: 166
End of month: 2011-Jun-30
ISO 8601 week number: 24, Day of year: 2455728
2011-Mar-16 2011-Jun-15 2011-Sep-21 2011-Dec-21
2012-Mar-21 2012-Jun-20 2012-Sep-19 2012-Dec-19
```

4.5   Posix Time System

This system represents a time system with nano-second and micro-second resolution with stable calculation properties. The most important class is `ptime` that contains functionality to create temporal objects having Gregorian date and hours, minutes, seconds, microseconds and nanoseconds components.

The other classes in this system are:
- `time_duration`: this is the base type that represents a length of time. A duration can be positive or negative. The resolution of `time_duration` is configurable at compile-time; for example, we can create its instances at microsecond or nanosecond resolution level.
- `time_period`: this class represents a range or interval between two times. It is useful because it allows us to simplify calculations involving time and time intervals.
- `time_iterator`: this class provides a mechanism for iterating through time. This iterator is similar to a *Bidirectional* iterator. In contrast to the latter iterator type, the iterators for `time_iterator` have no underlying sequence because all results are calculated quantities.

The functionality for the above classes is similar to that of dates, durations and periods in section 4.3 and for this reason we discuss what is necessary to deploy them in applications.

The functionality in `ptime` consists of:
- Default and copy constructors.
- Constructor with `date` and `time_duration` as input arguments.
- Construct from a string.
- Construct from the clock (both local time and universal time).
- Get the date and time offset from a `ptime` instance.
- Conversion to string format.
- Operators: comparison, addition and subtraction (to produce offsets).

The functionality in `time_duration` consists of:
- Constructor with hours, minutes, seconds and fractional seconds arguments. The last parameter is configurable to be micro-seconds or nano-seconds.
- Accessor functions for the components in `time_duration`.
- Conversion to string format.
- Operators: comparison, addition and subtraction (to produce offsets).

The functionality in `time_period` consists of:

- Constructor with two `ptime` arguments.
- Constructor with two `ptime` and `time_duration` arguments.
- Copy constructor.
- Accessor functions (similar to the functionality in `date_period`).
- Set-like functions (for example, union and intersection).
- Merge, span and shift functions.
- Conversion to string format.

The following code is an example of use:

```
#include <boost/date_time/posix_time/posix_time.hpp> // Types plus I/O.
#include <boost/date_time/posix_time/posix_time_types.hpp>

using namespace boost::posix_time;

int main()
{
    // Create ptime from components.
    int h = 1; int m = 2; int s = 3;
    ptime pt1(date(2011, May, 22), time_duration(h,m,s));

    // Create ptime from strings.
    string s1("2011-5-1 23:59:59:000");        // delimited string.
    ptime pt2(time_from_string(s1));
    Print(pt2.date(), "date from delimited string");

    string s2("201105011T235959");             // non-delimited string.
    ptime pt3(time_from_string(s1));
    Print(pt3.date(), "date from non-delimited string");

    // Get time from the clock.

    // Local time (computer).
    ptime currentTime(second_clock::local_time());
    cout<<"\nLocal time (second): "<<currentTime<<endl;

    // UTC time.
    ptime currentTime2(second_clock::universal_time());
    cout<<"Universal time (second): "<<currentTime2<<endl;

    // Local time on a sub-second clock.
    ptime currentTime3(microsec_clock::local_time());
    cout<<"Local time (micro): "<<currentTime3<<endl;

    // UTC time on a sub-second clock.
    ptime currentTime4(microsec_clock::universal_time());
    cout<<"Universal time (micro): "<<currentTime4<<endl;

    return 0;
}
```

The following code gives an example of how to use time durations and time periods:

```
// time_duration. The 4th parameter has resolution nanoseconds or
// microseconds depending on the Build-Compiler settings.

// 01:02:03:000000004 (ns) or 01:02:03:000004 (ms).
time_duration td1(1,2,3,4);
cout<<"Time duration: "<<td1<<endl;

ptime ptA(date(2011, May, 22), time_duration(1,2,3));
```

```
ptime ptB(date(2011, May, 23), time_duration(1,2,3));
time_period tp1(ptA, ptB);
cout<<"Time period: "<<tp1<<endl;
```

4.6   Local Time

This system supports the management of local time, for example:

- `local_date_time` : locally adjusted time point.
- `posix_time_zone` : a time zone that is supported by a Posix string.
- `time_zone_database` : getting time zones from a .csv file.
- `time_zone` : abstract time zone interface.

These classes define a time system adjusted for recording times related to a specific earth location. It uses all the features of the `posix_time` system that we discussed in section 4.5. Local time uses a time zone object to account for differences in time zones and daylight savings adjustments. The phrase *wall-clock* refers to the time that would be shown on a wall clock in a particular time zone at any point in time.

We conclude this section with some relevant code.

The following code has been taken from the Boost site and it shows the use of some of the classes in this section:

```cpp
#include <boost/date_time/gregorian/gregorian.hpp>
#include <boost/date_time/posix_time/posix_time.hpp>
#include <boost/date_time/local_time/local_time.hpp>
#include <iostream>
#include <locale>

int main()
{
    using namespace boost::gregorian;
    using namespace boost::posix_time;
    using namespace boost::local_time;

    tz_database tz_db;
    try
    {
        tz_db.load_from_file("date_time_zonespec.csv");
    }
    catch (data_not_accessible dna)
    {
        std::cerr << "Error with time zone data file: " << dna.what()
                << std::endl;
        exit(EXIT_FAILURE);
    }
    catch(bad_field_count bfc)
    {
        std::cerr << "Error with time zone data file: " << bfc.what()
                << std::endl;
        exit(EXIT_FAILURE);
    }

    time_zone_ptr nyc = tz_db.time_zone_from_region("America/New_York");
    local_date_time ny_time(date(2004, Aug, 30), hours(10), nyc, true);

    typedef boost::date_time::time_facet<local_date_time, char> ldt_facet;
    ldt_facet* timefacet = new ldt_facet("%Y-%b-%d %H:%M:%S%F %Z");
    std::locale loc(std::locale::classic(), timefacet);
```

```
    cout << ny_time << endl; // 2004-Aug-30 00:00:00 EDT.
    cout.imbue(loc);
    cout << ny_time << endl; // 2004-Aug-30 00:00:00 Eastern Daylight Time.

    // Deletion of facets is handled automatically!
    // Thus no need to delete the created facets.

    return 0;
}
```

The output from this code is:

```
2004-Aug-30 10:00:00 EDT
2004-Aug-30 10:00:00 Eastern Daylight Time
```

In the above code we used *facets* which will be discussed in section 4.8.

4.7   Date Generators and Algorithms

We now discuss *date generators* and *date algorithms*. These can be used as tools for generating other dates or schedules of dates. In general, these algorithms compute dates based on non-date input, for example determining the date corresponding to 'the first Sunday in October'.

The generators and algorithms typically correspond to the following functionality:
- Calculate the last Monday of January.
- Calculate the first Monday of January.
- Calculate the nth day of a given month.
- Create a partial date based on day and month and then calculate this day for a given year.
- Calculate the first Sunday after Jan 1, 2011.
- Calculate the first Sunday before Jan 1, 2011.
- Calculate the number of days from a given date until a given weekday.
- Calculate the number of days from a given date to a previous given weekday.
- Generate a date that represents the date of the following weekday from the given date.

Furthermore, it is possible to convert a date to a day number and vice versa; the following static functions are used for this purpose:
- Return the day of the week (0 = Sunday, 1 = Monday, ..., 6 = Saturday).
- Convert a *ymd* type to a day number. This day number is an absolute number of days since the *epoch start*.
- Given a year and month, determine the last day of the month.
- Convert a day number to a *ymd* struct.
- Determine if a year is a leap year.

We give some examples of how to use these functions:

```
int main()
{
    // Last day of a month.
    last_day_of_the_week_in_month ldm(Monday, May);
    date d = ldm.get_date(2011);
    Print(d,"last week in month");

    // First day of a month.
    first_day_of_the_week_in_month fdm(Monday, May);
    d = fdm.get_date(2011);
    Print(d,"first week in month");
```

```
// Generate a date from partial information.
partial_date pd(1, May);
d = pd.get_date(2011);
Print(d, "partial date");

// First Monday after and before a given date.
first_day_of_the_week_after fdaf(Monday);
d = fdaf.get_date(date(2011,May,22));
Print(d, "next date: ");

first_day_of_the_week_before fdbf(Monday);
d = fdbf.get_date(date(2011,May,22));
Print(d, "previous date: ");

return 0;
}
```

More examples can be found in the Boost online documentation.

4.8   Date/Time I/O and Serialisation

We now give a short overview of the I/O streaming system for temporal data. This system allows developers to control how dates and times are presented. It supports both narrow and wide streams. To this end, there are two ways to customise these I/O options:

- *Format flags*: these flags provide flexibility with regard to the order in which date elements are displayed. For example, the format %a denotes an *abbreviated weekday name* (for example, Mon) while %A denotes a *long weekday name* (for example, Monday).
- *String elements*: these are customisable and they allow the replacement of built-in-strings by month and week names as well as other strings.

Output is based on facets. A *facet* is an object that deals with a specific aspect of internationisation (Josuttis 1999). A *locale object* is a container for different facets. We use the facet type as the index to access an aspect of a locale. In general, a locale is a collection of parameters and functions used to support national or international conventions. Different locales will produce their own representations and formats for floating-point numbers, dates and monetary values, for example.

The format of the string delimiting a locale is:

   language[*_area*[*.code*]]

where *language* is a language (for example, English or German), *area* is the area, country or culture where the language is used and *code* defines the character encoding that is being used.

The output system is based on a date_facet (which is derived from std::facet) and the input system is based on a date_input_facet (which is also derived from std::facet). Then the time and local_time facets are derived from these two base types.

A simple example shows how to define date facets and then to print dates:

```
date d1(2011, Jan, 16);

// Define output options.

// 0. Default, prints: 2011-Jan-16.
```

```
cout << endl << "Default format: " << d1 << endl;

// 1. All date parts are shorthand, prints: Sun Jan 16, 11.
date_facet* facetA=new date_facet("%a %b %d, %y");

// Short day, month, day as decimal, 2-digit year.
cout.imbue(locale(cout.getloc(), facetA));

// Assign current locale to output stream.
cout << endl << "Short format: " << d1 << endl;

// 2. All date parts are longhand, prints: Sunday January 16, 2011.
date_facet* facetB=new date_facet("%A %B %d, %Y");

// Long day, month, day as decimal, 2-digit year.
cout.imbue(locale(locale::classic(), facetB));  // Classic C locale.
cout << endl << "Long format: " << d1 << endl;

// Deletion of facets is handled automatically!
// Thus no need to delete the created facets.
```

The class date_input_facet is used to allow users to control how dates and other Gregorian objects must be formatted for input. There are many format options in the system, for example:

- Set formats for dates.
- Set date format to ISO.
- Set date format to ISO extended.
- Set format to getting months, weekdays and years individually.

An example of defining input formats is:

```
// Date input options.
date_input_facet* inputFacet = new date_input_facet();
inputFacet->format("%m %d %Y");                // [01,12], [01,31], [yyyy]
cin.imbue(locale(cin.getloc(), inputFacet));   // Assign input facet.
cout << "Enter date (mm dd yyyy e.g. 03 05 2011): "; cin >> d1;
cout << "Input: " << d1 << endl;

inputFacet->set_iso_extended_format();         // %Y%-m-&d
cin.imbue(locale(cin.getloc(), inputFacet));   // Assign input facet.
cout << "Enter date (yyyy-mm-dd e.g. 2011-03-05): "; cin >> d1;
cout << "Input: " << d1 << endl;

// Deletion of facets is handled automatically!
// Thus no need to delete the created facets.
```

Furthermore, the library has support for time facet and time input facets and they are described in the Boost online documentation.

Finally, the Boost *date-time* library is compatible with the Boost Serialization library's text and xml archives. The serialisable classes are:

```
#include <boost/date_time/gregorian/gregorian.hpp>
#include <boost/date_time/gregorian/greg_serialize.hpp>
```

An example of use in a class is:

```
class TemporalClass
{
public:
    TemporalClass(date d = date(not_a_date_time), int i = 0)
        : my_date(d),  my_int(i) {}
```

```
        void Print(ostream& os) const
        {
            os << "TemporalClass= my_date is: " << my_date
               << " my_int is: " << my_int << endl;
        }

    private:
        friend class boost::serialization::access;

        template<class Archive>
        void serialize(Archive & ar, const unsigned int version)
        {
            ar & my_date;
            ar & my_int;
        }

        date my_date;
        int my_int;
    };
```

A test program is:

```
    try
    {
        date d(day_clock::local_day());

        // Serialise.
        std::ofstream ofs("date_demo.txt");
        boost::archive::text_oarchive oa(ofs);
        oa << d;

        cout << "Construct a Temporal Class" << endl;
        TemporalClass f(d, 1);
        f.Print(cout);
        oa << f;
    }
    catch(std::exception& e)
    {
        cout << "Caught Exception: " << e.what() << endl;
    }
```

4.9   Set-Like Operations

We conclude this chapter with some *set operations* on date and time objects. Typical code
is:

```
    // Comparing date periods.
    void ComparePeriods(const date_period& dp1, const date_period& dp2)
    {
        cout << endl;
        cout << dp1 << " contains " << dp2 << boolalpha << " "
             << dp1.contains(dp2) << endl;
        cout << dp2 << " contains " << dp1 << boolalpha << " "
             << dp2.contains(dp1) << endl;
        cout << dp1 << " intersects " << dp2 << boolalpha << " "
             << dp1.intersects(dp2) << endl;
        cout << dp2 << " intersects " << dp1 << boolalpha << " "
             << dp2.intersects(dp1) << endl;
        cout << "Intersection of " << dp1 << ", and " << dp2 << " ==> "
             << dp1.intersection(dp2) << endl;
    }

    // Interaction between date periods and other entities.
    cout << "**Interaction between date periods and other entities";
```

```
date myDateMiddle(day_clock::local_day());

date_duration duration(5);                          // 5 days duration.
date myDateLower = myDateMiddle - duration;
date myDateUpper = myDateMiddle + duration;

date_period dpFirst(myDateLower, myDateUpper);

// Does one period contain another period.
cout << dpFirst << " contains " << myDateMiddle << boolalpha << " "
     << dpFirst.contains(myDateMiddle);

// Merging periods (unions). The NULL set if the periods
// do not intersect.
date_period dpA(date(2011,Jan,1), date(2011,Jan,10));
date_period dpB(date(2011,Jan,9), date(2100,Jan,31));
date_period dpUnion = dpA.merge(dpB); Print(dpUnion, "union");

// Combine two periods and any gaps between them.
date_period dpC(date(2011,Jan,1), date(2011,Jan,5));
date_period dpD(date(2011,Jan,19), date(2100,Jan,31));
date_period dpSpan = dpC.span(dpD); Print(dpSpan, "span");

// Add a given number of days to begin and end of period.
days daysShift(7);                                  // Next week.
dpSpan.shift(daysShift); Print(dpSpan, "shifted period");

// Relationship between a period and a date.
date_period dpE(date(2011,Jan,1), date(2011,Jan,31));
date dateA(2010, Dec, 31); date dateB(2011, Feb, 1);
cout << "Period before date: " << dpE.is_before(dateA) << endl;
cout << "Period before date: " << dpE.is_before(dateB) << endl;

cout << "\n\n*** Comparing periods ***" << endl;

// Comparing periods.
date_duration duration2(2);                         // 2 days duration.
date myDateLower2 = myDateMiddle - duration2;
date myDateUpper2 = myDateMiddle + duration2;

date_period dpSecond(myDateLower2, myDateUpper2);

ComparePeriods(dpFirst, dpSecond);
```

You can run the above code and examine the output.

4.10 Application Areas

Once we have analysed the date-time library we are then ready to apply it, for example:
- Project planning and project monitoring.
- Bitemporal databases.
- Real-time scheduling and queueing systems.
- Financial applications, for example cashflow scheduling and business day conventions.
- Event-notification patterns based on temporal triggers.
- Using date-time with other Boost libraries, for example Asio and Thread.

4.11 Summary and Conclusions

In this chapter we have given an overview of the data structures and functionality in the Boost date-time library. It has support for a wide range of temporal data types including

Gregorian dates, durations, date periods in addition to Posix time, time duration and time period. It also supports I/O and serialisation operations.

Temporal data structures are ubiquitous in software applications.

5 Some Building Block Data Structures and Libraries

5.1 Introduction and Objectives

In this chapter we discuss four Boost libraries that can be used in combination with other libraries and in applications:

- *Timer*: this library contains classes for measuring elapsed time and reporting on program progress toward a predefined goal. This latter feature meets the human need of knowing how a program is progressing. It is useful for minor timing tasks and it is useful when we wish to know how long parts of program code take to complete.
- *Uuid*: this library allows us to generate universally unique identifiers in distributed environments. Uuids have many uses, ranging from network and database applications as well as being used as object identifiers (OIDs) in component-based software technologies (similar to Microsoft's Component Object Model (COM); see Rogerson 1997 for more details).
- *Dynamic Bit Set*: the class `dynamic_bitset` represents a set of bits. Its interface is almost identical to that of `std::bitset` except that in the former case the number of bits can be specified at run-time (that is, in the constructor of `dynamic_bitset`).
- *Circular Buffer*: this is an STL-compliant container that uses a single fixed-sized buffer as if it were connected end-to-end. It is useful for applications that need buffered data streams. This container is sometimes called a *cyclic buffer* or *ring buffer*. It is useful in *producer-consumer* applications, for example.

For each library, we give a discussion of the functionality and features that it offers. We then give a number of examples to show how to use the library.

5.2 Timer Library

This is a relatively simple and easy-to-use library and its main use is to time and report progress on program tests or batch jobs, for example. There are three classes in this library:

a) `timer`: this class measures elapsed time. It is useful for minor timing tasks such as testing the performance of an algorithm, comparing the cost of memory allocation and deallocation using the heap and finding performance bottlenecks in programs.

The main member functions are:

- Default constructor: start counting time in the timer. Time increases monotonically starting from t = 0.
- `restart()`: set the time to t = 0; time increases monotonically starting from t = 0.
- `elapsed()`: returns the elapsed time since creation time of the timer or since the last reset.

Constructors in `timer` may throw `std::bad_alloc` exception. Other member functions do not throw exceptions.

b) `progress_timer`: this class automatically measures elapsed time and then on destruction it displays an elapsed time message (for example, '4.5 s' where 's' is the official System International (SI) standard notation for seconds) in some appropriate form. The default 'form' (output) is the system console.

The main member functions are:

- Default constructor: start counting time in the timer. Time increases monotonically starting from t = 0.

- Destructor: this is called when an instance of `progress_timer` goes out of scope and then the total execution time is printed.

Constructors in `progress_timer` may throw `std::bad_alloc` exception. Other member functions do not throw exceptions.

c) `progress_display`: this class has functionality to display appropriate information pertaining to how far a program has proceeded in executing its goal. In particular, this class can report program execution status at appropriate times and code positions places in a running program. It is initialised with the expected count and the progress is incremented using the ++ operator. It outputs the progress to a stream which is by default the standard `cout` object.

We give a simple example of how to time the progress of computation in a program that also displays the progress:

```
#include <boost/shared_ptr.hpp>
#include <boost/array.hpp>
#include <boost/timer.hpp>
#include <boost/progress.hpp>

#include <iostream>

using namespace std;

int main()
{
    int count=1000000;
    const int N = 10000;

    // Start timer and progress_timer.
    boost::timer t;
    boost::progress_timer pt;

    // Create and print a progress_display.
    boost::progress_display display(count);

    // Create many shared pointers.
    boost::shared_ptr<boost::array<int, N> > ip;
    for (int i=0; i<count; i++)
    {
        // Allocate large array.
        ip=boost::shared_ptr<boost::array<int, N> >(
          new boost::array<int, N>);

        // Display progress.
        ++display;
    }

    // Print the elapsed time from the boost::timer.
    cout<<"Time for shared pointers: "<< t.elapsed() << endl;

    return 0;
} // The progress_timer prints the elapsed time automatically
  // when it goes out of scope here.
```

This approach is probably easier to use than system-level calls to `clock()` or creating your own timer classes, for example.

5.3   Uuid (Universally Unique Identifiers)

An *uuid* is an 128 bit (16 byte) identifier that is meant to function as a unique tag or piece of information in distributed applications and environments. Uuids are guaranteed to be unique and different from all other uuids in time and space. They are ubiquitous in software systems, for example Microsoft's Component Object Model (COM) (see Rogerson 1997 for a good introduction to COM).

Some applications of UUIDs are:
* *Databases*: we can use uuids to identify the rows or records of database tables to ensure that they are unique.
* *Network messaging*: a network message can be identified using an uuid to ensure that the fragments of a network message are properly reassembled when the message is sent between two computers in a network.
* *Distributed computing*: we can use an uuid to identify a remote procedure call.
* *Object persistency*: we can use uuids to define *oids* (*unique object identifiers*) in object-oriented databases.

5.3.1   Creating Uuids

There are a number of ways to create uuids in the Uuid library:
* From a string.
* From a namespace uuid and a name.
* From a random number generator in the *Random* library.
* The ability to create *nil* uuids, that is all values are initialised to zero.

To this end, the library has a number of generator classes. We first instantiate the appropriate generator and we then create the corresponding uuid based on it. We give some examples that show how to use these generators to produce uuids:

```
#include <boost/uuid/uuid.hpp>
#include <boost/uuid/uuid_generators.hpp>
#include <boost/uuid/uuid_io.hpp>

#include <boost/random.hpp>

#include <iostream>
using namespace std;

int main()
{
    using namespace boost::uuids;

    // Creating uuids.

    // From strings.
    string_generator strGen;
    uuid u1 = strGen("00000000-0000-0000-0000-000000000000");
    cout << u1 << endl;

    uuid u2 = strGen("0123456789abcdef0123456789ABCDEF");
    cout << u2 << endl;

    // Generate a 'nil' uuid.
    nil_generator nilGen;
    uuid u3 = nilGen();
    cout << "Nil uuid: " << u3 << endl;
```

```
    // Plan B to create a nil uuid.
    uuid u4 = boost::uuids::nil_uuid();
    cout << "Nil uuid: " << u4 << endl;

    // Creating uuids based on random number generators.
    basic_random_generator <boost::mt19937> rndGen;
    uuid u5 = rndGen();
    cout << "Random mt19937 number: " << u5 << endl;

    // Using an existing RNG.
    boost::mt19937 myRan2;
    basic_random_generator <boost::mt19937> rndGen2(&myRan2);
    uuid u6 = rndGen2();
    cout << "Random mt19937 number, II: " << u6 << endl;

    // Generate uuid from a namespace uuid and a name.
    uuid dnsId;
    name_generator namGen(dnsId);
    uuid u7 = namGen("datasim.nl");
    cout << "Namespace uuid: " << u7 << endl;

    return 0;
}
```

The output from this code is:

```
00000000-0000-0000-0000-000000000000
01234567-89ab-cdef-0123-456789abcdef
Nil uuid: 00000000-0000-0000-0000-000000000000
Nil uuid: 00000000-0000-0000-0000-000000000000
Random mt19937 number: fe12f4e5-57cd-416b-97cd-616b57cd616b
Random mt19937 number, II: 5cbb91d0-f69e-4e22-b69e-ae22f69eae22
Namespace uuid: 851b7cb1-e2a3-543a-a380-ea22bdb22a1e
```

5.3.2 Other Functionality

We conclude our discussion of Uuid with a short description of other functionality in the library. First, it is possible to iterate in an uuid; each element will be an 8-bit short and hence 16 of these types will be printed. An example is:

```
// Iterating in an uuid.
uuid::const_iterator it;
for (it = u7.begin(); it != u7.end(); ++it)
{
    cout << int(*it) << ", "; // 16 shorts printed.
}
cout << endl;
```

It is possible to compare uuids:

```
// Comparing uuids.
boolalpha( cout );
cout << (u1 == u2) << endl;
cout << (u1 != u2) << endl;
cout << (u1 < u2) << endl;
cout << (u1 > u2) << endl;
cout << (u1 <= u2) << endl;
cout << (u1 >= u2) << endl;
```

Finally, uuids are serialised as primitive types; this means that only the uuid value will be saved to, or loaded from an archive. We take the specific example of text input and output archives. In this case we create an uuid u1, serialise it to a text file and then we deserialise it to produce an uuid u2. We then compare the two values and these values should be the same:

```
#include <sstream>
#include <iostream>

#include <boost/uuid/uuid.hpp>
#include <boost/uuid/uuid_serialize.hpp>
#include <boost/uuid/uuid_io.hpp>

#include <boost/archive/text_oarchive.hpp>
#include <boost/archive/text_iarchive.hpp>


int main()
{
    using namespace std;
    using namespace boost::archive;
        using namespace boost::uuids;

    ostringstream o_stream;

    uuid u1 = {{0x12, 0x34, 0x56, 0x78, 0x90, 0xab, 0xcd, 0xef, 0x12, 0x34,
                0x56, 0x78, 0x90, 0xab, 0xcd, 0xef}};
    uuid u2;

    // Save.
    {
        text_oarchive oa(o_stream);
        oa << BOOST_SERIALIZATION_NVP(u1);
    }

    cout << "Stream: " << o_stream.str() << endl;

    // Load.
    {
        istringstream i_stream(o_stream.str());
        text_iarchive ia(i_stream);

        ia >> BOOST_SERIALIZATION_NVP(u2);
    }

    // Compare the deserialised value with the original value.
    if (u1 == u2)
    {
        cout << "Good, values are the same\n";
    }
    else
    {
        cout << "Something rotten!!\n";
    }

    return 0;
}
```

5.4   Dynamic Bitset and STL Bitsets

We discuss bitsets in this section. They model *fixed-sized arrays* (in the case of STL) and *dynamic arrays* (in the case of Boost). Bitsets are useful when we wish to manage sets of flags and use bitwise operations (such as AND, OR) on these sets.

We first discuss the STL class `bitset<N>`. This class models fixed-sized arrays of bits or Boolean values. The number of bits `N` is defined at compile time and this value cannot be changed thereafter. The member function categories in `bitset` are:

- Constructors: default and based on integer and string input arguments.
- Querying if one, some or all bits in a bitset have been set; comparing bitsets for equality or inequality.
- Setting, resetting and flipping the bits in a bitset.
- Bitwise operations on bitsets (and, or, nor, left and right shift, toggle bits).
- Type conversions: converting bitsets to `string` and to `long`.

We give some examples of how to use class `bitset`. We first create a default bitset, a bitset that we initialise using an integral value and then a bitset from a string:

```
#include <bitset>

// Constructors.
const int N = 10;
bitset<N> bsA;          // All bits set to 0.
cout << bsA << endl;    // Prints 10 zeroes.

int val = 7;
bitset<N> bsB(val);     // Init bitset with val's bit representation.
cout << bsB << endl;    // The binary form of val, i.e. 0000...111.

// Constructing bitsets based on strings.
bitset<N> bsC(string("0101010101"));      // String of length 10.
cout << bsC << endl;
```

Next, we create bitsets by extracting certain bits from input strings. In the first case we create a bitset of length 7 by extracting information starting at the third bit (index2) and continuing to the end of the string:

```
// Bitsets with start pos and/or size.
int index = 2;                            // 3rd bit, indexing starts at 0.
bitset<7> bsD(string("1111000"), index);  // From index to end.
cout << "Bitset with start index: " << bsD << endl;
```

The output in this case is '0011000'. We note that extra bits are *padded* from the left. The next example extracts 4 bits from beginning of the input string:

```
int num_bits = 4;
index = 0;
bitset<7> bsE(string("10111000"), index, num_bits);
cout << "Bitset with start index and number bits: " << bsE << endl;
```

The output in this case is '0001011'. In both cases we note that the bitset's elements are constructed *from right to left*.

We now discuss those operations that modify the bits in a bitset in some way. For example, we can set all the bits to `true`, set all the bits to a given value, set all the bits to `false`, flip all bits and flip at a certain position:

```
const int SZ = 4;
bitset<SZ> bsX(string("1010"));

bsX.set();              // Set all bits to true

// Set all the bits to bitValue.
bool bitValue = 1;      // True.
```

```
for (size_t j = 0; j < bsX.size(); ++j)
{
    bsX.set(j, bitValue);
}

bsX.reset();    // Set all bits to 0 (false).
bsX.flip();     // Set unset bits and vice versa.
bsX.flip(2);    // Toggle bit at position 2.
```

We have also created two utility functions to print the contents of a bitset and to compare two bitsets:

```
template <int N>
void ExamineBitset(const bitset<N>& bs)
{
    cout << "Number of total bits: " << bs.size() << endl;
    cout << "Number of set bits: " << bs.count() << endl;
    cout << "Is any bit set?: " << boolalpha << bs.any() << endl;
    cout << "Is no bit set?: " << boolalpha << bs.none() << endl;
}

template <int N>
void CompareBitsets(const bitset<N>& bs1, const bitset<N>& bs2)
{
    cout << "Bitsets equal?: " << boolalpha << (bs1 == bs2) << endl;
    cout << "BitSets not equal?: " << boolalpha << (bs1 != bs2) << endl;
}
```

You can test these functions. All the code is on the distribution medium.

5.4.1 Boolean Operations

We can perform bitwise binary and unary operations on bitsets. There are two binary forms, namely when the left-hand operand is modified and the second form is when two bitsets combine to form a new bitset. We take some examples of both forms:

```
const int M = 4;
bitset<M> bs1(string("1010")); cout<<"bs1: "<<bs1<<endl;
bitset<M> bs2(string("0011")); cout<<"bs2: "<<bs2<<endl;

// Boolean operators, non-modifying.
cout<<"~bs1: "<<~bs1<<endl;                    // Toggle all bits.
cout<<"bs1 ^ bs2: "<<(bs1 ^ bs2)<<endl;        // Bitwise XOR.
cout<<"bs1 | bs2: "<<(bs1 | bs2)<<endl;        // Bitwise OR.
cout<<"bs1 & bs2: "<<(bs1 & bs2)<<endl;        // Bitwise AND.

// Boolean operators, modifying.
bs1 ^= bs2; cout<<"bs1 ^= bs2: "<<bs1<<endl; // XOR .
bs1 |= bs2; cout<<"bs1 |= bs2: "<<bs1<<endl; // Bitwise OR.
bs1 &= bs2; cout<<"bs1 &= bs2: "<<bs1<<endl; // Bitwise AND.
```

Which option to choose depends on the application but in general the first form is more efficient than the second form.

We can also perform shift operations on bitsets. Again, there are two forms as in the previous case:

```
// Shift operators, non-modifying. Always zero's are shifted in.
int n=1;
bs1=bitset<M>(string("1001")); cout<<"bs1: "<<bs1<<endl;
cout<<"bs1>>n: "<<(bs1 >> n)<<endl;            // Shift n bits to the right.
cout<<"bs1<<n: "<<(bs1 << n)<<endl;            // Shift n bits to the left.
```

```
// Shift operators, modifying. Always zero's are shifted in.
bs1=bitset<M>(string("1001")); cout<<"bs1: "<<bs1<<endl;
bs1 >>= n; cout<<"bs1 >>= n: "<<bs1<<endl;   // Shift n bits to the right.
bs1 <<= n; cout<<"bs1 <<= n: "<<bs1<<endl;   // Shift n bits to the left.
```

5.4.2   Type Conversions

We conclude our discussion of `std::bitset` by showing how to return the integral and string values that a bitset represents. To this end, we use the member functions `to_ulong()` and `to_string()`. Here is an example:

```
// Type conversions.
const int P = 4;
bitset<P> bs(string("1011"));

// The integral value corresponding to the bits.
unsigned long value = bs.to_ulong();
string stringValue = bs.to_string();

cout << "Numeric value: " << value << ", String value: "
     << stringValue << endl;
```

5.4.3   dynamic_bitset

This class is almost identical to `std::bitset` and has an interface similar to that of `std::bitset`. There is however, one major difference; in the current case we can create bitsets of dynamic length at run-time. This is achieved in the constructors of `dynamic_bitset<Block, Allocator>`. It has two template parameters:

- *Block*: the integer type in which the bits are stored (default is `unsigned long`).
- *Allocator*: the allocator type used for all internal memory management (default is `std::allocator<Block>`).

An example of use is:

```
#include <iostream>
#include <boost/dynamic_bitset.hpp>

using namespace std;

int main()
{
    boost::dynamic_bitset<unsigned int> x(4); // All 0's by default.
    x[0] = 1;
    x[1] = 1;
    x[3] = 1;
    cout << x  << endl; // '1011'.

    boost::dynamic_bitset<unsigned int> y(4);
    cout << y << endl;  // '0000'.
    y = x;
    cout << y << endl;  // '1011'.

    return 0;
}
```

The other member functions are the same as those for `std::bitset`.

5.4.4   Applications of Dynamic Bitsets

There are many applications in which dynamic bitsets can be used. In general, their use results in efficient and compact code. Some applications are:

- Creating efficient and compact data structures.

- Memory allocation managers.
- Huffman coding, Bloom filters.
- Information retrieval.
- Raster graphics when we model pixels and bitmaps.
- Genetic algorithms, especially when modelling *selection, crossover* and *mutation* processes.
- When implementing security and access control policies.
- It can be an alternative to, and improvement to using `std::vector<bool>`.

Discussion of these topics is outside the scope of this book.

5.5   Circular Buffer

A *circular buffer* (also known as *cyclic buffer, circular queue* or *ring buffer*) is a data structure that uses a single fixed-sized buffer in which the end of the buffer is connected to its front. The buffer has thus a *front* and a *rear*. Indexing begins at zero and continues to the number of elements minus one in the buffer. For an empty buffer we have *front == rear == 0* as seen in Figure 5.1(a); *front* points one position counterclockwise from the element at the front of the queue. For non-empty buffers *rear* points to the position of the element at the rear of the queue. There are two major operations, namely:

- *enqueue*: add an element *x* to the buffer:
  rear = rear + 1 (mod Size)
  buffer[rear] = x
- *dequeue*: remove an element *x* from the buffer:
  front = front + 1 (mod Size)
  x = buffer[front]

In the above cases *Size* represents the number of elements in the buffer. We show the use of these operations in Figure 5.1. We show the state of the buffer after these operations have been executed:

- Figure 5.1(a): the circular buffer is empty.
- Figure 5.1(b): enqueue the values 'a', 'b' and 'c'.
- Figure 5.1(c): perform two dequeue and an enqueue of value 'd' in that order.
- Figure 5.1(d): perform two dequeue operations.
- Figure 5.1(e): enqueue the values 'e', 'f' and 'g'.
- Figure 5.1(f): enqueue the values 'x' and 'y'.

Circular buffers are used in a number of applications, for example:

- In a data acquisition application we store the most recently received samples; then the oldest samples are overwritten as new samples arrive.
- As a cache that stores a specified number of last inserted elements.
- As an efficient fixed capacity FIFO or LIFO queue that removes the oldest element when full.
- It can be used as an underlying container for other thread-safe containers such as `BoundedBuffer` that we discuss in section 5.5.2.
- Applicability to real-time, embedded and performance-critical applications. In particular, `circular_buffer` is compatible with the Boost Interprocess library that is used for interprocess communication.

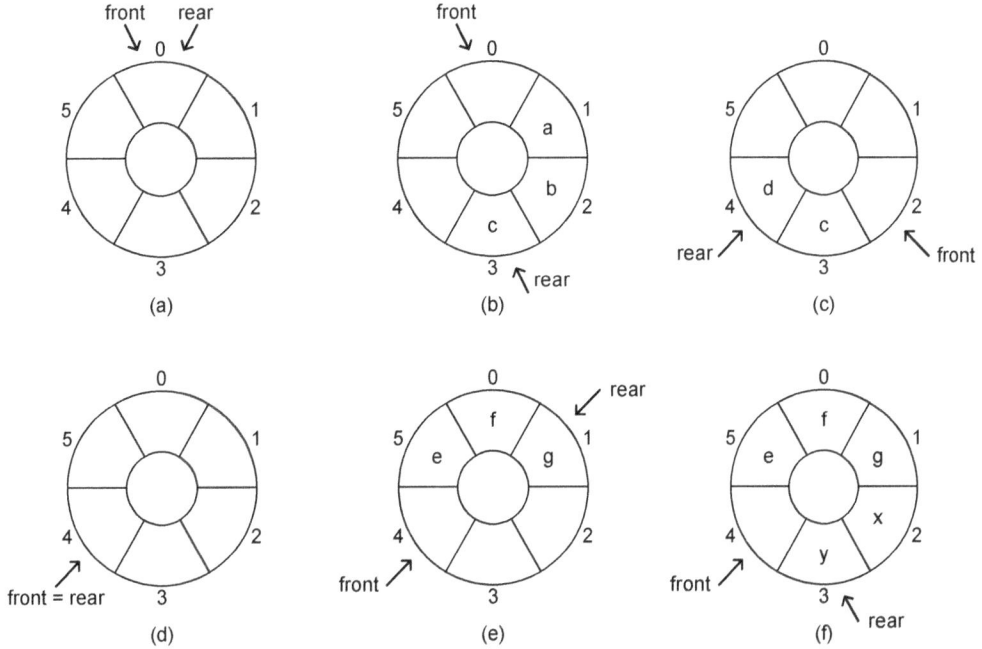

Figure 5.1 Circular buffer

5.5.1   The Boost Circular Buffer Class

In this section we give an overview of the class `circular_buffer<T, Alloc>`. We concentrate on a global description of its interface and we give some examples of use. More details can be found in the Boost online documentation and in later sections of this chapter. The container `circular_buffer<T, Alloc>` is a sequence container and is similar to `std::deque` and `std::list`. It has functionality for the following function categories:

- Constructors: there are several constructors, for example creating a circular buffer having a given size or *capacity*. For some real-time and embedded applications it is possible to specify a user-defined memory allocator.
- Sequential and random access iterators. In particular, it is possible to access the elements of a circular buffer using the operator `[]` and the member function `at()`.
- Add elements to, and remove elements from the front or back of the circular queue.
- Insert an element into the circular queue at a given (iterator) position; remove an element from a circular buffer at a given (iterator) position.
- Standalone functions for comparing circular buffers; these functions are the binary comparison operators such as `==` and `<`, for example. In general, two circular buffers are compared element-by-element.

We thus see that these categories are similar to those in STL and we do not discuss how to use them in any great detail. We do however, give a simple example of use. In this case we create a circular buffer of characters and we add elements to it and we remove elements from it. We also provide a function to print information pertaining to a circular queue:

```
#include <boost/circular_buffer.hpp>

template <typename T>
void Print(const boost::circular_buffer<T>& cb)
```

```
{
    cout << "Circular buffer size: " << cb.size() << endl;
    if (cb.size()==0) return;

    cout << "Front: " << cb.front() << ", Rear: " << cb.back()
        << ", Contents: ";

    // Print all elements.
    for (size_t j = 0; j < cb.size(); ++j)
    {
        cout << cb[j] << ",";
    }
    cout << endl;
}
```

The test program is:

```
cout<<"A: Create circular buffer with a size of 6."<<endl;
int size = 6;
boost::circular_buffer<char> cb(size);
Print<char>(cb);

cout<<"B: Enqueue 3 elements."<<endl;
cb.push_back('a');
cb.push_back('b');
cb.push_back('c');
Print<char>(cb);

cout<<"C: Dequeue 2 elements and queue 1 element."<<endl;
cb.pop_front();
cb.pop_front();
cb.push_back('d');
Print<char>(cb);

cout<<"D: Dequeue 2 elements."<<endl;
cb.pop_front();
cb.pop_front();
Print<char>(cb);

cout<<"E: Enqueue 3 elements."<<endl;
cb.push_back('e');
cb.push_back('f');
cb.push_back('g');
Print<char>(cb);

cout<<"F: Enqueue 2 elements."<<endl;
cb.push_back('x');
cb.push_back('y');
Print<char>(cb);

cout<<"Overflow buffer..."<<endl;
cout << "Size: " << cb.size() << endl;
for (int j = 0; j < 20; ++j)
{
    cb.push_back((char)(j+'A'));
}
Print<char>(cb);
```

Finally, the output from this code is:

```
A: Create circular buffer with a size of 6.
Circular buffer size: 0
B: Enqueue 3 elements.
Circular list size: 3
Front: a, Rear: c, Contents: a,b,c,
```

```
C: Dequeue 2 elements and queue 1 element.
Circular buffer size: 2
Front: c, Rear: d, Contents: c,d,
D: Dequeue 2 elements.
Circular buffer size: 0
E: Enqueue 3 elements.
Circular buffer size: 3
Front: e, Rear: g, Contents: e,f,g,
F: Enqueue 2 elements.
Circular buffer size: 5
Front: e, Rear: y, Contents: e,f,g,x,y,
Overflow buffer...
Size: 5
Circular buffer size: 6
Front: O, Rear: T, Contents: O,P,Q,R,S,T,
```

You can compare the code with the output that it produces.

The `boost::circular_buffer` has a fixed capacity. The size is specified in the constructor. Then *producers* update the values in the circular buffer while *consumers* read its elements. Newly inserted elements will cause elements at either the rear or at the front of the circular buffer to be overwritten when the capacity has been exhausted. Boost provides a number of *adapter classes* (for example, `circular_buffer_space_optimized`) that allocate memory when needed (the capacity grows) in contrast to `circular_buffer` that allocates memory when it is created.

For efficiency reasons, `circular_buffer` stores its elements in a contiguous region of memory. The consequences are:
- No implicit or unexpected memory allocation because memory is fixed.
- Constant-time insertion and removal of elements.
- Constant-time random access to elements.

5.5.2   Using Circular Buffer: Producer-Consumer Pattern

In Demming 2010 we developed a small application based on the *Producer-Consumer* pattern (see also Mattson 2005 for an introduction to *parallel design patterns*). We created a *thread-safe adapter* for `std::queue`. Producers write to the adapter while consumers read from the adapter. This solution is not as efficient as we might like for certain kinds of performance-critical applications. To this end, we now discuss a variation of the producer-consumer application in which the adapter is implemented using a circular buffer. The structure of the application is similar to the design in Demming 2010. We now discuss the main classes in the current case:

- `BoundedBuffer`: The adapter that contains an instance of `circular_buffer`. It has thread-safe member functions for adding elements to the rear of the buffer and for removing elements from the front of the buffer. The size of the buffer is fixed during its lifetime and is determined at creation time.
- `Consumer`: the class whose instances remove elements from the front of the buffer.
- `Producer`: the class whose instances add elements to the rear of the buffer.

We restrict the discussion to circular buffers having `double` as data for convenience:

```
// Bounded buffer of doubles; can be generalised to a template, later.
class BoundedBuffer
{
    boost::circular_buffer<double> m_container;
};
```

This allows us to concentrate on the essential multi-threading issues without our having to deal with template classes or template syntax. We use condition variables `cv_not_empty` and `cv_not_full` that threads use to wait on for an event to happen and to notify other threads when an event has happened. We also define a *mutex* that is used when locking code.

The member data of class `BoundedBuffer` is:

```
// Member data.
boost::mutex m_mutex;                   // Mutex for synchronising access
                                        // to the circular buffer.

// Condition variables.
boost::condition cv_not_empty;  // Buffer is not empty.
boost::condition cv_not_full;   // Buffer is not full.
```

We now discuss the operations for adding elements to and removing elements from the circular buffer. To this end, we first need two member functions that tell us if the buffer is not empty or not full:

```
bool is_not_empty() const { return !m_container.empty(); }
bool is_not_full() const  { return !m_container.full();  }
```

We first discuss how to add an element to the rear of a circular buffer in a thread-safe way:

```
// Add an element to the end of the buffer.
void push_back(double item)
{
    // 1. Obtain lock.
    boost::mutex::scoped_lock lock(m_mutex);

    // 2. Wait on the condition variable until the buffer is not full
    //    and add the element to the buffer.
    cv_not_full.wait(lock, boost::bind(&BoundedBuffer::is_not_full, this));
    m_container.push_back(item);

    // 3. Release lock.
    lock.unlock();

    // 4. Signal other that the buffer is not empty.
    cv_not_empty.notify_one();
}
```

We describe these steps as follows:
- Step 1: create a lock to ensure mutual exclusion to the code.
- Step 2: thread waits until the buffer is not full and then adds an element to the buffer.
- Step 3: step 2 has completed which means that the code can be unlocked.
- Step 4: notify other threads that they can proceed.

We now show how to remove an element from the front of a circular buffer in a thread-safe way. The steps are similar to those just discussed:

```
// Remove the first element from the buffer.
void pop_front(double* pItem)
{
    // 1. Obtain lock.
    boost::mutex::scoped_lock lock(m_mutex);

    // 2. Wait on the condition variable till the buffer is not empty
    // and retrieve element.
    cv_not_empty.wait(lock, boost::bind(&BoundedBuffer::is_not_empty,
```

```
                                 this));

        *pItem=m_container.front();
        m_container.pop_front();

        // 3. Release lock.
        lock.unlock();

        // 4. Signal others that the buffer is not full.
        cv_not_full.notify_one();
    }
```

We now show the producer and consumer classes:

```
// Producer class.
class Producer
{
private:
    BoundedBuffer* m_container;

public:
    // Constructor.
    Producer(BoundedBuffer* buffer): m_container(buffer) {}

    // Function run by another thread producing elements.
    void operator()()
    {
        cout << "Starting producer...\n";
        for (long i = 0; i < 100; ++i)
        {
            m_container->push_back(double(i));

            // Small delay.
            boost::this_thread::sleep(boost::posix_time::millisec(100));
        }
    }
};


// Consumer class.
class Consumer
{
private:
    BoundedBuffer* m_container;

public:
    // Constructor.
    Consumer(BoundedBuffer* buffer): m_container(buffer) {}

    // Function run by another thread consuming elements.
    void operator()()
    {
        cout << "Starting consumer...\n";
        double item;
        for (long i = 0; i < 100; ++i)
        {
            m_container->pop_front(&item); cout << item << ",";
        }
    }
};
```

We see that both of these classes implement the function call operator () and they will be used as the *callable objects* in a thread constructor. The code to create a simple producer-consumer application is:

```
// Create bounded buffer.
BoundedBuffer buffer(100);

// Put in some values into the circular buffer before
// consuming and producing.
for (long i = 0; i < 25 ; ++i)
{
    buffer.push_back(double(i));
}

cout << "Creating consumer and producer\n";
Consumer consumer(&buffer);
Producer producer(&buffer);

// Start the threads.
boost::thread consume(consumer);
boost::thread produce(producer);

// Wait for completion.
consume.join();
produce.join();
```

The details of how this code works has been discussed in detail in Demming 2010.

5.6   Summary and Conclusions

In this chapter we have discussed four specialised libraries that could be used as part of a larger application or in combination with other Boost libraries. They add to the general reliability and efficiency of applications. The libraries are used for timing program execution, creating specialised circular queues, generating unique IDS in time and space and when modelling dynamic bit sets.

6 Matrix Algebra in Boost Part I: uBLAS Data Structures

6.1 Introduction and Objectives

The Boost uBLAS library supports vector and matrix data structures and basic linear operations on these structures. The syntax closely reflects mathematical notation because operator overloading is used. Furthermore, the library uses *expression templates* to generate efficient code. The library has been influenced by a number of other libraries such as ATLAS, BLAS, Blitz++, POOMA and MTL. The main design goals are:

- Use mathematical notation whenever appropriate.
- Efficiency (time and resource management).
- Functionality (provide features that appeal to a wide range of application areas).
- Compatibility (array-like indexing and use of STL allocators for storage allocation).

The two most important data structures represent vectors and matrices. A *vector* is a one-dimensional structure while a *matrix* is a two-dimensional structure. We can define various *vector and matrix patterns* that describe how matrices are arranged in memory; examples are *dense*, *sparse*, *banded*, *triangular*, *symmetric* and *Hermitian*. These patterned structures are used in many kinds of applications. Furthermore, we can define primitive operations on vectors and matrices, for example:

- Addition of vectors and matrices.
- Scalar multiplication.
- Computed assignments.
- Transformations.
- Norms of vectors and matrices.
- Inner and outer products.

We can use these operations in code and applications. Finally, we can define *subvectors* and *submatrices* as well as *ranges* and *slices* of vectors and matrices.

Vectors and matrices are fundamental to scientific and engineering applications and having a well-developed library such as uBLAS with ready-to-use modules will free up developer time. Seeing that matrix algebra consumes much of the effort in an application we expect that the productivity gains will be appreciable in general. A discussion of applications of matrices is outside the scope of this book. However, we do present several methods to solve linear systems of equations in chapter 7 by basing them on uBLAS.

6.2 BLAS (Basic Linear Algebra Subprograms)

BLAS is a *de facto* application programming interface standard for libraries that perform basic linear algebra operations on vectors and matrices. They promote the readability, modularity and maintainability of software. BLAS promotes *modularity* by identifying frequently occurring operations of linear algebra and by specifying a standard interface to these operations. *Efficiency* is achieved by optimising the code within BLAS. It is important to identify and define a set of basic operations that is rich enough to allow us to model high-level algorithms on the one hand and simple enough to allow optimisation on a range of computers on the other hand.

The advantages of using BLAS are its robustness, portability and readability. The BLAS functionality consists of three levels that we now discuss.

6.2.1   BLAS Level 1

This level consists of low-level operations such as *inner products* (also known as *dot products*) of vectors and the addition of a multiple of one vector to another vector. These *vector-vector operations* are referred to as Level 1 BLAS such as:

$$y \leftarrow \alpha x + y$$
where x and y are vectors and α is a scalar.   (6.1)

These operations involve O(n) floating-point operations in general, where n is the length of the vectors. In equation (6.1) we see that the vector y is being updated and the operation is sometimes called *saxpy* ('scalar a x plus y').

6.2.2   BLAS Level 2

This level contains matrix-vector operations of the form:

$$y \leftarrow \alpha A x + \beta y$$
where x and y are vectors, A is a matrix α and β are scalars.   (6.2)

These matrix-vector operations occur during the implementation of many of the most common algorithms in linear algebra. The Level 2 BLAS involve O(mn) scalar operations where m and n are the dimensions of the matrix involved in the operations.

Other operations in BLAS Level 2 are:
- Rank-one and rank-two updates :

$$A = \alpha x y^T + A \text{ (rank-1 update)}$$

$$A = \alpha x y^T + \alpha y x^T + A \text{ (rank-2 update)}$$ (6.3)

    where y^T is the transpose of vector y.

- Solution of triangular equations of the form:

$$T y = x$$ (6.4)

where T is a non-singular *upper triangular matrix* (all elements below the main diagonal are zero) or *lower triangular matrix* (all elements above the main diagonal are zero).
In general – and when appropriate - the operations apply to general band, Hermitian, Hermitian band and triangular band matrices with real and complex coefficients in both single and double precision. We shall discuss these types of matrices in detail in later sections and in chapter 7.

6.2.3   BLAS Level 3

This level concerns *matrix-matrix operations* and they are similar to Level 2 operations. In general, we replace the vectors x and y in equations (6.3) by matrices B and C, for example. This approach keeps the design of the software as consistent as possible with the software of the Level 2 BLAS. It also helps users remember the calling sequences and parameter conventions. Some examples are:

- Matrix-matrix products:
$$C = \alpha AB + \beta C$$

$$C = \alpha A^T B + \beta C$$

$$C = \alpha AB^T + \beta C \tag{6.5}$$

$$C = \alpha A^T B^T + \beta C.$$

- Rank-k updates of a symmetric matrix C:

$$C = \alpha AA^T + \beta C \ (A^T \text{ is transpose of } A)$$

$$C = \alpha A^T A + \beta C$$

$$C = \alpha A^T B + \alpha B^T A + \beta C \tag{6.6}$$

$$C = \alpha AB^T + \alpha BA^T + \beta C.$$

- Multiplying a matrix B by a triangular matrix T:

$$B = \alpha TB$$

$$B = \alpha T^T B$$

$$B = \alpha BT \tag{6.7}$$

$$B = \alpha BT^T.$$

- Solving triangular systems of equations with multiple right-hand sides:

$$B = \alpha T^{-1} B \ (T^{-1} \text{ is inverse of } T)$$

$$B = \alpha BT^{-1} \tag{6.8}$$

where α and β are scalars; A, B and C are rectangular matrices; T is an upper or lower triangular matrix. Boost uBLAS supports the above BLAS operations and they are mapped to appropriate C++ function calls. We discuss these mappings in detail in this and the next chapter.

6.3 Dense Vectors

A *dense vector* of length n is one all of whose elements are explicitly given a value. In other words, there are no 'gaps' (missing values) in these vectors. To this end, the class vector<T, Alloc> has two parameters:
- The type T of the object stored in the vector.
- The type Alloc of storage array (dynamic, run-time storage fixed-size storage or compile-time storage.

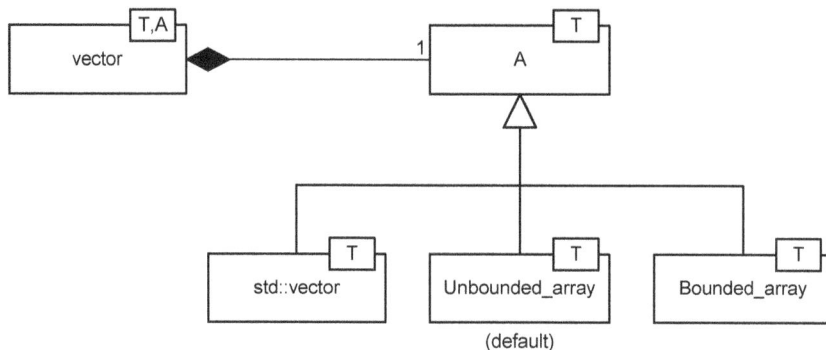

Figure 6.1 Dense Vector and its storage

We show the conceptual structure of this class in an UML class diagram in Figure 6.1. To use this class we instantiate its template parameters (the default allocator type is `unbounded_array<T>`).

The categories of member functions are:
- Constructors.
- Accessing the elements of the vector using the operators `()` and `[]`.
- Adding and subtracting two vectors.
- Multiply and divide a vector by a scalar.
- Constant and non-constant forward and reverse iterators.
- Resize a vector (*reallocate* a vector to hold a given number of elements).

Rather than giving extended examples of all the different member functions (many of which are easy if you are familiar with STL) we prefer to concentrate on critical member functions. We also mention that many STL algorithms can be used on uBLAS vectors.

6.3.1   Creating and Accessing Dense Vectors

We first create a number of dense vectors based on the options in Figure 6.1. We can create vectors having both numeric and non-numeric underlying data types and given storage arrays. Note that we use an alias for the uBLAS namespace:

```
#include <boost/numeric/ublas/vector.hpp> // The vector class.
#include <boost/numeric/ublas/io.hpp>     // Sending to IO stream.

namespace ublas=boost::numeric::ublas;

ublas::vector<double> v1(10);
ublas::vector<double, ublas::unbounded_array<double> > v2(10);
ublas::vector<double, ublas::bounded_array<double, 20> > v3(10);
ublas::vector<double> v4(5, 3.14);
ublas::vector<double, vector<double> > v5(10, 4.5);
cout<<"v5: "<<v5<<endl;

ublas::vector<char, vector<char> > v6(10, 'd');
cout<<"v6: "<<v6<<endl;
```

We can access and modify the elements of a vector using overloaded operators:

```
// Fill the vectors.
for (int i=0; i<10; i++)
{
```

```
    // Use the [] operator.
    v1[i]=i;

    // Use the () operator.
    v2(i)=i+10;
    v3(i)=i+20;
}
```

We now show the use of composite operators and the support for iterators:

```
// Operators.
// When adding/subtracting two vectors, they should have the same size.
cout<<endl<<"*** Operators ***"<<endl;
cout<<"v1+=v3:  "<<(v1+=v3)<<endl;
cout<<"v1-=v3:  "<<(v1-=v3)<<endl;
cout<<"v1*=2.5: "<<(v1*=2.5)<<endl;
cout<<"v1/=2.5: "<<(v1/=2.5)<<endl;

// Iterators.
cout<<endl<<"*** Iterators ***"<<endl;
transform(v1.begin(), v1.end(), v2.begin(), v3.begin(),
        multiplies<double>());
cout<<"Multiply v1 & v2 to v3 using transform algorithm ";
cout<<"and multiplies function object: "<<v3<<endl;
```

Finally, we can resize a vector as follows (notice the option to preserve the existing data in the vector):

```
v1.resize(8, false); cout<<".. to 8 (no data preserved): "<<v1<<endl;
v2.resize(8, true); cout<<".. to 8 (data preserved): "<<v2<<endl;
```

6.3.2 Special Dense Vectors

The uBLAS has support for special kinds of dense vectors:

- *Unit vector*: For a given vector size n, the kth *canonical vector* has value zero for all elements except for index k which has value 1. It is clear that there are n canonical *unit vectors* for vectors of size n and they form a *orthonormal basis* in n-dimensional Euclidean space. An example in three-dimensional space is:

```
// Create unit vectors. The first argument is the size,
// the second argument is the element that is 1.
ublas::unit_vector<double> uv1(3, 0);  // 1, 0, 0
ublas::unit_vector<double> uv2(3, 1);  // 0, 1, 0
ublas::unit_vector<double> uv3(3, 2);  // 0, 0, 1

cout<<"uv1: "<<uv1<<", index of 1: "<<uv1.index()<<endl;
cout<<"uv2: "<<uv2<<", index of 1: "<<uv2.index()<<endl;
cout<<"uv3: "<<uv3<<", index of 1: "<<uv3.index()<<endl;
```

- *Zero vector*: The n-dimensional zero vector has all its values equal to zero:

```
// All elements of a zero vector are always zero. Constructor accepts size.
ublas::zero_vector<double> zv(10);
cout<<"Zero vector (always contains all zeros): "<<zv<<endl;
```

- *Scalar vector*: This is a generalisation of the zero vector. A scalar vector of size n is one of whose elements all have the same value. An example of use is:

```
// A scalar vector has elements with the same value.
ublas::scalar_vector<double> sv1(5, 3.5);     // Size 5, contents 3.5.
ublas::scalar_vector<double> sv2(10, 9.0);    // Size 10, contents 9.0.
cout<<"Scalar vector with 3.5: "<<sv1<<endl;
cout<<"Scalar vector with 9.0: "<<sv1<<endl;
```

It is useful to have these special vectors at our disposal because they are needed in numerical linear algebra applications. Note that the elements of these special vectors are read-only.

6.4 Sparse Vectors

In general, most applications will use dense vectors but there may be a need for a *sparse vector*. With sparse vectors only non-zero elements are stored which can save memory when a vector only contains a few non-zero elements. Boost uBLAS provides various kinds of sparse vectors.

6.4.1 Mapped Vector

A *mapped vector* is one in which the non-relevant (or zero) elements are more numerous than the relevant (or non-zero) elements. uBLAS models the mapped vector using maps as shown conceptually in Figure 6.2. In this case the non-zero elements of the vector are mapped to consecutive elements of the corresponding associative container. Its interface is similar to that of the dense vector class. Internally, the type of the adapted array is essentially `std::map<std::size_t, T>`.

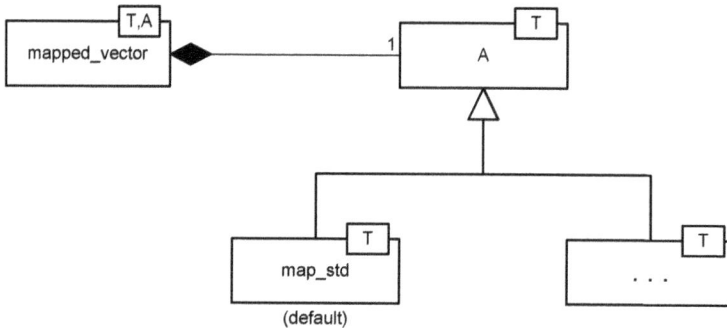

Figure 6.2 Sparse Vector

An example of use is:

```
#include <boost/numeric/ublas/vector_sparse.hpp>
#include <boost/numeric/ublas/io.hpp>

namespace ublas=boost::numeric::ublas;

// Mapped vector with 10 elements.
ublas::mapped_vector<double> mv1(10);

// Mapped vector with 10 elements where space is
// reserved for 6 non-zero elements.
ublas::mapped_vector<double> mv2(10, 6);

// Normal vector to be copied to mapped vector.
ublas::vector<double> v(10);

// Fill the (mapped) vectors.
for (int i=0; i<10; i++)
{
    // Only fill the odd elements.
    if (i%2==1)
    {
        // Use the [] operator.
```

```
            mv1[i]=i;

            // Use the () operator.
            mv2(i)=i*2;
        }

        v(i)=i%2*3;
    }

    // Normal vector (vector expressions) can be copied to mapped vector
    // (space reserved for 6 non-zero elements (optional)).
    // Uses a "map_array" as internal map datastructure instead of "map_std".
    ublas::mapped_vector<double, ublas::map_array<size_t, double> > mv3(v, 6);
```

We now carry out some arithmetic operations on mapped vectors; please note that the vectors must have the same size:

```
    // Operators.
    // Adding/subtracting two vectors, should have the same size.
    cout<<endl<<"*** Operators ***"<<endl;
    cout<<"mv1+=mv3: "<<(mv1+=mv3)<<endl;
    cout<<"mv1-=mv3: "<<(mv1-=mv3)<<endl;
    cout<<"mv1*=2.5: "<<(mv1*=2.5)<<endl;
    cout<<"mv1/=2.5: "<<(mv1/=2.5)<<endl;
```

Inserting elements into, and removing elements from a mapped vector is achieved as follows. The member function `insert_element()` does not insert a new element but overwrites the value of an existing element. For mapped vectors you can only insert at a position where there is a zero-value element. The member functions `erase()` and `clear()` do not remove elements but set their values to zero.

```
    mv2.insert_element(4, 3.14);
    cout<<"mv2.insert_element(4, 3.14): "<<mv2<<endl;
    mv2.erase_element(4);
    cout<<"mv2.erase_element(4): "<<mv2<<endl;

    try
    {
        mv2.insert_element(5, 3.14);
    }
    catch (ublas::bad_index)
    {
        cout<<"Err insert at pos 5, already has non-zero value."<<endl;
    }

    mv2.clear();
    cout<<"mv2.clear: "<<mv2<<endl;
```

Finally, iterators are defined for mapped vectors. Their use seems a bit odd at first sight because they iterate only in the used (non-zero) elements. But if an element is reset to zero, then that element is still used (still in the internal map) and will be iterated over. You have to take this iterator behaviour into account when using mapped vectors with algorithms, for example:

```
    ublas::mapped_vector<double> mv(10);
    mv[0]=30; mv[6]=20; mv[9]=10;
    cout<<"mv: "<<mv<<endl;

    // Iterate the mapped vector.
    int counter=0;
    for (ublas::mapped_vector<double>::iterator it=mv.begin();
         it!=mv.end(); it++)
    {
```

```
        cout<<*it<<"->";
        *it=1.5;
        cout<<*it<<", ";
        counter++;
    }
    cout<<endl<<counter<<" elements changed: "<<mv<<endl;

    // Set 1 extra element.
    mv[3]=99;
    cout<<endl<<"mv (element 3 set too): "<<mv<<endl;

    // Iterate the mapped vector again.
    counter=0;
    for (ublas::mapped_vector<double>::iterator it=mv.begin();
        it!=mv.end(); it++)
    {
        cout<<*it<<"->";
        *it=2.5;
        cout<<*it<<", ";
        counter++;
    }
    cout<<endl<<counter<<" elements changed: "<<mv<<endl;
```

6.4.2 Compressed Vector

A *compressed vector* is one in which the non-zero elements are mapped to consecutive elements of the index and value. It has four template parameters:

- The underlying data type T stored in the compressed vector.
- The index base IB of the compressed vector.
- The type IA of the adapted array for indices (default is the class unbounded_array<std::size_t>).
- The type TA of the adapted array for values (default is the class unbounded_array<T>).

An example of use with default parameters is:

```
    // The sparse vector classes (compressed vector).
    #include <boost/numeric/ublas/vector_sparse.hpp>
    namespace ublas=boost::numeric::ublas;

    // Compressed vector with 10 elements where space is reserved for 6
    // non-zero elements (more efficient).
    ublas::compressed_vector<double> cv2(10, 6);

    // Normal vector to be copied to compressed vector.
    ublas::vector<double> v(10);

    // Fill the (compressed) vectors.
    for (int i=0; i<10; i++)
    {
        // Only fill the odd elements.
        if (i%2==1)
        {
            // Use the () operator.
            cv2(i)=i*2;
        }

        v(i)=i%2*3;
    }
```

An example with user-specified values for the template parameters is:

```
// Normal vector (vector expressions) can be copied to compressed vector.
// Uses a "bounded_array" as internal datastructure.
ublas::compressed_vector<double, 0, ublas::bounded_array<double, 10>,
    ublas::bounded_array<double, 10> > cv3(v, 6);
```

Finally, the previous code examples above for a mapped vector will also work on compressed vectors. We do not repeat this code. It is available as software accompanying the book.

6.4.3   Coordinate Vector

A *coordinate vector* is similar to a compressed vector except that in a compressed vector the internal arrays are sorted, thus leading to faster lookups. An example of use is:

```
// Coordinate vector with 10 elements.
ublas::coordinate_vector<double> cv1(10);

// Compressed vector with 10 elements where space is reserved for
// 6 non-zero elements (more efficient).
ublas::coordinate_vector<double> cv2(10, 6);

// Fill the (coordinate) vectors.
for (int i=0; i<10; i++)
{
    // Only fill the odd elements.
    if (i%2==1)
    {
        // Use the [] operator.
        cv1[i]=i;

        // Use the () operator.
        cv2(i)=i*2;
    }
}
```

6.5   Dense Matrices

A *dense matrix* having n rows and m columns is one all of whose nXm elements are stored in memory. These types of matrices are used in many kinds of applications. The class matrix<T, F, Alloc> has three template parameters:
* T: the type of object stored in the matrix.
* F: the function object that describes the storage organisation, for example row order (the default is row_order).
* Alloc: the type of storage array (the default is unbounded_array<T>).

The conceptual UML class diagram is shown in Figure 6.3. The categories of member functions in this class are:
* Constructors.
* Accessing and modifying the elements of a matrix.
* Arithmetic operations, such as addition and multiplication of matrices.
* Multiplication and division by scalars.
* Iterators.

We now discuss dense matrices from a C++ perspective and we also give some examples of dense matrices.

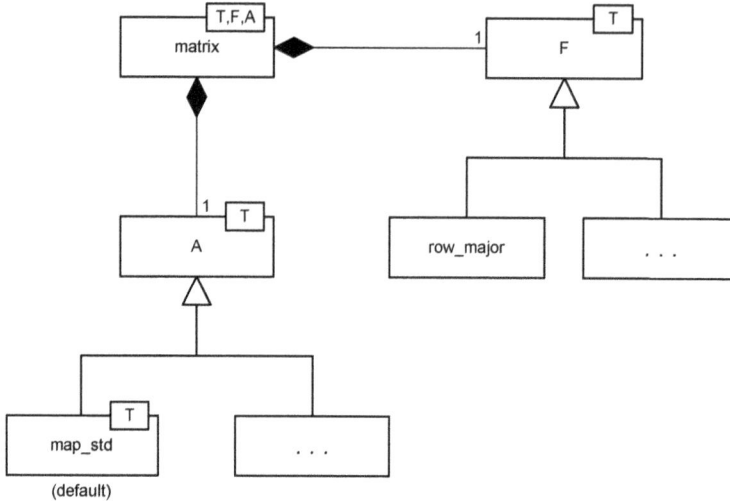

Figure 6.3 Dense Matrix Structure

6.5.1   Creating and Accessing Dense Matrices

We give some initial examples of creating dense matrices, accessing and modifying their elements and finally printing them:

```cpp
#include <boost/numeric/ublas/matrix.hpp>      // The matrix class.
namespace ublas=boost::numeric::ublas;

// Default matrix which stores data in the unbounded_array<T> class
// by default and has row major storage order.
ublas::matrix<double> m1(2, 3);

// Matrix which stores data in a bounded array and has column major
// storage order.
ublas::matrix<double, ublas::column_major,
    ublas::bounded_array<double, 6> > m2(2, 3);

// Matrix with all elements initialized to 3.14.
ublas::matrix<double> m3(2, 3, 3.14);

// Fill the matrices.
for (int row=0; row<2; row++)
{
    for (int column=0; column<3; column++)
    {
        m1(row, column)=10*row+column;
        m2(row, column)=m1(row, column)+5;
    }
}

// Display the matrices.
cout<<"m1: "<<m1<<endl;
cout<<"m2: "<<m2<<endl;
cout<<"m3: "<<m3<<endl;

// Sizes.
cout<<endl<<"*** Sizes ***"<<endl;
cout<<"m1 rows: "<<m1.size1()<<", columns: "<<m1.size2()<<endl;
cout<<"m2 rows: "<<m2.size1()<<", columns: "<<m2.size2()<<endl;
cout<<"m3 rows: "<<m3.size1()<<", columns: "<<m3.size2()<<endl;
```

The member functions `size1()` and `size2()` give the number of rows and columns in the matrix, respectively.

We can use arithmetic operations on dense matrices, as the following example shows:

```
// Operators.
// Adding/subtracting two matrices, they should have the same size.
cout<<endl<<"*** Operators ***"<<endl;
cout<<"m1+=m2:   "<<(m1+=m3)<<endl;
cout<<"m1-=m2:   "<<(m1-=m3)<<endl;
cout<<"m1*=2.5: "<<(m1*=2.5)<<endl;
cout<<"m1/=2.5: "<<(m1/=2.5)<<endl;
```

Finally, it is possible to resize dense matrices. We can modify the number of rows and columns by providing the appropriate integer parameters as well as a Boolean parameter that determines whether the values from the 'old' matrix should be preserved in the 'new' matrix:

```
// Resize the matrix.
// Matrices which use the bounded_array as storage always preserve data
// regardless of the "preserve" argument.
cout<<endl<<"*** Resize ***"<<endl;
m1.resize(2, 2, false);
cout<<"m1 resized to 2,2 (no data preserved): "<<m1<<endl;
m2.resize(2, 2, false);
cout<<"m2 resized to 2,2 (bounded_array always preserves): "<<m2<<endl;
m3.resize(2, 2, true);
cout<<"m3 resized to 2,2 (data preserved): "<<m3<<endl;
cout<<endl;
m1.resize(2, 3, false);
cout<<"v1 resized back to 2,3 (no data preserved): "<<m1<<endl;
m2.resize(2, 3, false);
cout<<"v2 resized back to 2,3 (bounded always preserves): "<<m2<<endl;
m3.resize(2, 3, true);
cout<<"v3 resized back to 2,3 (data preserved): "<<m3<<endl;
```

6.5.2   Special Dense Matrices

We now discuss three special kinds of matrices that are used in numerical linear algebra applications:

- `Identity matrix` : this is a *square matrix* (number of rows is the same as the number of columns) all of whose elements are zero except on the main diagonal of the matrix where the value is 1. An example of use is:

```
// Create identity matrices.
ublas::identity_matrix<double> m1(2);
ublas::identity_matrix<double> m2(3);

// Print the matrices.
cout<<"m1 (2x2): "<<m1<<endl;
cout<<"m2 (3x3): "<<m2<<endl;
cout<<"m1 rows: "<<m1.size1()<<", columns: "<<m1.size2()<<endl;
cout<<"m2 rows: "<<m2.size1()<<", columns: "<<m2.size2()<<endl;

// Resize the identity matrix. The data is always preserved even
// when preservation argument is false.
m2.resize(2, false);
cout<<"m2 resized to 2 (data always preserved)"<<m2<<endl;
m2.resize(3, false);
cout<<"m2 resized back to 3 (data always preserved)"<<m2<<endl;
```

- `Zero matrix`: this is a *rectangular matrix* (the number of rows is not necessarily equal to the number of columns) all of whose elements are zero. An example of use is:

```
// Create zero matrices.
ublas::zero_matrix<double> m1(2, 3);
ublas::zero_matrix<double> m2(3);

// Print the matrices.
cout<<"m1 (2x3): "<<m1<<endl;
cout<<"m2 (3x3): "<<m2<<endl;
cout<<"m1 rows: "<<m1.size1()<<", columns: "<<m1.size2()<<endl;
cout<<"m2 rows: "<<m2.size1()<<", columns: "<<m2.size2()<<endl;

// Resize the zero matrix. The data is always preserved even
// when preservation argument is false.
m1.resize(3, 2, false);
cout<<"m1 resized to 3x2 (data always preserved)"<<m1<<endl;
m1.resize(2, 3, false);
cout<<"m1 resized back to 2x3 (data always preserved)"<<m1<<endl;

cout<<endl<<"Swap the matrices"<<endl;
m1.swap(m2);
cout<<"m1: "<<m1<<endl;
cout<<"m2: "<<m2<<endl;
```

It is also possible to combine zero matrices with dense matrices, for example:

```
// Zero matrices can be used with normal matrices.
cout<<endl<<"Normal matrices can use zero matrices"<<endl;
ublas::matrix<double> m(2, 3, 5);
cout<<"m:     "<<m<<endl;
cout<<"m+=m2: "<<(m+=m2)<<endl;
```

- *Scalar matrices*: a scalar matrix is a rectangular matrix all of whose elements are equal to a given (single) value. An example of use is:

```
// Create scalar matrices.
ublas::scalar_matrix<double> m1(2, 3, 4);
ublas::scalar_matrix<double> m2(3, 2, 5);

// Print the matrices.
cout<<"m1 (2x3)=4: "<<m1<<endl;
cout<<"m2 (3x2)=5: "<<m2<<endl;
cout<<"m1 rows: "<<m1.size1()<<", columns: "<<m1.size2()<<endl;
cout<<"m2 rows: "<<m2.size1()<<", columns: "<<m2.size2()<<endl;
```

Note that the elements of these special vectors are read-only.

6.6   Other Kinds of Matrices

6.6.1   Sparse Matrices

A *sparse matrix* is one in which a small percentage of elements have values that we are interested in; in other words, most of the elements have zero values and we do not need to store these values in memory. One example of a sparse matrix is the `mapped_matrix` which stores the used elements in a map. It has the same structure as the class `matrix<T,F, Alloc>` as shown in Figure 6.3.

The main function categories are:
- Constructors.
- Accessing and modifying the elements of the matrix.
- Arithmetic operations such as addition and multiplication.
- Iterators.

Some examples of use are:

```
#include <boost/numeric/ublas/matrix_sparse.hpp>
namespace ublas=boost::numeric::ublas;

// Mapped matrix with 3x4 elements.
// As map datastructure it uses a "map_std<std::size_t, T>"
//(same as "std::map<std::size_t, T>") by default.
ublas::mapped_matrix<double> mm1(3, 4);

// Mapped vector with 3x4 elements where space is reserved
// for 7 non-zero elements
ublas::mapped_matrix<double> mm2(3, 4, 7);

// Normal matrix to be copied to mapped matrix.
ublas::matrix<double> m(3, 4);
for (int row=0; row<3; row++)
{
    for (int column=0; column<4; column++)
    {
        if ((row+column)%2==1)
        {
            mm1(row, column)=10*row+column;
            mm2(row, column)=mm1(row, column)+5;
        }

        m(row, column)=((row+column)%2)?mm1(row, column)+10:0;
    }
}
```

Another example using non-default template parameters is:

```
ublas::mapped_matrix<double, ublas::column_major,
    ublas::map_array<size_t, double> > mm3(m, 7);
```

In fact, the interface of mapped_matrix is similar to that of the class that models dense matrices. However, inserting elements into, and removing elements from a sparse matrix deserves special attention:

```
// Insert() does not insert a new element but overwrites the value of
// an existing element! For mapped matrices you can only insert at a
// position where there is a zero-value element. Inserting at a position
// where there is a non-zero value, will result in an runtime error.
// Erase() and clear() do not remove elements but makes them zero.
mm2.insert_element(0, 0, 3.14);
cout<<"mm2.insert_element(0, 0, 3.14): "<<mm2<<endl;
mm2.erase_element(0, 0);
cout<<"mm2.erase_element(0, 0): "<<mm2<<endl;

try
{
    mm2.insert_element(1, 0, 3.14);
}
catch (ublas::bad_index)
{
    cout<<"Error inserting at position (1,0), ";
        <<"position (1,0) already contain a non-zero value."<<endl;
}

mm2.clear();
cout<<"mm2.clear: "<<mm2<<endl;
```

The uBLAS library also has support for compressed and coordinate matrices but a discussion of these matrices is outside the scope of this book. They are discussed in the Boost online documentation.

6.6.2   Triangular Matrices

We now discuss an important class of matrices. These are called *triangular matrices* and we model only those values on the main diagonal and below it (in the case of a *lower-triangular matrix*) or those values on the main diagonal and above it (in the case of an *upper-triangular matrix)*.

Triangular matrices have specification `triangular_matrix<T, F1, F2, Alloc>` and thus accept four template parameters:

- The type `T` of object stored in the matrix.
- The function object `F1` that describes the type of the triangular matrix (choices are `lower` (default) and `upper`).
- The function object `F2` that describes the storage organisation (choices are `row_major` (default) and `column_major`).
- `Alloc`: the type of storage array (the default is `unbounded_array<T>`).

We give some illustrative examples on how to create upper and lower triangular matrices:

```
#include <boost/numeric/ublas/triangular.hpp>
using namespace boost::numeric::ublas;

// Lower triangular matrices.
triangular_matrix<double, lower> ml(3, 3);
for (unsigned i = 0; i < ml.size1(); ++i)
{
    for (unsigned j = 0; j <= i; ++j) ml(i, j) = 4.0;
}
cout << ml << endl;

// Upper triangular matrices.
triangular_matrix<double, upper> mu(3, 3);
for (unsigned i = 0; i < mu.size1(); ++i)
{
    for (unsigned j = i; j < mu.size2(); ++j) mu(i, j) = 3.0;
}
cout << mu << endl;
```

We also note that it is possible to add and multiply triangular and other kinds of matrices. Finally, it is possible to iterate in triangular matrices.

6.6.3   Triangular Adaptor

Given a rectangular dense matrix it is possible to define its upper and lower triangular *views*. In other words, we can define the upper and lower triangular parts of a matrix using an *adapter class*. Modifications to the adapters will be reflected in the adapted matrix and vice versa, as the following examples shows:

```
// Creating triangular matrix adaptors.

// 1. Create the matrix to be adapted.
matrix<double> m(3, 3);
for (unsigned i = 0; i < m.size1(); ++i)
{
    for (unsigned j = 0; j < m.size2(); ++j) m(i, j) = 4.0;
}
cout << "Matrix m: " << m << endl;
```

```
// 2. Create lower-triangular matrix.
triangular_adaptor<matrix<double>, lower> tal (m);
for (unsigned i = 0; i < tal.size1(); ++i)
{
    for (unsigned j = 0; j <= i; ++j) tal(i, j) = -2.0;;
}
cout << "Lower triangular adapter: " <<  tal << endl;

// 3. Create lower-triangular matrix.
triangular_adaptor<matrix<double>, upper> tau (m);
for (unsigned i = 0; i < tau.size1 (); ++i)
{
    for (unsigned j = i; j < tau.size2 (); ++j) tau(i, j) = -8.8;
}
cout << "Upper triangular adapter: " << tau << endl;

// 4. Print modified adapted matrix.
cout << "Matrix m: " << m << endl;

// 5. Modify the adapted matrix.
for (unsigned i = 0; i < m.size1(); ++i)
{
    for (unsigned j = 0; j < m.size2(); ++j) m(i, j) = 999.0;
}

// 6. See how the triangular views change.
cout << "Lower triangular adapter, II: " << tal << endl;
cout << "Upper triangular adapter, II: " << tau << endl;
```

6.7 Summary and Conclusions

In this chapter we have given an overview of the fundamental vector and matrix classes in Boost uBLAS. These are the building blocks for more advanced algorithms that we discuss in chapter 7 and indeed other applications. In particular, we discussed dense and sparse vectors and matrices as well as special data structures such as zero, unit and scalar-valued vectors and matrices. The main goal was to introduce the main functionality in the library.

7 Matrix Algebra in Boost Part II: Advanced Features and Applications

7.1 Introduction and Objectives

In this chapter we continue our discussion of the uBLAS library that we introduced in chapter 6. There we focused on the fundamental data structures and operations for vectors and matrices. In this chapter we discuss their structure and the operations that apply to them. In particular, we discuss the following topics:

- *Patterned matrices*, for example symmetric, banded and Hermitian matrices.
- *Vector and matrices expressions*, for example vector and matrix products and norms.
- *Vector and matrix proxies*, for example creating ranges and slices.

Having discussed these topics we can conclude that we have covered the most important functionality in Boost uBLAS. What's next? There are many applications of matrix theory and it is impossible to discuss them in this book. However, we discuss a particular application to the solution of matrix systems, namely LU and Cholesky decomposition and the Conjugate Gradient Method (CGM). We also devote a section to a short discussion of using uBLAS in conjunction with other Boost libraries.

We note that accessing the elements of a vector or a matrix outside their accepted ranges will result in *undefined behaviour*. It is then up to the developer to create exception handling code to avoid possible run-time errors. There are many applications that can be created using uBLAS as as substrate.

7.2 Patterned Matrices

We discuss how matrices are implemented in uBLAS.

a) General *rectangular full matrices* with n rows and m columns: this is a matrix with n x m elements in memory.
b) *Diagonal matrix*: a matrix all of whose elements are zero except for the main diagonal.
c) *Tridiagonal matrix*: a matrix all of whose elements are zero except for the main diagonal, the sub-diagonal and the super-diagonal. We need this type of matrix when we solve boundary value problems using finite difference methods (see Duffy 2006).
d) *Block tridiagonal*: a matrix whose diagonals are tridiagonal matrices.
e) *Lower triangular*: a matrix whose elements above the main diagonal are zero. An *upper triangular* matrix is one whose elements below the main diagonal are zero.
f) *Sparse matrix*: a matrix whose elements are mainly zero and that has a (small) percentage of non-zero elements. This is a special matrix category.

Some visual representations of various patterned matrices are shown in Figure 7.1 and 7.2.

7.2.1 Symmetric Matrices

A square matrix $A = (a_{ij})_{1 \leq i, j \leq n}$ is said to be *symmetric* if $a_{ij} = a_{ji}, \quad 1 \leq i, j \leq n$. In other words, the values above the main matrix diagonal are the same as their equivalents when mirrored in that diagonal. The class `symmetric_matrix<T, F1, F2, Alloc>` has four template parameters:

- The type of object T stored in the matrix.
- The function object F1 that describes the kind of symmetric matrix (default is `lower`).
- The function object F2 that describes the storage organisation (default is `row_major`).
- The type of adapted array `Alloc` (default is `unbounded_array<T>`).

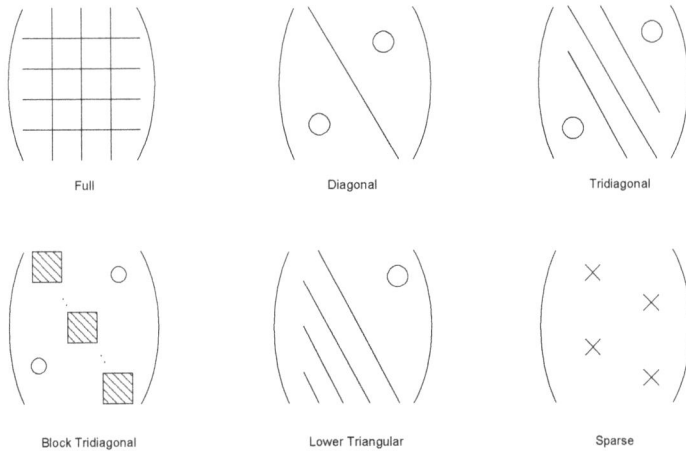

Figure 7.1 Matrix structures

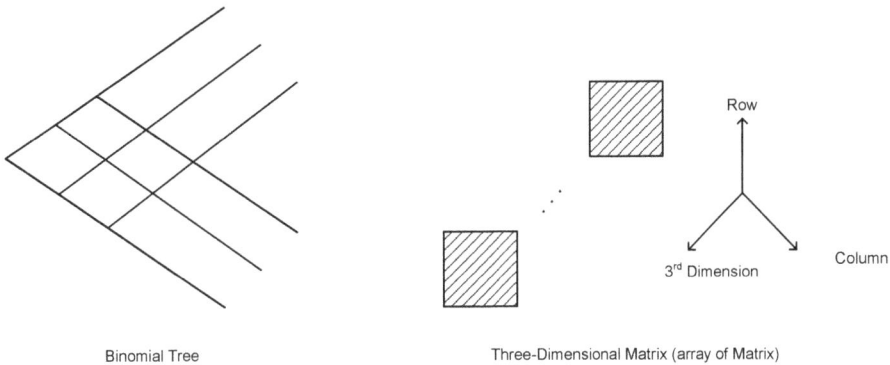

Figure 7.2 Special matrix structures

We give some examples on how to create and use symmetric matrices. First, we create and initialise upper and lower symmetric matrices that have row-major and column-major storage organisations:

```cpp
#include <boost/numeric/ublas/symmetric.hpp>
using namespace boost::numeric::ublas;

int sz = 3;
symmetric_matrix<int, upper, column_major>  m1(sz, sz);
symmetric_matrix<int, upper, row_major>     m2(sz, sz);
symmetric_matrix<int, lower, column_major>  m3(sz, sz);
symmetric_matrix<int, lower, row_major>     m4(sz, sz);

// Upper symmetric.
for (int i=0; i<sz; ++i)
{
    for (int j=i; j<sz; ++j)
    {
        m1(i,j) = 1;
        m2(i,j) = 2;
    }
}
cout << "Upper symmetric: " << m1 << endl;
```

```
cout << "Upper symmetric: " << m2 << endl;

// Lower symmetric.
for (int i=0; i<sz; ++i)
{
    for (int j=0; j <= i; ++j)
    {
        m3(i,j) = 7;
        m4(i,j) = -6;
    }
}
cout << "Lower symmetric: " << m3 << endl;
cout << "Lower symmetric: " << m4 << endl;
```

We see that it is only necessary to initialise the data above or below the main diagonal in a symmetric matrix. We can convince ourselves of this fact if we examine the output from the above code:

```
Upper symmetric: [3,3]((1,1,1),(1,1,1),(1,1,1))
Upper symmetric: [3,3]((2,2,2),(2,2,2),(2,2,2))
Lower symmetric: [3,3]((7,7,7),(7,7,7),(7,7,7))
Lower symmetric: [3,3]((-6,-6,-6),(-6,-6,-6),(-6,-6,-6))
```

We now discuss how to create *symmetric adaptors* for general dense matrices. In this case we can take a general matrix and create a symmetric matrix from its upper or lower triangular part. An example is:

```
// Symmetric adapters.
// Create the matrix to be adapted.
matrix<double> m (3, 3);
for (unsigned i = 0; i < m.size1(); ++ i)
{
    for (unsigned j = 0; j < m.size2(); ++ j) m (i, j) = 4.0;
}
cout << "Matrix m: " << m << endl;

// Create lower-symmetric matrix.
symmetric_adaptor<matrix<double>, lower> symm1(m);
cout << "Lower symmetric adapter, I: " <<  symm1 << endl;
for (unsigned i = 0; i < symm1.size1 (); ++i)
{
    for (unsigned j = 0; j <= i; ++j) symm1(i, j) = 2.0;;
}
cout << "Lower symmetric adapter, II: " <<  symm1 << endl;

// Create upper-triangular matrix.
symmetric_adaptor<matrix<double>, upper> symm2(m);
cout << "Upper symmetric adapter, I: " << symm2 << endl;
for (unsigned i = 0; i < symm2.size1(); ++i)
{
    for (unsigned j = i; j < symm2.size2(); ++j) symm2(i, j) = 8.0;
}
cout << "Upper symmetric adapter, II: " << symm2 << endl;
```

The output from this code is:

```
Matrix m: [3,3]((4,4,4),(4,4,4),(4,4,4))
Lower symmetric adapter, I: [3,3]((4,4,4),(4,4,4),(4,4,4))
Lower symmetric adapter, II: [3,3]((2,2,2),(2,2,2),(2,2,2))
Upper symmetric adapter, I: [3,3]((2,4,4),(4,2,4),(4,4,2))
Upper symmetric adapter, II: [3,3]((8,8,8),(8,8,8),(8,8,8))
```

7.2.2 Hermitian Matrices

A matrix is said to be *Hermitian* if it is equal to its own *Hermitian transpose*, that is its *complex conjugate transpose*. To this end, let $A = (a_{ij})_{1 \leq i,j \leq n}$ be a matrix with complex coefficients and let $\overline{A} = (\overline{a_{ij}})_{1 \leq i,j \leq n}$ be its complex conjugate matrix where $\overline{a}_{ij}$ is the complex conjugate of a_{ij}.

Then the Hermitian transpose of matrix A is defined by:

$$A^H \equiv \overline{A}^T$$

where in general A^T is the transpose of the matrix A. We say that a matrix A is *normal* if $AA^H = A^H A$.

An example of a normal matrix is:

$$C = \begin{pmatrix} 2 & 3 + 4i \\ 3 - 4i & -5 \end{pmatrix}.$$

Since Hermitian matrices have complex-valued elements we see that we need `std::complex<T>` when creating such matrices. Creating Hermitian matrices and Hermitian adapter matrices is very similar to how we did it for symmetric matrices in the previous section. We give some examples of upper and lower Hermitian matrices:

```
#include <boost/numeric/ublas/hermitian.hpp>
using namespace boost::numeric::ublas;

int sz = 2;
hermitian_matrix<complex<double>, upper, column_major> m1(sz, sz);
hermitian_matrix<complex<double>, upper, row_major>    m2(sz, sz);
hermitian_matrix<complex<double>, lower, column_major> m3(sz, sz);
hermitian_matrix<complex<double>, lower, row_major>    m4(sz, sz);

// Upper hermitian.
for (int i=0; i<sz; ++i)
{
    m1(i,i) = m2(i,i) = complex<double>(1.0, 1.0);
    for (int j=i+1; j<sz; ++j)
    {
        m1(i,j) = complex<double>(1,0);
        m2(i,j) = complex<double>(0,1);
    }
}
cout << "Upper hermitian: " << m1 << endl;
cout << "Upper hermitian: " << m2 << endl;

// Lower hermitian.
for (int i=0; i<sz; ++i)
{
    m3(i,i) = m4(i,i) = complex<double>(1.0, 1.0);
    for (int j=0; j < i; ++j)
    {
        m3(i,j) = complex<double>(1,0);
        m4(i,j) = complex<double>(0,1);
    }
}
cout << "Lower hermitian: " << m3 << endl;
cout << "Lower hermitian: " << m4 << endl;
```

We create Hermitian adaptor classes as follows:

```
// Hermitian adapters.
// Create the matrix to be adapted.
matrix<complex<double> > m (3, 3);
for (unsigned i = 0; i < m.size1(); ++ i)
{
    for (unsigned j = 0; j < m.size2(); ++ j)
    {
        m(i, j) = complex<double>(4.0, 4.0);
    }
}
cout << "Matrix m: " << m << endl;

// Create lower-hermitian matrix.
hermitian_adaptor<matrix<complex<double> >, lower> symm1(m);
cout << "Lower hermitian adapter, I: " <<  symm1 << endl;
for (unsigned i = 0; i < symm1.size1 (); ++i)
{
    for (unsigned j = 0; j <= i; ++j) symm1(i, j) = 2.0;
}
cout << "Lower hermitian adapter, II: " <<  symm1 << endl;
```

7.2.3   Banded Matrices

A *banded matrix* is a square matrix that has a given number of non-zero elements above the main diagonal and a given number of non-zero elements below the main diagonal. A well-known subcategory is the class of *tridiagonal matrices* that have one subdiagonal of non-zero elements above and below the main diagonal. A first example of a 3X3 tridiagonal matrix is:

```
#include <boost/numeric/ublas/banded.hpp>

int sz = 3;
int lowerBands = 1;
int upperBands = 1;
banded_matrix<double, column_major>  m1(sz, sz, lowerBands, upperBands);
banded_matrix<double, row_major>     m2(sz, sz, lowerBands, upperBands);


// Banded.
for (int i=0; i<sz; ++i)
{
    m1(i,i) = m2(i,i) = 1.0;
    for (int j = std::max(i-lowerBands, 0);
        j < std::min(i+upperBands+1, sz); ++j)
    {
        m1(i,j) = 3.0;
        m2(i,j) = -4.0;
    }
}
cout << "Column-major banded: " << m1 << endl;
cout << "Row-major banded: " << m2 << endl;
```

It is possible to create banded matrices in which the number of non-zero elements above the main diagonal is not necessarily equal to the number of non-zero elements below the main diagonal.

Finally, it is also possible to create *banded adaptor classes*, as the following example shows:

```
// Banded adapters.
// Create the matrix to be adapted.
```

```
matrix<double> m(3, 3);
for (size_t i = 0; i < m.size1(); ++i)
{
    for (size_t j = 0; j < m.size2(); ++j) m(i, j) = 4.0;
}
cout << "Matrix m: " << m << endl;

// Create lower-banded matrix.
size_t lowerB = 1;
size_t upperB = 1;
banded_adaptor<matrix<double> > band(m, lowerB, upperB);
cout << "Banded adapter, I: " <<  band << endl;
for (size_t i = 0; i < band.size1(); ++i)
{
    for (size_t j = std::max(i-lowerB, 0u);
         j < std::min(i+upperB+1, band.size2()); ++j)
    {
        band(i, j) = 2.0;
    }
}
cout << "Banded adapter, II: " <<  band << endl;
```

7.3   Vector and Matrix Proxies

We now discuss how to define certain views of vectors and matrices.

7.3.1   Vector Range

A *vector range* is a set of elements of a vector that are identified by a range. A *range* is a closed-open interval [i, j). This entails that indexing the vector range begins at i and ends at j-1. A simple example shows how to create a vector range:

```
#include <boost/numeric/ublas/vector_proxy.hpp>  // The vector range.
namespace ublas=boost::numeric::ublas;

ublas::vector<double> vA(6);
for (size_t j = 0; j < vA.size(); ++j) vA[j] = 6-j;   // Values 6,5,4,3,2,1
cout << "Vector: " << vA << endl;

ublas::vector_range<ublas::vector<double> > rangeA(vA, ublas::range(1, 5));
cout << "Range [1,5): " << rangeA << endl;       // Values in range are 5,4,3,2
```

uBLAS also provides two free functions to support the construction of vector ranges. The first function is called `subrange()` that accepts a vector, start index and end index (exclusive):

```
ublas::vector_range<ublas::vector<double> > rangeB =
    ublas::subrange(vA, 1, 3);
cout << "Subrange [1,3): " << rangeB << endl;    // Values are 5,4
```

The second free function is called `project()`. We use `subrange()` and `project()` functions instead of constructors to create a range; `project()` is more efficient when we create a view on a view since it combines the two ranges into one while `subrange()` piles the ranges (extra indirection). An example of use is:

```
ublas::vector_range<ublas::vector<double> > rangeC
    = ublas::project(rangeA, ublas::range(1, 3));
cout << "Project [1,3): " << rangeC << endl;     // Values are 4,3
```

7.3.2   Vector Slice

A *slice* can be seen as a generalisation of a range. It is also a view of a vector and it has three defining parameters, namely the *start index* of the slice, the *stride* that determines the next element of the slice and the *number of elements* in the slice. An example of use is to create a vector and extract a slice of size 4 from it starting at index one and taking each second element in the vector thereafter:

```
#include <boost/numeric/ublas/vector_proxy.hpp>    // The vector range.
namespace ublas=boost::numeric::ublas;

ublas::vector<double> vA(11);
for (size_t i=0; i<vA.size(); i++) vA[i]=i;
cout << "Vector: " << vA << endl;

// Create the vector slice.
int start = 1; int stride = 2; int length = 4;
ublas::slice mySlice(start, stride, length);
ublas::vector_slice<ublas::vector<double> > sliceA(vA, mySlice);
cout << "Vector slice: " << sliceA << endl;    // Output is 1,3,5,7
```

We see that we can define instances of `range` and `slice` independently of the vectors on which they operate. In general, we can consider a range to be a special slice having a stride equal to one.

7.3.3   Matrix Proxies: Rows and Columns

After having created a matrix, we may wish to access its individual rows or columns. In particular, uBLAS provides adapter classes to achieve these ends. This is a very useful feature to have and it has many applications in numerical linear algebra.

We take an example of a matrix and we extract its rows and columns. The following code shows how to use the functionality:

```
#include <boost/numeric/ublas/matrix_proxy.hpp>
namespace ublas=boost::numeric::ublas;

// Create matrix with 2 rows and 3 columns.
ublas::matrix<double> m(2, 3);

// Fill the matrix.
for (int row=0; row<2; row++)
{
    for (int column=0; column<3; column++)
    {
        m(row, column)=10*row+column;
    }
}

// Print the matrix.
cout<<"Matrix:    "<<m<<endl;

// Get a row and column
// The template argument to the matrix row/column is the type
// of the matrix to be adapted.
ublas::matrix_row<ublas::matrix<double> > r1(m, 1);
ublas::matrix_column<ublas::matrix<double> > c1(m, 1);
cout<<"Row 1    : "<<r1<<", size: "<<r1.size()<<", index="
    <<r1.index()<<endl;
cout<<"Column 1: "<<c1<<", size: "<<c1.size()<<", index="
    << c1.index()<<endl;

// Show all rows using row/column global function.
```

```
cout<<endl<<"All rows using row() global function."<<endl;
for (int i=0; i<2; i++)
{
    cout<<"Row "<<i<<"   : "<<ublas::row(m, i)<<endl;
}

// Show all columns.
cout<<endl<<"All columns using column() global function."<<endl;
for (int i=0; i<3; i++)
{
    cout<<"Column "<<i<<": "<<ublas::column(m, i)<<endl;
}
```

The output from this code is:

```
Matrix  : [2,3]((0,1,2),(10,11,12))
Row 1   : [3](10,11,12), size: 3, index=1
Column 1: [2](1,11), size: 2, index=1

All rows using row() global function.
Row 0   : [3](0,1,2)
Row 1   : [3](10,11,12)

All columns using column() global function.
Column 0: [2](0,10)
Column 1: [2](1,11)
Column 2: [2](2,12)
```

We conclude this section by showing that changing the value in a row or column proxy automatically changes the corresponding value in the underlying matrix. The converse is also true; changing an element in a matrix is visible in the corresponding row or column proxy. Here is an example:

```
// Change data through row/column.
r1[0]=8; c1(0)=9;
cout<<endl;
cout<<"r1[0]=8:             "<<r1<<endl;
cout<<"c1[0]=9:             "<<c1<<endl;
cout<<"Matrix changed too: "<<m<<endl;
```

The output in this case is:

```
r1[0]=8:             [3](8,11,12)
c1[0]=9:             [2](9,11)
Matrix changed too:  [2,3]((0,9,2),(8,11,12))
```

It is possible to use free functions called `row` and `column` to construct matrix rows and columns, respectively. In general, the complexity is linear depending on the size of the row or column. A discussion of these functions is outside the scope of this book.

7.3.4   Matrix Views: What are Options?

Given a matrix, it is possible to construct various kinds of views based on it:

- A subvector of the matrix.
- A sliced subvector of the matrix.
- A submatrix of the matrix.
- A sliced submatrix of the matrix.

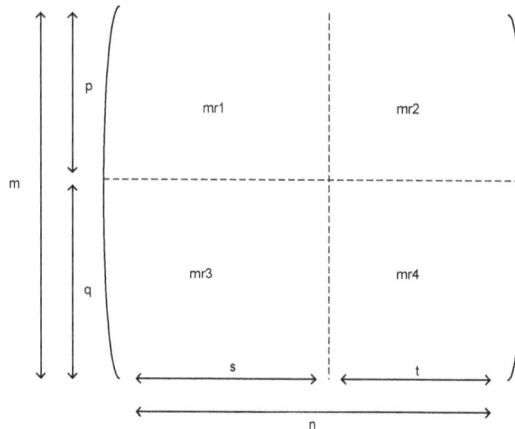

Figure 7.3 Matrix and submatrices

Much of the code that realises this functionality is easy to understand because it is similar to the code that we have discussed for the vector case.

We discuss how to create submatrices of a given matrix. It is a generalisation of how we created vector ranges except that we need two ranges in order to identify a submatrix. In order to make things precise we consider the case in Figure 7.3 in which we partition an mXn rectangular matrix mA into four sub matrices with the given numbers of rows and columns. To this end, we create four matrix ranges mr1, mr2, mr3 and mr4. This kind of problem occurs in many kinds of applications in numerical linear algebra and having a solution in uBLAS adds to the usefulness of this library. We note that the ranges are proxies which means that changes to the values of their elements will be seen in the underlying matrix and vice versa. In other words, the data in the ranges is not a copy of the data in the underlying matrix but rather they access the same data in the underlying matrix.

Referring to Figure 7.3 again, we first create and initialise the underling matrix mA as follows:

```
int m = 6; int n = 8;
ublas::matrix<double> mA(m, n);

// Fill the matrix.
for (size_t row=0; row < mA.size1(); row++)
{
    for (size_t column=0; column < mA.size2(); column++)
    {
        mA(row, column)= -9.0;
    }
}
```

We now create the four views of mA:

```
// Subdivision of main matrix dimensions.
int p = 3; int q = m-p;     // rows.
int s = 2; int t = n-6;     // columns.

// Create matrix ranges for each sub matrix.
ublas::matrix_range<ublas::matrix<double> > mr1(mA,
    ublas::range(0,p), ublas::range(0,s));
ublas::matrix_range<ublas::matrix<double> > mr2(mA,
    ublas::range(0,p), ublas::range(s,n));
ublas::matrix_range<ublas::matrix<double> > mr3(mA,
    ublas::range(p,m), ublas::range(0,s));
```

```
ublas::matrix_range<ublas::matrix<double> > mr4(mA,
    ublas::range(p,m), ublas::range(s,n));
```

Any changes in values of the elements of the ranges will be reflected in mA. For example, if we execute the following code and subsequently print mA we shall see that it has changed:

```
for (size_t row=0; row < mr1.size1(); row++)
{
    for (size_t column=0; column < mr1.size2(); column++)
    {
        mr1(row, column)= 1000.0;
    }
}
cout << "mA: " << mA << endl;
```

In applications we often perform operations on the elements of a matrix through its ranges and submatrices. To show what we mean, let us scale the elements of the ranges using the functionality provided in uBLAS:

```
// At this stage we perform numerical computations.
mr1 *= 0.25;
mr2 *= 0.25;
mr3 *= 0.25;
mr4 *= 0.25;
```

Finally, printing the matrix mA will prove that all its elements have been scaled by a factor of four.

The code in this section can be generalised in different ways. First, there are other strategies for partitioning a matrix into submatrices (for example, *strips* of columns or rows). Second, having partitioned the matrix we can parallelise the computation by assigning the workload on each sub matrix to a dedicated thread. At a design level, we use the *Geometric Decomposition* parallel design pattern to solve this problem (see Mattson 2005).

7.4   Vector Expressions

In this section we discuss the different kinds of mathematical operations that we can perform on vectors. These operations are used in numerical algorithms to manipulate vectors and matrices. The main operations are:

- Additive inverse of a vector; the vector corresponding the real and imaginary part of a complex vector; compute the complex conjugate vector of a vector; compute the transpose of a vector; compute the hermitian of a vector (that is the complex conjugate of the transpose of a vector expression).
- Adding and subtracting two vectors.
- The *inner product* and *outer (tensor) product* of two vectors. Let $u = (u_1, \ldots, u_m)$, $v = (v_1, \ldots, v_n)$ be two vectors of the same size. Then their inner product is defined by:

$$\sum_{j=1}^{n} u_j v_j.$$

The outer product of two vectors results in a matrix and is defined by:

$$uv^t = u \otimes v = A = \begin{pmatrix} u_1v_1 & u_1v_2 & \dots & u_1v_n \\ u_2v_1 & u_2v_2 & \dots & u_2v_n \\ \vdots & & & \\ u_mv_1 & u_mv_2 & \dots & u_mv_n \end{pmatrix}.$$

Inner and outer product calculations are very important in numerical linear algebra. The inner product produces a scalar result and the result of the outer product is a matrix. The outer product is a special case of the *Kronecker product* of two matrices

$$\begin{cases} A = (a_{ij}), & 1 \le i \le m, 1 \le j \le n \\ B = (b_{ij}), & 1 \le i \le p, 1 \le j \le q \end{cases}$$

is defined by:

$$A \otimes B = \begin{pmatrix} a_{11}B & \dots & a_{1n}B \\ \vdots & & \vdots \\ a_{m1}B & \dots & a_{mn}B \end{pmatrix}.$$

The Kronecker product matrix has mXp rows and nXq columns.

- *Scalar vector operations*: pre and post-multiplication of a vector by a scalar; dividing a vector by a scalar.
- *Vector reductions*: Computing the l_1, l_2 and l_∞ norms of a vector:

$$\text{Euclidean } (l_2) \text{ norm} \quad || \underline{x} ||_2 = \left(\sum_{j=1}^{n} x_j^2 \right)^{\frac{1}{2}}$$

$$l_1 \text{ norm} \quad || \underline{x} ||_1 = \sum_{j=1}^{n} | x_j |$$

$$l_\infty \text{ norm} \quad || \underline{x} ||_\infty = \max_{1 \le j \le n} | x_j |.$$

We take some examples to show how to use these operations. We first create a vector and we compute the additive inverse and the vector transpose:

```
ublas::vector<double> v1(4);
ublas::vector<double> v2(v1.size());

// Fill the vectors.
for (szie_t i=0; i < v1.size(); i++)
{
    // Use the [] operator.
    v1[i]=i+1;
    v2[i]=v2.size()-i;
}
cout << "v1: " << v1 << endl;
cout << "v2: " << v2 << endl;
```

```
// Unary operations.
cout << "Additive inverse of v1: " << -v1 << endl;
cout << "Transpose vector of v1: " << trans(v1) << endl;
```

The output from this code is:

```
v1: [4](1,2,3,4)
v2: [4](4,3,2,1)
Additive inverse of v1: [4](-1,-2,-3,-4)
Transpose vector of v1: [4](1,2,3,4)
```

We now discuss the operations in uBLAS for Hermitian vectors. In general, they are concerned with manipulating the real and imaginary parts of the vector in some way as the following example shows:

```
// Unary operations with Hermitian vectors.
ublas::vector<complex<double> > her(4);
for (int i=0; i < (int)her.size(); i++)
{
    her[i] = complex<double>(i+1, -i-1);
}

cout << "The original Hermitian vector: " << her << endl;
cout << "Real part of vector: " << real(her) << endl;
cout << "Complex part of vector: " << imag(her) << endl;
cout << "Complex conjugate vector: " << conj(her) << endl;
cout << "The Hermitian vector: " << trans(her) << endl;
```

The output from this code is:

```
The original Hermitian vector: [4]((1,-1),(2,-2),(3,-3),(4,-4))
Real part of vector: [4](1,2,3,4)
Complex part of vector: [4](-1,-2,-3,-4)
Complex conjugate vector: [4]((1,1),(2,2),(3,3),(4,4))
The Hermitian vector: [4]((1,-1),(2,-2),(3,-3),(4,-4))
```

The addition and subtract of two vectors is realised as follows:

```
// Binary operations on vectors.
cout << "v1: " << v1 << endl;
cout << "v2: " << v2 << endl;
cout << "v1 + v2: " << v1 + v2 << endl;
cout << "v1 - v2: " << v1 - v2 << endl;
```

while the inner and outer products are realised as follows:

```
// Different kinds of products.
cout << "Inner product of v1 and v2: " << inner_prod(v1,v2) << endl;
cout << "Outer product of v1 and v2: " << outer_prod(v1,v2) << endl;
```

The output from this code is:

```
v1: [4](1,2,3,4)
v2: [4](4,3,2,1)
v1 + v2: [4](5,5,5,5)
v1 - v2: [4](-3,-1,1,3)
Inner product of v1 and v2: 20
Outer product of v1 and v2:
[4,4]((4,3,2,1),(8,6,4,2),(12,9,6,3),(16,12,8,4))
```

Finally, we discuss how to calculate the norms of a vector. The sample code is:

```
// Vector reductions and vector norms.
cout << "L1 norm of v1: " << norm_1(v1) << endl;
```

```
cout << "L2 norm of v1: " << norm_2(v1) << endl;
cout << "L-infinity norm of v1: " << norm_inf(v1) << endl;
cout << "Index corresponding to L-infinity norm of v1: "
     << index_norm_inf(v1) << endl;
```

and the output is given by:

```
L1 norm of v1: 10
L2 norm of v1: 5.47723
L-infinity norm of v1: 4
Index corresponding to L-infinity norm of v1: 3
```

7.5   Matrix Expressions

We now discuss the following matrix operations in uBLAS:

- *Unary Operations*: additive inverse of a matrix, transpose of a matrix.
- *Binary Operations*: Addition and subtraction of two vectors.
- *Scalar Matrix Operations*: pre and post-multiplication of a matrix by a scalar; division of a matrix by a scalar.
- *Matrix-Vector Operations*: matrix-vector multiplication.
- *Matrix norm*: the l_1 and l_∞ norms.

Some examples are:

```
ublas::matrix<double> m1(2, 3);

// Matrix which stores data in a bounded array and has column
// major storage order.
ublas::matrix<double, ublas::column_major,
    ublas::bounded_array<double, 6> > m2(2, 3);

// Fill the matrices.
for (int row=0; row < (int)m1.size1(); row++)
{
    for (int column=0; column < (int)m1.size2(); column++)
    {
        m1(row, column)= row + column;
        m2(row, column)= row - column;
    }
}

// Unary operations.
cout << "Additive inverse of m1: " << -m1 << endl;
cout << "Transpose matrix of m1: " << trans(m1) << endl;
```

The output is:

```
Additive inverse of m1: [2,3]((-0,-1,-2),(-1,-2,-3))
Transpose vector of m1: [3,2]((0,1),(1,2),(2,3))
```

Mermitian matrices:

```
// Unary operations with Hermitian matrices.
ublas::matrix<complex<double> > her(4,4);
for (int row=0; row < (int)her.size1(); row++)
{
    for (int column=0; column < (int)her.size2(); column++)
    {
        her(row, column) = complex<double>(row, column);
    }
}
```

```
cout << "The original Hermitian matrix: " << her << endl;
cout << "Real part of matrix: " << real(her) << endl;
cout << "Complex part of matrix: " << imag(her) << endl;
cout << "Complex conjugate matrix: " << conj(her) << endl;
```

The output is:

```
The original Hermitian matrix:
[4,4]((((0,0),(0,1),(0,2),(0,3)),((1,0),(1,1),(1,2),(1,3)),((2,0),(2,1),(2,2
),(2,3)),((3,0),(3,1),(3,2),(3,3)))
Real part of matrix: [4,4]((0,0,0,0),(1,1,1,1),(2,2,2,2),(3,3,3,3))
Complex part of matrix: [4,4]((0,1,2,3),(0,1,2,3),(0,1,2,3),(0,1,2,3))
Complex conjugate matrix: [4,4]((((0,-0),(0,-1),(0,-2),(0,-3)),((1,-0),(1,-
1),(1,-2),(1,-3)),((2,-0),(2,-1),(2,-2),(2,-3)),((3,-0),(3,-1),(3,-2),(3,-
3)))
```

We can define binary operations on matrices:

```
// Binary operations on matrices.
cout << "m1: " << m1 << endl;
cout << "m2: " << m2 << endl;
cout << "m1 + m2: " << m1 + m2 << endl;
cout << "m1 - m2: " << m1 - m2 << endl;
cout << "2.0*m1: " << 2.0*m1 << endl;
cout << "m1*3.0: " << m1*3.0 << endl;
```

The output is:

```
m1: [2,3]((0,1,2),(1,2,3))
m2: [2,3]((0,-1,-2),(1,0,-1))
m1 + m2: [2,3]((0,0,0),(2,2,2))
m1 - m2: [2,3]((0,2,4),(0,2,4))
2.0*m1: [2,3]((0,2,4),(2,4,6))
m1*3.0: [2,3]((0,3,6),(3,6,9))
```

Code to calculate norms is:

```
// Matrix reductions and matrix norms.
cout << "L1 norm of m1: " << norm_1(m1) << endl;
cout << "L-infinity norm of m1: " << norm_inf(m1) << endl;
```

The output is:

```
L1 norm of m1: 5
L-infinity norm of m1: 6
```

Finally, here is an example of matrix-vector multiplication:

```
// Fill the vectors.
ublas::vector<double> vA(3);
for (int i=0; i < (int)vA.size(); i++)
{
    // Use the [] operator.
    vA[i]=i+1;
}

// Fill the matrices.
ublas::matrix<double> mA(3, 3);
for (int row=0; row < (int)mA.size1(); row++)
{
    for (int column=0; column < (int)mA.size2(); column++)
    {
        mA(row, column)= row + column;
    }
}
```

```
cout << "vA: " << vA << endl;
cout << "mA: " << mA << endl;
cout << "Product mA*vA: " << prod(mA, vA) << endl;
cout << "Product vA*mA: " << prod(vA, mA) << endl;
```

The output is:

```
vA: [3](1,2,3)
mA: [3,3]((0,1,2),(1,2,3),(2,3,4))
Product mA*vA: [3](8,14,20)
Product vA*mA: [3](8,14,20)
```

7.6   Applying uBLAS: Solving Linear Systems of Equations

We have now completed our discussion of uBLAS functionality, including data structures for vectors and matrices, views of these data structures and finally operations on these data structures. We now show to bring this functionality together. We focus on three important algorithms:

- The Conjugate Gradient Method (CGM) for symmetric and general matrices.
- LU decomposition of a general matrix.
- Cholesky decomposition.

There are many other applications that we could have taken but we feel that these three algorithms motivate the usefulness of uBLAS for the moment. The following *features* in uBLAS will be used in the ensuing discussion:

- Symmetric, lower triangular, upper triangular and general matrices.
- Inner product of two vectors.
- Matrix-vector multiplication.
- Sum and difference of two vectors.
- Vector norms (needed when testing for convergence of iterative methods).
- The transpose of a matrix.

We now discuss these matrix algorithms and their implementation using uBLAS.

7.6.1   Conjugate Gradient Method (CGM)

This method is used for solving a system of simultaneous linear algebraic equations:

$$AU = F$$

where A is a known nXn matrix, U is an $nX1$ vector of unknowns and F is a known $nX1$ vector. In this section we first discuss the CGM algorithm and corresponding C++ code when A is a symmetric matrix and we then discuss the steps of the algorithm when A is a general (not necessarily symmetric) matrix. The algorithm in the case of a symmetric matrix is given by:

$$r_0 = F - AU_0$$
$$p_0 = r_0$$

For $j = 1, \ldots, n$ compute

$$a_j = \| r_j \|_2^2 / p_i^T A p_i$$

$$U_{j+1} = U_j + a_j p_j$$

$$r_{j+1} = r_j - a_j A p_j$$

$$b_j = \frac{\|r_{j+1}\|_2^2}{\|r_i\|_2^2}$$

$$p_{j+1} = r_{j+1} + b_j p_j.$$

where r_j and p_j are vectors of length n for $j \geq 0$.

The code for this algorithm is:

```
// Solve Ax = b; 'x' is initial estimate.
template <typename TMatrix>
void ConjugateGradient(const TMatrix& A, const ublas::vector<double>& b,
                       ublas::vector<double>& x, double tol)
{
    // The size.
    const size_t n = b.size();

    // Step 0: init.
    ublas::vector<double> r(n);
    r = b - ublas::prod(A,x);
    ublas::vector<double> p(r);

    double a;
    double beta;
    double norm, norm2;
    ublas::vector<double> tmpVec(n);

    for (size_t j=1; j<=n; ++j)
    {
        // Step 1.
        norm = ublas::norm_2(r);
        norm *= norm;

        // Exit loop is convergence has been reached.
        if (norm <= tol) break;

        tmpVec = ublas::prod(A, p);
        a = norm / ublas::inner_prod(p, tmpVec);

        // Step 2.
        x += a*p;

        // Step 3.
        r -= a*tmpVec;

        // Step 4.
        norm2 = ublas::norm_2(r); norm2 *= norm2;
        beta = norm2 / norm;
        p = beta*p + r;
```

```
        }
    }
```

The CGM algorithm in the case of a general matrix A is:

$$r_0 = F - AU_0$$
$$p_0 = r_0$$

$$\text{for } j = 1, 2, \ldots, n$$

$$a_j = \|A^T r_j\|^2 / \|A p_j\|^2$$

$$U_{j+1} = U_j + a_j p_j$$

$$r_{j+1} = r_j - a_j A p_j$$

$$b_j = \|A^T r_{j+1}\|^2 / \|A^T r_j\|^2$$

$$p_{j+1} = A^T r_{j+1} + b_j p_j.$$

We leave it as an exercise to modify the CGM code for symmetric matrices so that it works in the case (non-symmetric) just given.

Test cases and code can be found on the software distribution medium.

7.6.2   LU Decomposition

This algorithm partitions a general matrix A into the product of a lower-triangular matrix L and an upper-triangular matrix U. The algorithm is documented in Dahlquist 1974 and Isaacson 1966, for example. The C++ code in combination with uBLAS given as a free function:

```cpp
// LU decomposition: A -> L*U
void InitLU(const ublas::matrix<double>& A,
            ublas::triangular_matrix<double, ublas::lower>& L,
            ublas::triangular_matrix<double, ublas::upper>& U)
{
    double sum;
    unsigned N = A.size1();

    // Common to make all diagonal elements == 1.0
    for (size_t k = 0; k < N; ++k)
    {
        L(k,k) = 1.0;
    }

    for (size_t j = 0; j < N; ++j)        // Loop over columns.
    {
        // U
        for (size_t i= 0; i <= j; ++i)    // Columns.
        {
            sum = 0.0;
            for (size_t k = 0; k < i; ++k)
            {
                sum += L(i,k)*U(k,j);
            }
            U(i,j) = A(i,j) - sum;
        }
```

```
        // L
        for (size_t i = j+1; i < N; ++i)      // Rows.
        {
            sum = 0.0;
            for (size_t k = 0; k < j; ++k)
            {
                sum += L(i,k)*U(k,j);
            }
            L(i,j) = (A(i,j) - sum) / U(j,j);
        }
    }
}
```

Having computed the matrices L and U we can then solve the following problem in two steps:

$$Ax = b$$

$$\Longleftrightarrow (LU)x = b$$
$$\Longleftrightarrow Ly = b$$

$$Ux \;\; = y.$$

The code for this sequence of steps is:

```
// Solve Ax = b
ublas::vector<double> SolveLU(const ublas::vector<double>& b,
    const ublas::triangular_matrix<double, ublas::lower>& L,
    const ublas::triangular_matrix<double, ublas::upper>& U)
{
    size_t N = b.size();
    ublas::vector<double> result(N);

    double sum;

    // Forward sweep Ly = b
    result[0] = b[0] / L(0,0);
    for (size_t i = 1; i < N; ++i)
    {
        sum = 0.0;
        for (size_t k = 0; k < i; ++k)
        {
            sum += L(i,k)*result[k];
        }
        result[i] = (b[i] - sum) / L(i,i);
    }

    // Backward sweep Ux = y
    result[N-1] = result[N-1]/U(N-1, N-1);
    for (size_t i = N-2; i >= 0 && i < N; --i)
    {
        sum = 0.0;
        for (size_t k = i+1; k < N; ++k)
        {
            sum += U(i,k)*result[k];
        }
        result[i] = (result[i] - sum) / U(i,i);
    }

    return result;
}
```

A simple example (null test) of use is:

```
unsigned N = 4;

// Input for Ax = b
ublas::matrix<double> A(N, N);
ublas::vector<double> b(N);
for (size_t i = 0; i < A.size1(); ++i)
{
    b[i] = 1.0;
    for (size_t j = 0; j < A.size2(); ++j)
    {
        A(i, j) = 0.0;
    }
    A(i,i) = 1.0;
}
std::cout << "Initial matrix A: " << A << std::endl;
cout << "Initial vector b: " << b << endl;

// Determine the L and U matrices.
ublas::triangular_matrix<double, ublas::lower> L(N,N); Init(L, 0.0);
ublas::triangular_matrix<double, ublas::upper> U(N,N); Init(U, 0.0);
InitLU(A, L, U);
cout << "Matrix L: " << L << endl;
cout << "Matrix U: " << U << endl;

// Solve 'Ax=b'.
ublas::vector<double> result = SolveLU(b, L, U);
cout << "Result vector Ax=b: " << result << endl;
```

You can experiment with different choices of A and b to test the accuracy of the method.

7.6.3 Cholesky Decomposition

For symmetric positive-definite matrices the LU decomposition algorithm takes on a particularly simple form, namely when the matrix U is the transpose of the matrix L:

$$A = LU = LL^T.$$

The algorithm to compute the matrix L is given by (see Dahlquist 1974):

$$l_{jj} = \left(a_{jj} - \sum_{k=1}^{j-1} l_{jk}^2 \right)^{1/2}, \quad 1 \le j \le n$$

$$l_{ij} = \left(a_{ij} - \sum_{k=1}^{j-1} l_{ik} l_{jk} \right) / l_{jj}, \quad i = j+1, \ldots, n.$$

The C++ code that implements this algorithm is:

```
// Cholesky decomposition.
void Cholesky(const ublas::matrix<double>& A,
    ublas::triangular_matrix<double, ublas::lower>& L)
{
    double sum;
    size_t N = A.size1();

    for (size_t j = 0; j < N; ++j)    // Loop over columns.
    {
        sum = 0.0;
        for (size_t k = 0; k < j; ++k)
```

```
        {
            sum += L(j,k)*L(j,k);
        }
        L(j,j) = sqrt(A(j,j) - sum);

        for (size_t i = j+1; i < N; ++i) // Rows.
        {
            sum = 0.0;
            for (size_t k = 0; k < j; ++k)
            {
                sum += L(i,k)*L(j,k);
            }
            L(i,j) = (A(i,j) - sum) / L(j,j);
        }
    }
}
```

Finally, an example of how to use the Cholesky algorithm is given by (notice we used a dense matrix but using a symmetric matrix would possibly have been more appropriate):

```
// Correlation matrix.
unsigned D = 4;
u::matrix<double> Corr(D,D);
Corr(0,0) = Corr(1,1) = Corr(2,2) = Corr(3,3) = 1.0;
Corr(0,1) = Corr(1,0) = 0.5;
Corr(0,2) = Corr(2,0) = 0.2;
Corr(0,3) = Corr(3,0) = 0.01;
Corr(1,2) = Corr(2,1) = 0.01;
Corr(1,3) = Corr(3,1) = 0.30;
Corr(3,2) = Corr(2,3) = 0.30;
cout << "Original matrix:" << endl << Corr << endl << endl;
```

A test case is:

```
// Cholesky decomposition.
cout << endl << "--- Do Cholesky decomposition ---" << endl << endl;
ublas::triangular_matrix<double, ublas::lower> L(D,D);
Cholesky(Corr, L);
cout << "L:" << endl << L << endl << endl;
```

Now we remark on stress-testing the Cholesky method. In particular, we wish to double-check our algorithm while at the same time use some of the functionality of uBLAS. We try to *recover* the original matrix that we used in the algorithm by multiplying the constructed lower-triangular matrix by its transpose:

```
// Recover the original matrix; a kind of check.
ublas::triangular_matrix<double, ublas::upper> U = LowerToUpper(L);
cout << "U:" << endl << U << endl << endl;
cout << "L*U (same as orignal matrix):" << endl << L*U << endl << endl;
```

where `LowerToUpper()` is a free function that converts a lower-triangular matrix to an upper-triangular matrix:

```
// Transpose a lower triangular matrix to form an upper triangular matrix.
ublas::triangular_matrix<double, ublas::upper> LowerToUpper(
    const ublas::triangular_matrix<double, ublas::lower>& L)
{
    ublas::triangular_matrix<double, ublas::upper> U(L.size2(), L.size1());

    for (size_t i = 0; i < U.size1(); ++i)
    {
        for (size_t j = i; j < U.size2(); ++j)
        {
            U(i,j) = L(j,i);
```

```
            }
        }

    return U;
}
```

We finish this section with recovering the original matrix by multiplying the upper and lower triangular matrix that was the result of LU decomposition:

```
// Create LU matrices.
cout << "--- Recover original matrix from LD & LD ---" << endl << endl;
ublas::triangular_matrix<double, ublas::lower> LD(D,D);
ublas::triangular_matrix<double, ublas::upper> UD(D,D);
InitLU(Corr, LD, UD);
cout << "LD: " << endl << LD << endl << endl;
cout << "UD: " << endl << UD << endl << endl;

// Recover original matrix in different ways.
cout << "LD*UD (same as orignal matrix): " << endl << LD*UD << endl;
cout << "UD*LD (same as orignal matrix): " << endl << UD*LD << endl;
```

where we have defined operators for multiplying lower and upper triangular matrices:

```
// Compute Lower*Upper.
ublas::matrix<double> operator * (
    const ublas::triangular_matrix<double, ublas::lower>& L,
    const ublas::triangular_matrix<double, ublas::upper>& U)
{
    ublas::matrix<double> result(L.size1(), L.size2());

    double sum; size_t r;

    for (size_t i = 0; i < result.size1(); ++i)
    {
        for (size_t j = 0; j < result.size2(); ++j)
        {
            sum = 0.0;
            r = std::min(i,j);
            for (size_t p = 0; p <= r; ++p)
            {
                sum += L(i,p)*U(p,j);
            }

            result(i,j) = sum;
        }
    }

    return result;
}

// Compute Upper*Lower.
ublas::matrix<double> operator * (
    const ublas::triangular_matrix<double, ublas::upper>& U,
    const ublas::triangular_matrix<double, ublas::lower>& L)
{
    // Rough and Ready, but it works; it is a test of uBLAS::transpose.
    ublas::triangular_matrix<double, ublas::upper> Upper = trans(L);
    ublas::triangular_matrix<double, ublas::lower> Lower = trans(U);

    return Lower*Upper;
}
```

We can run this code and see that the results are the same in all cases. Finally, another test is to subtract the original matrix from both products and then take the corresponding max norm:

```
// Look at matrix norms.
ublas::matrix<double> m1 = Corr - UD*LD;
ublas::matrix<double> m2 = Corr - LD*UD;
cout << "A - U*L max error: " << ublas::norm_inf(m1) << endl;
cout << "A - L*U max error: " << ublas::norm_inf(m2) << endl << endl;
```

These values should be very small.

7.7 Applications of uBLAS

Vectors and matrices are probably the most pervasive and useful data structures in mathematics and its applications. It is impossible to summarise their many applications but we give an overview of some situations in which we can apply uBLAS, in particular in combination with other Boost libraries and application areas:

- Parallelising uBLAS code by combining it with Boost Thread and OpenMP. In particular, we can apply and implement parallel design patterns (Mattson 2005) to improve the *speedup* of matrix operations.
- Vectors and matrices with specific data types such as `std::complex` and Boost *Rational*.
- Using uBLAS for non-numeric applications in the sense that the underlying data types are not necessarily numeric. For example, we can create vectors and matrices whose data are Boost functions and signals.
- Migrating legacy code that uses home-grown matrix classes to code that uses uBLAS data structures as substrate (Duffy 2004).
- Using uBLAS with Boost MultiArray and Boost Serialization. For example, two-dimensional slices of three-dimensional multi-arrays can result in uBLAS matrices. Furthermore, we can create multi-arrays whose elements are uBLAS data structures.
- We can create and use vectors and matrices of random numbers using uBLAS in combination with Boost Random. For example, block matrices can be modelled as two-dimensional multi-arrays whose values are matices.

7.8 Summary and Conclusions

In this chapter we continued from chapter 6 by discussing a number of advanced features in uBLAS. We introduced various kinds of banded matrices, vector and matrix expressions as well as ranges and slices of these data structures. Finally, we discussed some applications of uBLAS to solving linear systems of equations.

8 An Introduction to Network Programming Concepts and Protocols

8.1 Introduction and Objectives

The goal of this chapter is to give an introduction to network programming concepts and to discuss the TCP protocol suite. We do not assume knowledge of these concepts on the part of the reader but the principles should be easy to understand if the reader has some technical and software background.

This chapter is for the benefit of software developers. You may skip this chapter without loss of continuity if you are already familiar with TCP/IP.

8.2 Overview of OSI and TCP/IP Protocols and Services

The services of the TCP/IP protocol suite can be arranged according to the layers in Figure 8.1 outlined by the *International Standards Organization* (*ISO*) seven-level *Open Systems Interconnection* (*OSI*) *Reference Model*. This model describes the functions provided by any networking system in terms of *layers*. Each layer builds upon the layers below it. In particular, each layer provides a particular kind of *service* to the layers above it. In this sense the Reference Model is a *communication service specification*. In order to provide communication services each layer communicates with its *peer layer* in a different communications unit (called a *host*). To this end, *protocols* are the specifications that govern communication transactions between peer layers of the Reference Model.

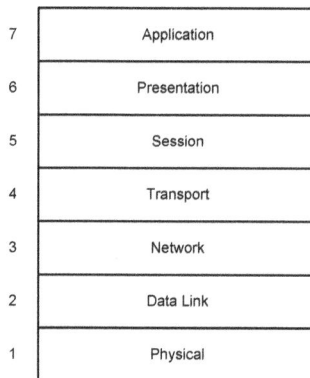

7	Application
6	Presentation
5	Session
4	Transport
3	Network
2	Data Link
1	Physical

Figure 8.1 Levels of OSI Reference Model

We now give a short overview of the responsibility of each of the layers in Figure 8.1. The *physical layer* defines electrical and physical specifications for devices. It defines the relationship between a device and a *transmission medium* (for example, an optical or copper cable) and including cable specification, hubs, repeaters, network adapters and much more. The *data link layer* provides the functional and procedural mechanisms to transfer data between network entities. It is also responsible for detecting and correcting errors that may occur in the physical layer. The *network layer* provides the functional and procedural mechanisms for transferring variable length data sequences from a source host on one network to a destination host on a different network. It also maintains the *quality of service* requested by the transport layer. The network layer performs network routing functions, possibly including fragmentation and reassembly. It also reports on delivery errors. Routers operate in the network layer. The *transport layer* provides transparent transfer of data between end users and it provides reliable data transfer services to the upper layers. It controls the reliability of a given link. TCP and UDP protocols operate in this layer. The *session layer* controls the dialogues (connections) between computers. It is responsible for the establishment, management and termination of the connections between local and remote applications. It supports simplex, half-duplex and full-duplex operations. A *duplex communication* is one consisting of two connected parties or devices that can communicate with each other in both directions. The term *multiplexing* is used when describing communication between more than two parties or devices. Devices that do not need the duplex capability use simplex communication. A *half-duplex* system provides communication in both directions but only in one direction at one time. Once a party begins receiving a signal it must wait for the transmitter to stop transmitting before replying. A *full-duplex* system allows communication in both directions and this communication can take place simultaneously. Typical examples are land-line telephone and mobile phone networks. The *presentation layer* establishes the context between application-layer entities. Higher-layer entities may use different syntax and semantics if the presentation service provides a mapping between them. This layer provides independence from data representation by translating between application and network formats. The presentation layer transforms data into the form that the application accepts. Finally, the *application layer* is the layer closest to the end user. This layer interacts with software applications that implement a communicating component.

TCP provides services at the Transport Layer and IP provides services at the Network Layer. The services of these two main protocols are augmented by application-like services in the higher layers as shown in Figure 8.2. For example, in layers 5 to 7 we have the following services:

- SMTP (*Simple Mail Transfer Protocol*): provides for the sending of text mail between hosts.
- DNS (*Domain Name System*): provides distributed directory services for mapping names to addresses. We introduce DNS in section 8.5.
- FTP (*File Transfer Protocol*): used to exchange files between computers.
- TELNET (*Telecommunications Network*): provides virtual terminal services for interactive access by terminal servers to hosts.

5 - 7	SMTP	DNS	FTP	TELNET
4	TCP		UDP	
3	IP	ICMP		
			ARP	RARP
2	Ethernet		Others	

Figure 8.2 Some TCP/IP Protocols and Services

Some of the other protocols in Figure 8.2 are:

- TCP (*Transmission Control Protocol*): a *connection-oriented* and reliable byte-stream protocol. TCP allows a process on one machine to send a stream of data to a process on another machine.
- IP (*Internet Protocol*): provides internet transaction services for Layer 4 clients. In general, IP is responsible for providing host-to-host datagram delivery.

- UDP (*User Datagram Protocol*): unacknowledged (unreliable) transaction-oriented protocol. UDP uses IP to deliver datagrams. UDP – in contrast to IP – includes a *protocol port number* that allows senders to distinguish between multiple destinations (application programs) on a remote machine. UDP also includes a checksum on the data being sent.
- ICMP (*Internet Control Message Protocol*): gateways and host computers use this protocol to send reports of problems about datagrams back to the original source that sent the datagrams. ICMP also includes an echo request/reply mechanism to test if a destination is reachable and responding.
- ARP (*Address Resolution Protocol*): map IP addresses into associated Ethernet addresses.
- RARP (*Reverse ARP*): maps Ethernet addresses to associated IP addresses.

We shall focus on the protocols TCP and UDP in this book, in particular from the viewpoint of the (novice) network software developer.

8.3   Internet Addresses

A TCP/IP network is a virtual network that is created by interconnecting physical networks by gateways. In order to hide physical network details and to make the internet appear as a single uniform entity the inventors of the technology came up with the idea of defining a globally accepted method of associating computers with unique identifiers that we call *IP addresses*. To this end, each computer (or *host*) is assigned an integer address (IP address) consisting of two parts; first, the part that identifies the specific network in which a host resides and second the part that uniquely identifies the host in that network. There are two versions:

- IPv4: each address is assigned a unique 32-bit internet address that is used by a host in all communications.
- IPv6: this standard succeeds IPv4. In this case each host is assigned a 128-bit address. One of the motivations for this new standard was the ability to define more addresses than is possible with IP4.

In this book we concentrate on IPv4 although we mention that Asio supports both IPv4 and IPv6 and has functionality for converting between them as well as supporting a version-independent IP address class mechanism.

We now discuss the structure of IPv4 addresses in more detail. As we already mentioned, each address has a network part and a host part, sometimes called *netid* and *hostid*, respectively. IP addresses can be categorised into one of the number of *classes*, for example:

- Class A: The first eight bits of the address are reserved for the netid and bit 0 has value '0'.
- Class B: The first sixteen bits of the address are reserved for the netid; the first two bits are '10'.
- Class C: The first twentyfour bits of the address are reserved for the netid; the first three bits are '110'. Thus, there are eigth bits for the hostid part.

We do not discuss class D and class E IP addresses in this book. Internet addresses need to be readable by humans and they are then written in *dotted decimal notation* consisting of four decimal integers separated by decimal points. Each value represents one byte (or *octet*) of the IP address. For example, the IP address 10000000 00001010 00000010 00011110 would be written as the class B address 128.10.2.30.

8.3.1 Some Special IP Addresses

We discuss a number of special IP addresses that are used in applications. First, the network address 127.0.0.1 is reserved for *loopback* when testing inter-process communication on the *local machine*. This address can be used when testing client-server and data-transfer applications. We can first test applications on the local machine before testing the software on a live network. Second, a *broadcast address* is one that refers to all hosts on a network. In general, any hostid consisting of all 1s is reserved for broadcast (IP address: 255.255.255.255).

A *multicast address* is a logical identifier for a group of hosts in a computer network. Multicast addresses can be used in the Data Link Layer (layer 2) in the OSI model, for example Ethernet multicast and in the Network Layer (layer 3) for IPv4 and IPv6. IPv4 multicast addresses are defined by the leading address bits of 1110 (class D address types).

8.4 Internet Addresses in Boost

Boost has three C++ classes that model IP addresses, namely classes for IPv4 and IPv6 addresses and a third class that implements version-independent IP addresses. We focus on the functionality for managing IPv4 addresses; the functionality for IPv6 addresses is similar.

The functions for the IPv4 C++ class are:
- Constructors (default, copy, from raw bytes, from unsigned integer in host byte order).
- Is the address an A, B or C type?
- Is the address a multicast or loopback address?
- Converting an address to a string; convert an address to an array of bytes.
- Compare IP addresses using operator overloading (!= , == , < , > , <= , >=).

We give an example. First, we have created a function to print information relating to IPv4 addresses. This function uses much of the functionality in the IP address class:

```cpp
#include <boost/asio/ip/address.hpp>

void ExamineIpAddress(const boost::asio::ip::address_v4& myIP,
                      const string& s = string(""))
{
    cout << "\n**IP4 ouput " + s << endl;

    // IP class.
    cout << "Class A: " << boolalpha << myIP.is_class_a() << endl;
    cout << "Class B: " << boolalpha << myIP.is_class_b() << endl;
    cout << "Class C: " << boolalpha << myIP.is_class_c() << endl;

    cout << "Multicast B: " << boolalpha << myIP.is_multicast();

    // Various representations.
    cout << endl << endl;
    boost::asio::ip::address_v4::bytes_type byteRep = myIP.to_bytes();
    for (size_t n = 0; n < byteRep.size(); ++n)
    {
        cout << int(byteRep[n]) << "/";
    }
    cout << endl;

    cout << "Long value: " << myIP.to_ulong() << endl;
    cout << "String value: " << myIP.to_string() << endl;
}
```

We create an IPv4 address using byte array values:

```
// v4 addresses.
boost::asio::ip::address_v4::bytes_type myAddress;
myAddress[0] = 127; myAddress[1] = 0;
myAddress[2] = 0; myAddress[3] = 1;

boost::asio::ip::address_v4 myIP(myAddress);
ExamineIpAddress(myIP);      // Default v4
```

The output from this code is:

```
**IP4 ouput
Class A: true
Class B: false
Class C: false
Multicast B: false

127/0/0/1/
Long value: 2130706433
String value: 127.0.0.1
```

We now discuss the class that implements *version-independent* IP addresses. Its member functions are:
- Constructors: default, copy, from an IPv4 address, from an IPv6 address.
- Create an address from an IPv4 string in dotted decimal form, or from an IPv6 address in hexadecimal notation.
- Determine if the address is an IPv4 or IPv6 address.
- Assign an address to another address.
- Convert an address to string format.

We give an example to show how to define and use version-independent addresses. We first have defined a convenience function to display information relating to a version-independent IP address:

```
void ExamineIpAddress(const boost::asio::ip::address& myIP,
                      const string& s = string(""))
{
    cout << "\n**IP version-independent ouput " + s << endl;

    cout << "Multicast?: " << boolalpha << myIP.is_multicast() << endl;
    cout << "Loopback?: " << boolalpha << myIP.is_loopback() << endl;

    // What is 'underlying' type?
    cout << "Was it a v4?: " << myIP.is_v4() << endl;
    cout << "Was it a v6?: " << myIP.is_v6() << endl;
    cout << "address: " << myIP << endl;

    // Display the different representations.
    if (myIP.is_v4()) cout << "IPv4 format: " << myIP.to_v4() << endl;
    if (myIP.is_v6()) cout << "IPv6 format: " << myIP.to_v6() << endl;
}
```

We now create a default IPv6 address and we then call this function:

```
// Create the 16 bytes for an IPv6 address.
boost::asio::ip::address_v6::bytes_type b1 =
    {1,2,3,4,5,6,7,8,9,10,11,12,13,14,15,16};

// Create Ipv6 address from bytes and scope ID.
boost::asio::ip::address_v6 myIPv6(b1, 12345);
ExamineIpAddress(myIPv6, "version-independent");
```

8.4.1   Implementing Endpoints

Boost supports the creation of endpoints for both TCP and UDP. An *endpoint* is an aggregation of an IP address and port number. The TCP and UDP protocols allow each IP address to be associated with 65,535 *ports* (a port is represented as an integer) and this means that a single address can run multiple applications, each one on its own port. Many applications have standard port assignments, for example HTTP (Hypertext Transfer Protocol) uses port 80, SMTP uses port 25 (used for e-mail routing between mail servers) and port 20 is FTP (File Transfer Protocol).

There are three ranges of port numbers defined. First the range [0, 1023] is the *well-known port* range which is used by the standard internet services like FTP, HTTP and DNS. The well-known ports should not be used unless the application implements the internet service assigned to that port. The second range [1024, 49151] is the *registered port* range. These port numbers are assigned by the *Internet Assigned Numbers Authority* (IANA) upon request however there are many applications that uses ports from this range unofficially. Finally, the range [49152, 65535] is the *private port* and *dynamic port* range. As these ports are unassigned they can be used for testing your deployments. This range is also used for dynamically generated port numbers. After a client connects to a well-know or registered port the communication is continued via a dynamically generated port number from the dynamic port range. We discuss ports in more detail in section 8.7 when we discuss sockets.

We focus on the TCP *endpoint class*. Its member functions are:

- Constructors: default, copy, from a port number (the address will be the *any* address corresponding to INADDR_ANY or `in6addr_any`), from a port number and IP address.
- Set and get the port and address associated with the endpoint.
- Comparison operators for endpoints.
- Output an endpoint as a string (using operator <<).

We now give some examples of how to define TCP endpoints:

```
#include <boost/asio.hpp>    // Convenience file.

#include <string>
#include <iostream>

using namespace std;

using namespace boost::asio;
using namespace boost::system;


int main()
{
    // The port number to use.
    unsigned short port=60000;

    ip::tcp::endpoint basicEndpoint;
    cout << basicEndpoint << endl;    // Output 0.0.0.0:0

    // Create local IP4 endpoint to listen to a certain port.
    ip::tcp::endpoint endPoint(ip::tcp::v4(), port);
    cout << endPoint << endl;         // Output 0.0.0.0:60000

    // Endpoint with IP address and port.
    boost::asio::ip::address_v4::bytes_type myAddress;
    myAddress[0] = 127; myAddress[1] = 0;
    myAddress[2] = 0; myAddress[3] = 1;
```

```
boost::asio::ip::address_v4 myIP(myAddress);
ip::tcp::endpoint endPoint2(myIP, port);
cout << endPoint2 << endl;

return 0;
}
```

We shall see in later chapters how endpoints are used in network applications.

8.5   Domain Name System (DNS)

We discussed IP addresses and their implementation in sections 3 and 4. They offer a convenient and compact representation for specifying hosts in a network. We now wish to assign more meaningful names to these hosts as well as providing mappings between these names and the corresponding IP addresses. Names for machines follow a hierarchical approach as show in Figure 8.3. The mechanism that implements this hierarchy is called the *Doman Name System* (DNS). In particular, it specifies the implementation of a distributed computing system that efficiently maps names to addresses. Each host in DNS is called a *domain name* and each name consists of a hierarchy of dot-delimited subnames, for example:

www.datasim.nl
www.ibm.com
www.ucla.edu

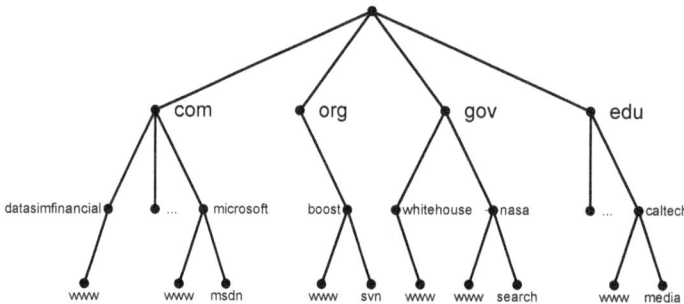

Figure 8.3 DNS Database

There are two main use cases when using DNS:
- Mapping domain names to addresses: in general, a set of *name servers* operating at multiple sites cooperatively solve this mapping problem. Most names can be mapped locally. The process of address-to-name mapping is trivial if we use *host tables* on the local machine.
- Mapping IP addresses to domain names (*reverse DNS*): given an IP address, determine its associated domain name. The address-to-name translation is not so simple.

The resolution of name-to-address is shown in Figure 8.4 by means of an example. In this case a client (called a *name resolver*) uses one or more *name servers* A, B, C and D. It queries a local name server A that then queries a number of other name servers in pursuit of an answer for the resolver. Finally, the local name server queries the authoritative name server A which then returns an answer. The steps in Figure 8.4 in which server A needs to query three other servers are:
1. Resolver host queries name server A.
2. A queries name server B.

3. B refers A to another name server C.
4. A queries C.
5. C refers to A to other name servers, for example D.
6. A queries D.
7. D sends a response to A.
8. A gives the answer to the resolver.

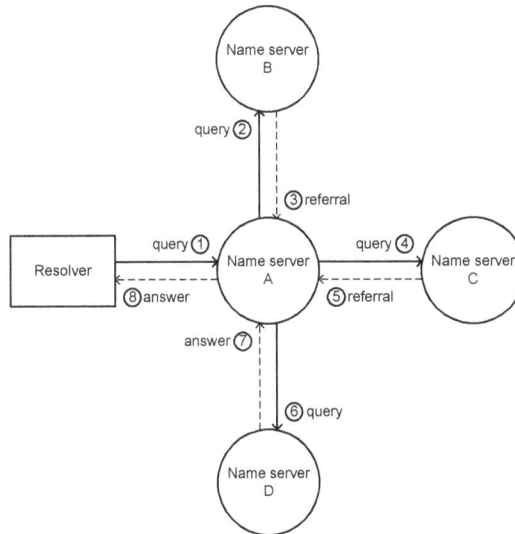

Figure 8.4 Resolution Process

Finally, name servers cache data which has a certain *time to live* (TTL). This is the amount of time that any name server is allowed to cache the data. After the TTL expires, the name server must discard the cached data and get new data from the *authoritative name server*. The value for TTL is determined by a trade-off between performance and consistency. A large value shortens the average time it takes to resolve information in a domain because the data is cached for for a longer period of time. On the other hand, the information will be inconsistent for a longer period of time if we change the data on name servers.

8.6   Client-Server Model of Interaction

From the application developer's viewpoint, a network application uses TCP/IP mechanisms to transfer data. To this end, TCP/IP provides a *peer-to-peer* communication mechanism to allow programmers to write communication software between two application programs and to pass data back and forth. The applications can execute on the same machine or on different machines. Applications communicate using the *client-server paradigm* in all cases. Fundamental to this paradigm is the problem of *rendezvous* and ensuring that client and server applications communicate in a predictable fashion. The client-server paradigm resolves this problem by demanding that one side starts execution and waits (indefinitely) for the other side to contact it. Thus, a program must be waiting to accept communication before any requests arrive. In other words, TCP/IP does not provide any mechanisms that automatically create running programs when a message arrives.

We now discuss some terminology. There are two roles in the paradigm, namely *client* and *server*. The direction of communication initiation determines which program is client and which program is server. In general, it is the client that initiates communication. A *client* is a conventional application program. It contacts a server when it executes, sends a request and then waits on a response. The client continues processing when the response arrives. A *server*, on the other hand is a program that waits for incoming communication requests from a client. It receives a client's requests, performs the necessary computation and then returns the result to the client.

8.6.1   Connectionless and Connection-Oriented Servers

There are two types of interaction styles in client-server applications:

- *Connectionless*: this treats each data packet or datagram as a separate entity that contains the source and destination addresses. It is possible that connectionless services drop packets or deliver them out of sequence. An *IP datagram* is the basic unit of information passed across a TCP/IP network. It contains a source address and destination address along with the data.
  UDP delivers a connectionless service. It does not guarantee reliable delivery. Requests from clients may be lost, delayed, duplicated or delivered out of order.
- *Connection-Oriented*: this represents a reliable service between client and server. TCP supports connection-oriented services and it provides the reliability that is needed to communicate across the internet. It computes checksums on the data to ensure that it is not corrupted during transmission and it uses sequence numbers to ensure that the data arrives in order. It also eliminates duplicate packets.

We need to discuss the issue concerning the status of ongoing interactions between client and server. This is called *state information*. Servers that contain state information are called *stateful servers*; otherwise they are called *stateless servers*. In general, stateful servers promote efficiency because they can store information on client-related data and they can compute incremental responses as each new request arrives. The downside is that state information may become stale or incorrect. In this sense we see that stateless servers are more reliable than stateful servers.

8.7   The Socket Interface

In this section we introduce the *socket abstraction* that serves as the basis for network I/O in client-server applications. It can be seen as a generalisation of the UNIX file access mechanism that provides an endpoint for communication. Both client and server create sockets without binding them to specific destination addresses. Similar to file operations, sockets have *read* and *write* operations. In particular, both clients and servers can send and receive datagrams.

Before we discuss the general steps when using socket calls with TCP we first need to introduce the port concept. A *port* is typically a small integer and it is used in combination with an IP address to define an *endpoint* through which applications communicate. First, the steps that the server executes are:

1. Create a socket.
2. Use *bind* system call to define a local address and port number.
3. *Listen*: prepare the server for incoming connections.
4. *Accept*: the server waits for a connection (the server *blocks* until a connection request arrives).
5. Receive data from the client (on a new dynamic port).
6. Send data to client.
7. Receive end message from client.
8. Close the socket.

The steps that the client executes are:
1. Create a socket.
2. Client connects to the destination address (the server).
3. Send data to server.
4. Receive data from server.
5. Close socket.

See Figure 8.5 for a visual representation of this use case, including the messages between client and server. In chapter 9 and 10 we shall discuss how the Asio library implements this functionality in C++.

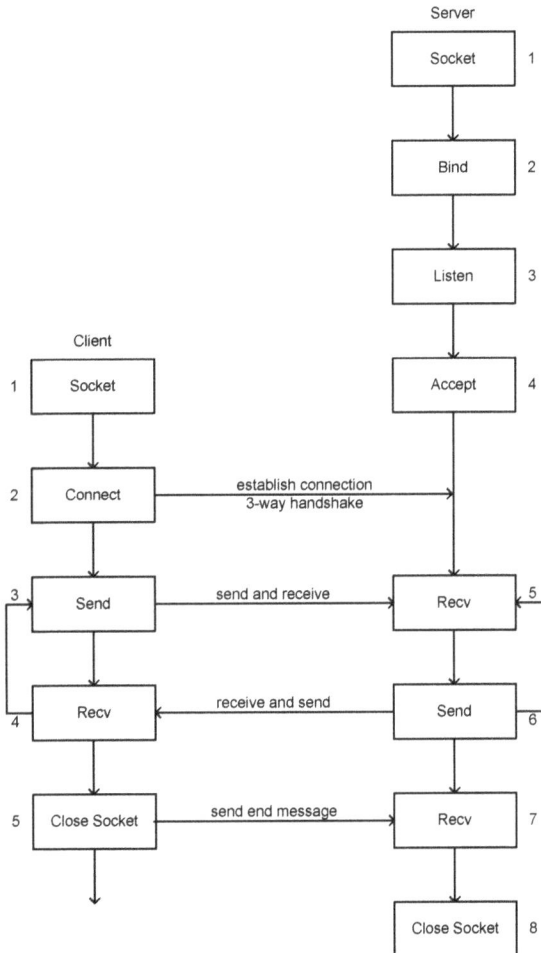

Figure 8.5 Socket call in TCP

8.8   Protocol for Acknowledgement and Retransmission

In Figure 8.5 we see that we use a so-called *three-way handshake* to establish TCP socket connections and to realise connections across the network. We describe the sequence of steps involved in this process (sometimes call SYN, SYN_ACK, ACK). The objective is to allow two computers attempting to communicate to negotiate the parameters of the network TCP socket connection before establishing a connection. The handshaking process is so flexible that both ends can initiate and negotiate separate TCP socket connections at the same time.

We now give a simple description of the three-way handshake process. Consider two hosts A and B with host A taking the initiative. The sequence is:
1. Host A sends a TCP SYNchronise packet to host B.
2. B receives A's SYN.
3. B sends a SYNchronise_ACKnowledgement to A.
4. A receives B'S SYN-ACK.
5. A sends ACKnowledge.
6. B receives ACK.

At this stage, the TCP socket is established. Finally, we note that TCP realises reliable stream delivery. The process that makes this possible is called *positive acknowledgement and retransmission*. Recipients must communicate with the source and they send back an acknowledgement message as they receive data. The source keeps a record of each packet that it sends and waits for an acknowledgement before sending the next packet. Furthermore, the sender starts a timer when it sends a packet and *retransmits* a packet if the timer expires before an acknowledgement arrives. Figure 8.6 depicts this use case. This shows the ideal case in which data is neither lost nor corrupted.

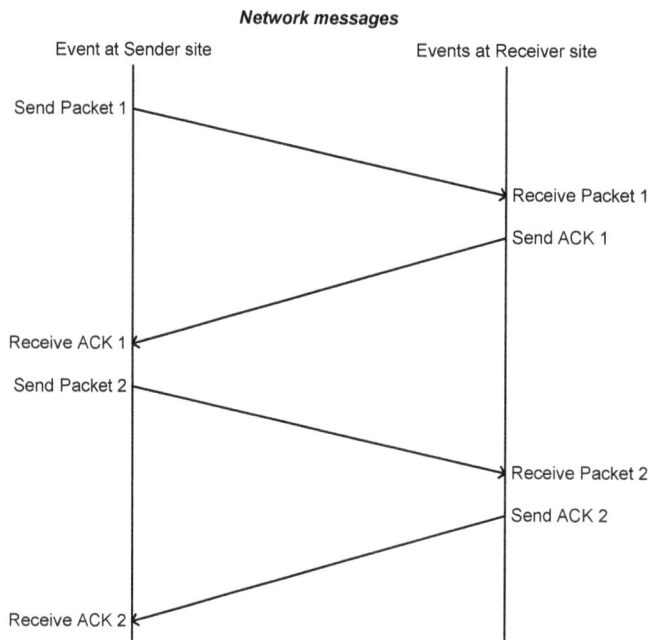

Network messages

Event at Sender site		Events at Receiver site
Send Packet 1		
		Receive Packet 1
		Send ACK 1
Receive ACK 1		
Send Packet 2		
		Receive Packet 2
		Send ACK 2
Receive ACK 2		

Figure 8.6 Protocol for acknowledgement and retransmission

8.9   Summary and Conclusions

We have given a short overview of some of the most important concepts in the TCP/IP protocol suite. We discussed layered protocols, IP addressing, the Domain Name System (DNS) and name-address resolution. Furthermore, we introduce the client-server programming model and its applications to network programming. Finally, we discussed the Socket Interface.

You should understand these topics before moving to chapters 9 and 10.

9 Boost ASIO: Synchronous Operations

9.1 Introduction

In this chapter we discuss how Boost implements the UDP and TCP socket interface that we introduced in chapter 8. When we wish to communicate between two computers we usually communicate over a network. In the past we needed to use C APIs that an Operating System (OS) provides. Furthermore a C API is usually harder to use than a C++ library and it is usually also platform-dependent.

The Boost ASIO library solves these problems. It provides platform-independent networking functionality. The goals of the ASIO library are:
- *Portability*: The library should support various platforms so that applications can run on those platforms without code changes.
- *Scalability*: The library should provide facilities to scale the application to thousands of concurrent connections. This is achieved by providing an *asynchronous model*.
- *Efficiency*: The library should be efficient. An example of this is the use of multiple buffers for I/O operations so that copying of data can be avoided.
- *Reuse concepts from existing APIs*: By using concepts from the BSD socket API the ASIO library feels familiar to network developers and it is also easy to learn for novice network developers.
- *Easy to use*: Users should be able to use the library with little effort.
- *Basis for further abstraction*: The library should be useable as basis for higher level abstractions such as modelling the HTML or FTP protocols, for example.

The ASIO library is also IP protocol-agnostic. In other words, the library works with both the IP4 and IP6 protocols.

To use the ASIO library we include the following code statements:

```
#include <boost/asio.hpp>
using namespace boost::asio;
```

The core class in the library is io_service. This class is used by the classes that abstract the networking communication. It is the bridge to the underlying operating system. Programs using ASIO should always create an io_service instance and ASIO needs it when creating the other networking objects (for example, a socket). We now describe this process in words. The process flow of a typical *synchronous* ASIO application is shown in Figure 9.1.

First, an io_service instance must be created which is necessary for all ASIO operations. This instance is passed as argument when an ASIO I/O object is created. When the I/O object has been created the general steps for a synchronous ASIO operation are (the numbers refer to those in Figure 9.1):
1. I/O operation is called e.g. a request to send data.
2. I/O object forwards request to io_service object.
3. io_service instance forwards request to OS. OS executes request.
4. OS returns result to the io_service.

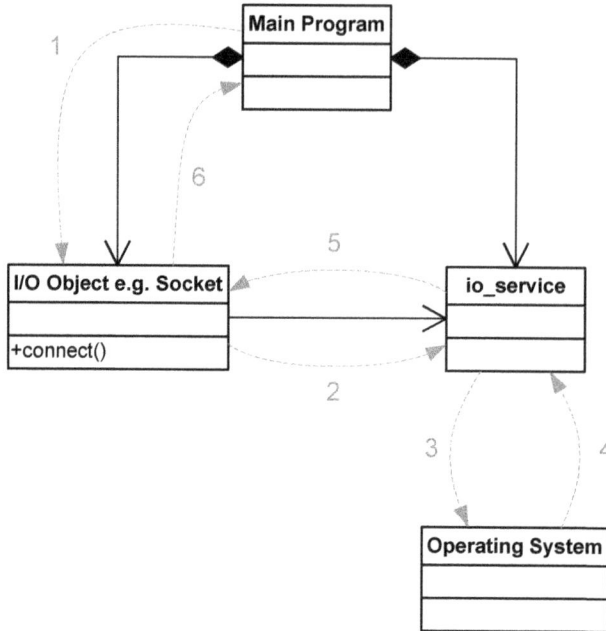

Figure 9.1 ASIO synchronous operation

5. `io_service` returns result to I/O object.
    *   Errors are converted to `boost::system::error_code`.
6. I/O object returns result to application.
    *   Errors can be thrown as `boost::system::system_error` exception.
    *   Errors can also be returned via an additional reference argument of type `boost::system::error_code`.

Handling errors can be done in two ways. When an error occurs the ASIO function can throw a `boost::system::system_error` exception which should then be caught in client code. Alternatively, most functions that can throw an exception also have an overloaded version that additionally accepts a `non-const` reference to an `boost::system::error_code` object. Instead of throwing an exception when there is an error the `error_code` object will be set and it can then be checked when the function completes.

9.1.1   Testing Network Applications and Troubleshooting

We do not necessarily need two computers in order to create and test network applications. Testing programs that eventually communicate with each other over the network can also be done on a single machine. We can run both server and client applications on the same machine during development. When the program needs the IP address of the remote machine we enter the IP address of the development machine. There is also a special IP address and host name that always refer to the local machine. The IP address 127.0.0.1 and host name *localhost* always refer to the local machine on every system. We normally use this address and host name when testing client/server applications on a single machine. When the application works correctly with the localhost as remote address it should also work with multiple machines if the network is correctly configured. Of course, we must test the program in this case as well.

When testing or deploying the application on multiple computers we can encounter some problems. Most machines run a firewall that monitors which applications are accessing the network. Firewalls can block programs that wish to access the network. They block applications that attempt to open a network port for listening (incoming network connections) since that could be a potential security hole. We explicitly tell the firewall that our application is allowed to open a network port for listening. Most firewalls will show a popup window when an application opens a network port so we simply can allow an application to open a port for listening. The next time the program starts the firewall will remember the application and should automatically give network access.

Each time we change the application the firewall will see it as a new application and will block it again.

More elaborate firewalls will also block outgoing connections, in particular applications that make a connection with a remote host. In this case most firewalls will display a popup and you can enable the program for outgoing connections.

We can set permissions in a firewall configuration when an application is denied network access and no popup is shown. Please refer to your firewall's documentation for details.

Besides software firewalls on the local computer there could also be a hardware firewall between the two computers that blocks network communication. Usually this firewall is part of the internet router or in large networks it could be another computer that connects the local network to the internet. These firewalls and routers must be configured to allow network traffic to pass through. In the case of server applications we must tell the router which computer on the local network is the server for a given internet port.

There are also firewalls that we have no control over. For example, internet providers or routers in organisations can block certain internet traffic. In some cases non-standard internet ports are blocked. In that case it could help to use a port from the well-know port range [0, 1023] (for example port 80 that is normally used by the http protocol) as long as it does not conflict with other programs running on the system that use this port. Using ports from the well-known range is not recommended unless the application is an implementation of the protocol that uses that port, for example when the application is a web server (port 80) or an FTP server (port 21).

9.2 DNS

Resolving a hostname to an endpoint (a combination of IP address and port number) is realised by the `resolver` class. For each internet protocol there is a corresponding resolver type. It is a template specialisation of the `basic_resolver` class. Each resolver type is nested in its protocol class:

```
class ip::basic_resolver;
typedef ip::basic_resolver<ip::tcp> ip::tcp::resolver;
typedef ip::basic_resolver<ip::udp> ip::udp::resolver;
typedef ip::basic_resolver<ip::icmp> ip::icmp::resolver;
```

The classes involved in resolving IP addresses are depicted in Figure 9.2.

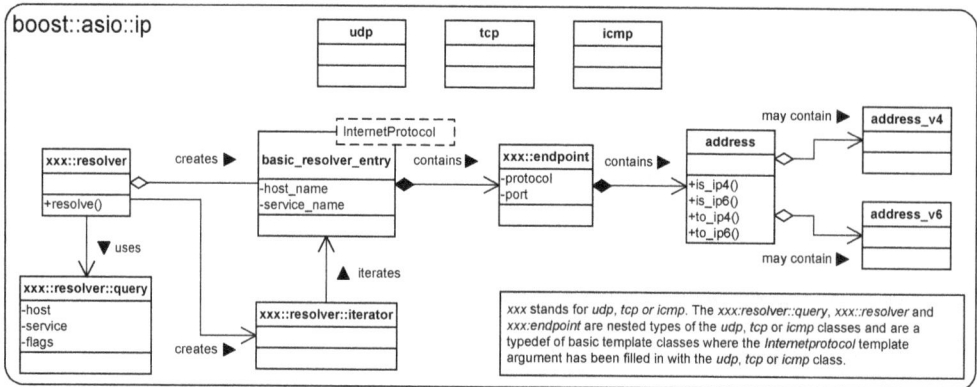

Figure 9.2 DNS Resolver and related classes

The resolver's `resolve()` function uses a `resolver::query` object. The resolver query contains the host name and the service name for the requested endpoint. It is possible that the *http* service for a host has a different IP address than that of the *ftp* service. The service can also be a port number in string format. When an empty string is passed as the service to use it will use port number 0. The port number can be modified later in the returned `endpoint` object.

Optionally, the query can specify if we desire to use ip4 or ip6 addresses. When not specified both v4 and v6 addresses will be returned.

A query can result in multiple IP addresses. This is the reason why the resolver returns an *iterator* to a collection of resolver entries. A resolver entry contains the endpoint object. The endpoint is then used when making connections.

We now show a function that resolves the end points for the TCP protocol and prints each endpoint:

```cpp
// Resolve an address for the TCP protocol.
void ResolveTCP(string host, string service)
{
    io_service ios;                     // IO service is always needed.
    boost::system::error_code ec;       // Space for the returned error code.

    // Create the resolver object and the query to pass to the resolver.
    ip::tcp::resolver r(ios);
    ip::tcp::resolver::query query(host, service);

    // Resolve the query and put it in an iterator.
    // Also create an interator indicating the end.
    ip::tcp::resolver::iterator it=r.resolve(query, ec);
    ip::tcp::resolver::iterator end;

    // Check if there was an error.
    if (ec)
    {
        cout<<"Error resolving host: "<<ec.message()<<endl;
        return;
    }

    // Display each entry found.
    while (it!=end) cout<<"IP end-point: "<<(it++)->endpoint()<<endl;
}
```

In this case we display the end points corresponding to the host name and service name.

The code for resolving the endpoint for UDP or ICMP protocols is similar to the above code. To this end, we replace `ip::tcp` by `ip::udp` or by `ip::icmp` respectively.

9.2.1   Reverse DNS

In some cases we wish to know the host or service name corresponding to a given endpoint. This can also be done using the `resolver` types. The `resolve()` function now accepts an endpoint object instead of a host name and service. It returns an iterator to a collection of resolver entries because a server can have multiple host names. The resolver entry contains the host and service name.

We now give a function that finds all the host and service names for a given TCP endpoint:

```
// Reverse DNS for the TCP protocol.
void ResolveTCP(string ip, int port)
{
    io_service ios;               // IO service is always needed.
    boost::system::error_code ec;  // Space for the returned error code.

    // Create the resolver object and the endpoint object
    // to pass to the resolver.
    ip::tcp::endpoint ep(ip::address::from_string(ip), port);
    ip::tcp::resolver r(ios);

    // Reverse DNS the address and put it in an iterator.
    // Als create an interator indicating the end.
    ip::tcp::resolver::iterator it=r.resolve(ep, ec);
    ip::tcp::resolver::iterator end;

    // Check if there was an error.
    if (ec)
    {
        cout<<"Error resolving ip address: "<<ec.message()<<endl;
        return;
    }

    // Display each entry found.
    while (it!=end)
    {
        cout<<"Host name: "<<it->host_name()<<endl;
        cout<<"Service name: "<<it->service_name()<<endl;
        it++;
    }
}
```

In this case, we display the host names and service names corresponding to the given endpoint.

9.3   Buffers

We need a buffer when receiving or sending data. A *buffer* is defined as a pair consisting of a pointer and a size. ASIO distinguishes between *read/write buffers* and *read-only buffers*. A read/write buffer can be converted to a read-only buffer but not the other way around. ASIO defines two buffer classes that are constructed with a pointer and a size:

```
class mutable_buffer;   // Read/write buffer.
class const_buffer;     // Read only buffer.
```

These classes wrap data created elsewhere and they do not manage the memory themselves. However, these classes are not directly accepted by the ASIO I/O functions. ASIO supports reading/writing to a collection of buffers using *scatter/gather operations*. Scatter/gather I/O is a method of input and output by which a singe procedure-call sequentially writes data from multiple buffers to a single data stream or recalls data from a data stream to multiple buffers. The ASIO functions accept a collection of buffers where the collection must adhere to the *MutableBufferSequence* or *ConstBufferSequence* concepts. These concepts require that a buffer class must provide `begin()` and `end()` functions. These functions return an iterator to a `mutable_buffer` or `const_buffer` depending on the type. For example, an `std::vector` or a `boost::array` can be used as collection of buffers.

We now discuss a `PrintBuffers()` function that accepts a buffer sequence and prints all the elements of each buffer in the sequence. The ASIO I/O functions use the buffer sequence in a similar way. The functions `buffers_begin()` and `buffers_end()` return iterators that enables us to iterate in the sequence of buffers as if it were a single continuous block of data. These iterators are used to create a string which is printed:

```
// Print the contents of a buffer sequence.
template <typename ConstBufferSequence>
void PrintBuffers(ConstBufferSequence buffer)
{
    cout<<" - "<<string(buffers_begin(buffer), buffers_end(buffer))<<endl;
}
```

We now create a collection of buffers and pass it to the `PrintBuffers()` function:

```
// Create two buffers.
char* s1="Datasim";
char* s2="Education";

// Create a array for two mutable buffers and fill it.
boost::array<mutable_buffer, 2> arr;
arr[0]=mutable_buffer(s1, 7);
arr[1]=mutable_buffer(s2, 9);

// Print the array with buffers (buffer sequence).
PrintBuffers(arr); cout<<endl;
```

If we only have a single buffer creating a buffer collection for it is extra work. Therefore ASIO provides subclasses of `mutable_buffer` and `const_buffer` that adhere to the *MutableBufferSequence* and *ConstBufferSequence* concepts, respectively but contains only a single buffer:

```
class mutable_buffers_1: public mutable_buffer;
class const_buffers_1: public const_buffer;
```

To ease creation of `mutable_buffers_1` and `const_mutable_buffers_1` instances ASIO provides several overloads of the `buffer()` global function. It creates the proper buffer sequence of various standard data types. The code below shows its usage:

```
// Create a few buffers.
char arr[]={'D', 'a', 't', 'a', 's', 'i', 'm', 0};
string str="Datasim";
boost::array<char, 8> ba={'D', 'a', 't', 'a', 's', 'i', 'm', 0};
vector<char> v;

// Fill the vector.
for (int i=0; i<8; i++) v.push_back(arr[i]);
// Wrap the buffers in a const_buffer or if possible in a mutable_buffer.
```

```
mutable_buffers_1 b1=buffer(arr);
const_buffers_1 b2=buffer(str);
mutable_buffers_1 b3=buffer(v);
mutable_buffers_1 b4=buffer(ba);

// Print the buffers.
PrintBuffers(b1);
PrintBuffers(b2);
PrintBuffers(b3);
PrintBuffers(b4);
```

It is also possible to wrap a subsection of an existing buffer in another buffer. First, we pass an extra argument to the `buffer()` function that limits the size of the buffer. Second, we add an integer to a buffer object to move the start point in the buffer while keeping the same size (the endpoint also moves). If the end overflows the buffer the size will be limited to the end of the buffer:

```
// Limit the buffer (b4=Datasim).
mutable_buffers_1 b11=buffer(b4, 4);      // Data
PrintBuffers(b11);
mutable_buffers_1 b12=buffer(b4+4);       // sim
PrintBuffers(b12);
mutable_buffers_1 b13=buffer(b4+2, 3);    // tas
PrintBuffers(b13);
```

9.4   UDP

The simplest form of communication in ASIO is using the UDP protocol. ASIO defines the `ip::udp::socket` class that is used for sending and receiving data in a buffer sequence. The client initiates communication while the server listens for clients. The data is sent as a datagram packet over the network. See Figure 9.3.

The communication is sometimes called 'fire and forget'. The data is sent but there is no provision in the UDP protocol to determine if a packet actually arrived. Furthermore, when sending multiple packets there is no guarantee that the receiving order is the same as the sending order. In other words, the packets can arrive out of sequence.

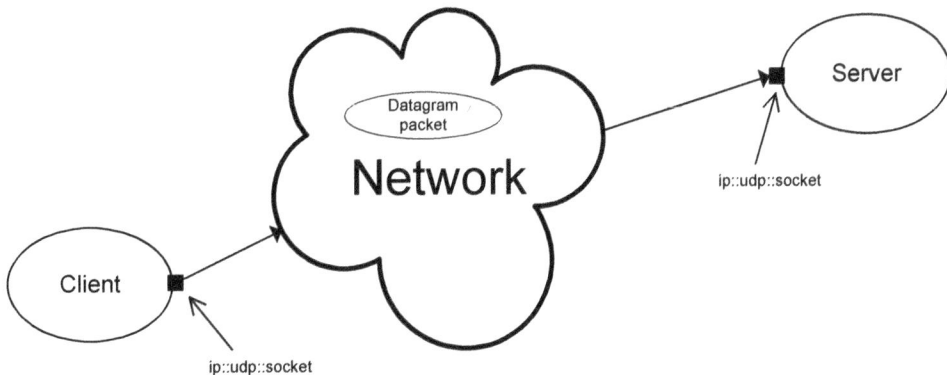

Figure 9.3 UDP Communication

The steps for a *server* to listen and receive data are based on the steps in section 8.7:
- Create an `ip::udp::socket` with arguments:
  - `io_service` object & local endpoint (port number).
- Prepare a buffer to hold the received data.

- Use `receive_from()` function on the socket to receive data:
  - Accepts buffer sequence.
  - Has a reference parameter that returns the client endpoint.
  - Returns the size of the received data.
- We can use the obtained client endpoint to send a reply.
- Use the `close()` function of the socket when finished.

The steps for the *client* to send a datagram are:
- Create an `ip::udp::socket` with an `io_service` object and the IP version to use.
- Prepare a buffer with data to send.
- Use `send_to()` function to send the data:
  - Accepts buffer sequence and an endpoint of the remote host (ip address + port number).
  - To obtain an endpoint from a host name we need the DNS resolver.
- Use the `close()` function when finished.

Note that when sending data we specify the remote endpoint for each send operation. Thus, there is no permanent connection between client and server.

9.4.1   Example: UDP Echo Server

We now implement an UDP echo server that listens for datagram packets and sends the same message with all characters converted to uppercase as reply. The server listens to all local network adapters with IP4 addresses. If we wish to listen to only one local network adapter then we need to create an endpoint with the IP address of that adapter.

Note that we use a `boost::array` as buffer that is passed to the `receive_from()` and `send_to()` functions using the `buffer()` function that wraps it in a buffer sequence:

```cpp
// The port number to use.
const unsigned int port=60000;

// Start opening socket.
cout<<"Opening UDP socket on port "<<port<<"..."<<endl;

// IO service is always needed.
io_service ios;

// Create local IP4 endpoint to listen to a certain port.
ip::udp::endpoint endPoint(ip::udp::v4(), port);

// Create and open the socket with the endpoint to listen to
// (all local addresses).
ip::udp::socket socket(ios, endPoint);
cout<<"Socket opened on: "<<endPoint<<endl;

// Buffer to store data and the endpoint of the client.
boost::array<char, 256> data;
ip::udp::endpoint client;

// Get the data.
cout<<"Waiting for data..."<<endl;
size_t size;
while (true)
{
    // Receive data.
    size=socket.receive_from(buffer(data), client);
    cout<<"Data received from "<<client
        <<": "<<string(data.data(), size)<<endl;
```

```
    // Send reply (uppercase string).
    for (size_t i=0; i<size; i++) data[i]=toupper(data[i]);
    socket.send_to(buffer(data, size), client);
}

// Never arrives here, but normally when finished, close the socket.
socket.close();
cout<<"Socket closed."<<endl;
```

9.4.2   Example: UDP Echo Client

We now discuss the client code. It reads strings from the console and then sends it to the server using UDP. It also waits for the answer and then prints it before reading the next line from the console.

```
// The port number to use.
const unsigned int port=60000;

// IO service is always needed.
io_service ios;

// Ask for host.
string host;
cout<<"Enter the host to connect to (empty=localhost): ";
getline(cin, host);

// If nothing entered, assume localhost.
if (host=="") host="localhost";

// Create the query and resolver. Get only IP4 addresses.
ip::udp::resolver::query query(ip::udp::v4(), host, "");
ip::udp::resolver r(ios);

// Resolve the query and put it in a resolver iterator.
ip::udp::resolver::iterator it=r.resolve(query);

// Get the endpoint of the first host from the resolver iterator.
ip::udp::endpoint endPoint=it->endpoint();
endPoint.port(port);

// Create and open socket for IP4.
cout<<"Opening socket..."<<endl;
ip::udp::socket socket(ios, ip::udp::v4());

// Connected.
string str;                      // String to send.
boost::array<char, 255> data; // Buffer for receiving answer.
do
{
    // Get the data to send.
    cout<<"Enter data to send (Enter to exit): ";
    getline(cin, str);

    // Send the data to the endpoint.
    cout<<"Sending '"<<str<<"' to endpoint '"<<endPoint<<"'"<<endl;
    socket.send_to(buffer(str), endPoint);

    // Get reply.
    ip::udp::endpoint serverEndPoint;
    size_t size=socket.receive_from(buffer(data), serverEndPoint);
    cout<<"Reply from "<<serverEndPoint<<" : "
        <<string(data.data(), size)<<endl;
}
while (str.length()!=0);
```

```
// Finished, close the socket.
socket.close();
cout<<"Socket closed"<<endl;
```

9.5   TCP

The TCP protocol is more reliable than UDP. It has provisions for resending lost or corrupt packets and for packet reordering. Thus for the user it seems like there is a permanent connection over which data is sent.

9.5.1   Example: TCP Echo Server

We now discuss the construction of a TCP server. The TCP protocol uses *logical connections*. This means that when the server handles more than one client it has a connection for each client. Therefore, creating a connection is a two-step process. We have already discussed this process in detail in section 8.7.

First, the server listens for clients using the `accept()` function on an `ip::tcp::acceptor` object.

When a client connects, a `ip::tcp::socket` object is configured that handles the communication with the client. See Figure 9.4.

The server can continue listening for other clients while the client is handled in a different thread. Alternatively, we can use asynchronous ASIO functions that we shall discuss in chapter 10.

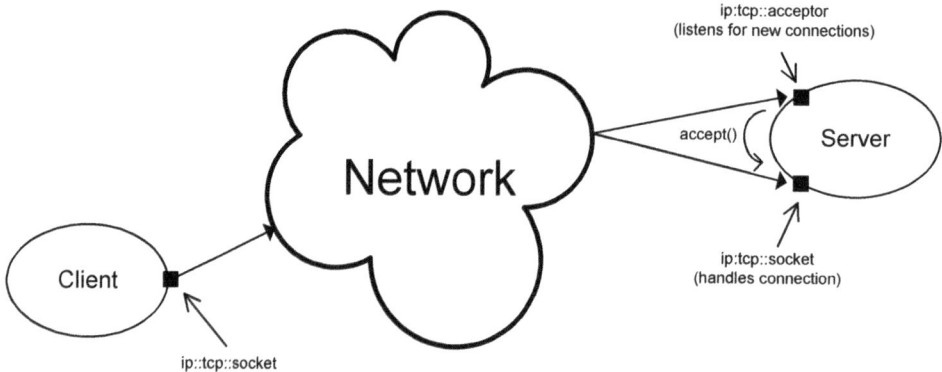

Figure 9.4 TCP Communication

The general steps for a multi-threaded TCP server are:

- Create an `ip::tcp::acceptor` object with arguments an `io_service` object and the local endpoint (port).
- Create an `ip::tcp::socket` object with the `io_service` object as argument.
- Call the `accept()` function on the `acceptor` object by passing the `socket` object. This will block until a client connects. The passed `socket` object is then configured to handle the connection.
- Pass the configured `socket` object to some code that handles the connection. The easiest approach is to create a connection handler class that we construct with the `socket` object and which runs in a separate thread.
- The server can now listen for other clients.

We now give an example of this process in the `Listen()` function of the `EchoServer` class. The `Listen()` function is actually a factory method that creates `EchoServer` objects with a connected client socket and with each object running in its own thread. Note that we use the smart pointer type `shared_ptr` to wrap a pointer to a `socket` object to ease memory management:

```cpp
// When a client connects, create new EchoServer object
// and run it using a thread.
static void Listen(unsigned int port)
{
    // IO service is always needed.
    io_service ios;

    // Create local IP4 endpoint to listen to a certain port.
    ip::tcp::endpoint endPoint(ip::tcp::v4(), port);

    // Start opening socket.
    cout<<"Listening to TCP socket on port "<<port<<"..."<<endl;
    ip::tcp::acceptor acceptor(ios, endPoint);

    // Never-ending loop that accepts new clients.
    while (true)
    {
        // Create and accept socket. The socket is assigned
        // to a shared pointer so we do not need to delete it explicitly.
        boost::shared_ptr<ip::tcp::socket> socket(
            new ip::tcp::socket(ios));
        acceptor.accept(*socket);

        // Create new EchoServer object to handle the connection and
        // run it in its own thread.
        // The server is copied to the thread, so as long the thread is
        // running, the echo server remains in memory.
        // Even when the thread object gets out of scope, the thread itself
        // won't be deleted. It is only detached from a thread object.
        boost::thread(EchoServer(socket));
    }
}
```

The TCP socket provides two member functions to read data into a mutable buffer sequence, namely `read_some()` and `receive()`. With `receive()`, we can optionally pass a `message_flags` to indicate how the receive operation should execute. Unfortunately, the possible values for the message flags are undocumented in the Boost online documentation. Furthermore, the `read_some()` and `receive()` functions seem to have the same functionality.

We use the member functions `write_some()` and `send()` to send data from a buffer sequence. With `send()` we can optionally pass a `message_flags` to indicate how the send operation should execute. Again, the possible values are undocumented in the Boost online documentation.

All the above read/write member functions return the number of bytes that are read or written. This can be different from the buffer size. There is no guarantee that the complete buffer has been read or sent in one operation. Thus we need to call these functions repeatedly until the correct number of bytes has been written. When there is no more data to read (for example, when the client has been disconnected) the read function will return with an 'eof' error.

Since there is no guarantee that the complete buffer has been sent or read, ASIO provides global `read()` and `write()` functions that repeatedly call the socket's `read_some()` or `write_some()` functions until the complete buffer has been read or written. These global functions accept the TCP socket and buffer sequence to use.

Finally, there is also a global `read_until()` function that reads data into the buffer until a certain character has been encountered or until a regular expression is true.

We now give the code of the `EchoServer` class that handles the connection with the client. This is a function object and it is constructed using the socket for the client. In the `operator ()` function (which is run in a separate thread) it reads characters from the socket using the `read_some()` member function. Then it converts the characters that have been read to upper case and finally it sends the characters back to the client using the global `send()` function. The `send()` function is used because this function guarantees that the requested number of bytes has been sent. This is repeated until an 'eof' error occurs after which time the socket is closed:

```
// TCP echo server class.
class EchoServer
{
private:
    // The client socket the server should use. No need to delete
    // the socket since it is encapsulated in a shared pointer.
    boost::shared_ptr<ip::tcp::socket> m_socket;

public:
    // Constructor with the socket to use.
    EchoServer(boost::shared_ptr<ip::tcp::socket> socket): m_socket(socket)
    {
    }

    // The function run by the thread.
    void operator () ()
    {
        // Display message.
        cout<<m_socket->remote_endpoint()<<": Connection accepted"<<endl;

        // Buffer, message size and error code.
        char buf[256];
        size_t size;
        boost::system::error_code ec;

        // Accept messages till client is disconnected (eof).
        do
        {
            // Read data from the socket.
            size=m_socket->read_some(buffer(buf, 255), ec);

            // Do only when there was no error.
            if (ec==0)
            {
                // Print received message.
                cout<<m_socket->remote_endpoint()<<": Message received: "
                    <<string(buf, size)<<endl;

                // Convert to uppercase and send reply.
                for (size_t i=0; i<size; i++) buf[i]=toupper(buf[i]);
                write(*m_socket, buffer(buf, size));
            }
        }
        while(ec!=error::eof);
```

```
            // Close connection.
            cout<<m_socket->remote_endpoint()<<": Connection closed"<<endl;
            m_socket->close();
        }
    };
```

9.5.2 Example: TCP Echo Client

We now discuss the construction of the TCP client. It uses a `ip::tcp::socket` to initiate a connection. The socket is created using the `io_service` object and a given IP version. Then the `connect()` function is called on the socket giving the endpoint to connect to. We use the same functions that the server uses to send and receive data.

We now show the client code for the `EchoServer` that we discussed in section 9.5.1. After having resolved the host endpoint using DNS we create a TCP socket and we connect to the server. Next the user is prompted to enter string data that is then sent to the server using the global `write()` function. In this way we are assured that the complete string has been sent. We then receive a reply from the server using the global `read()` function so we are sure that the complete reply has been read. This reading process is repeated until the user enters an empty string. Then the socket and thus the connection will be closed. The code is:

```
// The port number to use.
const unsigned int port=60000;

// IO service is always needed.
io_service ios;

// Ask for host.
string host;
cout<<"Enter the host to connect to (empty=localhost): ";
getline(cin, host);

// If nothing entered, assume localhost.
if (host=="") host="localhost";

// Create the query and resolver. Get only IP4 addresses.
ip::tcp::resolver::query query(ip::tcp::v4(), host, "");
ip::tcp::resolver r(ios);

// Resolve the query and put it in an resolver iterator.
ip::tcp::resolver::iterator it=r.resolve(query);

// Get the endpoint of the first host from the resolver iterator.
ip::tcp::endpoint endPoint=it->endpoint();
endPoint.port(port);

// Opening socket for IP4.
cout<<"Opening socket..."<<endl;
ip::tcp::socket socket(ios, ip::tcp::v4());
socket.connect(endPoint);

// Connected.
string str;                        // String to send.
boost::array<char, 255> data;     // Buffer for receiving answer.
do
{
    // Get the data to send.
    cout<<"Enter data to send (Enter to exit): ";
    getline(cin, str);
    size_t size=str.length();

    if (size>0)
```

```
        {
            // Send the data to the endpoint.
            cout<<"Sending '"<<str<<"' to endpoint '"<<endPoint<<"'"<<endl;
            write(socket, buffer(str, size));

            // Get reply.
            size=read(socket, buffer(data, size));
            cout<<"Reply from "<<socket.remote_endpoint()<<" : "
                <<string(data.data(), size)<<endl;
        }
    }
    while (str.length()!=0);

    // Finished, close the socket.
    socket.close();
    cout<<"Socket closed"<<endl;
```

9.5.3   Using Socket IOStreams to improve Ease of Use

The byte buffer-based TCP transport using sockets can be difficult to use. As an alternative ASIO provides an *iostream* interface as a layer on top of sockets. The *iostream* interface hides the complexities of host name resolution and buffer handling. Using the *iostream* interface we can open a stream by specifying a hostname and protocol. Then we can send and receive data using the standard iostream operators (<< and >>).

Below we show code for a TCP client that uses the tcp::iostream class to connect to an echo server. The constructor receives a host name and port number. Note that no io_service object is needed since it will be internally created. When the connection has been made it uses the << and >> operators to receive and send strings, respectively. When finished the network stream is closed.

```
    // Ask for host.
    string host;
    cout<<"Enter the host to connect to (empty=localhost): ";
    getline(cin, host);

    // If nothing entered, assume localhost.
    if (host=="") host="localhost";

    // Open a stream to the host on a certain port.
    ip::tcp::iostream stream(host, "60000");
    if (!stream)
    {
        cout<<"Could not make a connection."<<endl;
        return;
    }

    // Connected.
    string str;  // String to send.
    do
    {
        // Get the data to send.
        cout<<"Enter data to send (Enter to exit): ";
        getline(cin, str);
        size_t size=str.length();

        if (size>0)
        {
            // Send the data to the endpoint.
            cout<<"Sending '"<<str<<"' to endpoint '"
                <<stream.rdbuf()->remote_endpoint()<<"'"<<endl;
            stream<<str<<endl;
```

```
        // Get reply.
        stream>>str;

        cout<<"Reply from "
            <<stream.rdbuf()->remote_endpoint()<<" : "<<str<<endl;
    }
}
while (str.length()!=0);

// Finished, close the stream.
stream.close();
cout<<"Stream closed."<<endl;
```

The server consists of a listener that accepts connections and an object that handles the connection. The listener still uses a `tcp::acceptor` object but instead of a `tcp::socket` object the `accept()` function receives a `basic_socket_streambuf` object (subclass of `socket`) that is wrapped in a `tcp::iostream` object. The stream is passed to an `EchoServerStream` object that handles the connection. The code is:

```
// Listen for connections. When a client connects,
// create new EchoServer object and run it using a thread.
static void Listen(unsigned int port)
{
    // IO service is always needed.
    io_service ios;

    // Create local IP4 endpoint to listen to a certain port.
    ip::tcp::endpoint endPoint(ip::tcp::v4(), port);

    // Start opening socket.
    cout<<"Listening to TCP socket on port "<<port<<"..."<<endl;
    ip::tcp::acceptor acceptor(ios, endPoint);

    // Never ending loop that accepts new clients.
    while (true)
    {
        // Create and accept socket but assign it to a tcp::iostream.
        // The tcp::iostream is assigned to a shared pointer
        // so we do not need to delete it explicitly.
        boost::shared_ptr<ip::tcp::iostream>
            stream(new ip::tcp::iostream());
        acceptor.accept(*stream->rdbuf());

        // Create new EchoServer object to handle the connection and
        // run it in its own thread.
        // The server is copied to the thread, so as long the thread
        // is running, the echo server remains in memory.
        // Even when the thread object gets out of scope, the thread itself
        // won't be deleted. It is only detached from a thread object.
        boost::thread(EchoServerStream(stream));
    }
}
```

The `EchoServerStream` class receives the `tcp::iostream` object in its constructor. The function object is run in a different thread and it reads and writes messages from the network stream using the I/O << and >> operators:

```
// TCP echo server class using a stream.
class EchoServerStream
{
private:
    // The client socket the server should use.
    boost::shared_ptr<ip::tcp::iostream> m_stream;
```

```
public:
    // Constructor with the TCP IO stream to use.
    EchoServerStream(boost::shared_ptr<ip::tcp::iostream> stream)
    {
        m_stream=stream;
    }

    // The function run by the thread.
    void operator () ()
    {
        // Display message.
        cout<<m_stream->rdbuf()->remote_endpoint()
            <<": Connection accepted"<<endl;

        // Accept messages till client is disconnected (eof).
        string str;
        do
        {
            // Read data from the stream.
            str.clear();
            (*m_stream)>>str;

            // Do only when there was no error.
            if (str.length()>0)
            {
                // Print received message.
                cout<<m_stream->rdbuf()->remote_endpoint()
                    <<": Message received: "<<str<<endl;

                // Convert to uppercase and send reply.
                for (size_t i=0; i<str.length(); i++)
                {
                    str[i]=toupper(str[i]);
                }
                (*m_stream)<<str<<endl;
            }
        }
        while(str.length()>0);

        // Close connection.
        cout<<m_stream->rdbuf()->remote_endpoint()
            <<": Connection closed"<<endl;
        m_stream->close();
    }
};
```

9.6   Summary and Conclusions

In this chapter we discussed how ASIO can be used for resolving internet addresses and performing network communication using the UDP and TCP protocols. The *buffer* concept enables us to use many kinds of buffers for receiving and sending data. For example, a collection of several buffers can be used for a send or receive operation.

In this chapter we used synchronous functionality which is straightforward but which does not scale. In the next chapter we show how to make our code more scalable by using asynchronous functionality.

10 Boost ASIO: Asynchronous Operations

10.1 Introduction

In this chapter we discuss how Boost ASIO provides asynchronous network communication services. ASIO has asynchronous versions of many potentially long-lasting operations. By using these functions we do not have to wait before an operation has completed in order to do something else. The advantage of using asynchronous operations is that we can handle multiple operations simultaneously without having to create threads. Too many threads may impair performance.

The asynchronous functions are prefixed with *async_* (thus the functions have the form `async_xxx()`). They are *non-blocking* which means that they return immediately. When the asynchronous function has finished a *callback function* (functor) is called that was passed when initiating the asynchronous operation.

To run the asynchronous operations the `run()` function of the `io_service` object must be called which then calls all outstanding asynchronous operations. The `run()` function returns when all asynchronous operations are complete. It can be called from a new thread. It can also be simultaneously called by multiple threads. It is guaranteed that the asynchronous callback functions are executed in the same threads that run the `io_service` object.

Referring to Figure 10.1 the general steps when using asynchronous ASIO operation are:
- Create I/O object with an **io_service** object.
1. An asynchronous operation is started passing a callback function for example a request to send data.
2. I/O object forwards the request to `io_service` object.
3. `io_service` forwards the request to OS (Operating System). OS starts the request asynchronously.
4. Main program continues running.
5. OS places the result in a queue.

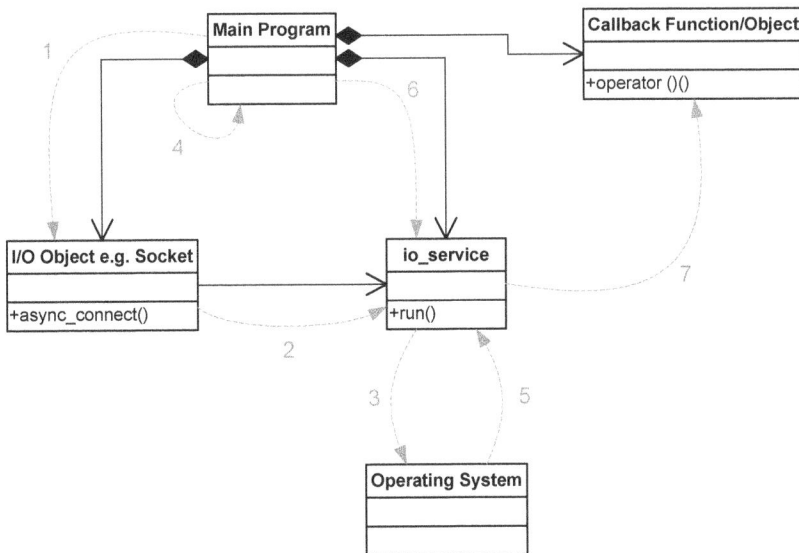

Figure 10.1 ASIO asynchronous operation

6. `io_service` picks up the result after its `run()` method is called.
   - Can be called from the main program.
   - Can be called from a separate thread(s).
7. `io_service` calls the given callback function.
   - Errors converted to `boost::system::error_code`.

10.2 Timers

The Boost ASIO library contains a *deadline timer*. We use it to wait until some time has elapsed or until a specific time has been reached. The deadline timer is used to detect *time-outs*.

We introduce asynchronous operations when discussing timers. Using asynchronous operations with timers prepares us for using asynchronous communication using UDP or TCP.

10.2.1 Synchronous Deadline Timer

Using a deadline timer in a synchronous fashion is easy. We create the deadline timer using an `io_service` object and we set the expiry time using the `expires_from_now()` member function.

When calling the `wait()` function it will block until the deadline has expired:

```
// IO service is always needed.
io_service ios;

// Create timer and set the expiry time relative from now.
deadline_timer t(ios);
t.expires_from_now(boost::posix_time::seconds(3));

// Wait for the timer synchronously.
cout<<"Waiting synchronously..."<<endl;
t.wait();
cout<<"Wait over."<<endl;
```

10.2.2 Asynchronous Deadline Timer

In some cases we may wish to use the deadline timer in an asynchronous fashion. Then we can wait for the timer to expire while simultaneously executing other tasks.

In the case of the deadline timer there is an `async_wait()` function that expects a functor (callback function or completion handler). The functor accepts an error code.
In the following example two asynchronous timers are started and the I/O service is run. When a timer expires the shared `HandleDeadline()` function is called. The second timer will expire first since it is created with a negative time offset relative to the first timer. There is no synchronisation needed since everything still runs from the main thread:

```
// Callback function when the timer expired.
void HandleDeadline(const boost::system::error_code& ec)
{
    // Check if there was an error.
    if (ec) cout<<"Error occured: "<<ec.message()<<endl;

    // Timer expired.
    cout<<"The time expired."<<endl;
}

// Using timer asynchronously.
void ASynchronousWait()
```

```
{
    // IO service is always needed.
    io_service ios;

    // Create timer and set the expiry time relative from now.
    deadline_timer t1(ios);
    t1.expires_from_now(boost::posix_time::seconds(3));

    // Create timer and set the expiry time on absolute value.
    deadline_timer t2(ios);
    t2.expires_at(t1.expires_at() - boost::posix_time::seconds(1));

    // Wait for the timers asynchronously.
    cout<<"Waiting asynchronously..."<<endl;
    t1.async_wait(&HandleDeadline);
    t2.async_wait(&HandleDeadline);

    // For asynchronous operations to run, the IO service must be run.
    // Calling run() will block until all asynchronous operations
    // are finished.
    ios.run();

    cout<<"All asynchronous operations completed."<<endl;
}
```

10.2.3 Binding Arguments

In some applications the handler function may need some extra data. In general, we can use a global variable but we can also pass the data to the handler function. The handler functions do not accept extra parameters in general but by using the *Boost Bind* library (that we discussed in Demming 2010) we can bind extra arguments to the handler function.

In the following example the handler function receives the name of the timer that expired as additional parameter. When passing the handler function to the async_wait() the library boost::bind is used to pass the timer name as first argument. The original error code is passed as second argument. In general, we would use the _1 syntax to indicate the original first argument but ASIO defines placeholder constants that make it more readable:

```
// Callback function when the timer expired.
void HandleDeadline(const string& timer,
                    const boost::system::error_code& ec)
{
    // Check if there was an error.
    if (ec) cout<<"Error occured: "<<ec.message()<<endl;

    // Timer expired.
    cout<<"The time expired for "<<timer<<endl;
}

// Binding arguments to handler function.
void BindingArguments()
{
    // IO service is always needed.
    io_service ios;

    // Create timer and set the expiry time relative from now.
    deadline_timer t1(ios);
    t1.expires_from_now(boost::posix_time::seconds(3));

    // Create timer and set the expiry time on absolute value.
    deadline_timer t2(ios);
    t2.expires_at(t1.expires_at() - boost::posix_time::seconds(1));
```

```
    // Wait for the timers asynchronously.
    // To pass an argument to the timer handler function,
    // we use boost::bind.
    // Asio already provides a placeholder for the error code so we
    // don't have to use the '_1' syntax.
    // The string object is copied to bind, so the handler receives
    // a copy and not a reference to an already deleted object.
    cout<<"Waiting asynchronously..."<<endl;
    t1.async_wait(boost::bind(&HandleDeadline, string("timer 1"),
                              boost::asio::placeholders::error));
    t2.async_wait(boost::bind(&HandleDeadline, string("timer 2"),
                              boost::asio::placeholders::error));

    // For asynchronous operations to run, the IO service must be run.
    // Calling run() will block until all asynchronous operations
    // are finished.
    ios.run();

    cout<<"All asynchronous operations completed."<<endl;
}
```

10.2.4 Binding to Member Functions

In many applications we use classes and in these cases we use a member function as handler function. This is possible by using `boost::bind`. When binding to a member function we also specify the object for the member function to bind to.

In the following example we have a `TimerClass` that has an embedded deadline timer. It uses the timer to print a counter every 500 milliseconds. The constructor of the class accepts an `io_service` object which is used to initialise the timer. Then an asynchronous wait is started in the constructor and by using `boost::bind` the `HandleDeadline()` member function for the current (this) object is used as handler function.

The `HandleDeadline()` handler function prints the counter and as long as the counter is less than 10 it will restart the deadline timer:

```
    // Class that uses a deadline timer to display a counter at regular
    // intervals.
    class TimerClass
    {
    private:
        // The deadline timer to use and the counter.
        deadline_timer m_timer;
        int m_counter;

    public:

        // Constructor with IO service.
        TimerClass(io_service& ios):
            m_timer(ios, boost::posix_time::millisec(500)), m_counter(0)
        {
            // Start the timer. Here we need to use boost::bind
            // to pass a member function as handler function.
            m_timer.async_wait(boost::bind(&TimerClass::HandleDeadline, this,
                                           boost::asio::placeholders::error));
        }

        // Callback function when the timer expired.
        void HandleDeadline(const boost::system::error_code& ec)
        {
            // Check if there was an error.
            if (ec) cout<<"Error occured: "<<ec.message()<<endl;
```

```
            // Do as long the counter is smaller than 10.
            if (m_counter<10)
            {
                // Print counter.
                cout<<"Count: "<<m_counter++<<endl;

                // Restart the timer. Here we need to use boost::bind to pass
                // a member function as handler function.
                m_timer.expires_from_now(boost::posix_time::millisec(500));
                m_timer.async_wait(boost::bind(&TimerClass::HandleDeadline,
                            this, boost::asio::placeholders::error));
            }
        }
};
```

Finally, we show the code that uses the TimerClass. We create an io_service object that is used to create the TimerClass object. Then the run() function is called on the io_service object to make the timer handler functions run:

```
// IO service is always needed.
io_service ios;

// Create an object of the timer class.
TimerClass o(ios);

// Run the timer asynchronously.
// Calling run() will block until all asynchronous operations
// are finished.
ios.run();
```

10.2.5 Thread Pooling and Synchronising Threads

Asynchronous functions incur less overhead than multiple threads, especially if there are more threads than cores in the computer. But solely using asynchronous operations is not scalable on multi-core systems. Therefore we can combine asynchronous operations with multiple threads in which a number of threads are pooled. In this way we prevent the overhead of creating too many threads while still making effective use of additional cores. To this end, we call the io_service::run() function from multiple threads. The handler functions are now called from multiple threads. Additional care is needed when the handlers access shared resources. In order to avoid race conditions we can apply the boost::thread synchronisation mechanisms by means of a *mutex* but it is easier to use an asio::strand. When a handler function is wrapped in an asio::strand object all handler functions that are called through the same asio::strand object are automatically synchronised. Wrapping is done by calling the wrap() function on the asio::strand object and passing the result as a handler function.

The advantage of *strands* is that they are easy to use. But the disadvantage is that the complete function is synchronised and not only that part of the function that accesses shared resources.

In the following example we create a class that uses two deadline timers that in their turn call the same handler. The code of the handler is synchronised by wrapping it in a strand instance when the asynchronous wait is initiated. The asio::strand object is a data member that is initialised in the constructor by passing the io_service object.

The handler function receives both the timer and the timer name. It restarts the input timer
for as long as the counter is less than 50:

```
// Class that uses a deadline timer and runs the IO service
// in a separate thread.
class TimerClassMt
{
private:
    // The strand used for synchronising calling the handlers.
    strand m_strand;

    // The deadline timers to use and the shared counter.
    deadline_timer m_timer1;
    deadline_timer m_timer2;
    int m_counter;

public:
    // Constructor with IO service.
    TimerClassMt(io_service& ios): m_strand(ios),
        m_timer1(ios, boost::posix_time::millisec(500)),
        m_timer2(ios, boost::posix_time::millisec(400)), m_counter(0)
    {
        // Start the timers. The handlers will be called through
        // a strand so they will be synchronised.

        m_timer1.async_wait(m_strand.wrap(
            boost::bind(&TimerClassMt::HandleDeadline, this, &m_timer1,
                "Timer 1", boost::asio::placeholders::error)));
        m_timer2.async_wait(m_strand.wrap(
            boost::bind(&TimerClassMt::HandleDeadline, this, &m_timer2,
                "Timer 2", boost::asio::placeholders::error)));
    }

    // Callback function when the timer expired.
    void HandleDeadline(deadline_timer* timer, const string& name,
                        const boost::system::error_code& ec)
    {
        // Check if there was an error.
        if (ec) cout<<"Error occured: "<<ec.message()<<endl;

        // Do as long the counter is smaller than 50.
        if (m_counter<50)
        {
            // Print thread ID, timer name and counter.
            cout<<"Thread: "<<boost::this_thread::get_id()<<" - ";
            cout<<name<<" - Count: "<<m_counter++<<endl;

            // Restart the timer. The handler is called through
            // a strand so it is synchronised.
            timer->expires_from_now(boost::posix_time::millisec(500));
            timer->async_wait(m_strand.wrap(
                boost::bind(&TimerClassMt::HandleDeadline, this, timer,
                    name, boost::asio::placeholders::error)));
        }
    }
};
```

Finally, the code that uses the `TimerClassMt` can now safely run the I/O service in
multiple threads. In this case it will be run by the main thread and one additional thread:

```
// IO service is always needed.
io_service ios;

// Create an object of the timer class.
```

```
TimerClassMt o(ios);

// Start the IO service in two thread. A new thread and the main thread.
boost::thread t(boost::bind(&io_service::run, &ios)); // Run IO service
                                                      // in new thread.
ios.run();                  // And in the main thread.

// Wait till the thread is also finished.
t.join();
```

10.3 Asynchronous UDP Server

The synchronous UDP server that we created in chapter 9 waited until the reply was completely sent before receiving the next message. By using the asynchronous `async_receive_from()` and `async_send_to()` functions we can now receive the next message while the reply is still being sent. This improves the responsiveness of our server when there are many clients.

We model the asynchronous UDP echo server as a class called `ASyncServer`. The UDP socket is now a data member. Since only one read or write operation can occur at the same time and not two simultaneous read operations or two simultaneous write operations we can make the client endpoint and receive buffer object as data members:

```
// Typedef for the buffer to use.
typedef boost::array<char, 256> TBuffer;

// Asynchronous UDP echo server.
class ASyncServer                 // Server class.
{
private:
    ip::udp::socket m_socket;     // The socket to use.
    ip::udp::endpoint m_client;   // The client endpoint.
    TBuffer m_buffer;             // The receive buffer.

    ...
};
```

The constructor of `ASyncServer` receives the `io_service` object to use and the port to listen on. The socket data member is initialised with the I/O service and a new local endpoint for IP4. Then the server class calls the `StartReceive()` member function that initiates an asynchronous receive:

```
// Constructor. Creates socket listening to IP4 addresses
// on a certain port.
ASyncServer(io_service& ios, unsigned int port):
    m_socket(ios, ip::udp::endpoint(ip::udp::v4(), port))
{
    cout<<"Socket opened on: "<<m_socket.local_endpoint()<<endl;

    // Start the receive.
    StartReceive();
}
```

The receive buffer data member is passed as a reference to the client endpoint data member. The passed handler function has the error code and the number of bytes that were received as arguments. This function uses `boost::bind` to bind a member function as handler. The function returns while the receive is done asynchronously:

```
// Start receiving data.
void StartReceive()
```

```
{
    cout<<"Start receiving..."<<endl;

    // Start receiving data.
    // We use bind to pass a member function as callback
    // instead of a global function or function object.
    m_socket.async_receive_from(buffer(m_buffer), m_client,
        boost::bind(&ASyncServer::HandleReceived, this,
                    boost::asio::placeholders::error,
                    boost::asio::placeholders::bytes_transferred) );

    cout<<"Waiting for data..."<<endl;
}
```

The HandleReceived() function is called by the I/O service when the asynchronous receive operation completes. The received data is printed after checking for an error.
To send a reply, a new buffer is needed since the receive buffer will be overwritten by another receive while the reply is still being sent. The reply buffer is filled with the uppercase version of the received data.

The buffer for the reply is wrapped in a shared pointer to ease memory management. Furthermore, an asynchronous send operation is started. We pass the shared pointer to the handler function because the send buffer must live as long as the send operation. In this way we are sure that the buffer will not be deleted when the HandleReceived() function returns.

When the asynchronous send operation has been started the StartReceive() member function is called again which then initiates an asynchronous receive. Thus sending the reply occurs at the same time as receiving new data:

```
// Called when the data is received.
void HandleReceived(const boost::system::error_code& ec, size_t size)
{
    // Exit if error.
    if (ec)
    {
        cout<<"Error while receiving data."<<endl;
        return;
    }

    cout<<"Data received from "<<m_client<<": "
        <<string(m_buffer.data(), size)<<endl;
    cout<<"Start sending reply..."<<endl;

    // For sending the reply, we can't use the same buffer because
    // that can be overwritten by another receive.
    // The lifetime of the send buffer must be bigger than this function,
    // so we wrap it in a shared pointer that must be passed to the
    // handle function.
    boost::shared_ptr<TBuffer> sendBuffer(new TBuffer());

    // Copy the message upper case to the send buffer.
    for (size_t i=0; i<size; i++) (*sendBuffer)[i]=toupper(m_buffer[i]);

    // Start sending reply. We use bind to pass a member function
    // as callback instead of a global function or function object.
    // We also use bind to pass the data buffer to send. This way we know
    // for sure the lifetime of the buffer is longer
    // than the send operation. Without it the local buffer would be
    // removed before the sending was complete.
    m_socket.async_send_to(buffer(*sendBuffer, size), m_client,
```

```
        boost::bind(&ASyncServer::HandleSent, this, sendBuffer,
                    boost::asio::placeholders::error,
                    boost::asio::placeholders::bytes_transferred) );

    cout<<"Waiting till reply sent..."<<endl;

    // Start receiving the next data concurrently while sending.
    StartReceive();
}
```

The `HandleSent()` member function is called by the I/O service when the asynchronous send operation completes. It will check for errors and then exit. Since the send buffer is passed as a shared pointer it will be automatically deleted when the `HandleSent()` function returns:

```
// Called when the data is sent.
void HandleSent(boost::shared_ptr<TBuffer> message,
                const boost::system::error_code& ec, size_t size)
{
    // Exit if error.
    if (ec)
    {
        cout<<"Error while sending data."<<endl;
        return;
    }

    cout<<"Reply sent: "<<string(message->data(), size)<<endl;
}
```

Finally, the `ASyncServer` class must be instantiated and the I/O service must be run:

```
// IO service is always needed.
io_service ios;

// Create asynchronous server.
ASyncServer server(ios, port);

// Run the events. Without this, the transfers are started,
// but the handlers are never called.
ios.run();
```

10.4 Asynchronous TCP Server

We have already seen that a TCP server uses a separate thread for each client. Since threads cause extra overhead the server performance can be affected if there are too many clients. Handling multiple clients in one thread is more efficient. This is possible by using *asynchronous ASIO calls*.

The asynchronous TCP server consists of two classes. First, `ASyncEchoServer` listens for clients and for each client that connects it creates an `ASyncConnection` object that handles further client communication. We also need some buffer and shared pointer typedefs to make the code more readable:

```
// Forward declaration.
class ASyncConnection;

// Typedef for the buffer type (shared_ptr).
typedef boost::array<char, 256> Buffer;
typedef boost::shared_ptr<Buffer> BufferPtr;

// Typedef for the ASyncConnection shared_ptr.
typedef boost::shared_ptr<ASyncConnection> ASyncConnectionPtr;
```

10.4.1   The ASyncEchoServer Class

We now continue with the `ASyncEchoServer` class. It has an `acceptor` object as data member which is initialised using the I/O service object and a local endpoint in the constructor. Then the `StartAccept()` member function is called, initiating an asynchronous accept of a client:

```
// Asynchronous echo server.
class ASyncEchoServer
{
private:
    // Acceptor object to use for listening to clients.
    ip::tcp::acceptor m_acceptor;

public:
    // Constructor to start the ASyncEchoServer.
    ASyncEchoServer(io_service& ios, unsigned int port):
        m_acceptor(ios, ip::tcp::endpoint(ip::tcp::v4(), port))
    {
        cout<<"Listening to TCP socket on port "<<port<<"..."<<endl;

        // Start accepting clients.
        StartAccept();
    }

    ...
};
```

The `StartAccept()` member function first creates an `ASyncConnection` object for the future client. The created object is wrapped in a shared pointer so that memory management is automatic. Note that because the `ASyncConnection` object destroys itself we cannot maintain a list of `ASyncConnection` objects. Then an asynchronous *accept* operation is initiated by calling the `async_accept()` function. The socket of the `ASyncConnection` object is passed that is initialised by the accept operation. The `ASyncConnection` object is bound to the handler function:

```
// Start accepting clients.
void StartAccept()
{
    // Create the connection handler object.
    // Put in shared pointer so memory management is automatic.
    ASyncConnectionPtr connection(
        new ASyncConnection(m_acceptor.get_io_service()));

    // Start accepting a client.
    m_acceptor.async_accept(connection->Socket(),
        boost::bind(&ASyncEchoServer::HandleAccept, this, connection,
                    boost::asio::placeholders::error));
}
```

The `HandleAccept()` member function is called by the I/O service when a new client connects. This function checks for errors and it starts the connection so that data can be asynchronously received and sent. Then the `StartAccept()` is again called to allow another client to connect:

```
// Client connected, handle the connection.
void HandleAccept(ASyncConnectionPtr connection,
                  const boost::system::error_code& ec)
{
    // Start the connection handler and continue accepting new connections.
    if (!ec)
    {
```

```
            connection->Start();
            StartAccept();
    }
    else
    {
        cout<<"Error: "<<ec.message()<<endl;
    }
}
```

The `ASyncEchoServer` must also be started:

```
// IO service is always needed.
io_service ios;

// Create asynchronous server.
ASyncEchoServer server(ios, port);

// Run the events. Without this, the transfers are started,
// but the handlers are never called.
ios.run();
```

At this stage the `ASyncEchoServer` class starts listening for clients by creating an `ASyncConnection` object for each connected client.

10.4.2 The ASyncConnection Class

The `ASyncConnection` class handles communication with the client. It is derived from the `boost::enable_shared_from_this` class because we need to wrap the `this` pointer in a shared pointer object from within a member function. The constructor initialises the socket with the I/O service object. There is also a getter function for the socket since the acceptor needs it to make a connection to a client:

```
// Class that handles the client.
// Derived from "enable_shared_from_this" so the 'this' object
// can be passed as shared_ptr to the callback function.
class ASyncConnection:
    public boost::enable_shared_from_this<ASyncConnection>
{
private:
    // The socket class for communication.
    ip::tcp::socket m_socket;

    // Constructor with the IO service to use.
    ASyncConnection(io_service& ios): m_socket(ios)
    {
    }

public:
    // Retrieve the socket used by this connection.
    // Need to be passed to acceptor.accept() function.
    ip::tcp::socket& Socket()
    {
        return m_socket;
    }

    ...
};
```

When the connection has been created the `ASyncServer` object calls the `Start()` member function which then initiates the reception of data. The `StartReceiving()` member function creates a new buffer in a shared pointer and starts an asynchronous read. The buffer is bound to the handler function in addition to the error code and bytes transferred arguments.

We note that instead of binding the `HandleReceived()` member function to the `this` object we can use the `shared_from_this()` global function to create a shared pointer containing the `this` object. The `ASyncServer::HandleAccept()` function holds a shared pointer to the `ASyncConnection` object when calling this function. When the `HandleAccept()` completes the shared pointer goes out of scope and then deletes the `ASyncConnection` object. To avoid deletion of the `ASyncConnection` object the `StartReceiving()` function passes a shared pointer containing the `ASyncConnection` object to the `HandleReceived()` member function. Just using the shared pointer constructor does not work correctly for `this` pointers. This is the reason that we need the `shared_from_this()` function that is part of the Boost *Smart Ptr* library:

```
// Start handling the connection.
void Start()
{
    cout<<m_socket.remote_endpoint()<<": Connection accepted"<<endl;
    StartReceiving();
}

// Start receiving data.
void StartReceiving()
{
    // Create receive buffer.
    BufferPtr receiveBuffer(new Buffer);

    // Start async read, must pass 'this' as shared_ptr, else the
    // 'this' object will be destroyed after leaving this function.
    m_socket.async_read_some(buffer(*receiveBuffer),
        boost::bind(&ASyncConnection::HandleReceived, shared_from_this(),
        receiveBuffer, boost::asio::placeholders::error,
        boost::asio::placeholders::bytes_transferred));
}
```

The I/O service calls the `HandleReceived()` member function when the asynchronous read has completed. If there are no errors it will then create a new buffer for the reply with the uppercase version of the data received and it then starts an asynchronous send operation. It uses the global `async_write()` function for sending and this guarantees that the complete buffer will be sent. The send buffer must be passed as a shared pointer to ensure that it remains in memory until the send operation completes. We note that `shared_from_this()` function is used again to make sure that the connection object remains in memory after returning from this function.

The socket is closed because the client disconnects if there was an *eof* error. The receive buffer is automatically deleted when the `HandleReceived()` function returns because it is passed as a shared pointer:

```
// Handle received data.
void HandleReceived(BufferPtr receiveBuffer,
                const boost::system::error_code& ec, size_t size)
{
    if (!ec)
    {
        // Print received message.
        cout<<m_socket.remote_endpoint()<<": Message received: "
            <<string(receiveBuffer->data(), size)<<endl;

        // Convert to uppercase. We can't use the same buffer because
```

```
                 // that could be overwritten by another receive.
                 BufferPtr sendBuffer(new Buffer);
                 for (size_t i=0; i!=size; i++)
                 {
                     (*sendBuffer)[i]=toupper((*receiveBuffer)[i]);
                 }

                 // Start sending reply, must pass 'this' as shared_ptr, else the
                 // 'this' object will be destroyed after leaving this function.
                 // We pass the buffer as shared_ptr to the handler so the buffer is
                 // still in memory after sending is complete. Without it, the
                 // buffer could be deleted before the send operation is complete.
                 async_write(m_socket, buffer(*sendBuffer, size),
                     boost::bind(&ASyncConnection::HandleSent, shared_from_this(),
                         sendBuffer, boost::asio::placeholders::error,
                         boost::asio::placeholders::bytes_transferred));
             }
             else if (ec==error::eof)
             {
                 // Client disconnected. Close the socket.
                 cout<<m_socket.remote_endpoint()
                     <<": Connection closed (handle received)"<<endl;
                 m_socket.close();
             }
             else
             {
                 cout<<"Error: "<<ec.message()<<endl;
             }
         }
```

The I/O service calls the `HandleReceived()` member function when the asynchronous read has completed. If there is no error it calls `StartReceiving()` again which then initiates the next asynchronous read operation. The send buffer is automatically deleted when the handler returns:

```
    // Handle for when the data is sent.
    void HandleSent(BufferPtr sendBuffer, const boost::system::error_code& ec,
                    size_t size)
    {
        if (!ec)
        {
            // Start receiving again.
            StartReceiving();
        }
        else if (ec==error::eof)
        {
            cout<<m_socket.remote_endpoint()
                <<": Connection closed (handle sent)"<<endl;
            m_socket.close();
        }
        else
        {
            cout<<"Error: "<<ec.message()<<endl;
        }
    }
```

10.5 Thread-Pooled Asynchronous TCP Server

Using asynchronous I/O operations is more efficient than creating a new thread for each newly created client. But asynchronous operations alone will not use any additional cores in a computer and hence this approach is less scalable. However, the I/O service can be run by multiple threads. We can combine the advantages of asynchronous I/O operations and multiple threads. In the following example we start the asynchronous TCP echo server and run the I/O service using the same number of threads as the number of cores in the system. Thus, there is a pool of threads that runs the scheduled handler functions:

```
// IO service is always needed.
io_service ios;

// Create asynchronous server.
ASyncEchoServerMt server(ios, port);

// How many cores do we have?
unsigned int noThreads=boost::thread::hardware_concurrency();

// Create a thread group for the threads and start threads all
// running the IO service.
boost::thread_group threads;
for (int i=0; i!=noThreads; i++)
{
    threads.create_thread(boost::bind(&io_service::run, &ios));
}

// Wait till all threads are finished.
threads.join_all();
```

The asynchronous calls will now be automatically scheduled among the created threads. We note that different threads can execute the asynchronous handlers and this implies that access to shared resources (for example, sockets) must be synchronised. This is possible by calling functions using a *strand*. Using a strand is more straightforward than using mutexes.

Both the ASyncServerMt and ASyncConnectionMt classes have an asio::strand data member. In the ASyncServerMt class the *strand* is used to synchronise access to the acceptor data member while in the ASyncConnectionMt class it is used to synchronise access to the socket data member. Note that in this example access to cout will not be synchronised because cout is used from multiple objects and thus not being synchronised by the strand.

We show some partial code for the ASyncConnectionMt class. The techniques are the same for the ASyncServerClassMt class and for other functions. The full code is available in the book's source code distribution. First, we show the ASyncConnectionMt class with the strand data member that is initialised with an io_service object in the constructor:

```
// Class that handles the client.
class ASyncConnectionMt:
    public boost::enable_shared_from_this<ASyncConnectionMt>
{
private:
    // The socket class for communication.
    ip::tcp::socket m_socket;

    // Strand object to synchronise calling handlers. Multiple treads might
    // access the socked at the same time since send and receive are
    // started asynchronously at the same time.
    strand m_strand;

public:
    // Constructor with the IO service to use.
    ASyncConnectionMt(io_service& ios): m_socket(ios), m_strand(ios)
    {
    }

    ...
```

```
};
```

Next we show the relevant section of the `HandleReceived()` member function. In the `async_write()` function call we see that the handler function is wrapped in a strand by a call to the strand's `wrap()` function. This is done for all asynchronous calls in the `ASyncServerMt` and `ASyncConnectionMt` classes. In this way it is guaranteed that only one handler function of the `ASyncConnectionMt` object is run at the same time.

We note that a call is made to `StartReceiving()` after initiating the asynchronous write. Thus, the next message can be read while the reply is still being sent:

```
// Handle received data.
void HandleReceived(BufferPtr receiveBuffer,
                    const boost::system::error_code& ec, size_t size)
{
    ...

    // Convert to uppercase. We can't use the same buffer because that
    // could be overwritten by another receive.
    BufferPtr sendBuffer(new Buffer);
    for (size_t i=0; i!=size; i++)
    {
        (*sendBuffer)[i]=toupper((*receiveBuffer)[i]);
    }

    // Start sending reply, must pass 'this' as shared_ptr, else the
    // 'this' object will be destroyed after leaving this function.
    // We pass the buffer as shared_ptr to the handler so the buffer is
    // still in memory after sending is complete. Without it, the buffer
    // could be deleted before the send operation is complete.
    // The HandleSent is now synchronised via the strand.
    async_write(m_socket, buffer(*sendBuffer, size),
        m_strand.wrap(boost::bind(&ASyncConnectionMt::HandleSent,
                    shared_from_this(), sendBuffer,
                    boost::asio::placeholders::error,
                    boost::asio::placeholders::bytes_transferred)));

    // Start receiving next bit.
    StartReceiving();

    ...
}
```

10.6 CRC Checksums and Time-outs

The TCP protocol has some built-in error detection code and built-in time-out functionality. But in some situations this might not be sufficient, for example when the remote server hangs. It can take a while before this error is detected.

In this section we discuss a TCP echo client/server that sends messages with *checksums* to detect errors. It uses timers and heartbeat messages to detect time-outs.

10.6.1 Message and CRC

Even though the TCP protocol uses a simple form of error detection it may need to be augmented with additional error detection features. This can be done by sending a checksum with the data. In this section we use the Boost CRC library to calculate a simple CRC-32 checksum.

For communication we define a `Message` class. A message consists of 4-bytes specifying the body length, a 4-byte CRC checksum and the message body which has the size specified in the first 4 bytes. Since we wish to send the message in one operation we define one buffer for all three parts of the message with additional pointers to each of the three parts. When the size is 0 we consider it to be a *heartbeat message* without any checksum. The SetPointers() function sets the pointers of each of the three parts when memory is created:

```
class Message
{
public:
    // The header and checksum lengths to use.
    static const long HeaderLength=4;
    static const long ChecksumLength=4;

private:
    char* m_data;        // Data for header, body and checksum.
    long* m_header;      // Pointer to the header data.
    long* m_checksum;    // Pointer to the checksum data.
    char* m_body;        // Pointer to the body data.

    // Helper function to set the pointers.
    void SetPointers()
    {
        m_header=(long*)m_data;
        m_checksum=(long*)(m_data+HeaderLength);
        m_body=m_data+HeaderLength+ChecksumLength;
    }

    ...
};
```

The default constructor is used to create an empty message object. This message object is used for receiving a new message or creating a heartbeat message (message with only the length part initialised to zero):

```
// Create empty "heartbeat" message or receive buffer.
Message()
{
    // Create memory block for header.
    m_data=new char[HeaderLength];
    SetPointers();

    // Set header to 0 (heartbeat meassage).
    *m_header=0l;
}
```

There is also a constructor that accepts a message string. It calculates a CRC-32 checksum using the boost::crc_32_type object which is a specialisation of the generic crc_optimal class. It calculates the checksum over the body part of the message that is then placed in the checksum part of the message. This constructor is:

```
// Create message and calculate checksum.
Message(const std::string& msg)
{
    // Create memory block.
    m_data=new char[msg.size()+HeaderLength+ChecksumLength];
    SetPointers();

    // Set header with the body size.
    *m_header=msg.size();

    // Copy the string to the message buffer.
    std::copy(msg.begin(), msg.end(), m_body);
```

```
    // Calculate and set CRC.
    boost::crc_32_type crc;
    crc.process_bytes(m_body, msg.size());
    *m_checksum=crc.checksum();
}
```

The destructor must delete the data buffer. Furthermore, there are functions to return the size of the body and the *receive length* (checksum and body length) that is used by clients to transfer the rest of the message after having received the header, and finally the *send length* (header size + checksum size and body length) that is used by clients to send the complete message:

```
// Destructor.
virtual ~Message()
{
    delete[] m_data;
}

// Get the body length.
long BodyLength() const
{
    return *m_header;
}

// Length of the body + checksum. In case of a heartbeat message,
// there is no checksum and body and thus returns 0. Clients use this
// length for receiving the message after receiving the header.
long ReceiveLength() const
{
    long bodyLength=BodyLength();
    return (bodyLength==0)?0:ChecksumLength+bodyLength;
}

// Length of the header + body + checksum. In case of a heartbeat message,
// there is no checksum and body and thus only returns the header length.
// Use this length for sending the complete message. Whole message must be
// send as one else it might be possible two message are interleaved.
long SendLength() const
{
    long bodyLength=BodyLength();
    return (bodyLength==0)?HeaderLength
                          :HeaderLength+ChecksumLength+bodyLength;
}
```

The data buffer needs to be resized to make space for receiving the checksum and body when a client receives the header with the message size. The Resize() functions takes care of this issue:

```
// Call this function to resize the buffer after receiving the header and
// before receiving the body.
void Resize()
{
    // Create new buffer.
    char* newData=new char[HeaderLength+ChecksumLength+BodyLength()];

    // Copy the header to the new buffer.
    *((long*)newData)=*m_header;

    // Delete old buffer.
    delete[] m_data;

    // Set buffer pointers.
    m_data=newData;
```

```
        SetPointers();
    }
```

The clients need access to the internal buffer in order to execute send and receive operations. The `HeaderData()` function returns the pointer to the beginning of the buffer used for receiving the header or for sending the complete message.

The `MessageData()` returns a pointer to the checksum part used for receiving the checksum and body after the header has been received. The `MessageData()` functions returns the body as a string:

```
// Return pointer to the start of the header, body + checksum data buffer.
// Client needs this to send the data or to receive header.
char* HeaderData() const
{
    return m_data;
}

// Return pointer to the start of the checksum + body data buffer.
// Client needs this to receive checksum + body.
char* MessageData() const
{
    return (char*)m_checksum;
}

// Return the message string.
std::string MessageString() const
{
    return std::string(m_body, BodyLength());
}
```

Finally, there is a `Checksum()` function to check if the received checksum matches the calculated checksum after having received the full message.

```
// Determine if the checksum is correct.
bool Checksum() const
{
    // Calculate CRC and compare with stored CRC.
    boost::crc_32_type crc;
    crc.process_bytes(m_body, BodyLength());
    long checksum1=crc.checksum();
    long checksum2=(long)(*m_checksum);
    return (checksum1==checksum2);
}
```

10.6.2 Heartbeats and Time-outs

The TCP protocol has a provision for *keep-alive* functionality. A *keep-alive* object is a short message that is sent once in a while to see if the other end is still responding. In ASIO this can be turned on by passing a `asio::tcp::socket::keep_alive` object to the `ip::tcp::socket::set_option()` function. Unfortunately, the default time-out of the system is quite long and there is no way to adjust the time-out using ASIO. Then it is better to have a keep-alive mechanism at the application layer.

The idea of detecting time-outs is based on the process that one end sends *heartbeat messages* at regular intervals in addition to the regular messages. The receiving end then starts a deadline timer. Each time a message is received the deadline timer is reset. As long as the heartbeat messages arrive on a regular basis the timer will never expire and thus normally the timer expire handler will never be called. But when the timer expiry handler is called this means that the heartbeat message did not arrive (in time) and then we concluded that something is wrong.

10.6.3 Sending messages

There are multiple *agents* in the system in the case of the echo server or echo client. The first agent is the deadline timer that detects time-outs if the other end does not respond in a timely manner. Second, there is an agent that sends heartbeat messages to the other end. Third, there is an agent that sends regular messages and finally there is an agent that receives messages. The time-out timer is reset every time a message is received.

There are two agents that send messages, namely the agent that sends heartbeat messages and the agent sending regular messages. Both agents can send at the same time. Since it is not guaranteed that a message is sent in one operation (remember the `write()` global function that sends data as multiple calls to `write_some()`) it might be possible that two sent messages will interleave and the data will arrive in the wrong order at the other end. Thus, having two agents sending messages at the same time may lead to problems. The solution is to use a *message queue*. The two agents generating heartbeat messages and the regular/response messages will put the messages in the queue in a thread-safe manner instead of sending them directly. In this way, the messages are not interleaved since there is only one agent that sends messages.

The process flow of the echo client is depicted in Figure 10.2. We see that after the *Start*, the time-out agent is started and a connect attempt is executed. When the connect succeeds this flow forks again into an agent that receives messages and into an agent that sends a heartbeat message and goes to sleep again. Furthermore, we see that the main program sends messages. Both the messages from the heartbeat agent and from the main program are queued and then sent by the *send message agent*. When the queue is empty the *send message agent* finishes but it can be restarted when a new message is queued. The flow for the echo server is along the same lines as in Figure 10.2.

10.6.4 Echo Client Implementation

We now discuss the implementation of the echo client. The implementation of the echo server is along the same lines and is available in the source code distribution of this book.

10.6.4.1 Echo Client Data Members

We first discuss the data members of the client class. In addition to the required `io_service` and `socket` members we store the remote endpoint that is later used for displaying information about the remote endpoint to which a connection was made.

Since there are multiple agents working independently we need a mechanism to indicate that they must stop. Therefore we need the `m_stop` member. Next, we need two deadline timers, one for detecting time-outs and one for the delay between sending consecutive heartbeat messages. Furthermore, we need a member for the message queue. The queue stores shared pointers so that memory management of the messages is automatically handled.

We also have two members that determine the time-out time and the heartbeat delay time. Finally, there is a constructor to initialise all the data members:

```
class Client
{
private:
    // Typedef for a shared pointer to a message.
    typedef boost::shared_ptr<Message> MessagePtr;

    // Typedef for a queue of messages.
    typedef std::queue<MessagePtr> MessageQueue;
```

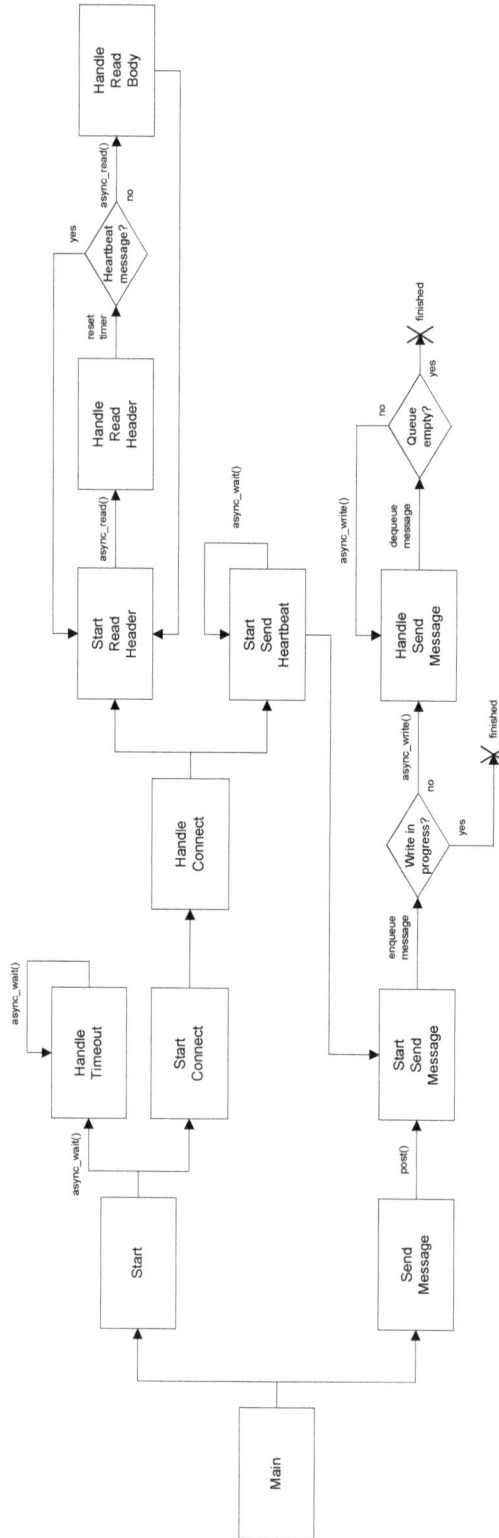

Figure 10.2 Flow diagram of the echo client

```
    // Data members.
    io_service& m_ios;                  // The IO service to use for ASIO.
    ip::tcp::endpoint m_endPoint;       // The endpoint to where we connected.
    ip::tcp::socket m_socket;           // The socket for communication
                                        // with the server.
    bool m_stop;                        // Boolean to indicate client must
                                        // stop.
    deadline_timer m_heartbeatTimer;    // Timer for scheduling
                                        // heartbeat messages.
    deadline_timer m_timeoutTimer;      // Timer for detecting time-outs
                                        // while connecting and reading
                                        // data.
    MessageQueue m_messageQueue;        // The queue for sending messages.
    int m_heartbeatDelay;               // The delay between sending
                                        // heartbeats in seconds.
    int m_timeoutTime;                  // The time-out time in seconds.

public:

    // Construct client object.
    Client(io_service& ios, int heartbeatDelay, int timeoutTime):
        m_ios(ios), m_socket(ios), m_stop(false), m_heartbeatTimer(ios),
        m_timeoutTimer(ios), m_messageQueue(),
        m_heartbeatDelay(heartbeatDelay), m_timeoutTime(timeoutTime)
    {
        // The heartbeat delay must be smaller than the time-out time.
        if (m_heartbeatDelay>=m_timeoutTime)
        {
            m_timeoutTime=m_heartbeatDelay;
        }
    }
};
```

10.6.4.2   Time-out Agent

The `Start()` member function starts the client. It receives the iterator from the DNS resolver that is passed to the function that makes the connection. It also starts an asynchronous wait on the time-out timer that will be set before other asynchronous operations are started. The handler will never be called if the time-out is reset before the timer runs out. But when the time-out is not set again in time the timer will run out and the `HandleTimeout()` function will be called:

```
// Start the client.
void Start(ip::tcp::resolver::iterator it)
{
    // Start making a connection.
    StartConnect(it);

    // Start time-out timer.
    // No time-out here since it was set in the StartConnect() function.
    // The HandleTimeout() function will only be called when there
    // was an time-out.
    // In normal situations, the time-out time will be reset after
    // every socket operation and thus never expire.
    m_timeoutTimer.async_wait(boost::bind(&Client::HandleTimeout, this));
}
```

The `HandleTimeout()` function is called by the I/O service when the time-out timer runs out. First, it will exit this function if the client needs to stop. Then it checks if indeed a time-out occured. It is possible that the timer has been reset before the handler was called. In that case the timer will be started again with a call to `async_wait()`. The alternative is that there was indeed a time-out; then a message will be printed and the client will be signalled to stop by calling to DoStop():

```
// When this function is called there was an time-out.
// In normal situations, the time-out timer will reset after each
// operation thus never expire.
void HandleTimeout()
{
    // Exit if the client must stop.
    if (m_stop) return;

    // First check if the deadline was really passed.
    // It could be possible that the timer was reset by a new
    // asynchronous operation in that time.
    if (m_timeoutTimer.expires_at()<=deadline_timer::traits_type::now())
    {
        std::cout<<"Time-out detected. Stopping client..."<<std::endl;

        // Set timer to infinite so it won't be called again.
        m_timeoutTimer.expires_at(boost::posix_time::pos_infin);

        // Make the client stop.
        DoStop();
    }
    else
    {
        // Enable the time-out timer again.
        m_timeoutTimer.async_wait(
            boost::bind(&Client::HandleTimeout, this));
    }
}
```

10.6.4.3   Connecting to the Server

The StartConnect() member function starts making a connection asynchronously. If the resolver iterator contains an endpoint it will try to connect to it asynchronously. But before that happens it will reset the time-out time value. If there was no endpoint, it will signal the client to stop:

```
// Start making a connection asynchronously.
void StartConnect(ip::tcp::resolver::iterator it)
{
    // Is there an end-point?
    if (it!=ip::tcp::resolver::iterator())
    {
        m_endPoint=it->endpoint();
        std::cout<<"Connecting to "<<m_endPoint<<"..."<<std::endl;

        // Reset the time-out time for connecting.
        // Heartbeat message should arrive earlier than the time-out.
        m_timeoutTimer.expires_from_now(
            boost::posix_time::seconds(m_timeoutTime));

        // Start asynchronous connect operation.
        m_socket.async_connect(*it, boost::bind(
                                  &Client::HandleConnect, this, it,
                                  boost::asio::placeholders::error));
    }
    else
    {
        // No more end-points to try. Stop the client.
        DoStop();
    }
}
```

The `HandleConnect()` member function is called by the I/O service when the connect operation finishes. It exits the function when the client was signalled to stop.

When the connecting was successful we initiates reading a message header operation and we start sending heartbeat messages:

```
// Connected, handle the connection.
void HandleConnect(ip::tcp::resolver::iterator it,
                   const boost::system::error_code& ec)
{
    // Exit if the client must stop.
    if (m_stop) return;

    // The async connect opens the socket.
    // If the socket is now closed, there was an time-out.
    if (!m_socket.is_open())
    {
        std::cout<<"Connect timed out\n"<<std::endl;

        // Try next end-point.
        StartConnect(++it);
        return;
    }

    // Check the error code.
    if (ec)
    {
        // Error making connection.
        std::cout<<"Connect error: "<<ec.message()<<std::endl;

        // Close the socket before attempting the next endpoint.
        m_socket.close();

        // Try next end-point.
        StartConnect(++it);
        return;
    }

    // Connection succeeded.
    std::cout<<"Connected to "<<it->endpoint()<<std::endl;

    // Start reading messages asynchronously.
    StartReadHeader();

    // Start writing heartbeat messages asynchronously.
    StartSendHeartbeat();
}
```

10.6.4.4 Receiving Messages Agent

The `StartReceiveMessage()` is an agent that is started when a connection is made. It first creates an empty message object and starts an asynchronous receive operation for the 4 bytes that make up the message header. The message header contains the length of the message. It resets the time-out time before starting the read operation:

```
// Start reading message header.
void StartReadHeader()
{
    // Exit if the client must stop.
    if (m_stop) return;

    // Create message.
    MessagePtr msg(new Message());
```

```
    // Reset the time-out time for reading header.
    // Heartbeat message should arrive earlier than the time-out.
    m_timeoutTimer.expires_from_now(
        boost::posix_time::seconds(m_timeoutTime));

    // Start an asynchronous read of the header.
    async_read(m_socket, buffer(msg->HeaderData(), Message::HeaderLength),
            boost::bind(&Client::HandleReadHeader, this, msg,
                        boost::asio::placeholders::error));
}
```

The I/O service calls the `HandleReadHeader()` member function when the header is read.
The handle function signals the client to stop if an error occurred. If the message received
was a heartbeat message (the size is 0), it will produce a beep and start receiving the next
message by calling `StartReceiveHeader()` again. Finally, if the received header contains
a non-zero length it will resize the message buffer and start an asynchronous receive
operation to read the message body. Note that the time-out time is reset before receiving the
message:

```
// Message header was read.
void HandleReadHeader(MessagePtr msg, const boost::system::error_code& ec)
{
    // Exit if the client must stop.
    if (m_stop) return;

    // Check the error code.
    if (ec)
    {
        // Transfer error.
        std::cout<<"Error receiving message header: "
                <<ec.message()<<std::endl;
        DoStop();
        return;
    }

    // Check if heartbeat message.
    if (msg->BodyLength()==0)
    {
        // When heartbeat message, read header again.
        StartReadHeader();

        // Do receive beep.
        Beep(1400, 200);

        return;
    }

    // Resize the message for receiving the body.
    msg->Resize();

    // Reset the time-out time for reading body.
    // Heartbeat message should arrive earlier than the time-out.
    m_timeoutTimer.expires_from_now(
        boost::posix_time::seconds(m_timeoutTime));

    // Start an asynchronous read of the checksum + body.
    async_read(m_socket, buffer(msg->MessageData(), msg->ReceiveLength()),
            boost::bind(&Client::HandleReadBody, this, msg,
                        boost::asio::placeholders::error));
}
```

The I/O service calls `HandleReadBody()` when the message body has been received. Then it prints the message and checks the CRC checksum of the message. Finally it will start a new receive operation:

```
// Message body was read.
void HandleReadBody(MessagePtr msg, const boost::system::error_code& ec)
{
    // Check the error code.
    if (ec)
    {
        // Transfer error.
        std::cout<<"Error receiving message body: "
                <<ec.message()<<std::endl;
        DoStop();
        return;
    }

    // Display the message.
    std::cout<<"Received: "<<msg->MessageString()<<std::endl;

    // Check CRC.
    if (!msg->Checksum())
    {
        std::cout<<"- Message has bad checksum!"<<std::endl;
    }

    // Exit if the client must stop.
    if (m_stop) return;

    // Read next message.
    StartReadHeader();
}
```

10.6.4.5 Send Heartbeat Message Agent

The `StartSendHeartbeat()` is an agent that is started when a connection is made. We recall that only one message can be sent at any given time. The `StartSendHeartbeat()` member function does not send the message itself but calls the `StartSendMessage()` message which queues the message for sending. Then it sets the heartbeat timer and starts an asynchronous wait operation on the heartbeat timer. In this way heartbeat messages will be sent at regular intervals:

```
// Send heartbeat message.
void StartSendHeartbeat()
{
    // Exit if the client must stop.
    if (m_stop) return;

    // Create and send heartbeat message.
    StartSendMessage(MessagePtr(new Message()));

    // Do send beep.
    Beep(700, 200);

    // Wait before sending next heartbeat.
    m_heartbeatTimer.expires_from_now(
        boost::posix_time::seconds(m_heartbeatDelay));
    m_heartbeatTimer.async_wait(
        boost::bind(&Client::StartSendHeartbeat, this));
}
```

10.6.4.6   Send Message Agent

Sending the messages in the message queue is realised by a separate agent. The *send message agent* can be active or inactive. It is initially *inactive* and will be started when the StartSendMessage() member function queues a message. The send message agent remains active as long as there are messages in the queue.

The StartSendMessage() function will push the incoming message onto the queue and when the send message agent is inactive it will be started by calling an asynchronous write operation that sends the current message. Note that the message will be removed from the queue after the message was sent because it needs to be in memory during the write operation. When the send message agent is already active the message in the queue will be sent by the HandleSendMessage() function.

```
// Send a message.
void StartSendMessage(MessagePtr msg)
{
    // As long as the queue is not empty, the 'sending agent' is
    // still alive.
    bool writeInProgress=!m_messageQueue.empty();

    // Queue the message.
    m_messageQueue.push(msg);
    if (msg->BodyLength()!=0)
    {
        std::cout<<"Sending '"<<msg->MessageString()
                <<"' to endpoint '"<<m_endPoint<<"'"<<std::endl;
    }

    // If the 'sending agent' is inactive, start it.
    if (!writeInProgress)
    {
        // Send message asynchronously. We leave the message on the queue
        // since it needs to be available during the async send.
        async_write(m_socket, buffer(msg->HeaderData(), msg->SendLength()),
            boost::bind(&Client::HandleSendMessage, this,
                    boost::asio::placeholders::error,
                    boost::asio::placeholders::bytes_transferred));
    }
}
```

The HandleSendMessage() member function will be called when a message has been sent. When there was no error the sent message is removed from the queue. When there are still messages in the queue the next message will be sent by starting a new asynchronous write operation. As long as there are messages in the queue the send message agent remains active. When the queue is empty the agent will become inactive until a new message is queued by calling the StartSendMessage() function:

```
// Message was sent.
void HandleSendMessage(const boost::system::error_code& ec, size_t size)
{
    // Check the error code.
    if (ec)
    {
        // Transfer error.
        std::cout<<"Error sending message: "<<ec.message()<<std::endl;
        DoStop();
        return;
    }

    // Remove the sent message from the queue.
    m_messageQueue.pop();
```

```
        // If the queue is not empty, send next message asynchronously.
        // We leave the message on the queue since it needs to be
        // available during the async send.
        if (!m_messageQueue.empty())
        {
            MessagePtr msg=m_messageQueue.front();
            async_write(m_socket, buffer(msg->HeaderData(), msg->SendLength()),
                boost::bind(&Client::HandleSendMessage, this,
                            boost::asio::placeholders::error,
                            boost::asio::placeholders::bytes_transferred));
        }
    }
```

The main program requests messages from the user. Then these messages are queued in the client object. That object runs in a different thread from the main program. This means that the message must be queued in a thread-safe manner. Instead of synchronising this ourselves the I/O service provides a `post()` function. This will run the given function in the same thread as the thread that is running the I/O service, thus avoiding the need for synchronising queuing messages from the main program. Thus the `SendMessage()` member function is called from the main program and schedules the `StartSendMessage()` function to be run from the I/O service thread. The message to send is bound to this function by using `boost::bind`:

```
    // Send a message. (called from main thread).
    // Since the IO service runs in its own thread,
    // the send is scheduled in the IO service.
    bool SendMessage(MessagePtr msg)
    {
        // Don't send if no message. Return false to quit.
        if (msg->BodyLength()==0) return false;

        // Schedule the StartSendMessage() function in the IO service.
        if (!m_stop)
        {
            m_ios.post(boost::bind(&Client::StartSendMessage, this, msg));
        }

        return !m_stop;
    }
```

10.6.4.7   Stopping the Client

All the agents of the client must be stopped when the client stops. This is achieved by having a data member m_stop which is checked by all agents. The `DoStop()` function sets the m_stop member and it also cancels the timers so they do not time-out anymore. Furthermore, it will shutdown the socket if it was open. This will ensure that the other end will receive an *end-of-file* error instead of the more crude *forced disconnection* error. Finally, when all agents have been stopped the client object will be removed from memory and the destructor will close the socket:

```
    // Stop the client.
    void DoStop()
    {
        std::cout<<"Stopping....."<<std::endl;

        // Set the stop variable so running functions stop themselves.
        m_stop=true;

        // Cancel the timers.
        m_heartbeatTimer.cancel();
```

```
      m_timeoutTimer.cancel();

      // Disable sending and receiving data for clean shutdown.
      // Without this, the server side will get a 'forced disconnection'
      // error instead of an neat 'end of file' error.
      if (m_socket.is_open())
      {
          m_socket.shutdown(ip::tcp::socket::shutdown_both);
      }
  }

  // Destructor.
  ~Client()
  {
      // Close the socket.
      m_socket.close();
      std::cout<<"Client closed."<<std::endl;
  }
```

When the main program wishes to stop the client it cannot call the `DoStop()` function
directly because it runs in another thread than the client. It must post the function to run on
the I/O service object. The `Stop()` function will do this:

```
  // Stop the client. (called from main thread). Since the IO service
  // runs in its own thread, the stop is scheduled in the IO service.
  void Stop()
  {
      // Schedule the DoStop() function in the IO service.
      m_ios.post(boost::bind(&Client::DoStop, this));
  }
```

10.6.4.8   Client Main Program

The last step is to show the main program. First, the user is asked to enter a host name that is
then resolved using the TCP DNS resolver. Then a client object is created and consequently
the I/O service object is run in a different thread. Furthermore, the user is asked to enter
strings which will be queued in the client object for sending by the 'send message' agent.
When an empty string is entered the client object is notified to stop and it waits until the
client has finished by joining on the thread that runs the I/O service:

```
  // Start the client.
  static void Start(int port, int heartbeatDelay, int timeoutTime)
  {
      // IO service is always needed.
      io_service ios;

      // Ask for host.
      std::string host;
      std::cout<<"Enter the host to connect to (empty=localhost): ";
      std::getline(std::cin, host);

      // If nothing entered, assume localhost.
      if (host=="") host="localhost";

      // Create the query and resolver. Get only IP4 addresses.
      std::stringstream service; service<<port;
      ip::tcp::resolver::query query(ip::tcp::v4(), host, service.str());
      ip::tcp::resolver r(ios);

      // Resolve the query and put it in an iterator.
      ip::tcp::resolver::iterator it=r.resolve(query);

      // Create and start client.
```

```
Client client(ios, heartbeatDelay, timeoutTime);
client.Start(it);

// Run the IO service in a separate thread.
boost::thread t(boost::bind(&boost::asio::io_service::run, &ios));

// Read lines and pass them to the client object.
std::string message;
std::cout<<std::endl<<"Enter text to send: "<<std::endl;
do
{
    // Get message from console.
    std::getline(std::cin, message);
}
while (client.SendMessage(MessagePtr(new Message(message)))); // Send.

// Stop the client and wait till the IO service thread is finished.
std::cout<<"Client stopping asynchronously..."<<std::endl;
client.Stop();
t.join();
}
```

10.7 Summary and Conclusions

In this chapter we have shown how asynchronous ASIO operations can improve efficiency and scalability because we can execute multiple I/O operations at the same time without the overhead of creating a thread for each client. Multiple processors and cores can still be used to improve the performance by using a thread pool for running the ASIO service object.

We also saw how we could detect transfer errors and connection problems by using message checksums and heartbeat timers.

11 Boost Interprocess: IPC Mechanisms

11.1 Introduction and Objectives

In this chapter we give an introduction to the Boost Interprocess Library. Applications running on a computer are called *processes*. Each process has its own resources such as memory and file handles. A process cannot directly access the resources of another process. This implies that processes cannot directly communicate with each other. In order to allow processes to exchange data we could let them communicate using networking operations (that we discussed in chapter 9 and 10). But this approach is inefficient in both memory usage and processing time.

To resolve these problems operating systems provide a number of mechanisms to allow two processes on the same machine to communicate. Using these mechanisms the processes can then communicate with each other more efficiently than using network operations. Communication between two processes is called *interprocess communication (IPC)*.

Interprocess communication entails information sharing between different processes. Some examples of communication mechanisms are *shared memory regions*, *shared files* and *shared kernel memory (message queues)*. Each mechanism has its advantages and disadvantages that we discuss in this chapter.

The Boost Interprocess Library wraps the operating system IPC mechanisms in a platform-independent way. All Boost IPC classes are defined in the namespace `boost::interprocess`. IPC provides mechanisms for sharing data between processes and for synchronising processes. The various IPC mechanisms for sharing data will be discussed in this chapter. Synchronisation mechanisms are discussed in chapter 12.

11.2 Persistence of IPC Mechanisms

The data that is shared between processes has a certain lifetime. It is important to know when data is created and destroyed. The lifetime (also known as *persistence*) depends on the IPC mechanism and on the OS (Operating System) used:

- *Process persistence*: The lifetime of the data lasts until all processes exit or until all processes explicitly close the IPC mechanism.
- *Kernel persistence*: The lifetime of the data lasts until the OS shuts down or until the IPC mechanism is explicitly deleted.
- *File system persistence*: The lifetime of the data lasts until the IPC mechanism is explicitly deleted.

The *boost::interprocess* IPC mechanisms and their lifetime are summarised in Figure 11.1. Note that the persistence level of some of the mechanisms that we discuss is OS-dependent.

Mechanism	Persistence
Shared memory	Kernel or file system
Memory mapped file	File system
Process-shared mutex types	Process
Process-shared semaphore	Process
Process-shared condition	Process

File lock	Process
Message queue	Kernel or file system
Named mutex	Kernel or file system
Named semaphore	Kernel or file system
Named condition	Kernel or file system

Figure 11.1 IPC Mechanisms and their persistence

11.3 Shared Memory

The most efficient way to exchange data between processes is by using *shared memory*. A block of physical memory (*memory segment*) will be mapped by the OS into the address space of several processes. The *shared memory segment* is created in one process and then opened in another process. Using a shared memory segment is a two-step process. When the shared memory segment was created or opened it will be mapped in the memory space of the process.

The shared memory segment remains in memory even when the process that created it terminates. The lifetime of shared memory can thus be longer than the lifetime of the processes that use it. The shared memory segment must be explicitly deleted by the last process.

The *boost::interprocess* library simulates shared memory using temporary shared files on platforms that do not natively support shared memory. This is why the persistence level can be of kernel or file system type.

To use shared memory with Boost we use the following include file:

```
#include <boost/interprocess/shared_memory_object.hpp>
```

A shared memory segment is modelled by the class:

```
boost::interprocess::shared_memory_object
```

Its constructor is defined as:

```
shared_memory_object(T cm, const char* name, mode_t mode,
                     const permissions& perm=permissions());
```

A shared memory object has a name. The parameter cm stands for creation mode and can have one of the following values:
- *create_only*: Creates a new shared memory segment. It will throw an interprocess_exception when the shared memory segment already exists.
- *open_or_create*: Create a new shared memory segment or it opens the existing one when it already exists.
- *open_only*: Open an existing shared memory region. It will throw an interprocess_exception when the region does not exist.

The parameter mode indicates the access mode and can have one of the following values:
- *read_write*: Shared memory segment can be read and written.
- *read_only*: Shared memory segment can only be read.

We can optionally pass a *permissions* object to limit which users can access the shared memory when a shared memory segment is created. The *permissions* object is created with Windows or Unix-specific permissions. When we use this object the application will not be platform-independent anymore. A discussion of this topic is outside the scope of the book and we refer the reader to the Boost online documentation.

A `shared_memory_object` instance cannot be directly used. When a shared memory object has been created its size must be set with the `truncate()` member function. Then the shared memory is mapped into memory using a `mapped_region` object whose interface is:

```
#include <boost/interprocess/mapped_region.hpp>

template<typename MemoryMappable>
mapped_region(const MemoryMappable& mapping, mode_t mode,
    offset_t offset=0, std::size_t size=0, const void* address=0);
```

The `mapping` argument is an instance of `shared_memory_object`. It is a template argument and thus the `mapped_region` class works with other types of IPC data objects. Several mappings having different lengths and different offsets can be made on the same shared memory segment. Mappings can also overlap. When no offset and size are given, the full memory segment will be mapped. Again the `mode` argument determines whether the mapping is read/write or read only. For example, on one read/write shared memory object we can simultaneously have a read/write mapping covering the first half of the shared memory object and a read-only mapping covering the complete shared memory object. Finally, we can give the mapping an explicit memory address. Using the address 0 (zero) will automatically determine a more efficient memory address. We discuss a scenario where an explicit address is needed later in this chapter.

The `mapped_region` object is thus the window to the shared memory segment. To use the mapped region we need to obtain its address using the `get_address()` member function. This returns a `void` pointer.

The following example shows how a shared memory object is created and then mapped in the process' memory. After the mapping a `string` message is then copied to the shared memory:

```
try
{
    // Ask the user to type in a string.
    cout<<"Creating new shared memory.\n"
        <<"Enter the text to store in the shared memory: ";
    string message; getline(cin, message);
    int stringLength=message.length()+1; // string length + trailing \0

    // Create a shared memory object called "MySharedMemory".
    // Initial size is 0.
    cout<<"Creating shared memory."<<endl;
    shared_memory_object sm(create_only, "MySharedMemory", read_write);

    // Set the size of the shared memory segment.
    sm.truncate(stringLength);

    // Map shared memory in process space.
    mapped_region mr(sm, read_write);

    // Get the address of the shared memory and fill it with the string.
    const char* source=message.c_str();
    const char* end=message.c_str()+stringLength;
```

```
    char* dest=(char*)mr.get_address();
    for (; source!=end; source++, dest++) *dest=*source;

    // Shared memory created.
    cout<<"Shared memory created with size: "<<mr.get_size()<<endl;
    cout<<"Message stored: "<<(char*)mr.get_address()<<endl;
}
catch (interprocess_exception& ex)
{
    cout<<"Creating shared memory failed.\n- "<<ex.what()<<endl;
}
```

The following example opens an existing shared memory region and maps it using a `mapped_region` object. Then it prints the size of both the shared memory object and the mapped region. Furthermore, it prints the message stored in the shared memory region. Finally, the shared memory region is removed from the system using the `remove()` function. Note that this is a static member of the `shared_memory_object` class:

```
// Try to open a shared memory segment.
try
{
    // Open shared memory object.
    shared_memory_object sm(open_only, "MySharedMemory", read_only);

    // Map shared memory in process space.
    mapped_region mr(sm, read_only);

    // Get the size of the complete shared memory.
    offset_t smSize; bool b=sm.get_size(smSize);

    // Display message in the shared memory region.
    cout<<"Shared memory found with length: "<<smSize<<endl;
    cout<<"The mapped region has length: "<<mr.get_size()<<endl;
    cout<<"Message: "<<(char*)mr.get_address()<<endl;

    // Remove the shared memory.
    if (shared_memory_object::remove("MySharedMemory")==true)
    {
        cout<<"Shared memory removed."<<endl;
    }
    else cout<<"Error while removing shared memory."<<endl;
}
catch (interprocess_exception& ex)
{
    cout<<"Opening shared mem failed. 'MySharedMemory' does not exist\n- "
        <<ex.what()<<endl;
}
```

Microsoft Windows supports shared memory natively but the lifetime is different than Unix shared memory. In Windows memory mapped files are automatically destroyed when the last process using the shared memory is destroyed. Thus Windows shared memory has process persistence while Unix shared memory has kernel or file system persistence. Because of the differences in this behaviour the Boost interprocess library uses shared files on Windows to simulate shared memory which ensures portability between Windows and Unix systems.

In some cases we really need native Windows shared memory, for example in order to communicate with processes that do not use Boost. We can realise this using the `windows_shared_memory` class. However, using this option makes our application Windows-specific and there are limitations such as that the opening process not knowing the size of the shared memory segment. When needed, the process that created the shared memory must transmit the size to the other process.

Since the native Windows shared memory is deleted when the last process is detached from the shared memory we conclude that another process must map the memory before the creating process exits. Thus, we need to use synchronisation mechanisms to be sure that shared memory has not been destroyed before a client can attach to it.

11.4 Memory Mapped File

Another IPC mechanism is *memory mapped files*. A file stored on disk can be (partially) mapped into the address space of a process. Access to the mapped memory constitutes access to the file. The file to be mapped must already exist and have the correct size. It may neither grow nor shrink when used as a memory mapped file and the file will not be automatically deleted when the memory mapped file object is deleted.

The use of a memory mapped file is similar to that with the `shared_memory_object` class. Multiple parts of the file can be mapped at the same time.

We can also use memory mapped files to access existing files in the same way as we do with local memory. This could simplify working with files compared to the standard file operations. The mapped file can be bigger than the logical memory capacity of the system in use, for example, a 9 GB DVD image which does not fit in the address space of a 32-bit system. In that case we can have multiple smaller mappings covering the whole file.

Updates written to the mapped file are directly visible to other processes but these updates are not immediately written to disk.

To use the memory mapped file, we create a `file_mapping` object:

```
#include <boost/interprocess/file_mapping.hpp>
file_mapping(const char* filename, mode_t mode);
```

The file must already exist and the mode can be `read_only` or `read_write`. We need to create one or more `mapped_region` instances before we can use the mapped file when creating the `file_mapping` object. This is similar to the case of the `shared_memory_object`.

We now give an example. To this end, we first create a file with the correct size using a custom `CreateFile()` function. We then create a `file_mapping` object and map it into the address space of the process using a `mapped_region` in the same way as with shared memory. When the memory is mapped a string is copied into the memory and the `flush()` function is called to make sure that the updates are written to disk. The *flush* function is needed when another process wishes to access the file directly without using the boost interprocess library:

```
try
{
    // Ask the user to type in a string.
    cout<<"Creating new memory mapped file.\n"
        <<"Enter the text to store in the memory mapped file: ";
    string message; getline(cin, message);
    int stringLength=message.length()+1;  // Size including trailing \0.

    // Create a new file of the right size.
    CreateFile(filename, stringLength);

    // Open the memory mapped file for writing.
```

```
        cout<<"Open memory mapped file in read/write mode"<<endl;
        file_mapping fm(filename.c_str(), read_write);

        // Map memory mapped file in process space.
        mapped_region mr(fm, read_write);

        // Get the address of the shared memory and fill it with the string.
        const char* source=message.c_str();
        const char* end=message.c_str()+stringLength;
        char* dest=(char*)mr.get_address();
        for (; source!=end; source++, dest++) *dest=*source;

        // Make sure the region is flushed to disk.
        mr.flush();

        // Memory mapped file created.
        cout<<"Memory mapped file created with size: "<<mr.get_size()<<endl;
        cout<<"Message stored: "<<(char*)mr.get_address()<<endl;
    }
    catch (interprocess_exception&)
    {
        cout<<"Creating memory-mapped file failed."<<endl;
    }
```

The next example opens the existing memory mapped file and maps it using a mapped_region object. Then it prints the size of the mapped region and it also prints the message in the memory mapped file. Finally, the file is removed from disk:

```
    // Try to open a memory mapped file.
    try
    {
        // Open the memory mapped file for reading.
        cout<<"Open memory mapped file in read mode"<<endl;
        file_mapping fm(filename.c_str(), read_only);

        // Map memory mapped file in process space.
        mapped_region mr(fm, read_only);

        // Display message in the mapped region.
        cout<<"The mapped region has length: "<<mr.get_size()<<endl;
        cout<<"Message: "<<(char*)mr.get_address()<<endl;

        // Remove the memory mapped file.
        file_mapping::remove(filename.c_str());
    }
    catch (interprocess_exception&)
    {
        cout<<"Opening memory mapped file failed. File does not exist."<<endl;
        return;
    }
```

11.5 Advanced Mapped Regions

Mapped region instances are independent of the underlying IPC memory mechanism that is being used. And once mapped, we can work with the memory as if it were regular memory. However, there are some issues we need to keep in mind when working with mapped regions because IPC mapped memory behaves differently from regular memory.

11.5.1 Pointers in Mapped Regions

The first thing we need to notice is the logical memory address of where the IPC memory is mapped to. By default this is system-defined and may not always be the same in all cases. It can differ between processes. For example, in process 1 the shared memory might be mapped at address 0x150000 while the same shared memory might be mapped at address 0x250000 in process 2. This has major consequences if we have pointers (or references) in the shared memory region. If you store a pointer to shared memory of process 1 it then points to a different memory address in process 2 if the address mappings are not the same. In general, pointers in a mapped region cannot be exchanged between two processes.

There are two ways to solve this problem:
* Use offset pointers.
* Fixed address mapping.

In both cases we can only store pointers to addresses in that mapped region. Pointers to normal memory have no meaning in another process and as such cannot be shared between processes.

11.5.1.1   Offset Pointers

Instead of storing regular (absolute) pointers we store *offsets* between addresses in the mapped region. The absolute addresses in a mapped region will be different for each process but offsets between addresses in a mapped region are the same for all processes. To this end, the interprocess library provides the `offset_ptr<T>` class. It is a special smart pointer that stores an offset instead of an absolute address. The offset stored is relative to the *this* pointer of the `offset_ptr<T>` object.

Offset pointers can also be used to point to objects in a mapped region and they can call member functions on them. But they cannot be used to call virtual functions. This is because the virtual function table is different from each process.

Representing a NULL pointer as an offset pointer can be problematic. An offset to address 0x00000000 would be different for each process. An offset of 0 cannot be used because then offset pointers that point to themselves cannot be created. Some structures need to point to themselves. Adding an extra member to the offset pointer to indicate a NULL pointer will work but it consumes extra memory and is bad for performance. This is why a null pointer is represented by an offset of 1. Thus this means you cannot have an offset pointer that points one byte after the *this* address but in practice this is never needed. We shall see examples of offset pointers later this chapter.

11.5.1.2   Fixed Address Mapping

Using offset pointers is less efficient than regular (absolute) pointers. To avoid problems with pointers in IPC memory we can also make sure that all processes map the IPC memory at the same address. When creating a mapped region object we specify the logical memory address to map the IPC memory as last argument to the mapped region constructor:

```
template<typename MemoryMappable>
mapped_region(const MemoryMappable& mapping, mode_t mode,
offset_t offset=0, std::size_t size=0, const void* address=0);
```

But there are limitations to the addresses that we can use. The mapping is based on the system's page size. The start address of a mapped region can only be on a page boundary. Both the address and the offset specified for the mapped region must be a multiple of the page size. More precisely, the *address-offset* must be on a page boundary. The page size of your system can be obtained by calling the static member function:

```
std::size_t page_size=mapped_region::get_page_size();
```

Furthermore, the page must not already be in use. The consumption of logical address space is per page. Thus, if we map a region with size 1 it will use a complete page that cannot be used elsewhere in the process.

We give an example of using different mappings. First, the `PrintRegionDetails()` function will print the region's size, start and end-addresses:

```
void PrintRegionDetails(mapped_region& region)
{
    cout<<"Region size:           "<<region.get_size()<<endl;
    cout<<"Region start address: "<<region.get_address()<<endl;
    cout<<"Region end address:    "
        <<(void*)((size_t)region.get_address()+region.get_size()-1)<<endl;
    cout<<"---------------------"<<endl;
}
```

The main program creates a shared memory segment that is twice the page size:

```
// Get the page size.
size_t pageSize=mapped_region::get_page_size();

// Create a shared memory object. Initial size is 0.
cout<<"Creating shared memory."<<endl;
shared_memory_object sm(create_only, "MySharedMemory", read_write);

// Set the size of the shared memory segment (2 times the page size).
sm.truncate(pageSize*2);

// Get the size of the complete shared memory.
offset_t smSize; bool b=sm.get_size(smSize);
cout<<"Size is: "<<smSize<<endl;
cout<<"Page size is: "<<pageSize<<endl;
```

Then we make various mappings. The first one is the *default mapping* where the address is determined by the system:

```
// 1: Create default mapping.
{
    cout<<endl<<"Create default mapped region (generated address)"<<endl;
    mapped_region mr(sm, read_write);
    PrintRegionDetails(mr);
}
```

Second, we create four mappings whose *size is half the page size* but where the address is determined by the system. Note that the memory ranges of the created mappings are not contiguous because each mapping must start at a page boundary. This implies that between two mappings there is a half page of unused addresses:

```
// 2: Create multiple mappings of half page size.
{
    cout<<endl<<"Create 4 mapped regions of 1/2 page size (generated "
        <<"address). Note the gap between region addresses."<<endl;
    mapped_region mr1(sm, read_write, 0, pageSize/2);
    mapped_region mr2(sm, read_write, 0, pageSize/2);
    mapped_region mr3(sm, read_write, 0, pageSize/2);
    mapped_region mr4(sm, read_write, 0, pageSize/2);
    PrintRegionDetails(mr1);
    PrintRegionDetails(mr2);
    PrintRegionDetails(mr3);
    PrintRegionDetails(mr4);
}
```

We now create a mapping with a *fixed address*. We multiply the page size by a factor to determine the address so that we are sure the mapping starts on a page boundary. We note that creating the mapping could still fail if the page is already in use by other parts of the process:

```
// 3: Create mapping with fixed address.
{
    cout<<endl<<"Create mapped region with fixed address "
        <<"(1000 times the page size)."<<endl;
    cout<<"This might fail if the page is already in use by "
        <<"other parts of the process."<<endl;
    mapped_region mr(sm, read_write, 0, pageSize, (void*)(1000*pageSize));
    PrintRegionDetails(mr);
}
```

Next, we create a mapping with a *fixed address and an offset*. In this case the address minus offset must be on a page boundary. Thus we add the offset to the base address:

```
// 4: Create mapping with fixed address and offset so the address-offset is
on a page boundary..
{
    int offset=100;
    cout<<endl<<"Create mapped region with fixed address and "
        <<"offset (address=1000 times the page size + offset)."<<endl;
    cout<<"This might fail if the page is already in use by "
        <<"other parts of the process."<<endl;
    mapped_region mr(sm, read_write, offset, pageSize,
                     (void*)(1000*pageSize+offset));
    PrintRegionDetails(mr);
}
```

Finally, we create a mapping were the address-offset is not on a page boundary. This will fail and an `interprocess_exception` is thrown:

```
// 5: Create mapping with fixed address (wrong).
{
    cout<<endl<<"Create mapped region with fixed address & "
        <<"offset 1 (1000 times the page size)."<<endl;
    cout<<"Should fail because address-offset not on page boundary."<<endl;
    mapped_region mr(sm, read_write, 1, pageSize, (void*)(1000*pageSize));
    PrintRegionDetails(mr);
}
```

Finally, the shared memory is deleted:

```
// Delete the shared memory
shared_memory_object::remove("MySharedMemory");
```

When using fixed address mapping we note that pointers can also be used to point to objects in a mapped region and we can call member functions on them. But they still cannot be used to call virtual functions. The virtual function table differs between processes because the pointers in the virtual function table point to regular memory and not to locations in the mapped region.

11.5.2 Static Members in Mapped Regions

We have to take special care when using static data members when we store objects in shared memory. Regular members of an object in a mapped region are stored in the mapped region but static data is actually global data and is stored in regular memory. Thus each process shares the regular object data but have their own copy of static data members.

This is not a problem if the static data member is a `const` member but if it is a non-`const` member writes to it will not seen by the other process.

11.6 Managed Memory Segments

Mapped regions are difficult to use because they are accessed at byte level. The memory management in the mapped region is done manually. Thus it is difficult to create complex objects and to handle dynamic memory creation and destruction. Furthermore, for other processes it can be difficult to find objects in the mapped region.

Managed memory segments solve these problems. They manage IPC memory and we can create objects in IPC memory similar to using the operators `new` and `delete`. Features include:
- Dynamic allocation of memory portions.
- Construction of C++ objects in IPC memory.
- Support for named objects so that objects can be found in memory by name.
- Atomic creation, thus preventing having two objects with the same name.

Unlike the `mapped_region` class that works with each type of IPC memory there are separate managed memory segment classes for each type of IPC memory. The supported types of memory are:
- Shared memory.
- Memory mapped files.
- Heap memory (operator *new* allocated).
- User provided fixed buffer.

The last two memory types allow us to use regular memory in the same way as with IPC memory.

11.6.1 Managed Shared Memory

The managed memory segment class for shared memory is called `basic_managed_shared_memory` and its header file and definition are:

```
#include <boost/interprocess/managed_shared_memory.hpp>

template
<
    typename CharType, typename MemoryAlgorithm,
    template<typename IndexConfig> typename IndexType
>
class basic_managed_shared_memory;
```

This class wraps `shared_memory_segment` and `mapped_region` objects. The complete shared memory segment is used by the managed shared memory object. But not all of it is available since some of that memory is used by the managed shared memory object for keeping track of memory usage.

The template arguments of the `basic_managed_shared_memory` class control various aspects of the managed segment. The `CharType` specifies the type of characters to use for the object names. In most cases this is `char` or `wchar_t`.
The `MemoryAlgorithm` template parameter specifies an algorithm class that determines how portions of a segment are allocated. It also determines the pointer type for addresses in the shared memory. Normally this is `void*` for an absolute address pointer or

`offset_ptr<void>` for offset pointers. The algorithm also determines the mutex type that we use to synchronise allocations. This can be a mutex, for example (or none if synchronisation is done externally). A description of the available algorithms is outside the scope of this book. We use the default algorithms.

Finally, the `IndexType` parameter specifies the data structure to use for the name-to-object address mapping.

There are several typedefs for frequently used template specialisations of the `basic_managed_shared_memory` class. These can be `offset_ptr` based or `void*` based and `char` or `wchar_t` based. All these typedefs use the default `IndexType`:

- `managed_shared_memory`   `// offset_ptr - char`
- `wmanaged_shared_memory`   `// offset_ptr - wchar_t`
- `fixed_managed_shared_memory`   `// void* - char`
- `wfixed_managed_shared_memory`   `// void* - wchar_t`

The constructor is defined as follows:

```
basic_managed_shared_memory(T cm, const char* name, size_t size,
                            const void* address=0);
```

The `name` and `size` parameters determine the name and size of the underlying shared memory object. The address must be specified when you use the *fixed* variants of the class to map the memory to a specific address. The `cm` parameter determines the creation mode of the underlying shared memory object and it can have the following values:

- *create_only*: Creates a new managed shared memory segment. An `interprocess_exception` will be thrown when a shared memory region with the specified name already exists.
- *open_only*: A managed shared memory segment will be opened with an existing shared memory region that has the specified name. If a memory region with the specified name does not exist an `interprocess_exception` will be thrown.
- *open_or_create*: If a shared memory region with the specified name already exists it will be opened in the managed shared memory segment. Otherwise, it will be created.

When all processes are finished with the managed segment we need to remove the shared memory object:

```
shared_memory_object::remove(const char* name);
```

11.6.2 Managed Memory Mapped File

The managed memory segment class for memory mapped files is called `basic_managed_mapped_file`. Its header file and definition are:

```
#include <boost/interprocess/managed_mapped_file.hpp>

template
<
    typename CharType, typename MemoryAlgorithm,
    template<typename IndexConfig> typename IndexType
>
class basic_managed_mapped_file;
```

This class wraps a `file_mapping` and `mapped_region` object. The complete file is mapped but some memory is used for housekeeping purposes. The meaning of the template arguments is the same as for the `basic_managed_shared_memory` class.

There are also a number of typedefs that make working with managed mapped files easier:
- `managed_mapped_file`   `// offset_ptr - char`
- `wmanaged_mapped_file`   `// offset_ptr - wchar_t`

There are no typedefs for a `void*` variant of managed mapped files.

The constructor is defined as follows:

```
basic_managed_mapped_file(T cm, const char* filename, size_t size);
```

The *filename* and *size* parameters specify the filename of the shared file and its size, respectively. The *cm* parameter represents the creation mode and can have the following values:
- *create_only*: Creates a new managed mapped file segment. An `interprocess_exception` will be thrown if the file already exists.
- *open_only*: A managed mapped file segment will be opened with an existing file. An `interprocess_exception` will be thrown if the file does not exist.
- *open_or_create*: If the specified file already exists it will be opened in the managed mapped file segment. Otherwise, it will be created.

The file to map can be automatically created while we have to provide an existing file when using the `mapped_file` object directly. The file will not be automatically deleted and thus it must be manually deleted.

11.6.3 Allocating Memory Fragments in Managed Memory

Allocating memory in a managed memory segment is the same for each managed memory segment type. The lowest level functionality allocates a number of bytes in the form of *memory fragments*. There are two versions:

```
void* allocate(std::size_t nbytes);
void* allocate(std::size_t nbytes, std::nothrow_t nothrow);
```

The first version throws an `interprocess::bad_alloc` exception if there is no more memory while the second returns a NULL pointer if there is no more memory.
When the memory is no longer needed it is deallocated:

```
void deallocate(void* addr);
```

Since working with plain memory fragments can be cumbersome we rarely allocate memory fragments directly. Usually we use the functions that allocate named objects as we shall discuss in the next section.

11.6.4 Allocating Objects in Managed Memory

The power of managed memory segments lies in the fact that we can create *named objects* and find existing named objects which makes using IPC memory much easier. All the managed memory segment classes have various functions to allocate, find and delete named objects and arrays of objects, as the following code shows:

```
// Construct single object or array of objects.
// Constructor arguments are passed as parameter list.
// If array, each object has same constructor arguments.
T* construct<T>(const CharType* name)(p1, p2, …);
T* construct<T>(const CharType* name)[count](p1, p2, …);

// Find object or array of objects. If not found, create it.
```

```
T* find_or_construct<T>(const CharType* name)(p1, p2, …);
T* find_or_construct<T>(const CharType* name)[count](p1, p2, …);

// Construct array of object taking the parameters from an iterator.
T* construct_it<T>(const CharType* name)[count](it1, it2, …);
T* find_or_construct_it<T>(const CharType* n)[cnt](it1, it2, …);

// Find object. Returns pointer plus the number of objects.
std::pair<T*, std::size_t> find<T>(const CharType* name);

// Destroy the object by name. Returns false if not present.
bool destroy<T>(const CharType* name);

// Destroy the object via pointer.
void destroy_ptr(void* ptr);
```

These functions throw an exception if an error occurs. However, they also have overloaded versions that accept an `std::nothrow` object as last argument that does not throw but returns a NULL pointer, for example.

In some cases an object does not need a name, for example when the object does not need to be found in another process. We then can create *anonymous objects* by passing the `anonymous_instance` constant as name. Objects without a name can only be destroyed via their pointer.

We now give an example that creates a managed shared memory segment and creates a new named `Point` object in that segment. We note that directly after creating the segment the free memory is smaller than the segment's size due to housekeeping data being created:

```
// Create managed shared memory and store a Point object.
try
{
    // Create the managed shared memory.
    managed_shared_memory segment(create_only, "MySharedMemory", 1024);
    cout<<"Segment size: "<<segment.get_size()<<endl;
    cout<<"Free memory: "<<segment.get_free_memory()<<endl;

    // Create a point called "MyPoint" in the managed memory segment.
    Point* point=segment.construct<Point>("MyPoint")(1.4, 5.9);
    cout<<"Point created: "<<*point<<endl;
    cout<<"Free memory: "<<segment.get_free_memory()<<endl;
}
catch (interprocess_exception& ex)
{
    cout<<"Failed to create managed shared memory"<<endl;
}
```

The next example opens an existing managed shared memory segment and tries to find the `Point` object by name. When found, it destroys the found object and tries to find it again (which should of course fail):

```
// Open the managed shared memory and find the Point object.
try
{
    // Open the managed shared memory.
    managed_shared_memory segment(open_only, "MySharedMemory");

    // Find the point called "MyPoint" in the managed memory segment.
    Point* point=segment.find<Point>("MyPoint").first;
    if (point!=NULL)
    {
        cout<<"Point found: "<<*point<<endl;
```

```
            // Remove the point.
            segment.destroy_ptr(point);
            cout<<"Point removed"<<endl;
        }
        else cout<<"Point not found"<<endl;

        // Try to find the point again in the managed memory segment
        // (should fail).
        point=segment.find<Point>("MyPoint").first;
        if (point!=NULL) cout<<"Point found: "<<*point<<endl;
        else cout<<"Point not found"<<endl;

        // Remove the shared memory.
        if (shared_memory_object::remove("MySharedMemory")==true)
        {
            cout<<"Shared memory removed."<<endl;
        }
        else cout<<"Error while removing shared memory."<<endl;
    }
    catch (interprocess_exception& ex)
    {
        cout<<"Opening shared memory failed. "
            <<"'MySharedMemory' does not exist."<<endl;
    }
```

11.6.5 Synchronisation of Object Construction and Retrieving

Synchronisation is important when two processes simultaneously access the same shared memory. For example, when we first call find() to get an object and then, if not found we call construct() to create a new object. This could result in an error if the object was created by another process between the find() and construct() calls. Thus, the *find* and *construct* may not be interrupted by another process (which must be *atomic*).

We can ensure atomicity by using one of the interprocess synchronisation classes. The find_or_construct() function is already guaranteed to be atomic. Internally it uses an interprocess_recursive_mutex which makes sure only one process can create the object.

11.6.6 Composite Objects

Objects containing pointers to other objects (these are called *composite objects*) cannot be directly stored in shared memory because addresses might be different between processes. Thus we need *fixed address mapping*, which can be complicated to use. Alternatively, we use *offset pointers*.

Using offset pointers is less efficient than regular pointers. However, we can define the pointer type as template argument. The pointer type can be a regular pointer when used in regular memory or an offset pointer when used in IPC memory.

As an example, we discuss a BasicLine class that has pointers to two Point objects. The template argument TPointer determines the pointer type to use to reference the points. We note that since it is not known how the points should be created (it can be in regular memory or IPC memory) the points must be created and deleted outside the BasicLine class. Because of this the copy constructor and assignment operator only make a *shallow copy*. We will see later that allocators can solve this limitation. The code that implements this line class is as follows:

```
template<typename TPointer>
class BasicLine
{
```

```
private:
    // The embedded points.
    TPointer m_p1;
    TPointer m_p2;

public:

    // Default constructor.
    BasicLine()
    {
        m_p1=NULL;
        m_p2=NULL;
    }

    // Constructor with points.
    BasicLine(TPointer p1, TPointer p2)
    {
        m_p1=p1;
        m_p2=p2;
    }

    // Copy constructor.
    // Shallow copy. Deep copy not possible because we do not know how
    // to allocate the new point (new or in managed memory segment).
    BasicLine(const BasicLine<TPointer>& source)
    {
        m_p1=source.m_p1;
        m_p2=source.m_p2;
    }

    // Destructor.
    ~BasicLine()
    {
        // Because we don't know how the points are created,
        // we can't delete them.
    }

    // Get the start-point.
    TPointer StartPoint() const
    {
        return m_p1;
    }

    // Get the end-point.
    TPointer EndPoint() const
    {
        return m_p2;
    }

    // Set the start-point.
    void StartPoint(TPointer p)
    {
        m_p1=p;
    }

    // Set the end-point.
    void EndPoint(TPointer p)
    {
        m_p2=p;
    }

    // Assignment operator.
    // Even when we can do a copy of the points (*m_p1=*source.m_p1)
    // since memory is already created, we do a shallow copy to make
    // it behave the same as the copy constructor.
```

```
        BasicLine<TPointer>& operator = (const BasicLine<TPointer>& source)
        {
            m_p1=source.m_p1;
            m_p2=source.m_p2;

            return *this;
        }

        // Send the line to an ostream.
        friend std::ostream& operator << (std::ostream& os,
                                          const BasicLine<TPointer>& l)
        {
            os<<"Line("<<*l.m_p1<<", "<<*l.m_p2<<")";
            return os;
        }
    };
```

We now use the `BasicLine` class. To allow us to switch between regular pointers and offset pointers we define a `Line` type using a *typedef*:

```
// Line with offset pointer (works always).
typedef BasicLine<offset_ptr<Point> > Line;
```

or:

```
// Line with normal pointer
// (works only when mapped addresses are the same).
typedef BasicLine<Point*> Line;
```

Now we create a managed segment and we create two `Point` instances in that segment. Note that since these are components of a line they are created without a name:

```
// Create the managed shared memory (force a specific address).
managed_shared_memory segment(create_only, "MySharedMemory", 1024,
    (void*)(1000*mapped_region::get_page_size()));
cout<<"Segment created. Address: "<<segment.get_address()<<endl;

// Create two anonymous points in the managed memory segment
Point* p1=segment.construct<Point>(anonymous_instance)(1.0, 2.0);
Point* p2=segment.construct<Point>(anonymous_instance)(4.0, 9.0);
```

We create the line object with these points as arguments. Then we print the line and its address. We also print the addresses of the points but this must be done in an indirect way. We cannot directly print an `offset_ptr`. Therefore we first dereference the offset pointer to get the point and then we take its address. This is the reason why we use the `&*` when printing the address. This essentially converts an `offset_ptr<Point>` to `Point*`. This has no influence if it already uses a regular pointer:

```
// Create a line called "MyLine" in the managed memory segment.
Line* line=segment.construct<Line>("MyLine")(p1, p2);
cout<<"Line created: "<<*line<<endl;
cout<<"Line address: "<<line<<endl;
cout<<"Start-point address: "<<&*line->StartPoint()<<endl;
cout<<"End-point address: "<<&*line->EndPoint()<<endl;
```

Another process can now find the line in the managed segment. We note that when deleting the line we should first delete the points in the line. We also need the `&*` to convert a potential `offset_ptr<Point*>` to `Point*`:

```
// Open the managed shared memory (force a specific address).
managed_shared_memory segment(open_only, "MySharedMemory",
    (void*)(1000*mapped_region::get_page_size()));
```

```
cout<<"Segment opened. Address: "<<segment.get_address()<<endl;

// Find the line called "MyLine" in the managed memory segment.
Line* line=segment.find<Line>("MyLine").first;
if (line!=NULL)
{
    cout<<"Line found: "<<*line<<endl;
    cout<<"Line address: "<<line<<endl;
    cout<<"Start-point address: "<<&*line->StartPoint()<<endl;
    cout<<"End-point address: "<<&*line->EndPoint()<<endl;

    // Remove the points.
    segment.destroy_ptr(&*line->StartPoint());
    segment.destroy_ptr(&*line->EndPoint());

    // Remove the line.
    segment.destroy_ptr(line);
}
else cout<<"Line not found"<<endl;
```

The offset pointer ensures that the Line class can be shared when the managed segment has different addresses in the processes. We can test this by specifying different addresses when creating and opening the managed shared memory. It still works when using the typedef that defines the Line using offset pointers. But when using the typedef for regular pointers the line does point to the wrong Point data.

11.6.7 Synchronising Composite Object Creation

Creating a composite object is a multi-step operation. It is possible that another process will use the *parent* object before the *child* objects have been created. In particular we wish to ensure that the parent object cannot be used until all child objects have been created. In other words, the complete creation process must be *atomic*.

The various segment manager classes also provide functionality to execute a functor atomically:

```
template<typename Func> void atomic_func(Func& f);
```

We do not need explicit synchronisation when we use the atomic_func() function. During this function calls to the following managed segment functions are blocked:
- construct(), construct_it() and find().
- find_or_construct() and find_or_construct_it().
- destroy() and destroy_ptr().

Instead of constructing the line with its points in the main program we wrap the creation process in a function object:

```
// Function object class to create a line atomically.
class CreateObjects
{
private:
    // The segment to use for allocation.
    managed_shared_memory* m_segment;

public:
    // The created line.
    Line* line;

    // Constructor with the segment to use for allocation.
    CreateObjects(managed_shared_memory* segment)
```

```
      {
          m_segment=segment;
      }

      // The function that creates a complex object.
      // This function will be called by atomic_func() so that
      // no others can create or find objects during this function.
      // The two points can't be used before the line is completely created.
      void operator () ()
      {
          // Create two named points.
          Point* p1=m_segment->construct<Point>("Point1")(9.0, 8.0);
          Point* p2=m_segment->construct<Point>("point2")(8.0, 9.0);

          // Create a line called "Line" in the managed memory segment.
          line=m_segment->construct<Line>("Line")(p1, p2);
      }
};
```

The function object can now be used to create the line with its component points:

```
// Create the managed shared memory
// (use the second version to force a specific address).
managed_shared_memory segment(create_only, "MySharedMemory", 1024);

// Create objects as atomic operation. During the execution of the
// function object, no others can create or find objects.
CreateObjects co(&segment);
segment.atomic_func(co);
cout<<endl<<"Line created atomically: "<<*co.line<<endl;
```

11.6.8 Using Allocators

We have already created a line class that has a template argument for the pointer type to use. The line class can be used with regular memory as well as in a managed segment. However, since the line class did not know if it was created in regular memory or in a managed segment it cannot allocate its start and end-points. These are created by the client. Now we require that the line class itself manages its embedded objects. The Boost interprocess library makes this possible by using the boost::interprocess::allocator class.

The allocator class has the same interface as std::allocator. A class can now create memory for its embedded objects using an allocator instead of using new or the managed segment's construct() functions. Normal memory is allocated or IPC memory is allocated depending on the allocator being used.

The boost::interprocess::allocator class has the following members:

```
template<typename T, typename SegmentManager>
class allocator
{
    // typedefs for easier handling (not all shown).
    typedef T* pointer;
    typedef const T& const_reference;

    // Constructor with segment manager and copy constructor.
    allocator(SegmentManager*);
    allocator(const allocator&);

    // Constructor with other allocator type. Used for conversion.
    // Using this, an allocator can be converted to an allocator that
    // allocates other types. So you only need to accept a void allocator.
    template<typename T2> allocator(const allocator<T2, SegmentManager>&);
```

```
    // Allocate a number of elements.
    pointer allocate(std::size_t, cvoid_ptr=0);

    // Deallocate a number of elements.
    void deallocate(const pointer&, std::size_t);

    // Copy construct an already allocated memory location.
    void construct(const pointer&, const_reference);

    // Call destructor of element without de-allocating memory.
    void destroy(const pointer&);
};
```

The `allocator` class has two template arguments, namely the type to be created and the `SegmentManager` type. Each managed memory segment class internally uses a segment manager object. This object manages the memory buffer and provides memory management functionality. It is also needed by an allocator and it is passed in the constructor. We use the `get_segment_manager()` function to obtain the segment manager from a managed memory segment. The segment manager type of a managed memory segment is available as a nested type definition called `segment_manager`. We now show how the segment manager object of a managed shared memory object is retrieved:

```
managed_shared_memory::segment_manager* sm;
sm=msm.get_segment_manger();
```

We now adapt the `BasicLine` class. The allocator is used to create, copy and destroy the start and end-points of the line. The allocator type is passed as a template argument instead of the pointer type argument. The pointer type is derived from the allocator type.

The constructors of `BasicLine` now accept an allocator object. If no allocator is passed it will create a new allocator object. This approach only works for allocators that have a default constructor such as the standard STL allocator (`std::allocator`). STL allocators are *stateless* and do not receive any data when created. However, the `boost::interprocess::allocator` does not have a default constructor because it is *stateful* (it needs the segment manager) and thus the allocator needs to be passed. The copy constructor copies the allocator from the source object. The assignment operator does not have to copy the allocator since the original allocator can be used.

We need to take care with the implementation of the destructor. The `deallocate()` function of the allocator does not call the destructor of the object but it only removes the memory. Thus before calling `deallocate()` we explicitly call the destructors of the object:

```
    // Use by default the STL heap allocator.
    template<typename TAllocator=std::allocator<Point> >
    class BasicLine
    {
    public:
        // Define typedefs for easing usage of Point allocator.
        typedef typename TAllocator::pointer            pointer;
        typedef typename TAllocator::const_pointer   const_pointer;
        typedef typename TAllocator::reference          reference;
        typedef typename TAllocator::const_reference const_reference;
        typedef typename TAllocator::size_type          size_type;
        typedef typename TAllocator::difference_type difference_type;

    private:
        // The embedded points.
        pointer m_p1;
        pointer m_p2;
```

```
    // The allocator to use.
    TAllocator m_allocator;

public:

    // Default constructor.
    BasicLine(const TAllocator& allocator=TAllocator()):
        m_allocator(allocator)
    {
        m_p1=m_allocator.allocate(1);
        m_p2=m_allocator.allocate(1);
    }

    // Constructor with points.
    BasicLine(const Point& p1, const Point& p2,
            const TAllocator& allocator=TAllocator()):
        m_allocator(allocator)
    {
        // Allocate points and copy the input points to it.
        m_p1=m_allocator.allocate(1); *m_p1=p1;
        m_p2=m_allocator.allocate(1); *m_p2=p2;
    }

    // Copy constructor (Deep copy).
    BasicLine(const BasicLine<TAllocator>& source):
        m_allocator(source.m_allocator)
    {
        // Allocate points and copy the source points to it
        m_p1=m_allocator.allocate(1); *m_p1=*source.m_p1;
        m_p2=m_allocator.allocate(1); *m_p2=*source.m_p2;
    }

    // Destructor.
    ~BasicLine()
    {
        // Deallocate does not call destructor thus we need to do that
        // first.
        m_p1->~Point();
        m_p2->~Point();

        // Deallocate the points using allocator object.
        m_allocator.deallocate(m_p1, 1);
        m_allocator.deallocate(m_p2, 1);
    }

    // Get the start-point.
    const Point& StartPoint() const
    {
        return *m_p1;
    }

    // Get the end-point.
    const Point& EndPoint() const
    {
        return *m_p2;
    }

    // Set the start-point.
    void StartPoint(const Point& p)
    {
        *m_p1=p;
    }

    // Set the end-point.
    void EndPoint(const Point& p)
```

```
    {
        *m_p2=p;
    }

    // Assignment operator (deep copy).
    BasicLine<TAllocator>& operator = (const BasicLine<TAllocator>& source)
    {
        // Copy the points (no need to copy allocator).
        *m_p1=*source.m_p1;
        *m_p2=*source.m_p2;

        return *this;
    }

    // Send the line to an ostream.
    friend std::ostream& operator << (std::ostream& os,
                                      const BasicLine<TAllocator>& l)
    {
        os<<"Line("<<*l.m_p1<<", "<<*l.m_p2<<")";
        return os;
    }
};
```

The line class can now be used by specifying the allocator type to use. We use typedefs to make the code easier to read. We define a `PointAllocator` type that allocates `Point` instances in managed shared memory which are then used to define a `Line` type that allocates its points in managed shared memory:

```
// Typedef for a managed shared memory Point allocator used by the line.
typedef allocator<Point, managed_shared_memory::segment_manager>
    PointAllocator;

// Typedef for a line using the point allocator.
typedef BasicLine<PointAllocator> Line;
```

These typedefs are now used to create `BasicLine` objects. In the following example we create a `managed_shared_memory` object and a `PointAllocator` for that memory. Furthermore, we create two `Line` objects using the normal `construct()` functions and they create their points using the given allocator. The two lines are deleted from the managed segment when finished:

```
// Create managed shared memory segment and allocator.
managed_shared_memory segment(create_only, "MySharedMemory", 1024);
PointAllocator allocator(segment.get_segment_manager());

// Create l1 and l2 that is a copy of l1.
// A PointAllocator is statefull and does not have a default constructor.
// So in this case we need to pass an allocator.
Line* l1=segment.construct<Line>("Line1")(Point(5, 10), Point(20, 30),
                                          allocator);
Line* l2=segment.construct<Line>("Line2")(*l1, allocator);
std::cout<<"Line1: "<<*l1<<std::endl;
std::cout<<"Line2: "<<*l2<<std::endl;

// Change l1.
l1->StartPoint(Point(99, 89));
l1->EndPoint(Point(77, 66));
std::cout<<"Line1 changed: "<<*l1<<std::endl;
std::cout<<"Line2 unchanged: "<<*l2<<std::endl;

// Delete the lines from the segments and remove shared memory.
segment.destroy_ptr(l1);
segment.destroy_ptr(l2);
```

```
shared_memory_object::remove("MySharedMemory");
```

When a `BasicLine` object is created without template arguments the default allocator (`std::allocator`) is used which of course allocates the points on the heap in the normal way:

```
// Line in normal memory.
// STL allocator is stateless and thus has a default constructor. In this
// case we do no need to pass an allocator because it can use the default
// created allocator.
BasicLine<> l3(Point(33, 44), Point(22, 11));
std::cout<<"Line in normal memory: "<<l3<<std::endl;
```

11.6.9 Other Allocators

The `allocator` class is a general purpose allocator and it is suitable in most situations. There are two other allocator types:

- *Segregated storage allocators*: `node_allocator`, `private_node_allocator`, `cached_node_allocator`
- *Adaptive pool allocators*: `adaptive_pool`, `private_adaptive_pool`, `cached_adaptive_pool`

Segregated storage allocators perform better when we allocate many objects of the same type. It also wastes less memory that is normally needed for housekeeping duties. The segregated storage allocator concepts are analogue to those in the boost::pool library that we discussed in chapter 14. The `node_allocator` is analogous to `boost::fast_pool_allocator`. The `private_node_allocator` has its own segregated storage pool and thus does not need synchronisation; however, it consumes more memory. The `cached_node_allocator` combines the previous two allocators by caching pieces for private use thus saving on synchronisation overhead while minimising memory usage.

The *adaptive pool allocator* solves one problem that node allocators experience, namely that the memory used by node allocators can only grow. When memory is deallocated it will be stored in the list of free nodes but the memory will never be returned to the segment manager. This memory can only be reused by objects that use the same node pool. The adaptive pool allocators can also return unused nodes to the segment manager at the cost of performance and space efficiency. The private and cached versions of the adaptive pool are analogous to the private and cached node allocators.

11.6.10 STL Compatible Containers

The STL containers cannot be placed in managed segments. This is because most STL implementations use raw pointers and cannot make use of offset pointers (`offset_ptr`). Therefore the Boost interprocess library provides the STL compatible containers `list`, `vector`, `map` and `string` among others that can be used in managed segments.

These containers are in the namespace `boost::interprocess` and the include files are stored in the '*boost/interproces/containers*' directory. For example, the `list` class is in the header file:

```
#include <boost/interprocess/containers/list.hpp>
```

We need to specify the data type stored in the container and the `boost::interprocess::allocator` type to use when creating an instance of a container. The `boost::interprocess::allocator` is a template class that has as template arguments the type to create and the type of the segment manager. In the example below we first define a typedef for a `Line` that uses an allocator for `Point` objects. Then it defines a list of `Line` objects using an allocator that creates `Lines`:

```
// Typedef for a managed shared memory Point allocator
// and a line using that allocator.
typedef allocator<Point, managed_shared_memory::segment_manager>
    PointAllocator;
typedef BasicLine<PointAllocator> Line;

// Typedef for a managed shared memory Line allocator
// and the list of lines using that allocator.
typedef allocator<Line, managed_shared_memory::segment_manager>
    LineAllocator;
typedef list<Line, LineAllocator> LineList;
```

The following example creates lists of lines in a shared memory segment and adds three lines to the lists. We only need to create one *allocator* object with a `void` as template argument which then can be used for both `PointAllocator` and `LineAllocator`. This is possible due to the fact that the *allocator* class has a conversion constructor that is used to create the right allocator from a `void` allocator.

The list can be created in two ways, first by passing the allocator and second by passing the segment manager of the managed segment. The second constructor automatically creates an allocator from the passed segment manager:

```
// Create the managed shared memory.
managed_shared_memory segment(create_only, "MySharedMemory", 5*1024);

// Display free memory.
std::cout<<"Free memory before list creation: "
        <<segment.get_free_memory()<<std::endl;

// Create an allocator with the segment manager to use.
// We create an allocator for voids.
// Since the allocator has a templated converting constructor,
// we can pass this one to both the list and line classes.
allocator<void, managed_shared_memory::segment_manager>
alloc(segment.get_segment_manager());

// Create a list called "MyList1" in the managed memory segment
// passing the allocator.
LineList* list1=segment.construct<LineList>("MyList1")(alloc);

// Create a list called "MyList2" in the managed memory segment passing
// the segment manager. It will create an allocator internally.
LineList* list2=
    segment.construct<LineList>("MyList2")(segment.get_segment_manager());

// Create some elements in the list.
for (int i=0; i<3; i++)
{
    list1->push_back(Line(Point(-i, -i), Point(i, i), alloc));
    list2->push_back(Line(Point(-i, i), Point(i, -i), alloc));
}

// Display free memory.
std::cout<<"Free memory after list creation: "
        <<segment.get_free_memory()<<std::endl;
```

These lists need to be created using the `construct()` function in a managed segment. When created in the regular way (on the stack or heap) the list itself will be in normal memory while the elements of the list will be in IPC memory.

Another process can now open the shared memory segment and find the lists. Note that unless we wish to add new lines to the lists we do not need to create an allocator because there is already an allocator associated with the existing lists and lines in the managed segment:

```
// Open the managed shared memory.
managed_shared_memory segment(open_only, "MySharedMemory");

// Display free memory.
std::cout<<"Free memory before list deletion: "
        <<segment.get_free_memory()<<std::endl;

// Find the lists called "MyList1" & "MyList2" in the
// managed memory segment.
LineList* list1=segment.find<LineList>("MyList1").first;
LineList* list2=segment.find<LineList>("MyList2").first;
if (list1!=NULL && list2!=NULL)
{
    std::cout<<"Lists found: "<<std::endl;

    // Print the lists.
    std::cout<<"List 1: "; Print(*list1);
    std::cout<<"List 2: "; Print(*list2);

    // Remove the lists, should also remove the lines & points.
    segment.destroy_ptr(list1);
    segment.destroy_ptr(list2);
    std::cout<<"Lists removed"<<std::endl;

    // Display free memory.
    std::cout<<"Free memory after list deletion: "
            <<segment.get_free_memory()<<std::endl;
}
else std::cout<<"Lists not found."<<std::endl;
```

The `Print()` function used above to print the list is defined as follows:

```
// Print the container.
template <typename T>
void Print(const T& container)
{
    T::const_iterator end=container.end();
    for (T::const_iterator it=container.begin(); it!=end; it++)
    {
        std::cout<<*it<<", ";
    }
    std::cout<<std::endl;
}
```

We summarise the available STL compatible containers in boost::interprocess:
* `vector` (boost/interprocess/containers/vector.hpp).
* `deque` (boost/interprocess/containers/deque.hpp).
* `list` (boost/interprocess/containers/list.hpp).
* `slist` (boost/interprocess/containers/slist.hpp) (single linked list, not in STL).
* `set` / `multiset` (boost/interprocess/containers/set.hpp).
* `map` (boost/interprocess/containers/map.hpp).
* `flat_set` / `flat_multi_set` (boost/interprocess/containers/flat_set.hpp) (not in STL, faster searching but slower insertions than regular set)).
* `flat_map` / `flat_multi_map` (boost/interprocess/containers/flat_map.hpp) (not in STL, faster searching but slower insertions than regular map).

- `basic_string` ((boost/interprocess/containers/string.hpp) `string` and `wstring` specialisations are only for regular memory.

11.6.11 Managed External Buffer and Managed Heap Memory

There are situations when we wish to use the functionality of managed segments but do not need to share them with other processes, for example if we create complex structures in memory and serialise the structure as one memory block to disk. This approach would be more efficient than serialising the whole object graph using the Boost serialisation library, for example.

In some (embedded) systems dynamic memory may be too expensive to use while a managed segment is more efficient. In these situations the boost interprocess library provides managed segments for regular memory buffers that are called `basic_managed_external_buffer` and `basic_managed_heap_memory`. These managed segment classes work with regular memory instead of IPC memory. Thus, it is not shared between processes and it does not need process synchronisation.

11.6.11.1 Managed External Buffer

The *managed external buffer* wraps a memory buffer and provides managed segment functionality. The memory buffer can be static (global) memory, a memory buffer on the stack (local array) or it can even be a buffer created on the heap. We can use this class for direct access to the memory for example, when we need to save the memory to disk or send it over a network. The header file and definition are as follows:

```
#include <boost/interprocess/managed_external_buffer.hpp>

template
<
    typename CharType, typename MemoryAlgorithm,
    template<typename IndexConfig> typename IndexType
>
class basic_managed_external_buffer;
```

There are typedefs to make working with managed external buffers easier. Both use the default index type:
- `managed_external_buffer`   `// offset_ptr - char`
- `wmanaged_external_buffer`   `// offset_ptr - wchar_t`

There are no typedefs for a `void*` version of the managed external buffer. We note that these typedefs use a `MemoryAlgorithm` type that does not use any synchronisation mechanism because they can only be used inside a single process.

The constructor of a managed external buffer receives the address and the size of a static memory buffer that it manages. However, the address of the buffer cannot be arbitrary. The memory algorithm used by the managed segment expects a certain alignment of the memory address; for example the address must be on an 8 byte boundary.

We give an example of a vector of lines stored in a new managed external buffer. We note that the pointer to the buffer is aligned correctly by retrieving the alignment value from the managed external buffer. This is the reason why the size of the created buffer is incremented with the alignment value. Next, the memory buffer is assigned to a managed external buffer. Finally, we allocate a vector in the managed segment and we write the buffer to a disk file:

```
// Typedef for a managed shared memory Point allocator
```

```cpp
// and a line using that allocator.
typedef allocator<Point, managed_external_buffer::segment_manager>
    PointAllocator;
typedef BasicLine<PointAllocator> Line;

// Typedef for a managed shared memory Line allocator and the vector of
lines using that allocator.
typedef allocator<Line, managed_external_buffer::segment_manager>
    LineAllocator;
typedef vector<Line, LineAllocator> LineVector;

// The size of the buffer.
const int size=2048;

// Create a file from a managed external buffer segment.
void CreateFile()
{
    // Create buffer. The memory algorithm needs to have the
    // memory aligned at a certain boundary.
    // Thus we create a few extra bytes and make sure the buffer
    // passed to the manageed buffer is properly aligned.
    const int alignment=
        managed_external_buffer::memory_algorithm::Alignment;
    char data[size+alignment-1];
    char* buffer=data+(int)data%alignment;

    // Create the managed external buffer.
    managed_external_buffer segment(create_only, buffer, size);

    // Create an allocator with the segment manager to use.
    // We create an allocator for voids.
    // Since the allocator has a templated converting constructor,
    // we can pass this one to both the list and line classes.
    allocator<void, managed_external_buffer::segment_manager>
        alloc(segment.get_segment_manager());

    // Create an empty vector called "Lines" in the
    // managed memory segment passing the allocator.
    LineVector* lines=segment.construct<LineVector>("Lines")(alloc);

    std::cout<<"Vector adress: "<<(void*)lines<<", "
            <<((int)lines)%4<<std::endl;

    // Create some elements in the vector.
    for (int i=0; i<3; i++)
    {
        lines->push_back(Line(Point(-i, -i), Point(i, i), alloc));
    }

    // Save the buffer to a file.
    std::ofstream os("data.bin");
    if (os)
    {
        os.write(buffer, size);
        std::cout<<"File written..."<<std::endl;
    }
    else std::cout<<"Error writing file..."<<std::endl;
}
```

When the file is saved another program can load the file in a buffer, open a managed external buffer and find the vector. We note that when the managed external buffer is created the parameter open_only is passed since the buffer already contains the data:

```cpp
// Load a file in a managed external buffer segment.
bool LoadFile()
```

```
{
    // Create buffer. The memory algorithm needs to have the
    // memory aligned at a certain boundary.
    // Thus we create a few extra bytes and make sure the buffer
    // passed to the manageed buffer is properly aligned.
    const int alignment=managed_external_buffer::
        memory_algorithm::Alignment;
    char data[size+alignment-1];
    char* buffer=data+(int)data%alignment;

    // Load the file into the buffer.
    std::ifstream is("data.bin");
    if (is)
    {
        is.read(buffer, size);
        std::cout<<"File read..."<<std::endl;
    }
    else
    {
        std::cout<<"Error opening file..."<<std::endl;
        return;
    }

    // Create the managed external buffer.
    managed_external_buffer segment(open_only, buffer, size);

    // Find a vector called "Lines" in the managed memory segment
    // passing the allocator.
    LineVector* lines=segment.find<LineVector>("Lines").first;

    // Print the lines in the vector.
    if (lines!=NULL)
    {
        for (int i=0; i!=lines->size(); i++)
        {
            std::cout<<(*lines)[i]<<std::endl;
        }
    }
}
```

11.6.11.2 Managed Heap Memory

The managed heap memory creates a buffer on the heap. The base address of this memory cannot be retrieved. For this reason it is not suitable if we need direct access to this memory. But it can be used in situations when allocating memory using new/delete operations is too slow. The header file and definition are:

```
#include <boost/interprocess/managed_heap_memory.hpp>

template
<
    typename CharType, typename MemoryAlgorithm,
    template<typename IndexConfig> typename IndexType
>
class basic_managed_heap_memory;
```

There are some typedefs that make working with managed heap memory easier. Both use the default index type:

- managed_external_buffer   // offset_ptr - char
- wmanaged_external_buffer   // offset_ptr - wchar_t

There are no typedefs for a `void*` version of the managed heap memory. Note that these typedefs use a `MemoryAlgorithm` type that does not use any synchronisation mechanism because they can only be used inside a single process.

The constructor of the managed heap memory receives the size of the memory block to be created. The memory is allocated internally on the heap.

The size of the managed heap memory buffer can be incremented by calling the `grow()` function. This will create a new buffer and copy the data. This will only work if you use offset pointers since regular pointers will become invalid when the data is moved.

11.6.12 Other Managed Segment Functionality

We have concentrated on the basic functionality of managed segments to get you started. Managed segments provide more functionality that are useful in advanced scenarios, for example:
- Raw handles to allocated memory blocks.
- Unique instance construction (*Singleton* objects).
- Growing managed segments.
- Memory reservation in segments.
- Allocating aligned memory in segments.
- Resizable memory blocks (`allocation_command`).
- Private managed segments (`open_copy_on_write`).

11.7 Summary and Conclusions

We have introduced shared memory and memory mapped files as a means to support interprocess communication (IPC). We also saw that managed memory segments make it possible to create complex structures in IPC memory and that they also help with synchronisation. Finally, we saw that the functionality provided by managed segments can also be used with regular memory buffers.

We will discuss *process synchronisation* in chapter 12.

12 Boost Interprocess II: Process Synchronisation

12.1 Introduction and Objectives

In this chapter we discuss process synchronisation mechanisms in IPC. In chapter 11 we saw that processes can communicate with each other using shared memory and memory mapped files. The managed segment classes also provide mechanisms to let us atomically create complex structures in IPC memory. But when multiple processes are accessing the same data we need to synchronise code as in the case of multiple threads.

Boost interprocess provides several synchronisation mechanisms that have many similarities with synchronisation mechanisms used with threads. The difference here is that the interprocess synchronisation mechanisms also work when the threads are in different processes. We discussed multithreading in a single process in Demming 2010.

The interprocess synchronisation mechanisms can be divided into named and anonymous mechanisms. We discuss them here.

With *named synchronisation mechanisms* one process creates the synchronisation mechanism with a name while the other process opens the existing synchronisation mechanism by specifying that name. When creating a synchronisation object we specify the creation mode (`create_only`, `open_only`, etc.).

When using named synchronisation mechanisms both processes use their own synchronisation object that accesses the same underlying synchronisation resource.

The advantage of named mechanisms is that they are easy to use, in particular for simple synchronisation tasks where there is no need to create IPC memory.

Anonymous synchronisation mechanisms do not have a name. That means that the synchronisation mechanism must be passed to another process by storing the synchronisation object in IPC memory. When using anonymous synchronisation mechanisms both processes use the same synchronisation object. In contrast to named mechanisms anonymous mechanisms can be created only. When we wish to get an existing anonymous synchronisation object we need to find it in a mapped region.

The advantage of mechanisms stored in IPC memory is that they can be saved to disk and are still available after a reboot of the system when an IPC mechanism is used with file system persistence.

12.2 Mutexes

A basic synchronisation mechanism is the *mutex* (mutual exclusion) mechanism and it has named and anonymous versions. A mutex guarantees that only one thread (no matter which process the thread resides in) can lock the given mutex object at any given time. There can be only one thread executing the code protected by the mutex. The other threads are blocked.

We can differentiate between recursive and non-recursive mutexes. A *recursive mutex* can be locked multiple times by the same thread. It must then be unlocked the same number of times to release it. A *non-recursive mutex* can only be locked once by the same thread. The results are undefined when a non-recursive mutex is locked for a second time by a thread.

12.2.1 Mutex Operations

A mutex has the following functions:
- `void lock();`
  Gets ownership of the mutex. When a thread has ownership of this mutex the `lock()` function will block a second thread until the first thread releases the mutex.
- `bool try_lock();`
  Gets ownership of the mutex when it is not already owned by another thread. When another thread already has ownership of the mutex it returns immediately. The return value indicates if ownership was taken.
- `bool timed_lock(const boost::posix_time::ptime& abs_time);`
  Gets ownership of the mutex when it is not already owned by another thread. When another thread already has ownership of this mutex it will block until the other thread releases the mutux or until the specified time expired (time given is the absolute end time, not a duration). The return value indicates if ownership was taken.
- `void unlock();`
  The calling thread releases ownership of the mutex.

12.2.2 Named Mutex

There are two named mutex classes, namely a *normal mutex* (named_mutex) and a *recursive mutex* (named_recursive_mutex). The required header files are:

```
#include <boost/interprocess/sync/named_mutex.hpp>
#include <boost/interprocess/sync/named_recursive_mutex.hpp>
```

We will now give an example of a named mutex. In this case multiple processes write logging information to a file. Of course only one process can write to the file at a given time. Since there is no need to share data we use a named mutex for synchronisation. The named mutex is created with the `open_or_create` option. Thus the first process will create the named mutex while the other processes opens this mutex. The code that opens and writes to a file is between mutex `lock()` and `unlock()` calls.

The `sleep()` function is used to create a small delay that enables us to see that a process waits for another process to unlock the mutex:

```
// Create or open a named mutex.
named_mutex mutex(open_or_create, "MyMutex");

// Repeat.
for (int i=0; i<10; i++)
{
    // First aquire a lock the mutex.
    cout<<"Trying to get lock..."<<endl;
    mutex.lock();
    cout<<"- Mutex taken."<<endl;

    // Open or create file and append data to it.
    ofstream os("data.txt", ios_base::app);
    if (os)
    {
        os<<"Thread id: "<<boost::this_thread::get_id()
          <<", iteration: "<<i<<endl;
    }

    // Wait for a second to see if other processes are blocked.
    boost::this_thread::sleep(boost::posix_time::seconds(1));

    // Release the lock.
    mutex.unlock();
```

```
        cout<<"Lock released."<<endl<<endl;;
}
```

We need to remove the mutex when finished. This is done by the static `remove()` function of the named mutex:

```
// Ask to delete the file.
cout<<"Delete file & mutex? (y/n): ";
char c; cin>>c;

// Delete the file and remove mutex.
if (c=='y' || c=='Y')
{
    // Delete file.
    if (remove("data.txt")) cout<<"File deleted."<<endl;
    else cout<<"Deletion failed."<<endl;

    // Remove mutex from system.
    if (named_mutex::remove("MyMutex")) cout<<"mutex removed."<<endl;
    else cout<<"Mutex remove failed."<<endl;
}
```

12.2.3 Anonymous Mutex

There are two anonymous mutex classes, namely a *normal mutex* (`interprocess_mutex`) and a *recursive mutex* (`interprocess_recursive_mutex`). The required header files are:

```
#include <boost/interprocess/sync/interprocess_mutex.hpp>
#include <boost/interprocess/sync/interprocess_recursive_mutex.hpp>
```

Below we see an example of an anonymous mutex. In this example an `Account` object is shared between processes by storing it in shared memory. Since the account is not allowed to have a negative balance the combination of the balance checking and withdraw functions must execute as an atomic operation. This is done by using a mutex. In this case the mutex is stored in the `Account` object and thus in shared memory. Therefore an anonymous mutex can be used.

The `Account` class has a data member for an interprocess mutex. The mutex object is used to synchronise the `Withdraw()` function. The `sleep()` function is used to create a small delay so that it is possible to see one process waiting for the other before it can withdraw money:

```
class Account
{
private:
    // The account number, balance and the mutex to synchronise on.
    double m_accountNumber;
    int m_balance;
    interprocess_mutex m_mutex;

public:
    // Nested class for exception.
    class NoFundsException { };

    // Default constructor.
    Account()
    {
        m_accountNumber=0;
        m_balance=0;
    }
```

```
    // Constructor with account number and initial balance.
    Account(int accountNumber, double balance)
    {
        m_accountNumber=accountNumber;
        m_balance=balance;
    }

    // Get the account number.
    int AccountNumber()
    {
        return m_accountNumber;
    }

    // Get the balance.
    double Balance()
    {
        return m_balance;
    }

    // Set the balance.
    void Balance(double value)
    {
        m_balance=value;
    }

    // Withdraw an amount. Synchronised with mutex.
    void Withdraw(double amount)
    {
        // Acquire lock on mutex. If the lock is already locked,
        // it waits till unlocked.
        m_mutex.lock();

        if (m_balance-amount>=0)
        {
            // For testing we now give other threads a change to run.
            boost::this_thread::sleep(boost::posix_time::seconds(1));

            // Withdraw the money.
            m_balance-=amount;
        }
        else
        {
            // Before throwing an exception, don't forget the unlock
            // the mutex.
            m_mutex.unlock();
            throw NoFundsException();
        }

        // Release lock on mutex. Forget this and it will hang (deadlock).
        m_mutex.unlock();
    }
};
```

Now we can use the Account class in shared memory. The following example repeatedly withdraws money from the account until a NoFundsException is thrown. The mutex object of an account object will be automatically removed from memory when the account object is deleted from shared memory because the mutex is a data member of the account class. Therefore there is no need to explicitly remove the mutex as in the named mutex example.

```
    // The amount the withdraw each time.
    double amount=50.0;

    // Create or open the managed shared memory.
```

```
managed_shared_memory segment(open_or_create, "MySharedMemory", 1024);

// Create or find the account object (is already synchronised).
Account* account=segment.find_or_construct<Account>("MyAccount")(0, 1000);

// Print start balance.
cout<<"Balance at startup: "<<account->Balance()<<endl;

try
{
    while(true)
    {
        // Withdraw money. This is synchronised inside the Withdraw()
        // function.
        account->Withdraw(amount);
        cout<<"Withdrawn "<<amount<<". Balance: "
            <<account->Balance()<<endl;

        // Wait a little for the next iteration.
        boost::this_thread::sleep(boost::posix_time::millisec(100));
    }
}
catch (Account::NoFundsException& ex)
{
    cout<<"Can't withdraw anymore. No balance."<<endl;
}
catch (interprocess_exception& ex)
{
    cout<<"Interprocess error:"<<ex.what()<<endl;
}

// Wait for <enter>.
cout<<"Press a <enter> destroy account and removed shared memory."<<endl;
cin.get();

// Remove the account.
segment.destroy_ptr(account);

// Remove the shared memory.
if (shared_memory_object::remove("MySharedMemory")==true)
{
    cout<<"Shared memory removed."<<endl;
}
else cout<<"Error while removing shared memory."<<endl;
```

12.2.4 Scoped Lock

A mutex must be unlocked after the thread has finished working with the shared resource in order to avoid deadlock situations. But programming mistakes are easily made especially when some code inside the synchronised block throws an exception. It is easy to forget to unlock the mutex in the exception handling/throwing code.

To resolve these potential problems, a mutex is normally used in combination with a *scoped lock*. The scoped_lock class wraps a mutex and unlocks the mutex in its destructor. When a scoped lock is created on the stack the mutex will automatically be unlocked when the scoped lock goes out of scope.

To use the scoped lock we include the following header file:

```
#include <boost/interprocess/sync/scoped_lock.hpp>
```

This is a template class that receives the type of mutex it should wrap as template argument. The mutex must be passed when a scoped lock is constructed. The constructor will immediately try to lock the passed mutex and block until the lock has been acquired. When we pass `try_to_lock_type` as second argument to the constructor it will use a *try lock* to lock the mutex. When a posix time is passed as second argument it will use a *timed lock*. Since a try lock and timed lock are non-blocking we need to check if a lock was taken by using the `owns()` member function.

Below we see a section of the named mutex example using a scoped lock. We note that it is not necessary to unlock the mutex. It is automatically unlocked when the scoped lock goes out of scope:

```
// Create or open a named mutex.
named_mutex mutex(open_or_create, "MyMutex");

// Repeat.
for (int i=0; i<10; i++)
{
    // First aquire a lock the mutex using a scoped_lock.
    cout<<"Trying to get lock..."<<endl;
    scoped_lock<named_mutex> lock(mutex);
    cout<<"- Mutex taken."<<endl;

    // Open or create file and append data to it.
    ofstream os("data.txt", ios_base::app);
    if (os) os<<"Thread id: "<<boost::this_thread::get_id()
            <<", iteration: "<<i<<endl;

    // Wait for a second to see if other processes are blocked.
    boost::this_thread::sleep(boost::posix_time::seconds(1));

} // Mutex released here by scoped_lock.
```

An interprocess mutex can also be wrapped by the scoped lock. As an example, we discuss the account's `Withdraw()` function using a scoped lock. It is not necessary to unlock the mutex when an exception is thrown since it will be automatically unlocked when the scoped lock goes out of scope.

```
// Withdraw an amount. Synchronised with mutex.
void Withdraw(double amount)
{
    // Acquire lock on mutex using scoped_lock.
    // If the lock is already locked, it waits till unlocked.
    scoped_lock<interprocess_mutex> lock(m_mutex);

    if (m_balance-amount>=0)
    {
        // For testing we now give other threads a change to run.
        boost::this_thread::sleep(boost::posix_time::seconds(1));

        // Withdraw the money.
        m_balance-=amount;
    }
    else
    {
        // Mutex is automatically unlocked because scoped_lock
        // goes out of scope.
        throw NoFundsException();
    }

} // Mutex automatically released because scoped_lock goes out of scope.
```

It is recommended to use a mutex in combination with a scoped lock since it reduces the chance of a programming mistake that can cause a *deadlock*.

12.3 Condition Variables

Mutexes are useful for regulating access to shared resources but they are not very suitable as a mechanism for notifying other processes. For notification of other processes the Boost interprocess library provides *condition variables*. One process waits until a condition is met by waiting on a condition variable. Another process can then notify the waiting process to tell it that it can continue by using the condition variable.

A condition variable works in conjunction with a mutex to provide synchronisation functionality. First, the process that needs to wait for a condition locks the mutex. Then the process waits on the condition variable which unlocks the mutex and waits atomically until another process performs a *notify* on the condition variable. When a notification is sent the lock on the mutex is acquired again before the wait is over. Thus before and after the wait it is guaranteed that we have locked the mutex.

Boost provides a *named condition variable class* (`named_condition`) and an *anonymous condition variable class* (`interprocess_condition`). They need to be used with the corresponding mutex type. Thus a named condition variable must use the named mutex and it may not use the anonymous mutex. The header files are:

```
#include <boost/interprocess/sync/named_condition.hpp>
#include <boost/interprocess/sync/interprocess_condition.hpp>
```

An application of condition variables is the *Producer/Consumer pattern* that we introduced in Demming 2010 in the context of Boost Thread. The producer creates data that will be processed by the consumer. The data is stored in a queue which must be safe to access by multiple processes. When the queue is empty the consumer must wait until the producer puts some more data into the queue. The consumer is then woken up by sending a *notify* using a condition variable. The producer-consumer pattern is depicted in Figure 12.1.

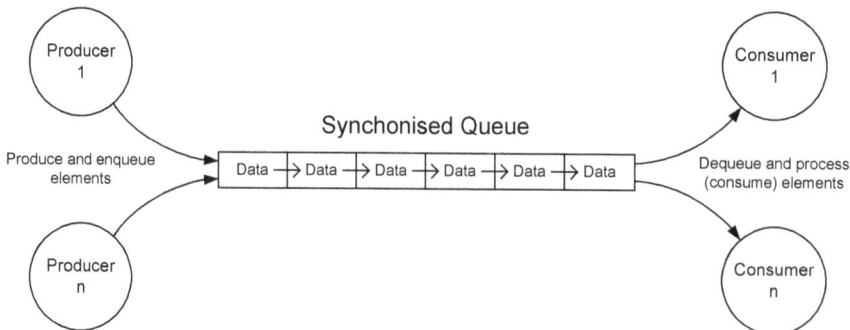

Figure 12.1 Producer-Consumer Pattern

All the synchronisation and notification is done in the `SynchronisedQueue` class. Since an STL queue cannot allocate its elements in IPC memory, we use a `boost::interprocess::deque` to store the data. The `SynchronisedQueue` has two template arguments; namely, the type to store and the allocator to use for allocating elements. There is one constructor that initialises the internal deque with the allocator to use.

For synchronisation and notification the class contains an `interprocess_mutex` and `interprocess_condition` as data member:

```
// Queue class that has interprocess synchronisation and notification.
template <typename T, typename TAllocator>
class SynchronisedQueue
{
private:
    deque<T, TAllocator> m_queue;      // Use boost::interprocess deque
                                       // to store data.
    interprocess_mutex m_mutex;        // The mutex to synchronise on.
    interprocess_condition m_cond;     // The condition to wait for.

public:

    // Constructor with the allocator to use for the queue.
    SynchronisedQueue(const TAllocator& a): m_queue(a)
    {
    }

    ...
};
```

The consumer uses the `Dequeue()` function of the `SynchronisedQueue` class. It first aquires a lock on the mutex data member for save access to the internal deque member. When the queue is empty it waits on the condition variable. Note that the `wait()` function accepts the locked mutex. The `wait()` function releases the lock so others can access the deque member. Optionally, we can pass a Posix time specifying the maximum time to wait. When a notification is sent the lock on the mutex is required and the `wait()` function is exited. Again there is a check to test if there is data in the queue since the data inserted in the queue that caused the notify could already have been dequeued by another process. If there is data in the queue it will be removed from the queue and returned. The lock will be automatically released when exiting the `Dequeue()` function:

```
// Get data from the queue. Wait for data if not available.
T Dequeue()
{
    // Acquire lock on the queue.
    scoped_lock<interprocess_mutex> lock(m_mutex);

    // When there is no data, wait till someone fills it. Lock is
    // automatically released in the wait and obtained again after the
    // wait.
    while (m_queue.size()==0) m_cond.wait(lock);

    // Retrieve the data from the queue
    T result=m_queue.front(); m_queue.pop_front();
    return result;

} // Lock is automatically released here.
```

The producer uses the `Enqueue()` function of the `SynchronisedQueue` class. It aquires a lock on the mutex data member and pushes data onto the internal `deque` member. Then it calls the `notify_one()` function on the condition variable to notify one of the waiting processes. When `notify_all()` is used all waiting processes will be notified. The lock will be automatically released when exiting the `Enqueue()` function:

```
// Add data to the queue and notify others.
void Enqueue(const T& data)
{
    // Acquire lock on the queue.
```

```
scoped_lock<interprocess_mutex> lock(m_mutex);

// Add the data to the queue.
m_queue.push_back(data);

// Notify others that data is ready.
m_cond.notify_one();

} // Lock is automatically released here.
```

The synchronised queue can now be used to send data from one process (*producer*) to another process (*consumer*). A regular STL string cannot be used in IPC memory when we wish to send strings between two processes. Therefore we use a specialisation of the `boost::interprocess::basic_string` class. The `basic_string` class needs an allocator. To make things simpler we use typedefs to define a `char` allocator for shared memory that is used by a string of characters.
We also define a string allocator for shared memory that is used by the specialisation of the `SynchronisedQueue` class:

```
// Regular strings can't be put in IPC memory
// so we use a boost::interprocess::basic_string.
// The interprocess string needs an allocator for chars.
typedef allocator<char, managed_shared_memory::segment_manager>
    CharAllocator;
typedef basic_string<char, std::char_traits<char>, CharAllocator>
    shm_string;

// Typedef for a managed shared memory allocator used by
// the synchronised queue of shm_strings.
typedef allocator<shm_string, managed_shared_memory::segment_manager>
    StringAllocator;
typedef SynchronisedQueue<shm_string, StringAllocator> StringQueue;
```

The queue for strings can now be used by the producer. It opens an existing shared memory segment. If the segment does not already exist it will create a new shared memory segment. Then it tries to find an existing queue in the segment and when not found it creates a new queue. It then adds strings to the queue using a looping mechanism. Finally, an empty string is queued to indicate that there is no more data:

```
// Create or open the managed shared memory.
managed_shared_memory segment(open_or_create, "MySharedMemory", 1024);

// Create an allocator with the segment manager to use.
// We create an allocator for voids.
// Since the allocator has a templated converting constructor,
// we can pass this one to both the string and queue classes.
allocator<void, managed_shared_memory::segment_manager>
    alloc(segment.get_segment_manager());

// Create or find the string queue object (is already synchronised).
StringQueue* queue=
    segment.find_or_construct<StringQueue>("MyQueue")(alloc);

// Producer started.
std::cout<<"Producer started. Putting data in the queue."<<std::endl;

// Put strings in the queue.
int data=0;
while (data!=10)
{
    // Produce a string and store in the queue.
    std::stringstream tmp; tmp<<"Number: "<<data++;
```

```
    shm_string str(tmp.c_str(), alloc);
    queue->Enqueue(str);
    std::cout<<"Data produced: "<<str<<std::endl;

    // Sleep a second.
    boost::this_thread::sleep(boost::posix_time::seconds(1));
}

// Insert empty string to indicate end.
queue->Enqueue(shm_string("", alloc));
```

The consumer also creates or opens a shared memory segment with the same name and creates or finds the named queue of strings. Due to the fact that both producer and consumer use the `open_or_create` option when creating the shared memory segment and the `find_or_construct()` function when creating the queue it does not matter which process starts first. The first process creates the shared memory with the queue and the second process opens the existing shared memory with the queue. Then the consumer retrieves strings from the queue until an empty string is returned after which it deletes the queue and shared memory:

```
// Create or open the managed shared memory.
managed_shared_memory segment(open_or_create, "MySharedMemory", 1024);

// Create an allocator with the segment manager to use.
// We create an allocator for voids. Since the allocator has a
// templated converting constructor,
// we can pass this one to both the string and queue classes.
allocator<void, managed_shared_memory::segment_manager>
    alloc(segment.get_segment_manager());

// Create or find the string queue object (is already synchronised).
StringQueue* queue=
    segment.find_or_construct<StringQueue>("MyQueue")(alloc);

// Consumer started.
std::cout<<"Consumer started. Wating for data..."<<std::endl;

// Retrieve strings from the queue.
shm_string data(alloc);
do
{
    // Retrieve data from the queue.
    data=queue->Dequeue();

    // Display the extracted data.
    if (data!="") std::cout<<"Data consumed: "<<data<<std::endl;
}
while (data!="");

// The queue and shared memory can now be deleted.

// Remove the queue.
segment.destroy_ptr(queue);

// Remove the shared memory.
if (shared_memory_object::remove("MySharedMemory")==true)
std::cout<<"Shared memory removed."<<std::endl;
else std::cout<<"Error while removing shared memory."<<std::endl;
```

12.4 Message Queue

We created our own synchronised queue in the previous section. Boost Interprocess library also provides a `message_queue` class. As the name implies the queue is used for sending messages to another process. A *message* consists of the length of the message and the data in the message. The message is thus raw bytes and not an object. An object can be sent when it is binary serialisable.

Each message also has a priority. The `message_queue` is thus a *priority queue*. Messages with the highest priority will be returned from the queue first.

To use the message queue we use the following include file:

```
#include <boost/interprocess/ipc/message_queue.hpp>
```

The message queue is a named IPC mechanism. To create a queue we specify the name, the maximum number of messages in the queue and the maximum message size. Another process can then open the queue using its name. As with shared memory, the message queue must be removed after use by calling the static `remove()` function specifying the queue's name.

There are three modes for sending and receiving messages:
- *Blocking* (`send()` and `receive()`):
  When the queue is full (when sending) or empty (when receiving) the thread is blocked until there is space in the queue or when there is a new message.
- *Try* (`try_send()` and `try_receive()`):
  Sending or receiving messages will return immediately. When the queue is full (when sending) or empty (when receiving) an error (`bool`) is returned.
- *Timed* (`timed_send()` and `timed_receive()`):
  When the queue is full (when sending) or empty (when receiving), the operation is retried until it succeeds or until the specified time-out (Posix time) is reached in which case an error is returned.

Below we see a message queue example in which a process sends integers to another process. The producer opens an existing queue or creates a new queue if the queue does not already exist. The maximum number of elements is 10 and the size of a message is the size of an integer. Then it queues 20 numbers using the `send()` function which blocks until the message can be queued. We note that a priority is also given. When an element is extracted from the queue the element with the highest priority will be returned first when there is more than one element:

```cpp
// Open exisiting or create a message queue.
message_queue queue(open_or_create, "MyQueue", 10, sizeof(int));

// Send a sequence of numbers. Also priority is generated.
for (int i=0; i!=20; i++)
{
    // Generated a priority.
    unsigned int priority=i+10;

    // Enqueue the sequence number.
    queue.send(&i, sizeof(i), priority);
    std::cout<<"Number queued: "<<i<<", priority: "<<priority<<std::endl;

    // Sleep a second.
    boost::this_thread::sleep(boost::posix_time::seconds(1));
}
```

The consumer also opens or creates a message queue with the same name. It does not matter which process starts first. Then it will dequeue 20 numbers using the `receive()` function. Note that we first need to create space for the message. Since it is a simple integer we can pass the address of an integer variable. The second argument is the size of the receive buffer. The third argument will be filled with the actual received number of bytes. Finally, the fourth argument will be filled with the priority of the element.

When all elements have been extracted the message queue is removed from the system as the following code shows:

```
// Open exisiting or create a message queue.
message_queue queue(open_or_create, "MyQueue", 10, sizeof(int));

// Variable to receive data in.
int number;               // The number.
std::size_t size;         // The number of bytes received.
unsigned int priority;    // The priority of the received message.

// Dequeue the numbers.
for (int i=0; i!=20; i++)
{
    // Dequeue the number.
    queue.receive(&number, sizeof(number), size, priority);
    std::cout<<"Nuber dequeued: "<<number<<", priority: "<<priority
            <<", size: "<<size<<std::endl;
}

// Remove the message queue.
message_queue::remove("MyQueue");
```

12.5 Semaphores

A *semaphore* is an IPC synchronisation mechanism that combines a mutex with a counter. It can be used to control access to resources that have some kind of a maximum. For example, a resource that may only be accessed by a maximum number of clients at the same time. A semaphore can also be used to control access to a buffer that has a maximum number of elements.

The Boost Interprocess library provides a *named semaphore* (`named_semaphore`) and an *anonymous semaphore* (`interprocess_semaphore`). The required include files are:

```
#include <boost/interprocess/sync/named_semaphore.hpp>
#include <boost/interprocess/sync/interprocess_semaphore.hpp>
```

When a semaphore is created it must be set to an initial value. A semaphore provides two basic operations:
- *Wait* (`wait()` / `try_wait()` / `timed_wait()`)
  Test the current count value. Wait when the value is less or equal than zero. Otherwise the count is decremented and the wait function is exited.
- *Post* (`post()`)
  Increment the current count value. If there is one or more blocked threads in a wait, one of them is woken up.

When the initial semaphore counter value is set to one, it effectively works as a mutex (wait is lock, post is unlock). A difference is that the *wait* and *post* can be executed by different threads while with mutexes *lock* and *unlock* must be executed by a single thread.

We now show an example where we implement a *circular buffer* that can be shared between processes. A circular buffer has a finite capacity and will overwrite the last element when the buffer is full. Thus we avoid adding an element when the buffer is full and removing an element when the buffer is empty. We could solve this using mutexes and condition variables but using semaphores is usually more efficient.

The `CircularBuffer` class has template arguments for the type to store and the allocator to use. Internally it uses an *interprocess vector* (not STL vector) to store the data. It has data members to keep track of the current head and tail elements. Furthermore, we have one semaphore that is used to block adding an element when the buffer is full and one semaphore that is used to block removing an element when the buffer is empty. We also need a mutex to synchronise access to the buffer.

The constructor is used to initialise the data members. The `m_full` semaphore is initialised to the capacity of the buffer. The semaphore will block when the counter is decreased to zero. The `m_empty` semaphore is initialised to zero. It blocks initially until adding an element increases the semaphore's counter.

We pass an initial value for the buffer elements to the vector. This is needed because the allocator needs to allocate memory for the buffer but some types for `T` need to be created with an allocator (e.g. `Line` class or `interprocess::string` class) but some do not (e.g. `int, double`). Since the vector class cannot know if an allocator is needed for creating an instance of `T` the initial element value is created externally to the vector and the circular buffer class and the copy constructor of the type takes care of allocation of the type's internal data:

```
// A circular buffer storing Ts. The allocator must create Ts.
template <typename T, typename TAllocator>
class CircularBuffer
{

private:
    vector<T, TAllocator> m_data;     // The vector with data.
    std::size_t m_capacity;           // The capacity of the circular buffer.
    int m_currentIn;                  // The current input element in
                                      // the circular buffer.
    int m_currentOut;                 // The current output element
                                      // in the circular buffer.

    interprocess_mutex m_mutex;       // Synchronisation mutex.
    interprocess_semaphore m_full;    // Semaphore to control access
                                      // in case buffer is full.
    interprocess_semaphore m_empty;   // Semaphore to control access in
                                      // case buffer is empty.

public:
    // Create a circular buffer. The "full" semaphore must block (count==0)
    // when the buffer is full thus the initial value is the capacity.
    // The "empty" semaphore must block (count==0) when the buffer
    // is empty thus the initial value is 0.
    // We need to pass the initial value for the vector elements. We can't
    // create it here since some types need an allocator and some not.
    CircularBuffer(std::size_t capacity, const T& initial,
                   const TAllocator& alloc):
        m_data(capacity, initial, alloc), m_capacity(capacity),
        m_currentIn(0), m_currentOut(0), m_mutex(),
        m_full(capacity), m_empty(0)
    {
    }
};
```

The `Enqueue()` member function adds an element to the buffer. It uses the `m_full` semaphore to block when the buffer is full. The `wait()` function call will block when the semaphore's counter is zero. When the counter is not zero it will decrement the counter and continue. A lock on the buffer is obtained and the data is added to the buffer. Finally, it will call `post()` on the `m_empty()` semaphore that increments the semaphore's counter so `Dequeue()` will not block anymore (the buffer is not empty now):

```
// Enqueue an element.
void Enqueue(const T& data)
{
    // Block if the buffer is full.
    m_full.wait();

    // Obtain lock on the buffer and store the data.
    {
        scoped_lock<interprocess_mutex> lock(m_mutex);
        m_data[m_currentIn++]=data;
        if (m_currentIn==m_capacity) m_currentIn=0;
    } // Lock released here.

    // Increase the empty semaphore counter
    // (not empty anymore if it was empty).
    m_empty.post();
}
```

The `Dequeue()` member function removes an element from the buffer. It uses the `m_empty` semaphore to block when the buffer is empty (if the semaphore's counter is zero). Otherwise, it decrements the counter and continues to remove the element from the buffer. Finally the `m_full` semaphore is incremented so that the `Enqueue()` function will not block anymore (the buffer is now not full):

```
// Dequeue an element.
T Dequeue()
{
    // Block if the buffer is empty.
    m_empty.wait();

    // Obtain lock on the buffer, remove the data and unlock buffer again.
    m_mutex.lock();
    T result=m_data[m_currentOut++];
    if (m_currentOut==m_capacity) m_currentOut=0;
    m_mutex.unlock();

    // Increase the full semaphore counter (not full anymore if it was
    // full).
    m_full.post();

    // Return the data.
    return result;
}
```

The `CircularBuffer` class can now be used in shared memory, for example. We use typedefs to declare a circular buffer for interprocess strings with the needed allocators:

```
// Regular strings can't be put in IPC memory so
// we use a boost::interprocess::basic_string.
// The interprocess string needs an allocator for chars.
typedef allocator<char, managed_shared_memory::segment_manager>
    CharAllocator;
typedef basic_string<char, std::char_traits<char>, CharAllocator>
    shm_string;
```

```
// Typedef for a managed shared memory allocator used by the
// synchronised queue of shm_strings.
typedef allocator<shm_string, managed_shared_memory::segment_manager>
    StringAllocator;
typedef CircularBuffer<shm_string, StringAllocator> StringCircularBuffer;
```

We show code that opens or creates a circular buffer. Then it adds interprocess strings to the buffer that were entered by the user. We see that the `Enqueue()` blocks when the buffer is full. An empty string stops adding strings to the buffer:

```
// Create or open the managed shared memory.
managed_shared_memory segment(open_or_create, "MySharedMemory", 1024);

// Create an allocator with the segment manager to use.
// We create an allocator for voids. Since the allocator
// has a templated converting constructor,
// we can pass this one to both the string and queue classes.
allocator<void, managed_shared_memory::segment_manager>
alloc(segment.get_segment_manager());

// Create or find the string queue object (is already synchronised).
// We pass the size of the buffer, the initial value of the elements
// and the allocator to use.
StringCircularBuffer*
buffer=segment.find_or_construct<StringCircularBuffer>("MyBuffer")
    (size, shm_string(alloc), alloc);

std::string str;
do
{
    // Get string from user.
    std::cout<<"Enter string (empty==exit): ";
    std::getline(std::cin, str);

    // Add the string to the circular buffer.
    std::cout<<"- Adding string to buffer. "
            <<"Will block if buffer is full."<<std::endl;
    shm_string tmp(str.c_str(), alloc);
    buffer->Enqueue(tmp);
    std::cout<<"- String added."<<std::endl<<std::endl;
}
while (str!="");
```

Finally, we show the client code that opens or creates a circular buffer and then removes strings from the circular buffer. We see that `Dequeue()` blocks when the buffer is empty. When an empty string is read from the buffer it stops reading from the buffer and removes the circular buffer from shared memory:

```
// Create or open the managed shared memory.
managed_shared_memory segment(open_or_create, "MySharedMemory", 1024);

// Create an allocator with the segment manager to use.
// We create an allocator for voids. Since the allocator
// has a templated converting constructor,
// we can pass this one to both the string and queue classes.
allocator<void, managed_shared_memory::segment_manager>
alloc(segment.get_segment_manager());

// Create or find the string queue object (is already synchronised).
// We pass the size of the buffer, the initial value of the
// elements and the allocator to use.
StringCircularBuffer* buffer=
    segment.find_or_construct<StringCircularBuffer>("MyBuffer")
        (size, shm_string(alloc), alloc);
```

```
shm_string str(alloc);
do
{
    // Wait for user.
    std::cout<<"Press enter to get string from buffer.";
    std::cin.get();

    // Retrieve string.
    std::cout<<"- Getting string from buffer. "
            <<"Can block if buffer is empty."<<std::endl;
    str=buffer->Dequeue();
    std::cout<<"- String retrieved: "<<str<<std::endl<<std::endl;
}
while (str!="");

// Destroy circular buffer.
segment.destroy_ptr(buffer);

// Remove the shared memory.
if (shared_memory_object::remove("MySharedMemory")==true)
std::cout<<"Shared memory removed."<<std::endl;
else std::cout<<"Error while removing shared memory."<<std::endl;
```

12.6 Upgradable Mutexes

12.6.1 Introduction to Upgradable Mutexes

Let us imagine the situation in which one thread is writing data in a shared data structure and multiple threads are reading data from the shared data structure without modifying it.
When one process is writing the other processes may not read the data. We can enforce this constraint using mutexes. But this has the disadvantage that a process that is reading data will also lock the mutex and thus block other readers. Processes that only read data will then be sequentially executed while it would be safe for them to execute concurrently. Thus we wish to have the possibility to block only when there is a write operation in progress and not when there is a read operation in progress.

The solution to this problem is to use an *upgradable mutex* which has three levels of locking:

- *Exclusive lock*: This is similar to a regular mutex lock. If a thread acquires an exclusive lock then no other thread can acquire any type of lock. If some other thread has already acquired any type of lock this thread will block until the other threads release their lock. This lock is acquired by threads that wish to modify the shared data.
- *Sharable lock*: When a thread acquires a sharable lock other threads can still immediately obtain a sharable lock or upgradable lock. But if another thread tries to obtain an exclusive lock it will block until all other locks are released. When there is already an exclusive lock or upgradable taken by another thread obtaining a sharable lock will block until the exclusive lock and/or upgradable lock are released. This lock is acquired by threads that only read the shared data.
- *Upgradable lock*: An upgradable lock is similar to a sharable lock but it can be atomically upgraded to an exclusive lock. There can be only one upgradable lock at any given time. Thus when there are only sharable locks and no upgradable or exclusive locks the upgradable lock will be taken immediately; otherwise it will block. This lock is used by threads that mainly read the shared data but may also need to write to the shared data as well. The advantage is that an upgradable lock is promoted to an exclusive lock atomically and thus shared data cannot be changed in the transition. When you release a shared lock and then obtain an exclusive lock the shared data could have been changed in the meantime.

Summarising, when a thread obtains an exclusive lock, no other thread can have a lock. But when nobody has an exclusive lock multiple threads can hold a shared lock (if they were obtained earlier than an upgradable lock) and one thread can hold an upgradable lock.

An upgradable mutex is more flexible than a regular mutex but it has more overhead. It can improve concurrency when shared data is read more often than being written. If write access is needed most of the time or when the synchronised section is very short it is more efficient to use a regular mutex.

12.6.2   Upgradable Mutexes in Boost Interprocess

The   Boost   Interprocess   Library   provides   a   named   upgradable   mutex (`named_upgradable_mutex`)   and   anonymous   upgradable   mutex (`interprocess_upgradable_mutex`). The required header files are:

```
#include <boost/interprocess/sync/named_upgradable_mutex.hpp>
#include <boost/interprocess/sync/interprocess_upgradable_mutex.hpp>
```

An upgradable mutex provides the following functionality:
* Exclusive locking:
  - `lock()`, `try_lock()` and `timed_lock()`
    Blocks or returns error when already sharable, upgradable or exclusive lock taken.
  - `unlock()`
* Sharable locking:
  - `lock_sharable()`, `try_lock_sharable()` and `timed_lock_sharable()`
    Blocks or returns error when already upgradable or exclusive lock taken.
  - `unlock_sharable()`
* Upgradable locking:
  - `lock_upgradable()`, `try_lock_upgradable()` and `timed_lock_upgradable()`
    Blocks or returns error when already upgradable or exclusive lock taken.
  - `unlock_upgradable()`
* Lock demotions:
  - `unlock_and_lock_upgradable()`
    exclusive->upgradable (atomically & non-blocking)
  - `unlock_and_lock_sharable()`
    exclusive->sharable (atomically & non-blocking)
  - `unlock_upgradable_lock_sharable()`
    upgradable->sharable (atomically & non-blocking)
* Lock promotions:
  - `unlock_upgradable_and_lock()`, `try_unlock_upgradable_and_lock()` and `timed_unlock_upgradable_and_lock()`
    upgradable->exclusive (atomically & blocks or returns error when still sharable locks are active but will maintain upgradable lock)
  - `try_unlock_sharable_and_lock()`
    sharable->exclusive (atomically & returns error when still shareable or upgradable locks are active but will maintain sharable lock)
  - `try_unlock_sharable_and_lock_upgradable()`
    sharable->upgradable (atomically & returns error when still sharable or upgradable locks are active but will maintain sharable lock)

As with regular mutexes, releasing a lock is essential. In the past we used the `interprocess::scoped_lock` to automatically release a lock but this provides exclusive locking only. Therefore the interprocess library also provides `interprocess::sharable_lock` and `interprocess:upgradable_lock` classes. These obtain a sharable lock or upgradable lock in the constructor and they are automatically released the lock in the destructor.

The required header files are:

```
#include <boost/interprocess/sync/sharable_lock.hpp>
#include <boost/interprocess/sync/upgradable_lock.hpp>
```

We can now use the upgradable mutex in an example. One process is publishing its current status (progress) in shared memory. Multiple processes can read this status. The upgradable mutex ensures that readers only block when data is being written and not when other readers are reading data.

Since we store a string in shared memory we need to define an allocator and string type for shared memory:

```
// Regular strings can't be put in IPC memory so we use a
boost::interprocess::basic_string.

// The interprocess string needs an allocator for chars.
typedef allocator<char, managed_shared_memory::segment_manager>
    CharAllocator;
typedef basic_string<char, std::char_traits<char>, CharAllocator>
    shm_string;
```

The server writes its status to a shared string variable in shared memory. For synchronisation it uses a named upgradable mutex. When updating the string it takes an exclusive lock on the mutex using the `scoped_lock` class that automatically releases the mutex when it goes out of scope. The exclusive lock will block readers. We added a small time delay in order to show that the readers are blocked during the update:

```
// Create or open the managed shared memory.
managed_shared_memory segment(open_or_create, "MySharedMemory", 1024);

// Create an allocator with the segment manager to use.
// We create an allocator for voids.
// Since the allocator has a templated converting constructor,
// we can pass this one to both the string and queue classes.
allocator<void, managed_shared_memory::segment_manager>
    alloc(segment.get_segment_manager());

// Create or find the string object (is already synchronised).
// We pass the the initial value of the string and the allocator to use.
shm_string* buffer=segment.find_or_construct<shm_string>("MyBuffer")
    ("Not started", alloc);

// Create or find named upgradable mutex.
named_upgradable_mutex mutex(open_or_create, "MyMutex");

// Update the progress.
for (int i=0; i<=100; i+=10)
{
    // Create progress string.
    std::stringstream tmp;
    if (i<100) tmp<<"Progress: "<<i<<"%"; else tmp<<"Finished";

    // Print progress.
    std::cout<<tmp.str()<<std::endl;
```

```
    // Write progress string. Sync with upgradable mutex.
    {
        // We take an exclusive lock since we update the data.
        scoped_lock<named_upgradable_mutex> lock(mutex);

        // Update string.
        *buffer=shm_string(tmp.str().c_str(), alloc);

        // Time delay to show readers will now block.
        boost::this_thread::sleep(boost::posix_time::seconds(1));

    } // Lock automatically released here.

    // Time delay for next update.
    boost::this_thread::sleep(boost::posix_time::seconds(3));
}
```

The clients read the status from the string in shared memory. As with the server it uses the same named upgradable mutex as the server. When reading the string it takes a sharable lock on the mutex using the `sharable_lock` class that automatically releases the lock when it goes out of scope. The sharable lock does not block other readers but it will block the writer. We added a small time delay to show that the other readers are not blocked during the read operation:

```
// Create or open the managed shared memory.
managed_shared_memory segment(open_or_create, "MySharedMemory", 1024);

// Create an allocator with the segment manager to use.
// We create an allocator for voids. Since the allocator has
// a templated converting constructor,
// we can pass this one to both the string and queue classes.
allocator<void, managed_shared_memory::segment_manager>
    alloc(segment.get_segment_manager());

// Create or find the string object (is already synchronised).
// We pass the initial value of the string and the allocator to use.
shm_string* buffer=segment.find_or_construct<shm_string>("MyBuffer")
        ("Not started", alloc);

// Create or find named upgradable mutex.
named_upgradable_mutex mutex(open_or_create, "MyMutex");

// Temporary string for storing status.
std::string tmp;

// Read status updates.
do
{
    // Read progress string. Sync with upgradable mutex.
    {
        // We take a sharable lock since we only read the data.
        sharable_lock<named_upgradable_mutex> lock(mutex);

        // Read and print the string.
        tmp=std::string(buffer->c_str());
        std::cout<<tmp<<std::endl;

        // Little time delay to show readers will NOT block
        // (but writers do block).
        boost::this_thread::sleep(boost::posix_time::milliseconds(500));

    } // Lock automatically released here.
}
while (tmp!="Finished");
```

12.6.3 Lock Transfer

We saw in section 12.6.2 how a lock can be promoted or demoted. This can cause problems when we need to unlock the mutex after an exception has occurred. Imagine the following pseudocode:

```
// Create upgradable mutex.
named_upgradable_mutex mutex(open_or_create, "MyMutex");

try
{
    // Obtain exclusive lock.
    mutex.lock();

    // Modify data.
    // ...

    // Finished update, demote atomically the mutex to sharable lock.
    mutex.unlock_and_lock_sharable();

    // Read data.
    // ...

    // Explicit unlocking.
    mutex.unlock_sharable();
}
catch (...)
{
    // What should we call?
    mutex.unlock();
    mutex.unlock_sharable();
}
```

We see that in this case, the catch handler does not know which unlock function to call. Thus we need to split it into multiple try...catch blocks.

When we use the scoped_lock, sharable_lock and upgradable_lock classes we cannot call the lock's demote or promote functions. Releasing the lock and immediately obtaining another kind of lock is less efficient and is not an atomic operation.

In this case we actually wish to transfer the lock from a scoped_lock to a sharable_lock instance. The interprocess library provides this feature using the move() function.

The above code could be rewritten as:

```
// Create upgradable mutex.
named_upgradable_mutex mutex(open_or_create, "MyMutex");

try
{
    // Obtain exclusive lock.
    scoped_lock<named_upgradable_mutex> lock1(mutex);

    // Modify data.
    // ...

    // Finished update, demote atomically the mutex to sharable lock.
    sharable_lock<named_upgradable_mutex> lock2(move(lock1));

    // Read data.
    // ...
```

```
} // Lock automatically released here no matter
  // what type of lock is currently active.
catch (...)
{
    // No unlocking needed here.
}
```

Demotions always succeed and are inmediately executed, but *promotions* can fail or can block. A promotion from upgradable to exclusive lock can block or fail. In this case we can use a *try* or *timed* transfer. A promotion from sharable to exclusive lock will never block but instead returns an error. In this case you can only use a *try* transfer.

Below we show a promotion from an upgradable lock to an exclusive lock using a time-out. Note that the end time is given (and not duration):

```
// Promotion transfer (upgradable->exclusive)
// with time-out (current time + 2 seconds).
upgradable_lock<named_upgradable_mutex> upg_lock(mutex);
boost::posix_time::ptime time_out=
    boost::posix_time::second_clock::local_time()+
    boost::posix_time::seconds(2);
scoped_lock<named_upgradable_mutex> scp_lock(move(upg_lock), time_out);
```

We give an example of a promotion from an upgradable lock to an exclusive lock using the *try* option. It will not block but it returns immediately.

```
// Promotion transfer (upgradable->exclusive) using try.
sharable_lock<named_upgradable_mutex> shr_lock(mutex);
scoped_lock<named_upgradable_mutex> scp_lock(move(shr_lock), try_to_lock);
```

After a promotion transfer we should check if it succeeded by checking if the lock is owned. To this end, we use the lock's `owns()` member function:

```
// Check if transfer worked.
if (scp_lock.owns()) std::cout<<"Transfer succeeded"<<std::endl;
else std::cout<<"Transfer failed"<<std::endl;
```

12.7 Summary and Conclusions

We have seen that the interprocess library provides the same kinds of synchronisation mechanisms as we see with multi-threading. The interprocess synchronisation mechanisms also work when the threads are in different processes while the threading synchronisation mechanisms only work when the threads are in the same process.

The synchronisation mechanisms could be stored in IPC memory but in situations where no IPC memory is needed the synchronisation mechanism can also be created and found by name without having to store them in IPC memory.

13 Interval Arithmetic

13.1 Introduction and Objectives

Interval Arithmetic is used in calculations in which the physical parameters of a problem are not known with certainty, due to measurement errors for example. It is used to find reliable and guaranteed solutions to several kinds of equations and in particular it has applications to optimisation problems and to problems in which underflow and overflow can occur. Interval Arithmetic has applications to problems in which no exact estimates are available. However, it is possible to quantify how accurate an estimate is by computing an interval that contains the exact (unknown) value. The width of the interval determines how accurate this estimate is. It may be possible to reduce the size of this interval when it is used in an algorithm, thus giving us a more precise estimate of the true value. Some of the general scenarios are:

- *Controlling rounding errors* arising in an algorithm or computation. After each operation in the algorithm we get an interval that includes the true result with certainty. The distance between the interval boundaries (the so-called interval *width*) gives us a direct error estimate.
- *Tolerance analysis*: we allow certain tolerances in the measurement of parameters in many simulation applications. Furthermore, some constants are not precisely known. In contrast to *point methods*, using interval arithmetic ensures that no part of the solution area can be overlooked. Computer Aided Manufacturing (CAM) measurements usually involve working with interval numbers.
- *Fuzzy interval arithmetic*: this can be seen as an extension of traditional interval arithmetic. But in this case we can state if a value is in an interval to a certain degree.

Interval analysis became popular in the 1960s. One of the first textbooks are Moore 1966 and Moore 1979 and he applied the method to matrix computation, function evaluation, root-finding, integral equations and as well as to convex and nonlinear optimisation. In general, interval analysis techniques can be used when we wish to keep track of and handle rounding errors directly during calculations and in the presence of measurements errors. It can also be used when we use devices with limited accuracy. Finally, interval arithmetic is useful for finding reliable and guaranteed solutions.

A readable and clear introduction to interval analysis and applications to numerical analysis is given in Alefeld 2000.

13.2 What is Interval Analysis, Interval Arithmetic, Interval Mathematics?

Interval analysis is a branch of numerical analysis that is concerned with the quantification of bounds on rounding and measurement errors in numerical computation with the goal of obtaining reliable results from algorithms and processes. Instead of providing a single outcome as an estimate, interval analysis provides an estimate as a *range* or *interval* of values. For example, we can estimate someone's height as being 1.86 metres but this value may be inaccurate due to measurement errors. Interval analysis, on the other hand would model with certainty the exact height as lying somewhere in the interval (1.845, 1.87), for example.

One of the first mathematicians to use interval analysis was Archimedes in the third century BC. He used 'two-sided approximations' to calculate π by inscribing and circumscribing a circle by regular polygons with n sides, n = 4,5,6,... We stop the process when the difference between the areas of the circumscribed and inscribed polygons is less than some given tolerance. To give an idea of the process, we take the examples n = 4 (circumscribed and inscribed squares) and n = 6 (circumscribed and inscribed hexagons). Of course, we need to know the formulae for the areas of these regular polygons. To this end, we consider a circle of radius one. The lower and upper bounds for π can be computed using analytic geometry:

- Square: in the interval [2.0, 4.0].
- Hexagon: in the interval [2.596, 3.464].
- Regular 96-sided polygon: in the interval [3.062, 3.312].

We see that the interval containing the exact value of π shrinks as the number of edges of the polygon increases. In general, there is a certain amount of *uncertainty* in the answer because all we can say is that the answer lies somewhere in an interval. The degree of uncertainty is determined by the *width* of the interval containing the exact answer; the smaller the width the better the approximation. Then we can take the midpoint of the interval as an estimate of the true answer.

To take another example, we calculate the human *body mass index* (BMI). This is the body weight in kilograms divided by the square of the height in metres. Using bathroom scales to measure body weight may lead to inaccuracies, for example of the order of one kilogram. In general, we usually round the weight to the nearest whole number. Furthermore, inaccuracies in calculation of height will also lead to inaccuracies in the formula for BMI:

$$\text{BMI} = w/L^2 \text{ where } w = \text{weight and } L = \text{height.} \tag{13.1}$$

To test the accuracy of this formula, let us assume that height is in the interval [1.80, 1.90] == [A, B] and weight is in the interval [79, 81] == [C,D]. There are five possibilities to calculate the BMI using equation (13.1), namely the four points (A,C), (A, D), (B, C), (B,D) and finally using interval arithmetic. The results of the calculations in these five cases are:

- (A,C): 24.3827
- (A,D): 25.0
- (B,C): 21.8837
- (B,D): 22.4377
- Interval solution: [21.8837, 25.0].

We see that the solution based on interval arithmetic contains the first four solutions based on the endpoints (A,C), (A, D), (B, C) and (B,D). In other words, the interval arithmetic solution contains all combinations of all possible intermediate values. It can be overly *conservative* in general and in some applications we may need to reduce the width of the interval containing the exact solution.

The code that produced the above results used the Boost Interval library is:

```
#include <boost/numeric/interval.hpp>
#include <boost/numeric/interval/utility.hpp>

typedef boost::numeric::interval<double> Range;

int main()
{
    double A = 1.80; double B = 1.90;   // Heights.
    double C = 79.0; double D = 81.0;   // Weights.

    Range height(A, B);
    Range weight(C, D);

    cout << "(A,C): " << C/(A*A) << endl;
    cout << "(B,C): " << C/(B*B) << endl;
    cout << "(A,D): " << D/(A*A) << endl;
    cout << "(B,D): " << D/(B*B) << endl;
```

```
    // Using interval arithmetic operators.
    Range bmi = weight/ (height*height);
    cout << "Interval BMI): "; Print(bmi); cout << endl;

    return 0;
}
```

Another important application is when we wish to quantify the propagation of rounding errors. We can get strange results when using normal floating-point arithmetic. We take the example of the ***nonlinear recurrence relationship***:

$$x_{n+1} = x_n^2, \quad n \geq 1$$

$$x_0 = 1 - 10^{-21}.$$

(13.2)

The exact solution converges monotonically to zero. However, due to finite computer precision (for example, a computer that stores numbers with ten-place decimal significant digits) the approximate solution of equation (13.2) gives $x_0 = x_1 = x_2 = \ldots = x_{75} = 1$. Using interval arithmetic, on the other hand we are able to determine the precision of the algorithm by producing an (possibly large) interval in which the solution is situated. In this case the solution will be the interval [0,1] after n = 20 iterations, for example. The code is:

```
#include <boost/numeric/interval.hpp>
#include <boost/numeric/interval/utility.hpp>

typedef boost::numeric::interval<double> Range;

int main()
{
    int n = 40;                // Number of iterations.
    int counter = 1;
    int exponent = -21;
    double xOld = 1.0 - pow(10.0, exponent);
    double xNew;

    // Recursive procedure using 'exact' arithmetic.
    do
    {
        xNew = xOld*xOld;
        cout << xNew << ", ";

        xOld = xNew;
    } while (counter++ < n);

    // Recursive procedure using interval arithmetic.
    double tol = pow(10.0, -3);
    double A = xOld - tol; double B = 1.0; // Initial estimate.
    counter = 1;

    Range iOld(A, B);
    Range iNew;

    do
    {
        iNew = iOld*iOld;
        Print(iNew); cout << endl;

        iOld = iNew;
    } while (counter++ < n);

    return 0;
}
```

The function to print the interval is:

```
template <typename T>
void print(const boost::numeric::interval<T>& interval)
{
    cout << "[" << interval.lower() << "," << interval.upper() << "]";
}
```

13.3 Interval Arithmetic: Mathematical Foundations

In this section we introduce the mathematical foundations of interval arithmetic. An interval is a closed bounded set of real numbers, denoted by:

$$[a, b] = \{x : a \leq x \leq b\}. \tag{13.3}$$

We see that the interval contains an *uncountable* number of values. This is the usual interpretation. We can also regard an interval as a number represented by the ordered pair {a, b} of its endpoints. This is similar to how rational numbers (the quotient a/b) are defined, for example. We shall see how to define arithmetic operations for intervals. Intervals have a *dual nature* because set and arithmetic operations can also be applied to them.

An n-dimensional *interval vector* is an ordered n-tuple $(X_1, X_2, \ldots, X_n)$ where each X_j is an interval for $j = 1, \ldots, n$. We normally represent intervals by capital letters. Similarly, an *interval matrix* is a matrix whose elements are interval numbers. If the real number x is in the interval X, we write $x \in X$.

Some definitions and properties are:
1) Two intervals $X = [\underline{X}, \overline{X}], Y = [\underline{Y}, \overline{Y}]$ are *equal* if their corresponding endpoints are equal, that is $\underline{X} = \underline{Y}$ and $\overline{X} = \overline{Y}$.
2) The *intersection* of two intervals X and Y is empty $(X \cap Y = 0)$ if either $\underline{X} > \overline{Y}$ or $\underline{Y} > \overline{X}$. Otherwise, the intersection of X and Y is an interval defined by: $X \cap Y = [\max(\underline{X}, \underline{Y}), \min(\overline{X}, \overline{Y})]$.
3) The *union* of two intervals X and Y having non-empty intersection is given by $X \cup Y = [\min(\underline{X}, \underline{Y}), \max(\overline{X}, \overline{Y})]$.
4) We can extend the *transitive order relation* < on real numbers to intervals, that is: $X < Y \Longleftrightarrow \overline{X} < \underline{Y}$.
5) Set *inclusion*: this is a transitive order relation for intervals: $X \subseteq Y \Longleftrightarrow \underline{Y} \leq \underline{X}$ and $\overline{X} \leq \overline{Y}$.
6) The *width* of an interval $X = [\underline{X}, \overline{X}]$ is defined by $w(X) = \overline{X} - \underline{X}$.
7) The *absolute value* of an interval X is defined by $|X| = \max(|\underline{X}|, |\overline{X}|)$. We see that $|x| \leq |X| \ \forall x \in X$.
8) If X is a vector interval then the *vector norm* is given by $\|x\| = \max(|X_1|, \ldots, |X_n|)$.
9) The *midpoint* of an interval X is defined by $m(X) = (\underline{X} + \overline{X})/2$.
10) Let $A = (a_{ij}), \ 1 \leq i \leq n, \ 1 \leq j \leq m$ be an interval matrix. Its *matrix norm* is then defined by $\|A\| = \max_{1 \leq i \leq n} \sum_{j=1}^{m} |a_{ij}|$. This norm is the extension of the maximum row sum for real matrices.

We now discuss interval arithmetic. It is an extension of real number arithmetic. In the sequel, we let $X = [a, b]$, $Y = [c, d]$ represent two intervals. We then define the following operations:

- *Addition*: $X + Y = [a + c, b + d]$.
- *Subtraction*: $X - Y = [a - d, b - c]$.
- *Multiplication*: $X * Y = [\min(ac, ad, bc, bd), \max(ac, ad, bc, bd)]$.
- *Division*: $[\min(a/c, a/d, b/c, b/d), \max(a/c, a/d, b/c, b/d)]$.

We note that division by an interval containing zero is not defined in interval arithmetic. Finally, we discuss some algebraic properties of interval number. Let X, Y and Z be intervals. Then:

$$X + (Y + Z) = (X + Y) + Z$$
$$X(YZ) = (XY)Z$$
$$X + Y = Y + Z$$
$$XY = YX$$

where the product of two intervals X and Y is defined by:

$$XY = \{xy; x \in X, y \in Y\}.$$

You can verify that;

$$\underline{XY} = \min(\underline{XY}, \underline{X}\overline{Y}, \overline{X}\underline{Y}, \overline{XY})$$

$$\overline{XY} = \max(\underline{XY}, \underline{X}\overline{Y}, \overline{X}\underline{Y}, \overline{XY}).$$

For addition and multiplication the following rules hold:

$$0 + X = X + 0 = X$$
$$1X = X1 = X$$

for any interval X. Finally, the *subdistributivity property* holds for intervals:

$$X(Y + Z) \subseteq XY + XZ$$

for any intervals X, Y and Z. We see this relationship is a combination of algebraic and set theoretic constructions.

This has been a short introduction to the essential properties of interval numbers.

13.4 Boost Interval Library: Functionality and Initial Examples

In this section we give a high-level overview of the class `interval<T>` and related free functions in the Boost Interval library. The class `interval<T>` has two template parameters:

```
template<class T, class Policies>
class interval
{
    // ...
};
```

The template parameter `T` is the *base number type* and it is assumed to be *totally ordered* by which is meant that any two elements x and y can be compared; the only choices are $x < y, x == y$ or $x > y$. This rules out `std::complex<T>` (for example) as a base

number type in the library. We also demand that if $x >$ and $y > z$, then $x > z$. This total
order also rules out the use of *modulo types* in the library.

The second template parameter `Policies` is mainly used for specialised implementations
of rounding policies for `float` and `double` primitive types. It is possible to round *upward*
or *downward*. We use default policy only and a discussion of specialised policies is outside
the scope of this book. In the version that we used we found that certain policies of Boost
did not work which meant that we are unable to discuss some of the functionality in the
library.

The class `interval<T>` has functionality for creating intervals, accessing their properties
and performing addition, subtraction and multiplication. In general, interval arithmetic
subsumes real arithmetic in the sense that a real number x is viewed as a degenerate interval
$[x, x]$. Some example code is:

```
#include <boost/numeric/interval.hpp>
typedef boost::numeric::interval<double> Range;

// Real numbers are a special case of interval numbers.
double val = 3.0;
Range r0(val);
cout << "Degenerate interval: " << r0 << endl;

// Create and manipulate some numbers.
Range r1(0.0, 1,0);
cout << "Lower boundary: " << r1.lower() << endl;
cout << "upper boundary: " << r1.upper() << endl;

Range rCC(r1);
cout << "Copy constructor: " << rCC << endl;

// Interval with number arithmetic.
double t = 2.0;
r1 += t; r1 -= t; r1 *= t; r1 /= t;

// Interval with interval arithmetic.
Range rTmp(2.0, 3.0);
r1 += rTmp; r1 -= rTmp; r1 *= rTmp; r1 /= rTmp;
```

In addition, the library has support for a range of global functions that we can classify as
follows:

- Arithmetic operators involving intervals: +, -, *, /.
- Algebraic functions: `abs()`, `sqrt()`, `square()`, `nth_root()`.
- Transcendental functions: `exp()`, `log()`.
- Trigonometric functions: `sin()`, `cos()`, `tan()`, `asin()`, `acos()`, `atan()`.
- Hyperbolic trigonometric functions: `sinh()`, `cosh()`, `tanh()`, `asinh()`, `acosh()`,
  `atanh()`.
- Bounds-related interval functions: `lower()`, `upper()`, `width()`, `median()`, `norm()`
  `empty()`, `equal()`, `in()`, `subset()`, `proper_subset()`.
- Set manipulation interval functions: `intersection()`, `hull()`, `bisect()`.
- Interval comparison operators: <, <=, >, >=, == and != . We note that the operands for
  these binary operators can be any combination of intervals and real numbers.

Most of the above functions are easy to understand and to use. The bounds-related interval
functions are probably less obvious and they relate to essential 'generic' properties of
intervals and set-like operations on intervals. First, we give some examples of functions in
the other categories:

```
Range r1(1.5, 3.0);
Range r2(-10.0, 20.0);
cout << "r1: " << r1 << endl;
cout << "r2: " << r2 << endl;

// Numeric operations.
cout << "r1+r2: " << (r1+r2) << endl;
cout << "r1-r2: " << (r1-r2) << endl;
cout << "r1*r2: " << (r1*r2) << endl;
cout << "r1/r2: " << (r1/r2) << endl;

// More numeric operations.
double t = 3.0;
cout << endl;
cout << "t: " << t << endl;
cout << "r1+t: " << (r1+t) << endl;
cout << "r1-t: " << (r1-t) << endl;
cout << "r1*t: " << (r1*t) << endl;
cout << "r1/t: " << (r1/t) << endl;

// Algebraic functions.
cout << endl;
cout << "abs(r1): " << abs(r1) << endl;
cout << "sqrt(r1): " << sqrt(r1) << endl;
cout << "square(r1): " << square(r1) << endl;
cout << "pow(r1, 2): " << pow(r1, 2) << endl;
cout << "nth_root(r1, 4): " << nth_root(r1, 4) << endl;
```

Some other functions are:

```
// Set manipulation interval functions.
Range rA(0.0, 10.0);
Range rB(5.0, 15.0);
Range rX = hull(rA, rB); // [0.0, 15.0]
cout << "rA: " << rA << endl;
cout << "rB: " << rB << endl;
cout << "Hull(rA, rB): " << rX << endl;

// Modifiers and properties.
Range rD(-100.0, 200.0);
cout << endl << "rD: " << rD << endl;
cout << "Width: " << width(rD) << endl;
cout << "Median: " << median(rD) << endl;
double stretch_factor = 400.0;
Range rE = widen(rD, stretch_factor);  // Stretch out in both directions.
cout << "rE=widen(rD, 400)" << rE << endl;

// Set manipulation.
Range rF = intersect(rD, rE);
cout << "rF=intersect(rD, rE): " << rF << endl;
```

We have created a function to print an interval, namely:

```
template<typename T, typename Policies>
std::ostream& operator << (std::ostream &os,
    const boost::numeric::interval<T, Policies>& x)
{
    os << "[" << x.lower() << ", " << x.upper() << "]";
    return os;
}
```

You can choose which option to use in a given context.

13.5 Application: Matrix Computations with Intervals

In this section we discuss the solution of linear algebraic systems:

$$Ax = b \tag{13.4}$$

where A is a given interval square matrix and b is a known interval vector when the number of columms of A is equal to the number of elements in b. The objective is to find an interval vector x that satisfies the equation (13.4). Let us examine the 2X2 case:

$$A = \begin{pmatrix} a_{11} & a_{12} \\ a_{21} & a_{22} \end{pmatrix}$$
$$Ax = b, \quad x = {}^t(x_1, x_2), \quad b = {}^t(b_1, b_2) \tag{13.5}$$

whose solution is given by:

$$x_1 = \frac{b_1 a_{22} - b_2 a_{12}}{a_{11} a_{22} - a_{12} a_{21}}$$
$$x_2 = \frac{a_{11} b_2 - a_{21} b_1}{a_{11} a_{22} - a_{12} a_{21}}. \tag{13.6}$$

We now discuss the implementation of these formula. First, we initialise the structures in (13.5) as follows (note that we use the matrix classes from uBLAS):

```
namespace ublas = boost::numeric::ublas;
typedef boost::numeric::interval<double> Range;

// Solve a 2X2 system of equations using interval arithmetic.
typedef ublas::matrix<Range> Matrix;
typedef ublas::vector<Range> Vector;

// Create a matrix with elements that are intervals.
int NR = 2; int NC = 2;
Matrix A(NR, NC);

// Fill the matrix.
for (size_t row=0; row<A.size1(); row++)
{
    for (size_t column=0; column<A.size2(); column++)
    {
        A(row, column)= Range(0.0, 1.0);
    }
}

A(0,0) = 1.0; A(1,0) = 1.0;
A(0,1) = 2.0; A(1,1) = Range(10.0, 12.0);
cout << "Matrix A: "; Print(A);

Vector b(2);
b[0] = 1.0;
b[1] = 0.0;
cout << endl;
cout << "Vector b: "; Print(b);
```

The output from this code is:

```
Matrix A:
a(0,0) == [1,1], a(0,1) == [2,2],
a(1,0) == [1,1], a(1,1) == [10,12],

Vector b:
v[0] == [1,1], v[1] == [0,0],
```

The C++ function to solve system (13.4) using the formula (13.6) is:

```
// Ax = b ==> find x
Vector Solve(const Matrix& A, const Vector& b)
{
    Vector result(2);

    Range denominator = (A(0,0)*A(1,1) - A(0,1)*A(1,0));

    result[0] = (A(1,1)*b[0] - A(0,1)*b[1]) / denominator;
    result[1] = (A(0,0)*b[1] - A(1,0)*b[0]) / denominator;

    return result;
}
```

We solve for the solution of (13.4):

```
Vector x = Solve(A, b);
cout << "Solution vector: "; Print(x);
```

and the output now becomes:

```
Solution vector:
v[0] == [1,1.5], v[1] == [-0.125,-0.1],
```

We now discuss the computation of the inverse of A using the formula:

$$A^{-1} = \begin{pmatrix} a_{22} & -a_{12} \\ -a_{21} & a_{11} \end{pmatrix} / (a_{11}a_{22} - a_{12}a_{21}).$$ \hfill (13.7)

The corresponding function is:

```
// Ax = b ==> find x
Matrix Inverse(const Matrix& A)
{
    Matrix result(A.size1(), A.size2());

    Range determinant = (A(0,0)*A(1,1) - A(0,1)*A(1,0));

    result(0,0) = A(1,1) / determinant;
    result(0,1) = -A(0,1) / determinant;
    result(1,0) = -A(1,0) / determinant;
    result(1,1) = A(0,0) / determinant;

    return result;
}
```

We have tested this function and we have pre and postmultiplied A by inverse(A); using real arithmetic we would get an identity matrix (1's on diagonal and 0's off the diagonal) but in this case we get an interval answer. The code is:

```
Matrix B = Inverse(A);
cout << "Inverse matrix: "; Print(B);

Matrix C = prod(A,B);
Matrix D = prod(B, A);

cout << "\n\nC == A*B and D == B*A should be identity\n";
Print(C);
Print(D);
```

The output from this code is:

```
Inverse matrix:
a(0,0) == [1,1.5], a(0,1) == [-0.25,-0.2],
a(1,0) == [-0.125,-0.1], a(1,1) == [0.1,0.125],
C == A*B and D == B*A should be identity

a(0,0) == [0.75,1.3], a(0,1) == [-0.05,0.05],
a(1,0) == [-0.5,0.5], a(1,1) == [0.75,1.3],
```

and

```
a(0,0) == [0.75,1.3], a(0,1) == [-1,1],
a(1,0) == [-0.025,0.025], a(1,1) == [0.75,1.3],
```

It is possible to generalise the above discussion to general systems of linear equations, for example using LU decomposition as discussed in chapter 7 in which we use interval matrices instead of matrices whose elements are real numbers. A discussion of this topic is outside the scope of this book.

Finally, we give a simple example to show how to create *multidimensional intervals* and compute their volume:

```
// Multidimensional intervals
long N = 3;
vector<Range> multiInterval(3);
multiInterval[0] = Range(-1.0, 1.0);
multiInterval[1] = Range(-1.0, 1.0);
multiInterval[2] = Range(-1.0, 1.0);

double volume = 1.0;
for (size_t i = 0; i < multiInterval.size(); ++i)
{
    volume *= width(multiInterval[i]);
}
cout << "Volume: " << volume << endl;
```

In general, we can use this approach in applications, for example by defining data structures that are composed of intervals and collections of intervals.

13.6 Function Evaluation in Interval

Interval Arithmetic is a large field of research. It is impossible to discuss all aspects in this chapter but we would like to describe how to evaluate interval-valued functions with interval arguments. To motivate the use of this topic, we consider the problem of finding roots of the quadratic equation:

$$Ax^2 + Bx + C = 0 \tag{13.8}$$

where A, B and C are given interval numbers and x is the interval number that satisfies (13.8), namely:

$$x = \frac{-B \pm \sqrt{B^2 - 4AC}}{2A}. \tag{13.9}$$

We experiment with various values of A, B and C to determine what the roots will be. In the exact case (that is, using real numbers) we took $A = 1, B = -3, C = 2.0$ and the roots were $x = 1$ and $x = 2$. We perturbed these parameters somewhat to see how different the resulting computed roots were compared to the exact values. You just run the code from the software distribution medium.

We now describe the code using Interval in order to compute the roots of (13.8) as given by formulae (13.9). The focus is one producing readable code that uses the functionality in Boost Interval. The formulae for (13.9) is realised by the following code:

```
// Compute ax^2 + bx + c
Range RootQuadraticPolynomialFirst(const Range& A, const Range& B,
                                   const Range& C)
{
    Range result1 = (-B + sqrt(B*B - Range(4.0)*A*C))/(Range(2.0)*A);
    return result1;
}

// Compute ax^2 + bx + c
Range RootQuadraticPolynomialSecond(const Range& A, const Range& B,
                                    const Range& C)
{
    Range result2 = (-B - sqrt(B*B - Range(4.0)*A*C))/(Range(2.0)*A);
    return result2;
}
```

Furthermore, the following function computes the quadratic polynomial for any value of x:

```
// Compute ax^2 + bx + c
Range QuadraticPolynomial(const Range& A, const Range& B, const Range& C,
                          const Range& X)
{
    return A*X*X + B*X + C;
}
```

We note that both the input parameters and result type are interval numbers. We take a specific example of equation (13.8). As an initial *sanity check*, we take an example whose coefficients are real numbers and in this case the roots are equal to 1 and 2. We create degenerate interval coefficients and the roots will be [1,1] and [2,2] when we run the code:

```
// Roots of x^2 - 3x + 2 = (x - 1)(x - 2)
Range a(1.0, 1.0); Range b(-3.0, -3.0); Range c(2.0, 2.0);
Range root1 = RootQuadraticPolynomialFirst(a, b, c);
Range root2 = RootQuadraticPolynomialSecond(a, b, c);
cout << "Root1 "; Print(root1); cout << endl;
cout << "Root2 "; Print(root2); cout << endl;
```

We perturb the coefficient c to see what the roots will be:

```
Range a(1.0); Range b(-3.0); Range c(1.9, 2.1);
```

The resulting roots will be **[1.8873, 2.09161]** and **[0.908392,1.1127]**. You can run the code and experiment with various values of a, b and c.

Another issue involves reducing the number of occurrences of a variable before interval evaluation. This can reduce the width of the interval in which a solution lies. We take the example based on an interval number A and we use the relationship:

$$\frac{A}{A-2} = 1 + \frac{2}{A-2}.$$

We see that the expression on the left-hand of this equation involves evaluating A twice while the expression on the right-hand of the equation involves evaluating A once. When evaluated, we see that the second form results in an interval number with a smaller width (which is better) than the width from the first form. Sample code is:

```
// Simple test.
Range rA(19.0,20.0);
Range factor1 = rA /(rA - 2.0);
Range factor2 = 1.0 + 2.0/(rA - 2.0);
cout << "Factors:\n";
cout << "Factor 1: " << factor1 << endl;
cout << "Factor 2: " << factor2 << endl;
```

The output from this code is:

```
Factors:
Factor 1: [1.05556, 1.17647]
Factor 2: [1.11111, 1.11765]
```

We see that the interval `factor2` is contained in the interval `factor1` and thus gives sharper bounds. More detailed discussions of *interval-reducing techniques* can be found in Moore 1966 and Moore 1979.

We conclude this section by computing the range value of the quadratic equation (13.8). We can evaluate it in different ways, for example:

$$(Ax + B)x + C \text{ (method I)}$$
$$Ax^2 + Bx + C \text{ (method II)}.$$

(13.10)

Method I corresponds to *Horner's method* while Method II corresponds to a straightforward computation of the quadratic equation. Due to subdistributivity $(Ax + B)x + C \subset Ax^2 + Bx + C$ we expect Method I to give a tighter interval than that for Method II.

Again, you can check the results by running the code from the distribution kit.

13.7 Advanced Functions and Related Data Structures

In this section we discuss using the Boost Function library in conjunction with Boost Interval. In general, we are interested in mappings from a general *domain D* to a general *range R*:

$$f : D \rightarrow R.$$

(13.11)

All functions that we model in applications are specialisations of this mapping. For example, the spaces D and R can be n-dimensional real or complex spaces. In the current case we are interested in mappings from interval numbers to interval numbers. Other combinations are possible (for example, from real numbers to interval numbers) but a discussion of these topics is outside the scope of this book.

For the moment, let us suppose that the mapping f in (13.11) maps (scalar) interval numbers to interval numbers. We assume that the body of f is composed by using elementary operations +, -, *, / and standard trigonometric and other functions. We replace real numbers x by interval numbers [X] when computing this function. Then, *the range of f over* [X] (denoted by $R(f; [X])$) is the interval number obtained by applying f to the boundaries of [X].

We can also *evaluate f at* [X] by using the rules for interval arithmetic as described in section 3.

We take an example:

$$f(x) = \frac{x}{1-x}. \tag{13.12}$$

We can implement this functionality in C++. To this end, we create a global function that computes the quantities of interest:

```
typedef boost::numeric::interval<double> Range;

// Compute f([X]) and the range of f over [X]
void Print(const boost::function<Range (const Range& x)> f, const Range& x)
{
    // Compute f([x])
    Range interval = f(x);
    cout << "f[x]: "<<interval.lower()<<","<<interval.upper() << endl;

    // Compute the range of f
    Range lowerVal = f(Range(x.lower(), x.lower()));
    Range upperVal = f(Range(x.upper(), x.upper()));

    cout << "Range lower: " << lowerVal.lower() << ","
         << lowerVal.upper() << endl;
    cout << "Range upper: " << upperVal.lower() << ","
         << upperVal.upper() << endl;

    Range range(lowerVal.lower(), upperVal.upper());
    cout << "Range of f[x]: " << range.lower() << ","
         << range.upper() << endl;
}
```

We now return to the example (13.12) by invoking `Print()` in a specific case:

```
Range TestFunc(const Range& x)
{
    return x / (1.0 - x);
}

// Create and manipulate some numbers
Range x(2.0, 3.0);
Print(TestFunc, x);
```

You can modify the code in order to convince yourself of the following facts:

$$f(x) = \frac{x}{1-x}, \quad x \neq 1$$

$$[X] = [2, 3]$$

$$R(f; [X]) = [-2, -3/2] \tag{13.13}$$

$$f([X]) = [-3, -1].$$

We conclude this section by showing how to create functions that have an STL `vector` and `boost::function` instance as input arguments and an interval as return type. To illustrate the syntax, we deliver a free C++ function:

```
// Evaluation of a scalar interval function at [x]
void Print(const boost::function<Range (const vector<Range>& arr)>& f,
           const vector<Range>& arr)
{
    Range result = f(arr);

    cout << "scalar f[x]: [" << result.lower() << ","
```

```
        << result.upper() << "]" << endl;
    }
```

In order to show how to use this function we must instantiate the input arguments:

```
Range TestFuncArray(const vector<Range>& arr)
{
    // Just a test to show use of interval vectors
    return (arr[0] + arr[1])/2.0;
}
```

and

```
vector<Range> myArr(2);
myArr[0] = 1.0;
myArr[1] = 2.0;
```

Finally, we can call the function:

```
Print(TestFuncArray, myArr);
```

It is possible to generalise the above code to suit many requirements, function types and data structures.

13.8 Solution of Nonlinear Equations

We now discuss the application of interval arithmetic to finding the roots of nonlinear equations. We focus on scalar problems, in other words real-valued functions of a single real variable. There are many nonlinear solvers to find the zeroes of these kinds of equations but our interest in this section is when both input argument and return type are interval numbers. To this end, we examine the *Newton-Raphson method* in interval arithmetic. The full details are given in the works of Moore that we have already referred to. The interval Newton-Raphson method is an example of an *interval contraction method* resulting in a nested sequence of intervals that converge to a fixed point of the restriction to real numbers of the nonlinear function whose zeroes we wish to find.

In general, we wish to find a zero of the nonlinear equation $f(x) = 0$ in some interval. First, we note:

$$x \in [X] \Rightarrow f(x) \in f([X])$$

$$R(f;[X]) \subseteq f([X]).$$

$$m(X) = \text{midpoint (centre of } [X])$$

$$N(X) = m(X) + \left(\frac{1}{-f'(X)}\right) f(m(X))$$

The iterative scheme is:

(13.14)

(13.15)

$$X_{k+1} = N(X_k) \cap X_k, \quad k \geq 0; \quad X_0 \text{ given}$$

where $f'(X) = \frac{df}{dX}$.

This scheme is similar to the traditional Newton-Raphson method with the twist that the current algorithm produces a sequence of shrinking intervals at each iteration that contain the zero of the nonlinear equation:

$$X_0 \supset X_1 \supset X_2 \supset \ldots \supset X_k. \tag{13.16}$$

Boost Interval supports functionality that allows us to implement the above algorithms. We need to satisfy the following constraints:

$$f'(X) \text{ does not contain zero and } f(m(X)) \text{ is defined.} \tag{13.17}$$

We now present the code. We need two functions f and fd (representing the function and its derivative, respectively), an initial interval and a tolerance as input:

```cpp
// Interval Newton Raphson solver.
Range NRSolver(const boost::function<Range (const Range& x)>& f,
               const boost::function<Range (const Range& x)>& fd,
               Range& x0, double TOL)
{
    Range xnp1;
    double diff = 10.0 * TOL;
    double centre;                 // Centre (median) of interval.

    int counter = 1;
    while (diff > TOL)
    {
        centre = median(x0);         // Midpoint of current interval.
        xnp1 = centre - f(centre) * (1.0/fd(x0));  // NR algorithm.
        xnp1 = intersect(xnp1, x0);  // Decrease the interval.

        diff = width(xnp1);
        x0 = xnp1;

        counter++;
    }

    cout << "Number of iterations: " << counter << endl;

    return x0;
}
```

We give an example of how to compute $\sqrt{2}$. Note that the interval given must contain the solution. The two input functions are:

```cpp
// Functions for NR method to calculate sqrt(2).
Range Func(const Range& x)
{
    return x*x - 2.0;
}
```

and

```cpp
Range FuncDerivative(const Range& x)
{
    return 2.0*x;
}
```

A test program is:

```cpp
int main()
{
    double tol = 0.004;

    // The interval where we know the solution is.
    Range x0(0.0, 100.0);

    Range r = NRSolver(Func, FuncDerivative, x0, tol);
    cout << "Final Root sqrt: [" << r.lower() << ","
```

```
        << r.upper() << "]" << endl;
    double cen = median(r);
    cout << "Solution is: " << cen << ", " << endl;

    return 0;
}
```

You can run the code to test the accuracy of the algorithm.

13.9 Summary and Conclusions

We have given an introduction of the Boost Interval library. Interval Arithmetic is a branch of numerical analysis and its main applications are to problems with inaccurate input data or when we wish to quantify round-off error during computations. It can also be used in other applications where it is needed to model intervals and collections of intervals. In this case it might be worth having a look at the Interval Container Library (ICL) that we discuss in chapter 18.

We have not discussed trigonometric and transcendente functions for interval numbers because some code is not supported in the version of Boost Interval we used. It seems as if this is a major bug in the library. A discussion of using Boost Interval with other Boost libraries is outside the scope of this book.

14 User-defined Memory Allocation: Boost Pool

14.1 Introduction and Objectives

In this relatively short chapter we discuss the Boost Pool library that allows us to perform dynamic memory allocation and deallocation in much the same way as we are accustomed to with the C functions *malloc* and *free* or the C++ operators `new` and `delete`. However, these implementations lead to memory fragmentation problems due to the fact that blocks of variable size are allocated and deallocated at run-time. This makes them unsuitable for some real-time and embedded software systems because of the ensuing performance problems and response unpredictability. In order to resolve these problems the Boost Pool library allows developers to *preallocate memory blocks* in which each block consists of a number of *chunks* of fixed and equal size. The advantages are that there is little memory administration overhead and that allocation/deallocation is fast. These advantages come at a price, however all chunks have the same size and they are limited to one data type. Furthermore, we need a separate storage for each data type in an application. On the other hand, the advantages could outweigh the disadvantages, especially for *hard real-time* and *embedded* applications where *timeliness* is mandatory. For application developers this may be less of a concern but nonetheless we should try to avoid creating and destroying many small objects, as this can lead to performance degradation.

In this chapter we introduce the functionality in Pool and we discuss the various options that promote efficient memory management based on various user requirements and performance scenarios. We also discuss Boost Timer (that we introcuded in chapter 5) and we use it as a simple means of comparing the relative performance of Pool memory management against *malloc* and *new*, for example.

14.2 Dynamic Memory Allocation in C++ and STL Allocator Requirements

In C++ it is possible to handle the allocation and deallocation of memory using special objects called *allocators*. These are abstractions for translating a need to use memory into a raw call for memory. We can choose between different allocators thus allowing us to use different memory models in an application. The default allocator in STL is based on `new` and `delete` operators. In most cases application developers do not have to be concerned with allocators and can ignore them as they have default template argument values. For real-time and embedded systems this default situation may need to be modified if performance becomes an issue.

The fundamental operations in an STL allocator class are:
- `allocate(num);` allocate memory for `num` elements.
- `construct(p);` initialise the elements to which p refers.
- `destroy(p);` destroy the elements to which p refers.
- `deallocate(p,num);` deallocate memory for `num` elements to which p refers.

It is possible to create user-defined allocators as described in Josuttis 1999, for example. The main issue is to allocate and deallocate memory. In general, we create a base implementation and specialised allocator classes that implement the member functions `allocate()`, `deallocate()` and `max_size()` (this member function returns the maximum number of elements that can be allocated). Let us assume that we have created such a user-defined allocator class `UserAlloc`. We can then use it as follows:

```
int main()
{
```

```
std::vector<long,UserAlloc<long> > v;

for (long j = 0; j < 10; ++j)
{
    v.push_back(j);
}

return 0;
}
```

To recall, the details of constructing the class `UserAlloc` are discussed in Josuttis 1999.

We now shall see that Pool objects request memory blocks from the system. These blocks are split into chunks that are then given to the user. To this end, the various Pool interfaces have a template parameter `UserAllocator` that controls how system memory blocks are allocated and deallocated. Pool supports two allocator types based on `new/delete` (the default for Pool interfaces) and on `malloc/free`, respectively. They are defined as follows:

```
// The default case in Pool.
struct default_user_allocator_new_delete
{
    typedef std::size_t size_type;
    typedef std::ptrdiff_t difference_type;

    static char * malloc(const size_type bytes)
    { return new (std::nothrow) char[bytes]; }

    static void free(char * const block)
    { delete [] block; }
};

struct default_user_allocator_malloc_free
{
    typedef std::size_t size_type;
    typedef std::ptrdiff_t difference_type;

    static char * malloc(const size_type bytes)
    { return reinterpret_cast<char *>(std::malloc(bytes)); }

    static void free(char * const block)
    { std::free(block); }
};
```

We shall see examples of use in later sections.

14.3 Pool Concepts

We discuss some of the problems associated with standard memory allocation and deallocation in C++. First, it must support memory blocks of different sizes which can lead to memory waste and performance problems. Second, keeping track of used and unused memory becomes problematic and the memory manager needs to maintain internal data structures that hold this information. This in its turn leads to extra memory and time overhead. Finally, creating and destroying many *small-grained objects* has a performance impact on a running program. To resolve these problems Pool employs a *simple segregated storage* mechanism that results in the elimination of memory overhead. All allocations take place in a small amount of time. The downside is that simple segregated storage can only allocate chunks of a single fixed size.

14.3.1 Simple Segregated Storage Concept

Simple Segregated Storage is a very simple and fast memory allocation/deallocation algorithm. Given a *memory block*, the algorithm partitions it into fixed-size *chunks*. A *pool* is an object that uses Simple Segregated Storage in this way. The chunks all have the same size and it is thus not possible to ask for chunks of different sizes. For example, it is not possible to ask a Pool of integers for a character or a Pool of characters for an integer.

A free list is interleaved with unused chunks. A *free list* is a data structure that is used for dynamic memory allocation. It connects unused allocated regions of memory together in a linked list. Each unallocated region has a pointer to the next unallocated region. This makes allocation and deallocation operations very simple. To free a region we just add it to the free list. To allocate a region, we remove a region from the end of the free list and subsequently use it. There are several disadvantages of using free lists but for simple applications they are useful.

Another algorithm is the *buddy memory allocation algorithm* (see Knuth 1997). The algorithm requires that the block sizes be some power of 2. If a block is not of size 2^k for some k then the next power of 2 is chosen and extra unused space is allocated accordingly. The method keeps separate lists of blocks of each size 2^k for $0 \le k \le m$. The memory pool consists of 2^m words and initially a block of 2^m words is available. If a block of size 2^k is needed at a later time and if nothing is available then a larger available block is split into two equal parts and at some stage a block of the right size 2^k will become available. When a block splits into two equal sub-blocks (and the sub-block size is half that of the original block) we say that the two sub-blocks are called *buddies*. When the buddies become available again they are coalesced into a single block.

We conclude this section with a summary of using memory pools compared to using `malloc()`:

- Memory allocation execution time with memory pools is constant because there is no *fragmentation*. Furthermore, memory release for many objects in a pool is one operation, in contrast to `malloc()` which releases objects one by one.
- Fixed-size block memory pools do not need to store metadata for each allocation which is needed because we need to know the size of allocated blocks, for example.
- It is possible to group memory pools in hierarchical tree structures which makes it suitable for programming structures such as loops and recursions.

The flexibility of Pool is determined by the interfaces it provides. First, *Object Usage* is the method whereby each Pool is an object that may be created and destroyed. When a Pool is destroyed it implicitly frees all chunks that have been allocated from it. *Singleton Usage* is the method whereby each Pool is an object with *static duration*, that it is destroyed at program exit time. Pool objects when using Singleton Usage can be shared and access to them is thread-safe. It is possible to free Pool objects when using Singleton Usage by calling `release_memory()` or `purge_memory()` as we shall see in later sections.

As far as exception handling is concerned, some Pool interfaces throw an exception when memory is depleted while others return 0; in general Pool interfaces always prefer to return 0 instead of throwing an exception.

In the following sections we discuss specific Pool classes.

14.4 Pool

This is a fast memory allocator and it guarantees proper alignment of all allocated chunks. It extends the functionality of the simple segregated storage solution and it provides two `UserAllocator` classes that we discussed in section 14.2.

We take an example of allocating and deallocating memory using `malloc()` / `free()`, `new` / `delete` and the pool class. The objective is to compare the relative speed of memory allocation and deallocation in C and C++ of each option. You can then compare the results with the corresponding memory allocation and deallocation functions in Pool. The code is:

```cpp
#include <iostream>
#include <boost/pool/pool.hpp>
#include <boost/timer.hpp>

using namespace std;

int main()
{
    int count=1000000;
    int* ip;

    // Create using malloc/free.
    {
        boost::timer t;
        int size=sizeof(int);
        cout << "Size of int: " << size << endl;

        for (int i=0; i<count; i++)
        {
            ip=(int*)malloc(size);
            free(ip);
        }

        cout<<"Time for malloc/free: "<<t.elapsed()<<endl;
    }

    // Create using new/delete.
    {
        boost::timer t;

        for (int i=0; i<count; i++)
        {
            ip=new int;
            delete(ip);
        }

        cout<<"Time for new/delete: "<<t.elapsed()<<endl;
    }

    // Create using pool.
    {
        boost::timer t;
        boost::pool<> p(sizeof(int));

        for (int i=0; i<count; i++)
        {
            ip=(int*)p.malloc();
            p.free(ip);
        }

        cout<<"Time for pool, default new allocator: "<<t.elapsed()<<endl;

    } // Memory not released by free but will be freed here when pool
      // goes out of scope. Also internal memory will be released.
```

```
    // Create using pool with explicitly new/delete allocator.
    {
        boost::timer t;
        boost::pool<boost::default_user_allocator_new_delete>
            p(sizeof(int));

        for (int i=0; i<count; i++)
        {
            ip=(int*)p.malloc();
            p.free(ip);
        }

        cout<<"Time for pool, explicit new allocator: "<<t.elapsed()<<endl;
    }

    // Create using pool with explicitly malloc allocator.
    {
        boost::timer t;
        boost::pool<boost::default_user_allocator_malloc_free>
            p(sizeof(int));

        for (int i=0; i<count; i++)
        {
            ip=(int*)p.malloc();
            p.free(ip);
        }

        cout<<"Time for pool, explicit malloc allocator: "
            <<t.elapsed()<<endl;
    }

    // Create using pool with explicitly own allocator.
    {
        boost::timer t;
        boost::pool<Datasim::MyAllocator> p(sizeof(int));

        for (int i=0; i<count; i++)
        {
            ip=(int*)p.malloc();
            p.free(ip);
        }

        cout<<"Time for pool, explicit my allocator: "<<t.elapsed()<<endl;
    }

    return 0;
}
```

We have defined our own allocator object and it could be useful for customisation purposes:

```
namespace Datasim
{
    struct MyAllocator
    {
        typedef std::size_t size_type;
        typedef std::ptrdiff_t difference_type;

        static char * malloc(const size_type bytes)
        { return new (std::nothrow) char[bytes]; }

        static void free(char * const block)
        { delete [] block; }
    };
```

```
}
```

We ran this program on a normal laptop; in general, we found that `pool` allocation/deallocation for integers is twice as fast as allocation/deallocation using `malloc()` or `new`. Also when the size of the data that is being allocated gets bigger, new and `malloc()` get slower while the allocation time for pool is independent of the size. You can experiment on other hardware platforms to compare the relative performance.

Some final remarks concerning the `pool` class:
- It returns 0 when out-of-memory.
- We use overloaded `malloc()` to allocate a chunk of memory and overloaded `free()` to deallocate a chunk.
- We use `release_memory()` to release unallocated blocks.
- We use `purge_memory()` to release all memory. In this case all pointers to allocated chunks are invalidated.

14.5 Singleton Pool

The *Singleton Pool* class is similar to `pool` except that instances of the former class have static lifetime by default. In other words, memory is destroyed when the program ends but it is also possible to explicitly release all internal memory in the pool before program end by calling the static member function `purge_memory()`. It uses `pool` internally.

The class interface is:

```
template <typename Tag, unsigned RequestedSize,
          typename UserAllocator, typename Mutex, unsigned NextSize>
struct singleton_pool
{
    // etc.
};
```

This class is a *Singleton* in the Design Pattern sense (see GOF 1995). It is thread-safe if there is only one thread running before `main()` begins and after `main()` ends. In particular, all static member functions of `singleton_pool` synchronise their access to the underlying pool. We also note that the `Tag` template parameter allows different sets of singleton pools to exist (as with the Boost Flyweight library we discussed in Demming 2010).

We take an example of use and we create and destroy some `array<int, N>` instances. When we ran the program, we saw that Singleton Pool was slighty slower than the regular pool. This is probably because the Singeton Pool adds synchronisation so allocating memory from different threads is safe. On our test machine allocating very small blocks with Singleton Pool is slower than with `malloc()` or `new` but for larger blocks the Singleton Pool is faster because its allocation time is independent of the size:

```
#include <boost/pool/singleton_pool.hpp>

// Class just for tagging a singleton pool.
struct MyTag1 {};
struct MyTag2 {};

// Typedef for the data to allocate.
typedef boost::array<int, 10000> Data;
// Define a singleton pool to create chunks for "Data".
typedef boost::singleton_pool<MyTag1, sizeof(Data)> Pool1;
typedef boost::singleton_pool<MyTag2, sizeof(Data)> Pool2;
```

```
int main()
{
    int count=1000000;
    Data* ip;

    // Create using malloc/free.
    {
        boost::timer t;
        int size=sizeof(Data);
        cout << "Size of Data: " << size << endl;

        for (int i=0; i<count; i++)
        {
            ip=(Data*)malloc(size);
            free(ip);
        }

        cout<<"Time for malloc/free: "<<t.elapsed()<<endl;
    }

    // Create using new/delete.
    {
        boost::timer t;

        for (int i=0; i<count; i++)
        {
            ip=new Data;
            delete(ip);
        }

        cout<<"Time for new/delete: "<<t.elapsed()<<endl;
    }

    // Create using singleton pool #1.
    {
        boost::timer t;

        for (int i=0; i<count; i++)
        {
            ip=(Data*)Pool1::malloc();
            Pool1::free(ip);
        }

        cout<<"Time for singleton pool #1: "<<t.elapsed()<<endl;

    } // Singleton pool memory still available here.

    // Create using singleton pool #2.
    {
        boost::timer t;

        for (int i=0; i<count; i++)
        {
            ip=(Data*)Pool2::malloc();
            Pool2::free(ip);
        }

        cout<<"Time for singleton pool #2: "<<t.elapsed()<<endl;

    } // Singleton pool memory still available here.

    // Explicitly release all internal memory in the pool.
    Pool1::purge_memory();
    Pool2::purge_memory();
```

```
        return 0;
    }
```

14.6 Object Pool

This is the *Object Usage* pool for object chunks. It is type-aware and it returns a pointer to
an object rather to `void*`. No casting is needed and 0 is returned when memory is depleted.
The *Object Pool* `malloc()` function allocates objects but it does not call a constructor.
Therefore we normally allocate an object using a call to `construct()` that also calls a
constructor. In a similar vein, `free()` frees the object but it does not call its destructor. We
use `destroy()` to free an object which calls the destructor. Finally, objects that have not
been freed or destroyed will be destroyed (including a call to the destructor) when the pool
goes out of scope.

An example of use is now given:

```cpp
#include <boost/pool/object_pool.hpp>

int main()
{
    int count=1000000;
    Point* point;

    // Create using new/delete.
    {
        boost::timer t;

        for (int i=0; i<count; i++)
        {
            point=new Point;
            delete(point);
        }

        cout<<"Time for new/delete: "<<t.elapsed()<<endl;
    }

    // Create using pool (malloc/free).
    {
        boost::timer t;
        boost::object_pool<Point> p;

        for (int i=0; i<count; i++)
        {
            point=p.malloc();    // No constructor called.
            p.free(point);       // No destructor called.
        }

        cout<<"Time for object pool (malloc/free): "<<t.elapsed()<<endl;

    } // Memory not released by free, will be released here when pool goes
      // out of scope. Destructors are called for all unreleased objects
      // no matter if they were created with malloc() or construct().

    // Create using pool (construct/destroy).
    {
        boost::timer t;
        boost::object_pool<Point> p;

        for (int i=0; i<count; i++)
        {
            point=p.construct();  // Calls default constructor.
```

```
        p.destroy(point);       // Calls destructor.
    }

    cout<<"Time object pool(construct/destroy): "<<t.elapsed()<<endl;

} // Memory not released by destroy will be released when pool goes
  // out of scope. Destructors are called for all unreleased objects
  // no matter if they were created with malloc() or construct().

cout<<endl<<"Test calling of constructor/destructor"<<endl;
{
    boost::object_pool<Point2> p;
    Point2* pt;

    cout<<"Create with malloc()"<<endl;
    pt=p.malloc();
    cout<<"Destroy with free()"<<endl;
    p.free(pt);

    cout<<endl<<"Create with construct()"<<endl;
    pt=p.construct(10.0, 20.0);
    cout<<"Destroy with destroy()"<<endl;
    p.destroy(pt);

    cout<<endl<<"Create with malloc() but no free()"<<endl;
    p.malloc();
    cout<<"Create with construct() but no destroy()"<<endl;
    p.construct(10.0, 20.0);
    cout<<"Is the destructor called when going out of scope?"<<endl;
}
cout<<"Object pool out of scope"<<endl;

return 0;
}
```

14.7 Pool Allocator and Fast Pool Allocator

These classes are *Singleton Usage* pools for object chunks. They throw the exception
`std::bad_alloc` when out of memory. Of particular interest is that they are compatible
with STL containers and their main use is as an allocator for these containers. The two
classes are:

- `pool_allocator`: Regular pool allocator. Is more efficient when allocating a number
  of contiguous chunks at the time, for example when used with an `std::vector`.
- `fast_pool_allocator`: Is faster when allocating one chunck at the time, for example
  when used with `std::list`.

Tags are used for the underlying *Singleton Pool*, that is `pool_allocator_tag` and `fast_pool_allocator_tag`. You can use these tags to access the underlying singleton directly
to explicitly release the memory for example.

An example of use using the STL list container is:

```
#include <iostream>
#include <list>

#include <boost/pool/pool_alloc.hpp>
#include <boost/timer.hpp>

using namespace std;

int main()
```

```
{
    int count=10000;

    // Normal allocator.
    {
        boost::timer t;

        list<int> l;
        for (int i=0; i<count; i++) l.push_back(i);

        cout<<"Time for list regular alloc: "<<t.elapsed()<<endl;
    }

    // Pool allocator.
    {
        boost::timer t;

        list<int, boost::pool_allocator<int> > l;
        for (int i=0; i<count; i++) l.push_back(i);

        cout<<"Time for list with pool allocator: "<<t.elapsed()<<endl;
        cout<<"It takes some time when the list goes out of scope, "
            <<"before the memory is freed."<<endl;
    }

    // Explicitly release internal memory.
    // Use underlying singleton pool.
    boost::singleton_pool<boost::pool_allocator_tag,
                          sizeof(int)>::release_memory();

    // Fast pool allocator.
    {
        boost::timer t;

        list<int, boost::fast_pool_allocator<int> > l;
        for (int i=0; i<count; i++) l.push_back(i);

        cout<<"Time list fast pool alloc: "<<t.elapsed()<<endl;
    }

    // Explicitly release internal memory.
    // Use underlying singleton pool.
    boost::singleton_pool<boost::fast_pool_allocator_tag,
                          sizeof(int)>::release_memory();

    return 0;
}
```

14.8 Summary and Conclusions

We have introduced Boost Pool that gives real-time and embedded programmers more control over how memory is managed in a program when compared to heap-based memory management using the C++ operators new and delete. Pool is limited in its general applicability but it is very fast.

15 An Introduction to Graph Theory and Graph Algorithms

15.1 Introduction and Objectives

In this chapter we introduce a class of data structures called graphs. The origins of graph theory can be traced to the work of Leonhard Euler (1707-1783) and in recent years there has been a great interest in the theory and its applications to economics, telecommunications, computer science and optimisation.

A *graph* is a collection of *nodes* (or *vertices*) that are connected by *edges*. There are various types of graphs. We discuss how to represent graphs in this chapter. Having done that we discuss a number of operations on graphs:

- *Searching* in a graph (discovering information about a graph G).
- Finding the *shortest path* between two vertices in a graph (in this case each edge has a numerical weight assigned to it).
- *Minimum spanning tree* (find a subset of the edges of G that connects all its vertices and whose total weight is a minimum).
- *Maximum flow problems* (how much of a quantity can move through a network of nodes?).
- Partitioning a graph into *connected components*; a connected component is a group of vertices in a graph that are mutually reachable from one another.

We give a number of examples to motivate what graphs are and the operations that are defined on them. Furthermore, we implement these operations using the functionality of the Boost Graph Library (BGL) in chapter 16 and we give more advanced examples and applications in chapter 17.

15.2 Directed and Undirected Graphs; Terms and Definitions

A *graph* $G = (V, E)$ is a data structure consisting of a finite set V of *vertices* (or *nodes*) and a finite set E of *edges* such that each edge e is associated with a pair of vertices u and v. We say that the graph is *undirected* if there is no distinction between the edge from u to v and the edge from v to u; it is the same edge. A *directed graph* $G = (V, E)$ (or *digraph* for short) is one in which the vertex set is as in an undirected graph but the set E represents directed arcs such that each arc in E is associated with an *ordered pair* of vertices u and v. We write $e = (u, v)$ to denote that e is an *arc* from u to v. In general, edges and arcs are represented by lower case letters while we can use either upper-case or lower-case letters for vertices. We represent graphs and digraphs pictorially by modelling vertices as circles or points and edges as straight or curved lines connecting the vertices. An example of an undirected graph with four vertices and six edges is shown in Figure 15.1(a) while a digraph with four vertices and seven arcs is shown in Figure 15.1(b).

We introduce some terminology. First, let u and v be vertices in a graph and let e be an edge connecting them. We can write $e = \{u, v\}$ or equivalently $e = \{v, u\}$ since the graph is undirected by definition. We say that e is *incident* on both u and v and that u and v are *adjacent vertices*. These vertices are also incident on e. An edge joining a vertex to itself is called a *loop*. If there is more than one edge joining the pairs of vertices then the graph is called a *multigraph*. If two or more edges join the same pairs of edges in a multigraph, these

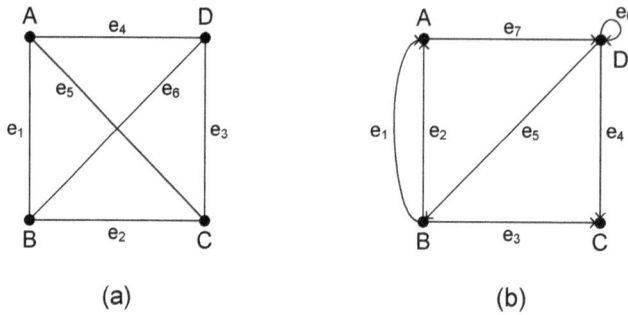

Figure 15.1 Graph and Digraph

edges are called *multiple edges*. An example of a multigraph is shown in Figure 15.1(b) where we see two edges e_1 and e_2 between vertices A and B. We also note the loop e_6 at vertex D. We say that a graph is *simple* if it has no multiple edges and no loops. An example of a simple graph is given in Figure 15.1(a) while the directed graph in Figure 15.2 is not simple because it has a loop at vertex A. It is possible to associate auxiliary information with a graph's edges; normally this corresponds to some numeric or physical quantity. In this case we say that a graph is a *network* or *weighted graph*. These special graphs are important in applications. The weights correspond to domain-specific information such as duration of a project activity or the distance between two adjacent cities. Figure 15.3 is an example of a weighted graph.

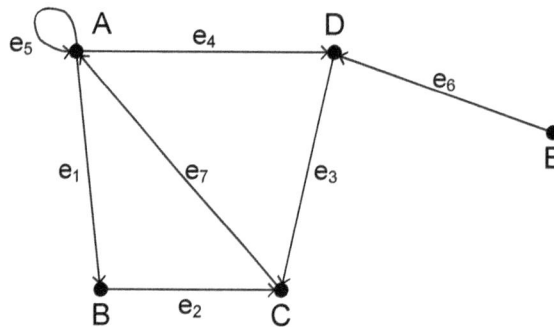

Figure 15.2 Multigraph

Now let u and v be vertices in a digraph. We write $e = (u, v)$ to describe the arc from u to v ; we then say that u *is adjacent to* v or that v *is adjacent from* u. We also say that e is *incident from u* or *incident to v*. We also say that two vertices are adjacent if there is an arc from one vertex to the other vertex. A *weighted digraph* or *weighted network* is a digraph in which each arc has a real number assigned to it. We remark that an arc from vertex u to vertex v in a diagraph does not imply the existence of an arc from v to u.

15.2.1 Further Properties of Graphs and Digraphs

If we treat every arc of a digraph as an edge (rather than an arc), the resulting structure is called the *underlying graph* of the digraph. A simple graph with n vertices is said to be *complete* if there is an edge between each pair of vertices. The graph is then denoted by K_n. A digraph is a *complete digraph* if its underlying graph is complete.

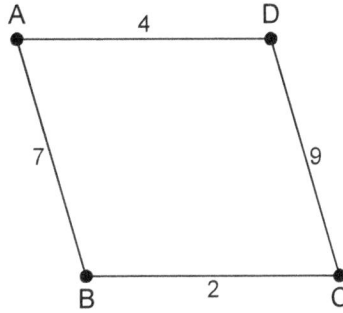

Figure 15.3 Weighted graph

The *degree* of a vertex in a graph is the number of edges incident on that vertex. A vertex is *odd* if its degree is odd; otherwise, it is *even*. For example, the degree of vertex A in Figure 15.1(a) is odd because it has three incident edges whereas vertex C in Figure 15.3 is even. The *indegree* of a vertex in a digraph is the number of arcs incident to that vertex. The *outdegree* of a vertex is the number of arcs incident from that vertex. For example, the indegree of vertex C in Figure 15.2 is two while its outdegree is one.

A graph $G' = (V', E')$ is called a *subgraph* of $G = (V, E)$ if V' is a subset of V and E' is a subset of E. If W is any subset of V, then the *subgraph of G induced* by W is the graph $H = (W, F)$ where f is an edge of F if $f = \{u, v\}$ where f is in E and u and v are in W. For example, in Figure 15.4 the vertex set $W = \{1, 2, 4, 5\}$ is a subset of the vertex set $V = \{1, 2, 3, 4, 5\}$ and the subgraph of G induced by W is H. A *complete subgraph* of G is called a *clique* in G. For example, the subgraph of G with vertices $\{1, 2, 3\}$ is a clique.

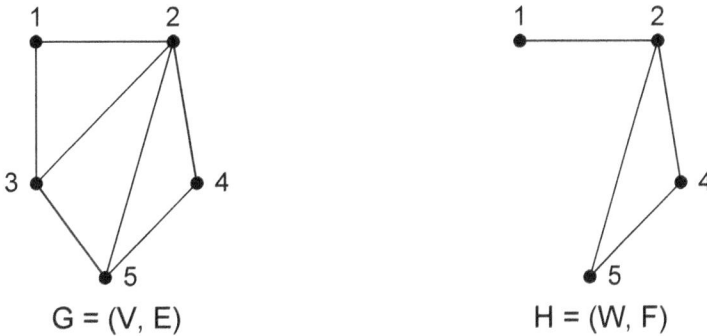

Figure 15.4 Graph and Subgraph

15.2.2 Paths and Connectivity

A *path* in a multigraph between two vertices v_0 and v_n is a finite sequence of vertices and edges in the form $v_0, e_1, v_1, e_2 \ldots, e_n, v_n$ where e_k is an edge between v_{k-1} and v_k for $k = 1, \ldots, n$. The vertices and edges in a path need not be distinct. The number of edges in a path is called its *length* (we then call it an *n-path)* and we say that the path connects its endpoints. We have included both the vertices and edges in the definition of a path but when there is no danger of ambiguity we can denote a path solely by its vertices. For example, in Figure 15.1(a) the sequence of vertices $\{A, B, D\}$ is a path of length 2. A path is *simple* if its vertices are distinct. It is easy to check that all edges in a simple graph are distinct but a path with distinct edges can have repeated vertices. A path between a vertex and itself is called a *closed path*. A *circuit* is a closed path in which all edges are distinct. A *cycle* is a circuit in which all vertices are distinct. Finally, a *walk* is an alternating sequence of edges and vertices, beginning and ending with a vertex, where each vertex is incident to both the edge that precedes it and the edge that follows it in the sequence.

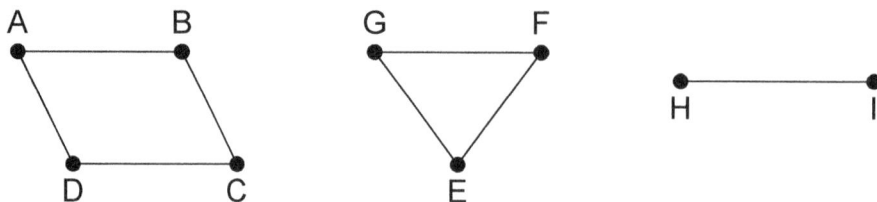

Figure 15.5 Non-connected graph

A graph is *connected* if there is a path between any two of its vertices. The graphs in Figures 15.1(a) and 15.2 are connected while the graph in Figure 15.5 is not connected because there is no path from vertex E to vertex C, for example. In this latter case we say that the graph has three *connected components* that are the subgraphs induced by the vertex sets {A, B, C, D}, {E, F, G} and {H, I}.

Let G be a connected graph. The *distance* between vertices u and v in G, written as $d(u, v)$, is the length of the shortest path between u and v. The *diameter of a graph* G, written diam(G), is the maximum distance of the shortest paths between any two vertices in G. For example, in Figure 15.6 d(A, C) = 2 and diam(G) = 14 (F to D).

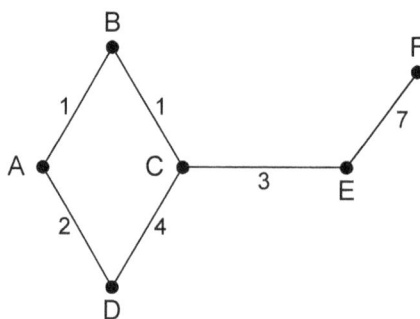

Figure 15.6 Distance and Diameter

15.2.3 Special Types of Graphs

We give a short introduction to a number of special graph types. A *bipartite graph* G is a graph whose vertices V can be partitioned into two disjoints subsets M and N such that each edge of G connects a vertex of M to a vertex of N. A *complete bipartite graph* connects each vertex of M with each vertex of N. If M has m vertices and N has n vertices we denote the bipartite graph by $K_{m,n}$. Such graphs have mn edges. An example in the case $m = 2, n = 3$ is given in Figure 15.7. Bipartite graphs are used in *matching problems* (for example, matching m people to n jobs), Petri nets in concurrent software systems and Coding Theory in which each code is associated with a unique meaning.

A *tree graph* T is a connected graph having no cycles. A tree containing n vertices has $n - 1$ edges. A *forest* is a graph with no cycles and its connected components are trees. A subgraph T of a connected graph G is called a *spanning tree* of G if T is a tree and T includes all the vertices of G. A graph can have several spanning trees, as shown in *Figure 15.8.*

Now let G be a connected weighted graph. Then we can compute a *total weight* for each spanning tree T by adding the weights of all the edges of T. A *minimum spanning tree* (MST) of a weighted digraph G is a spanning tree whose total weight is a minimum. For small weighted graphs we can find the minimum spanning tree by inspection. In such cases you can convince yourself that this is indeed the MST by comparing its weight value with the total weights of the other spanning trees of the graph.

A graph or digraph is called *labeled* if its edges and/or vertices are assigned some kind of data. Special cases are weighted graphs and weighted digraphs.

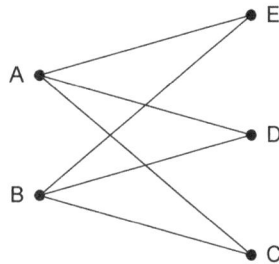

Figure 15.7 Bipartite $K_{2,3}$ graph

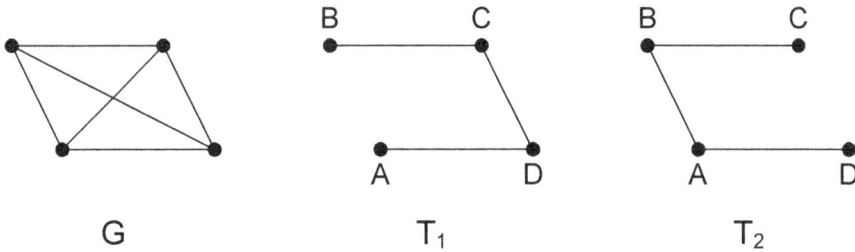

Figure 15.8 Graph G and two spanning trees T_1 and T_2

15.3 Graph Data Structures

We now discuss how to represent graphs and digraphs as datastructures. To this end, the most common data structures are matrices and lists. We introduce a number of matrix structures that describe properties of graphs and digraphs.

Let G be a graph with n vertices $v_1, \ldots, v_n$. Then the *adjacency matrix* $A = (a_{ij})_{1 \le i, j \le n}$ is a symmetric matrix of size n and it consists of zeroes and ones:

$$a_{ij} = \begin{cases} 1, \text{ if } v_i \text{ is adjacent to } v_j, \quad i \ne j \\ 0, \text{ otherwise.} \end{cases}$$

We give an example of an adjacency matrix for the graph in Figure 15.9. The matrix is symmetric in this case. In the case of a digraph the situation is slightly different. In this case the adjacency matrix is not symmetric. An example is given in Figure 15.10.

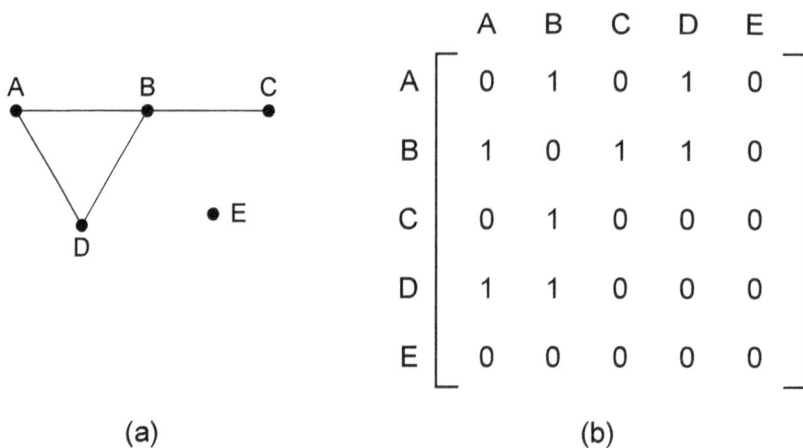

$$
\begin{array}{c c c c c c}
 & A & B & C & D & E \\
A & 0 & 1 & 0 & 1 & 0 \\
B & 1 & 0 & 1 & 1 & 0 \\
C & 0 & 1 & 0 & 0 & 0 \\
D & 1 & 1 & 0 & 0 & 0 \\
E & 0 & 0 & 0 & 0 & 0
\end{array}
$$

(a)   (b)

Figure 15.9 Adjacency matrix for a graph

There is a relation between the number of paths between pairs of vertices in a graph and the powers of its adjacency matrix, namely:

If A is the adjacency matrix of a graph then the (i, j)-entry of the kth power A^k of A is the number of k-paths between vertex i and vertex j.

The second data structure is the *adjacency list* which is a representation of all edges in a graph or of all arcs in a digraph. For each vertex, we enumerate its adjacent vertices. The adjacency list for the graph in Figure 15.10 is given in Figure 15.11.

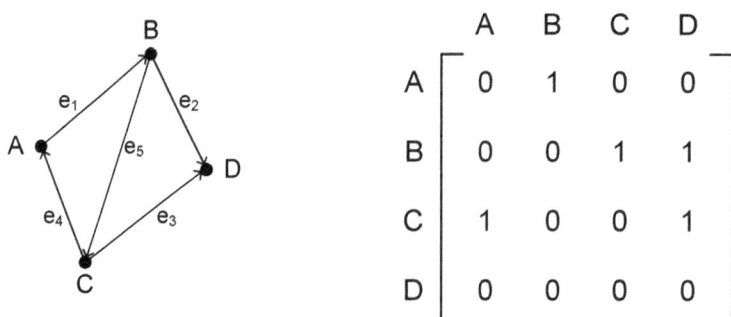

$$
\begin{array}{c c c c c}
 & A & B & C & D \\
A & 0 & 1 & 0 & 0 \\
B & 0 & 0 & 1 & 1 \\
C & 1 & 0 & 0 & 1 \\
D & 0 & 0 & 0 & 0
\end{array}
$$

Figure 15.10 Adjacency matrix for a digraph

Vertex	Adjacency List
A	B
B	C, D
C	A, D
D	ø (none)

Figure 15.11 Adjacency list for digraph

Another representation for a graph is the *incidence matrix*; in this case the number of rows is the same as the number of vertices in the graph and the number of columns is the same as the number of edges in the graph. For a graph, the values are:

$$a_{ij} = \begin{cases} 1, \text{ if vertex } v_i \text{ and edge } e_j \text{ are adjacent} \\ \\ 0, \text{ otherwise.} \end{cases}$$

For a digraph, if the kth arc is (i,j) then the kth column of this matrix has +1 in the ith row, -1 in the jth row and 0 everywhere else. Examples of incidence matrices are given in Figures 15.12 and 15.13, for graphs and digraphs, respectively.

Finally, we discuss some other matrix representations:
- The degree matrix.
- The Laplacian (or Kirchoff, Admittance) matrix.
- The distance matrix.

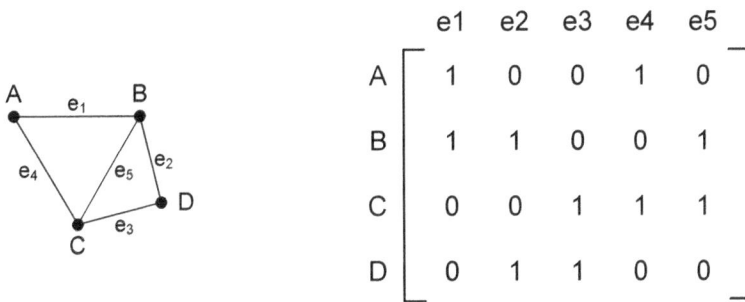

	e1	e2	e3	e4	e5
A	1	0	0	1	0
B	1	1	0	0	1
C	0	0	1	1	1
D	0	1	1	0	0

Figure 15.12 Incidence matrix for a graph

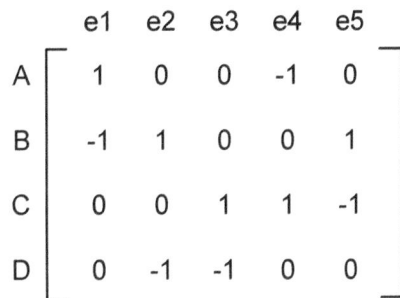

	e1	e2	e3	e4	e5
A	1	0	0	-1	0
B	-1	1	0	0	1
C	0	0	1	1	-1
D	0	-1	-1	0	0

Figure 15.13 Incidence matrix for digraph of Figure 15.10

The *degree matrix* is a diagonal matrix (all off-diagonal values are zero) whose diagonal elements contain information about the degree of each vertex. The *Laplacian matrix* L is the difference between the degree matrix D and the adjacency matrix A, that is L = D – A. The *distance matrix* of a weighted graph is a square symmetric matrix whose size is the same as the number of vertices in the graph and contains element values that represent the shortest path between two vertices. The distance between two vertices that are not connected is infinity by default. We shall use the distance matrix in chapter 17.

We conclude with some remarks. For graphs having a *sparse adjacency matrix* the adjacency list takes up less memory because it does not use space to represent edges that do not exist. For other cases, each entry in an adjacency matrix requires one bit. Furthermore, it is easy to find all vertices adjacent to a given vertex when using the adjacency list representation. This operation takes O(n) time using an adjacency matrix representation where n is the number of vertices in the graph. On the other hand, it is easy to determine if two vertices have an edge between them.

15.4 Operations on Graphs

Having discussed what graphs and digraphs are and how they are represented we now show what can be done with them. In particular, we discuss operations on graphs and we shall progress to applications in BGL in chapters 16 and 17.

Some important classes of algorithms are:
• Minimum spanning trees (MST).
• Basic algorithms (depth-first search, breadth-first search).
• Shortest paths in graphs.
• Maximum flows in networks.
• Computing connected components.

We describe each of these categories in the following sections and we give worked examples (which can be computed by hand) to help us in our understanding of fundamental concepts.

15.5 Minimum Spanning Tree (MST) Problems

We recall the MST problem; for a connected weighted graph G find that spanning tree whose total weight is as small as possible. Three popular algorithms are:
• *Reverse-delete* algorithm.
• *Kruskal's* algorithm (supported in BGL).
• *Prim's* algorithm (supported in BGL).

What is common to these three algorithms is that they find the MST for a given weighted graph, but they go about it in different ways. We now discuss each one.

The *reverse-delete* algorithm starts with the original graph and it deletes edges from it until the minimal spanning tree has been found. The steps are:
1. Start with graph G containing the list of weighted edges E.
2. Iterate over E in descending order (that is, starting with the largest weight).
3. For each visited edge, check if deleting it will disconnect the graph. If it does not, then delete it. In general, a graph is disconnected if it has more than one connected component.
4. Process all edges and delete those that do not lead to additional disconnection.

This algorithm is easy to understand and to visualise, especially for small graphs. For larger graphs, we implement the graph in software. We take an example as shown in Figure 15.14. The sorted edge weights are {10, 5, 5, 4, 2, 1}. If we now navigate in this list and delete the corresponding edges that do not disconnect the graph, we end up with the set of vertices {1, 2, 4, 3} that form the MST. You can go through the steps and convince yourself that this is indeed the MST.

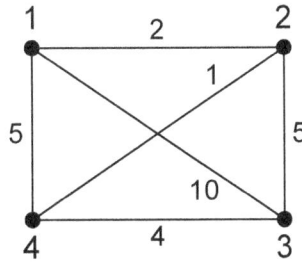

Figure 15.14 Minimal Spanning Tree example

Kruskal's algorithm starts with an empty graph (no edges) and it adds edges rather than removing them. The steps are:
1. Initialise the graph G with n vertices and no edges/arcs.
2. Create a list L from the set of edges E in *ascending order* of length (arbitrarily rank those edges/arcs with the same length).
3. Select the edge/arc from the head of L. We delete it if it forms a circuit in G and we repeat step 2. Otherwise, we transfer the edge/arc from L to G.
4. If G is a tree, then we are finished; otherwise repeat step 2.

As an example, we apply Kruskal's algorithm to the weighted graph in Figure 15.14. First, we need to sort the list of edges based on their weight values; thus L = { {2,4}, {1,2}, {3,4}, {1,4}, {2,3}, {1,3} }. The first edge {2,4} does not form a circuit in G, thus we add it to G. Next, the edge {1, 2} does not form a circuit, so we add it to G and then we add edge {3,4} to G. Finally, adding the edges {1,4}, {2,3} and {1,3} would cause a circuit to be formed, hence we delete them. The resulting MST is shown in Figure 15.15.

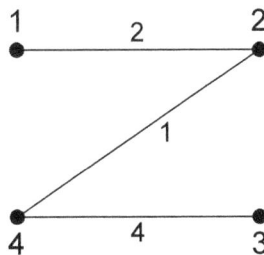

Figure 15.15 Minimal spanning tree

Prim's algorithm is a 'greedy' algorithm in the sense that the MST is grown steadily from one initial arc; at each stage of the algorithm the arc that is added is the shortest arc remaining that has one vertex in the tree. Thus, to select an arc, we scan those arcs that are not yet in the partial tree and we divide them into two sets corresponding to those that have one and only one vertex in the tree and those that have none or two. The steps are:

1. Initialise the graph (G,E) with one vertex (arbitrarily selected) having no arcs.
2. Select the arc (i,j) whose length is least, from among the arcs (i,q) that have i in G and q not in G. We add this arc to G and we add j to the node set of G.
3. If G is a spanning tree for the graph (G,E) we stop; otherwise, repeat step 2.

As an example, we take Figure 15.14 again and we select vertex 1 as the initial vertex. The corresponding arcs are {1,2}, {1,3} and {1,4}. Arc {1,2} has the smallest weight value and we add it to E as well as adding vertex 2 to G. G is not a spanning tree (step 3) and hence we execute step 2 again. The corresponding arcs are {1,3}, {1,4}, {2,3} and {2,4}. The last arc is {2,4} and we add it to E and we add vertex 4 to G. At this stage the corresponding arcs are {1,3}, {1,4}, {2,3} and {3,4}. The last arc is {3,4} and we add it to and we add vertex 3 to G. We are now finished because adding any new arcs will lead to a circuit. We are now finished and the resulting MST is in the case of Kruskal's algorithm, namely the graph in Figure 15.15.

15.6 Depth-First and Breadth-First Searches in Graphs

In many applications it is necessary to discover all of the vertices that are reachable from a given start or *source vertex*. To this end, there are two fundamental algorithms that satisfy this requirement; both algorithms need a source vertex from which to commence the search. First, *Breadth-First-Search (BFS)* expands from the source vertex to those vertices 'closest' to it. We take the example in Figure 15.16 which is a tree with four levels. The vertex j is the root of the tree. With this vertex as source vertex, application of the BFS algorithm visits the vertices in the order $\{j, f, k, a, h, z, d\}$. In other words, all vertices at a given level are visited before any vertices at a lower level. With *Depth-First-Search (DFS)* we process the start vertex j and then we process the neighbours of j, then the neighbours of the neighbours of j, and so on. After arriving at a 'terminal' vertex (that is, one that has no unprocessed neighbour), we backtrack on the path until we can continue on another path, until each vertex is processed once and only once. For example, applying DFS to the tree in Figure 15.16 gives the vertex list $\{j, f, a, d, h, k, z\}$.

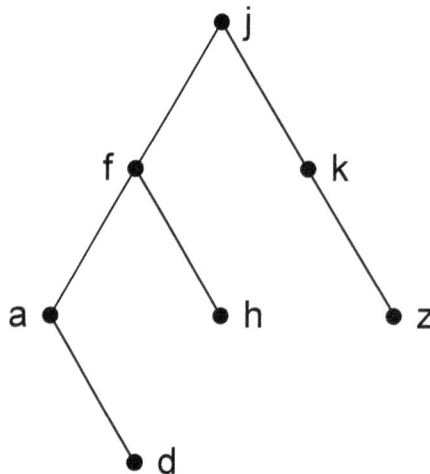

Figure 15.16 Searching in a tree

A *tree edge* is one connecting two adjacent vertices. For example, in Figure 15.16, there is a tree edge between vertex j and vertex k, the former being called the *predecessor* or *parent* and the latter is called the *successor* or *descendent*. A *back edge* is one that connects a vertex to one of its ancestors (for example, parent, grandparent,..) in a search tree. Loops (edges starting and ending at a single vertex) are considered to be back edges. A *forward edge* is a non-tree edge that connects a vertex to a *descendent*. Finally, a *cross-edge* is an edge that does not fall in any one of the first three categories. A pictorial representation of these edge categories is given in Figure 15.17.

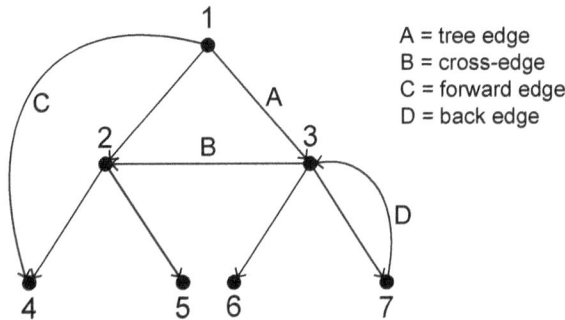

Figure 15.17 Types of edges

15.7 Shortest Path Problems

In some applications we are interested in computing the shortest path between two given vertices in a graph/digraph or more generally, in a weighted graph/digraph with non-negative path costs. In the first case the shortest path represents the number of edges between the source and destination vertices. In the second case the shortest path is the smallest total cost between these vertices. This algorithm was originally conceived by the Dutch computer scientist Edsger Dijkstra in 1959. A typical application of the algorithm is to find the distance between two cities that are connected by a net of highways. The cities represent the vertices while the edges represent the routes between the cities. The edge weights are the inter-city distances. Another example is shown in Figure 15.18. In this case we have a network of Internet routers (vertices) and edges that represent direct connections between routers. Delay and bandwidth information in milliseconds are the weights corresponding to each edge. Thus, the network problem of routing packets (messages) from a sender to a receiver can be formulated as a shortest-path problem.

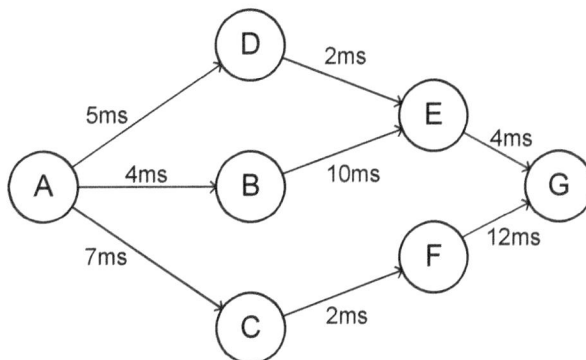

Figure 15.18 Computation time in a software process

The *shortest path algorithm* can be generalised to cases in which we wish to compute all shortest paths from a given vertex to every other vertex. This is called the *Floyd-Warshall algorithm*. A discussion of this algorithm is given in chapter 17.

We now discuss the *Dijkstra algorithm*. We first associate a distance with each pair of vertices in the network. This distance is the arc length if there is an arc between the vertices, zero for the distance from a vertex to itself and it is ∞ for the distance between two vertices that are not linked by an arc. Next, each vertex is assigned a *label* which is the distance to that vertex from the *start vertex (s)* along the shortest path found thus far. The label has two states namely *permanent*, in which case the distance found is along the shortest of all paths or *temporary*, in which case there is some uncertainty as to whether the path found is shortest. The algorithm gradually changes temporary labels into permanent ones. Given a set of vertices with temporary labels we wish to make these labels smaller by finding paths to these vertices using the shortest paths to permanently labeled vertices, followed by an arc from a vertex having a permanent label. Then, the vertex with the smallest temporary label is selected and its label is made permanent. We repeat this process until the *terminal vertex t* gets a permanent label.

The steps in the *Dijkstra algorithm* to find the shortest path between source vertex s and terminal vertex t are:
1. Assign a temporary label L(i) = ∞ to all vertices $i \neq s$. Set $L(s) = 0$ and $p = s$, where p is the last node to be given a permanent label. Make $L(s)$ permanent.
2. For each vertex i with a temporary label, redefine $L(i)$ to be $\min(L(i), L(p) + d(p, i))$ where $d(p, i)$ is the weight of arc (p, i). Find the vertex i with the smallest temporary label; set p to this i and make the label $L(p)$ permanent.
3. Go to step 2 if the terminal vertex t has a temporary label. Otherwise, t has a permanent label and we are finished because this label corresponds to the length of the shortest path from s to t through the network.

We take a specific example of a digraph with five vertices. In particular, we take the digraph in Figure 15.19 consisting of the vertices A,B,C,D and E. We rename them so that they conform to Dijkstra's notation: s = A, 1 = B, 2 = D, 3 = C, t = E. The arcs and their weights remain the same as in Figure 15.19.
We fill in the steps 1-3 for this particular case. As we shall see, we execute step 1 once and step 2 four times. As reader, you may wish to check the steps. We define the vectors M as $(L(s), L(1), L(2), L(3), L(t))$ and S that denote whether a vertex is permanent (Y) or not (N), that is $S = (Y/N, Y/N, Y/N, Y/N, Y/N)$. Let $d(u, v)$ be the weight of arc (u, v) where u and v are vertices.

Step 1:
Choose $p = s$; $M = (0, \infty, \infty, \infty, \infty)$, $S = (Y, N, N, N, N)$.

Step 2:
$\quad L(1) = \min(L(1), L(p) + d(p, 1)) = 5$; $L(2) = \infty$; $L(3) = 1$; $L(t) = \infty$
$\quad$ Then $p = 3$, $M = (0, 5, \infty, 1, \infty)$ and $S = (Y, N, N, Y, N)$
$\quad$ Vertex t still is a temporary vertex, so we continue.

Step 2:
$\quad L(1) = 5$; $L(2) = \infty$; $L(t) = 11$
$\quad$ Then $p = 1$, $M = (0, 5, \infty, 1, 11)$ and $S = (Y, Y, N, Y, N)$

Vertex t still is a temporary vertex, so we continue.

Step 2:
 $L(1) = 14; L(2) = 6.3; L(t) = 8$
 Then $p = 2, M = (0, 5, 6.3, 1, 8)$ and $S = (Y, Y, Y, Y, N)$
 Vertex t still is a temporary vertex, so we continue.

Step 2:
 $L(t) = 6.7$
 Then $p = t, M = (0, 5, 6.3, 1, 6.7)$ and $S = (Y, Y, Y, Y, Y)$
 Vertex t still is a permanent vertex, so we are finished. The shortest path has length 6.7.

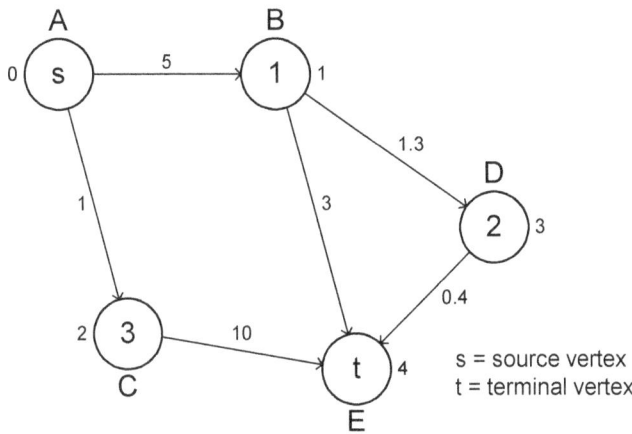

Figure 15.19 Digraph for Dijkstra's algorithm

There are a number of other shortest-path algorithms, some of which are supported in BGL. First, the *Bellman-Ford label-correcting algorithm* is less efficient than the Dijkstra algorithm but in the former case the weights are allowed to be negative. Bellman-Ford is used in routing applications, for example *Routing Information Protocol* (RIP). Second, *Johnson's* and *Floyd-Warshall algorithm* computes the shortest paths between all pairs of vertices in dense and sparse directed graphs. We discuss these algorithms in chapter 16 and 17.

15.8 Connected Components

We already know that a graph G is connected if there is a path between any two of its vertices. A connected subgraph H of G is a *connected component* of G if H is not contained in any larger connected subgraph of G. It is thus a *maximal connected subgraph*. We are interested in a number of issues relating to connectedness:
• Determine whether a given graph is connected.
• Compute all the connected components of a graph.
It is easy to answer these questions for small graphs that can be visualised (on paper, for example). For larger graphs and networks, however this is not possible and we then apply software algorithms that we discuss in chapter 17.

In order to compute the connected components of an undirected graph we employ the depth-first search (DFS) algorithm. We run DFS on the graph and we mark all vertices in the same DFS tree that belong to the same connected component. In BGL, the process is:
1. Read the network into memory.
2. Represent the network as a BGL graph.
3. Call the `connected_components()` function.

The number of connected components is an important *topological invariant* of a graph. In algebraic graph theory it is the multiplicity of 0 as an eigenvalue of the Laplacian matrix of the graph. A directed graph is called *strongly connected* if there is a path from each vertex in the graph to every other vertex. The *strongly connected components* of a directed graph are its maximal strongly connected subgraphs. We say that a digraph is *weakly connected* if its underlying graph is connected.

15.9 Applications of Graph Theory

We discuss some applications of graph theory.

15.9.1 Project Planning

Graph theory has been used to model the *events* and *tasks* (or *activities*) in project management and systems analysis since the early 1950s. The first applications were called *PERT (Project Evaluation and Review Technique)* method and the related *CPM (Critical Path Method)* and were developed to simplify the planning and scheduling of large and complex projects to support the U.S. Navy's Polaris nuclear submarine project. Nowadays, we see an implementation of the PERT method in Microsoft Project, for example.

We discuss the following topics in this section:
• The major components in a PERT network and their properties (attributes).
• Creating a PERT network and initialising its properties.
• Getting project-related information from a PERT network.

The two main components in PERT networks are *events* and *activities*. An *event* represents a milestone in a project and it occurs at a point in time. An *activity* represents the actual operations, tasks or activities in the real-life project. In general, an event represents the beginning and/or end of zero or more activities. We represent events as circles and activities as directed arcs between events. Activities are identified by their start and end events. An example of a network with 6 events is given in Figure 15.20. We see that the activities connect these events. The arrows depict the *precedence relationships* between events. For example, activities 2-3 and 2-4 can only be executed after activity 1-2 has completed while activities 2-3 and 2-4 may be executed in parallel. Similarly, activity 5-6 cannot begin until completion of both activities 3-5 and 4-5. In general, we say that activity i-j has *start event* i and *end event* j.

Inspecting Figure 15.20 again, we notice the arc weights and these represent the time (in days, weeks or months, for example) it takes to complete each activity. We consider the source event to begin at time zero (0). Then we can compute how long it takes to complete a given activity. For example, activity 3-5 will be completed at the end of 7 days, activity 4-5 at the end of 8 days. Hence, activity 5-6 starts at time 8 since activities 3-5 and 4-5 must both be completed before it can start.

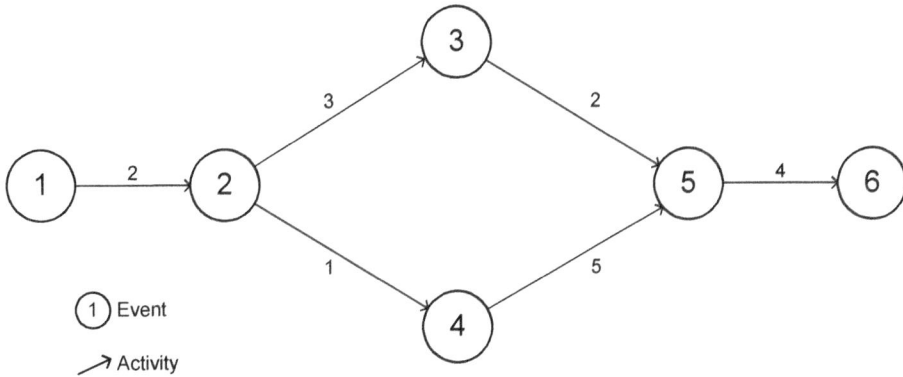

Figure 15.20 Simple PERT-CPM network

We now discuss the problem of estimating activity times. In general, estimating how long it takes to complete an activity is not easy as it demands insight and experience. The CPM network method assumes that a single value estimate of the time required for each activity is available. The PERT technique, on the other hand includes an explicit recognition of the uncertainty associated with activity time estimates and to this end it models activity duration as a *triangular probability distribution* having three *uncertainty parameters*:

- Variable a = the *most optimistic (shortest) time* to complete the project. We assume that everything proceeds better than is normally expected.
- Variable b = *most likely (modal) time*. We assume that everything proceeds as normally expected.
- Variable c = *most pessimistic (longest) time*. We assume that everything goes wrong (but at the same time avoiding major catastrophes).

We note that Boost supports the triangular distribution and its statistical properties in the Math Toolkit library and the Random library that allows us to generate random variates of the triangular distribution. Continuing, based on the above three estimates we compute the *expected time* or the best estimates to complete an activity by the formula:

$$T_e \equiv (a + 4b + c)/6.$$

In general, we apply this formula to each activity in the project. This expected time is analogous to the single value estimate in the CPM method.

The next issue is to discuss event attributes. The three most important attributes are:

- *Earliest expected event time* (T_E): the time based on the latest completion of an activity terminating at that event.
- *Latest allowable event time* (T_L): the latest 'calendar' time at which the event can take place (be realised) and still keep the project on time.
- *Event slack* (S): this is a computed value as the difference between the latest allowable time and the earliest expected time, that is $S = T_L - T_E$.

We now compute these quantities for the network in Figure 15.21. We compute the earliest expected time by starting at the *terminal event* (where $T_L = 9$). We then set T_E to this terminal value. Then the activity values terminating at the last event are subtracted from the last T_L value. For the case in which two activities start from an event, we must compare the values and T_L will be the earlier of the alternatives yielded. For example, the value of T_L for event 3 is 2.

In general, the first event has a T_E of zero. To compute the earliest expected event time for a general event in which one or more activities terminate on an event, the latest activity completion time determines the T_E for that event. Finally, event slack S is the difference between the latest allowable time and the earliest expected time for a given event.

The *critical path* of a network is the sequence of activities that constitutes the longest time path through the network. It determines the minimum expected time in which the project can be completed. It is a lower bound and it can be traced through the zero slack events. For such nodes there is no difference between earliest expected time and the latest allowable time (for example, the nodes 1, 3, 4 and 6 in Figure 15.21). In other words, there is no time to spare on the critical path. For example, the critical path for the network in Figure 15.21 is the activity sequence {1-3, 3-4, 4-6}.

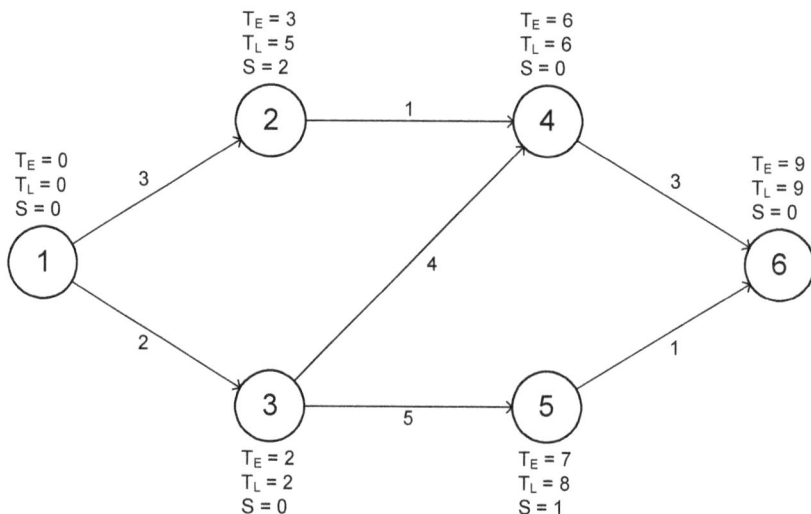

Figure 15.21 Network with Event Times and Slack

We conclude this section with a discussion of how we can give probabilistic conclusions concerning project completion time. We assume that activity times are independent random variables. Appealing to the *Central Limit Theorem* allows us to assume that the distribution of the overall project time will be normal (Gaussian distribution). Let us assume that there are n activities in a project. Then the *project standard deviation* is given by:

$$\sigma_{cp} = \sqrt{\sigma_j^2}$$

where

$$\sigma_j^2 = \frac{a_j^2 + b_j^2 + c_j^2 - a_j b_j - a_j c_j - b_j c_j}{18}$$

is the *variance* of the jth activity whose uncertainty parameters are (a_j, b_j, c_j), for the jth activity $j = 1, \ldots, n$.

We now wish to make probability statements about completing a project on or before a specified time or after a specified time based on the assumption that the overall project can be approximated by a normal distribution. The formula to calculate the probability that the project will be completed before a certain time is:

$$Z = \frac{target - cpt}{sd}$$

where

- Z = probability of completion.
- *target* = time before which we wish to complete project.
- *cpt* = expected project time (critical path time).
- *sd* = standard deviation of project.

Having computed Z we can then find the probability of completion by mapping the standard deviation to a probability. For example, if Z = 1.37 then we have a 91.47 probability of completing a project within 60 weeks whose critical path time is 52 weeks and whose standard deviation is 5.83 weeks.

We conclude this section with a remark on how to compute the critical path in PERT networks. In fact, this is the longest simple path in the network; in other words no repeated events (vertices) are allowed in the path. The longest path problem is related to the shortest path problem by exploiting the *duality of optimisation*; in this case the longest path in graph G is the same as the shortest path in the graph H which has the same nodes and arcs as G but with arc weights negated.

15.9.2 Some Specific Graphs

In this section we give examples of graphs that occur in various kinds of applications. They are meant for motivational purposes and they can be applied to other similar applications.

In a round-robin judo tournament each judoka must compete with every other judoka. Let each vertex in a digraph represent a judoka and an arc from vertex v to vertex w if judoka v defeats judoka w. This is a complete digraph since its underlying graph is complete. This is called the *dominance digraph* of a tournament. These digraphs have applications to social and biological sciences. Some use cases are to determine who is the 'winner' or 'leader' in the dominance graph. The answer is the vertex whose outdegree is maximum. An example with four judokas is given in Figure 15.22; in this case, judoka '2' is the overall winner.

We now consider the assignment problem consisting which m job applicants $p_1, p_2, \ldots, p_m$ and n jobs $q_1, q_2, \ldots, q_n$. Let V be the set of job applicants and W the set of jobs. If applicant $p_i, i = 1, \ldots, m$ is qualified for job $q_j, j = 1, \ldots, n$ then draw an edge between the two vertices (p_i, q_j) and let $c_{ij}, i = 1, \ldots, m, j = 1, \ldots, n$ be the salary to be paid to $p_i, i = 1, \ldots, m$ if she is hired for job $q_j, j = 1, \ldots, n$. The model is a weighted bipartite network and the optimisation problem is to find a job assignment for the applicants such that all the jobs are filled and the total salary to be paid is a minimum.

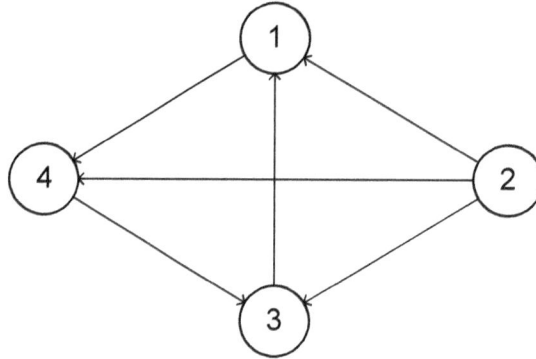

Figure 15.22 Tournament Graph

15.9.3 Eulerian, de Bruijn and Hamiltonian Digraphs

A path in a graph is an *Eulerian path* if every edge of the graph appears as an edge in the path exactly once. A closed Eulerian path is called an *Eulerian circuit*. A graph is called an *Eulerian graph* if it has an Eulerian circuit. It can be proved that a finite connected graph is Eulerian if and only if each vertex has even degree.

There are many applications of Eulerian graphs to operations research, Computer Science and transportation, for example. We give one example here. This is the *de Bruijn digraph*. To this end, consider binary words and vertices of the form $v = a_1, \ldots, a_{n-1}, n > 1$. We then create two arcs to vertices $a_2, a_3, \ldots, a_{n-1}0$ and $a_2, a_3, \ldots, a_{n-1}1$ by defining them as $v1v0$. Thus, the 2^n arcs of the digraph represesent the set of binary words of length n, that we denote by $G(2, n)$. An example of a $G(2, 3)$ digraph is shown in Figure 15.23. An example of a $G(2, 4)$ digraph is shown in Figure 15.24.

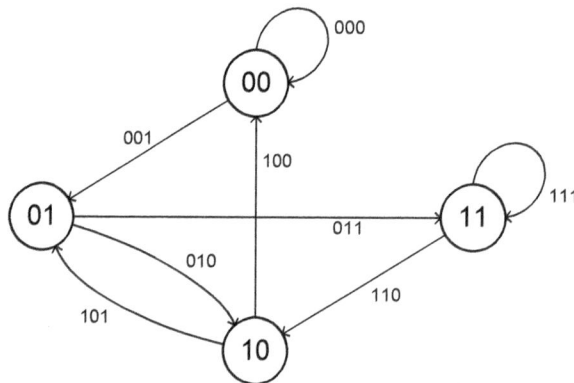

Figure 15.23 De Bruijn digraph G(2,3)

We can generalise to the case of an alphabet of p letters to form the de Bruijn graph $G(p, n)$ having p^{n-1} vertices and p^n arcs such that the indegree and outdegree are both equal to p. Since the sum of the indegree and outdegree is even we then know that $G(p, n)$ is Eulerian since this condition is necessary and sufficient for a path to be Eulerian.

A path between two vertices in a graph is called a *Hamiltonian path* if it passes through each vertex exactly once. A *Hamiltonian cycle* is a closed path that passes through each vertex exactly once and in which all the edges are distinct. A *Hamiltonian graph* is one having a Hamiltonian cycle. For digraphs, a directed graph between two vertices is a *directed Hamiltonian path* if it passes through each vertex exactly once. Finally, a closed directed Hamiltonian path is a *directed Hamiltonian cycle*. Hamilton cycles have applications to the *Travelling Salesman Problem* and scheduling applications. For example, consider a machine shop with n different machines. We wish to run a job through all these machines but not in any particular order. Each machine is the vertex of a digraph and we draw an arc from each vertex to every other vertex. Then any directed Hamilton path in the digraph is a schedule. If c_{ij} is the setup time required when the job goes from machine i to machine j then the optimisation problem is to find a schedule that takes the least amount of time.

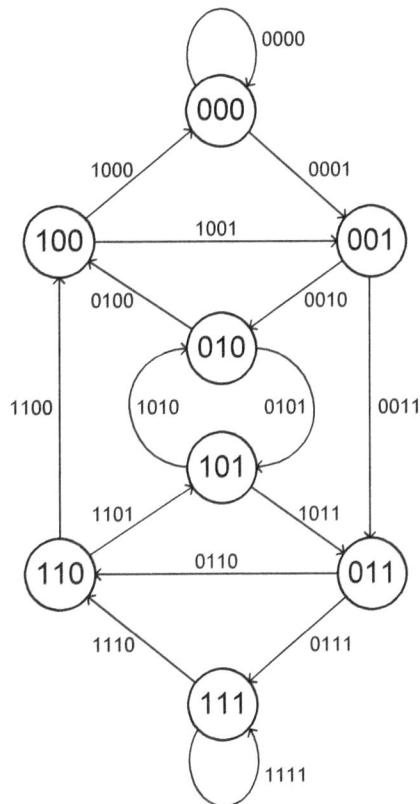

Figure 15.24 G(2,4)

15.9.4 Random Graphs

A *random graph* is a graph that is generated by some random process. We start with a set of n vertices and we then add edges between them at random. Different graph models produce different probability distributions on graphs. An example is the graph G(n,p) containing n vertices in which every possible edge occurs independently with probability p. Another model is G(n,M) which assigns equal probabilities to all graphs with exactly M edges. This is a snapshot at a particular time M of a random process which is a stochastic process starting with n vertices and no edges. At each step we add a new edge chosen uniformly from the set of missing edges. We discuss random graphs in more detail in chapter 17.

15.10 Flow Networks

A *flow network* is a special kind of digraph in which each edge has a *capacity* and each edge receives a *flow*. The capacity is an upper limit on the amount of flow on an edge. In general, the amount of flow into a node (vertex) is equal to the amount of flow exiting it. A *source* is a special node that has more *outgoing flow* than *incoming flow* while a *sink* is a node that has less outgoing flow than incoming flow.

Let u and v be two nodes. The *capacity* $c(u, v)$ defined between these adjacent nodes is a real-valued function; if the nodes are not adjacent its value is zero. A *flow network* f is a real-valued function on the Cartesian product $V \times V$ (where V is the set of vertices of the graph) having the following properties:

- *Capacity constraints*: $f(u, v) \leq c(u, v)$. In other words, the flow along an edge cannot exceed its capacity.
- *Skew symmetry*: $f(u, v) = -f(u, v)$. In other words, the net flow from u to v is the opposite in value to the net flow from v to u.
- *Flow conservation*: for nodes that are neither source nor sink nodes we claim that the net flow at a node u is zero, that is:

$$\sum_{w \in V} f(u, w) = 0.$$

Source nodes 'produce' flow while sink nodes 'consume' flow. We note that $f(u, v)$ represent the net flow from u to v. For example, if $c(u, v) = 10$, and if there is a real flow of 6 from u to v, then $f(u, v) = 10-6 = 4$ and $f(v, u) = -f(u, v) = -4$.

The *residual capacity* of an edge (u, v) is defined by $c_f(u, v) = c(u, v) - f(u, v)$. From this definition it is possible to construct a residual network depicting the amount of available capacity.

We give a generic example of a flow network in Figure 15.25. Note the presence of source node s and sink node t. We employ the notation f/c to denote the flow and capacity on an edge. For example, 3/5 denotes a flow of 3 and a capacity of 5.

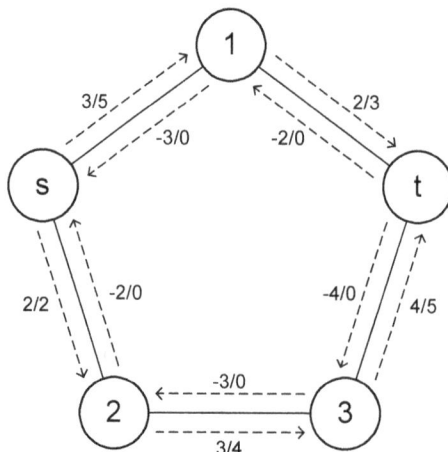

Figure 15.25 Flow Network

We now discuss the main issue called the *maximum flow problem* that is concerned with determining how much of some quantity (for example, water or a commodity) can move through a network. There are many algorithms that solve this problem, two of which are supported in BGL:

- *Ford-Fulkerson*: this algorithm sends flow along paths having a capacity. In general, a path with available capacity is called an *augmenting path*.
- *Edmunds-Karp*: this is a refinement of the Ford Fulkerson algorithm and is based on the BFS algorithm.

BGL supports the Edmunds-Karp and push-relabel maximum flow algorithms.

We conclude this secion with a short description of a practical application of flow networks, namely providing cities with a reliable water supply. We consider a network of *water pipes*, each one having a diameter, thus allowing an amount of water to flow through them. The pipes are connected at *junctions* and the amount of water flowing into a given junction is equal to the amount of water flowing out of it. In general we shall have a number of pumps P (*source nodes*) from which water is transported to *reservoirs* R (*sink nodes*). When pump conditions suddenly change a pressure discontinuity is created that propagates in the pipes. This phenomenon – called *waterhammer* – can cause serious damage to the water system and to prevent this from occurring we introduce air vessels or surge tanks T at strategic locations in the network. An example of such a network is given in Figure 15.26. A *surge tank* is often used to control the pressure spikes resulting from rapid changes in the flow. For example, when the turbine gates at a power station are closed the water level in the surge tank rises above its original level as the kinetic energy of the rejected flow is converted into potential energy. Similarly, when the turbine gates are opened the surge tanks provide energy for the immediate demand of the turbine. This action reduces the waterhammer effects in the network. An *air chamber* is a closed tank in which the lower portion contains water while the upper part contains compressed air. When power failure occurs both the pressure head and the flow decrease rapidly. Then the compressed air in the chamber forces water out of the bottom of the chamber into the discharge line, thus minimising the velocity changes and waterhammer effects in the discharge line.

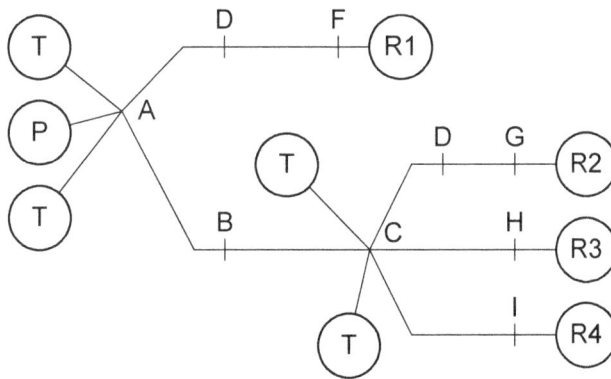

Figure 15.26 Water network

A simulation program to calculate the pressure discontinuity uses the following system of semi linear first-order partial differential equations in the space variable x and the time variable t (see Parmakian 1963):

$$\frac{\partial h}{\partial t} + \frac{1}{g}\frac{\partial v}{\partial t} = -\frac{\alpha}{2g}v|v| - \frac{1}{g}v\frac{\partial v}{\partial x}$$

$$\frac{\partial h}{\partial t} + \frac{a^2}{g}\frac{\partial v}{\partial x} = 0 \qquad\qquad (15.1)$$

where

$\alpha =$ Fanning friction factor.

$g =$ constant of gravity.

$h =$ $h(x,t)$ (hydrostatic pressure).

$v =$ $v(x,t)$ (mean velocity over a cross-section of a pipe in the network).

$|v| =$ absolute value of v.

$a =$ wave speed of water in the pipe.

The first equation in (15.1) is called the *equation of motion* while the second equation is called the *continuity equation* (vd Riet 1964).

The objective of the simulation program is to compute the pressure $h(x,t)$ and velocity $v(x,t)$ at discrete mesh points in the x and t directions using numerical methods (for example, the *Method of Characteristics (MOC)*) but we also have taken the boundary conditions at junctions into consideration. Each conduit has a length L and hence is bounded by $x = 0$ (entrance) and $x = L$ (exit). We call a boundary point a *junction point of the first kind* when the conduit is connected solely to other conduits (for example, points B, and D in Figure 15.26). The conduit can also be connected to some mechanism (for example a pump, surge tank or reservoir) and we call this a *junction of the second kind* (for example A, C, F, G, H and I in Figure 15.26). The velocity and pressure satisfy certain boundary conditions at these junction points.

15.11 Summary and Conclusions

We have given an introduction to graph theory, the main concepts and a discussion of a number of graph algorithms. Graph theory and its applications is a vast area of research and we have covered some essentials that should help us to appreciate the functionality in BGL. Furthermore, we introduce small and illustrative examples to support the theory and we show the steps in each algorithm in this chapter. For larger graphs we automate this manual process and this is the subject of chapters 16 and 17 when we introduce the Boost Graph Library.

16 The Boost Graph Library Data Structures and Fundamental Algorithms

16.1 Introduction and Objectives

In this chapter we introduce the Boost BGL. The focus is on showing how the foundations of graph theory that we introduced in chapter 15 are realised by the data structures and algorithms in BGL. To this end, we give an overview of the *building blocks* that we can use to help us write applications in BGL:

- The Boost Property Map library.
- The Boost Graph interface.
- Graph classes, iterators and adapters.
- Some basic algorithms.

Since this is an intimidating list of topics to discuss we introduce them by first discussing some of the examples from chapter 15, in particular those involving graphs with a small number of vertices. The algorithms discussed in this chapter concern the most common ones for the calculation of shortest paths, and minimum spanning trees. Chapter 17 deals with more advanced algorithms.

One of the goals of chapter 16 is to introduce the core functionality in BGL and how to use it.

16.2 An Overview of the Functionality in BGL

Before we introduce the interfaces, its data structures and algorithms in BGL we first give an overview of the main *functionality*. In particular, we discuss what can be done with graphs, for example:

- Core search algorithms, for example breadth-first, depth-first search and visit.
- Topological sort and transitive closure.
- Shortest paths/cost minimisation algorithms (Dijkstra, Bellman-Ford, Johnson, Floyd-Warshall).
- Deterministic and random minimum spanning tree algorithms.
- Connected components algorithms.
- Maximum flow and matching algorithms.
- Sparse matrix ordering algorithms.
- Graph metrics.
- Graph structure comparisons.
- Layout algorithms.
- Planar graph algorithms.
- Graph Input/Output.

In this chapter we focus mainly on shortest-path and minimum spanning tree algorithms. chapter 17 discusses more advanced algorithms.

16.3 Boost Property Map Library

This library contains a number of interface specifications for map datastructures that can then be used in a range of applications. Our interest here lies in using this library in combination with BGL. These specifications are described in the form of *concepts*, similar to the approach taken with *iterator concepts* in STL. It is not the goal of the library to provide map implementations as such because this is the responsibility of client code. However, the library provides map adapters to the generic map interface as we shall see later in this section.

The property map interface consists of a set of concepts. We recall that a *concept* is a set of requirements that types must satisfy (Demming 2010). These concepts define a syntax for mapping key objects to corresponding value objects. The property operations are global functions:

- `get(map, key)`: retrieve the value corresponding to a given key in `map`.
- `put(map, key, value)`: modify the `value` corresponding to a given key in `map`.
- `operator[key]`: retrieve the value corresponding to a given `key` in the map. This function cannot be defined globally because it must be defined as either a member function or as friend function of the map class under construction.

The library provides various property map types that implement these functions. We shall use them later but we now give the example `associative_property_map<>` to show how to use the code. This class is an adapter for `std::map<>` because this latter class does not support the property map concepts. The initial example that shows the syntax features:

```
#include <map>
#include <string>
#include <iostream>

#include <boost/property_map/property_map.hpp>

using namespace std;

int main()
{
    // First associative & const associative map.

    // Create std::map and fill it.
    map<string, string> names;
    names["Mickey"]="Mouse";
    names["Donald"]="Duck";
    names["Mimi"]="Mouse";

    // The std::map does not implement the property map concepts.
    // Wrap the std::map in the boost::associative_property_map adapter.
    boost::associative_property_map<map<string, string> > namesMap(names);

    cout << "[Mickey]: " << namesMap["Mickey"]<<endl;
    namesMap["Mickey"] = "Mouse";
    put(namesMap, "Donald", "Duck");
    cout << "[Mickey]: " << namesMap["Mickey"] << endl;
    cout << "get(Donald): " << get(namesMap, "Donald") << endl;

    return 0;
}
```

In general, it is possible to create your own specialised property map classes by implementing the three functions above. A discussion of this topic is outside the scope of this book.

16.3.1 Boost Property Map Category Tags and Traits

There are four categories of property maps, each one dealing with some aspect of access:
- *Readable*: the associated property data can only be read. The data is return-by-value.
- *Writeable*: the associated property data can only be written.
- *Read/write*: the associated property data can be read and written.
- *Lvalue*: the associated property is represented in memory and it is possible to get a reference to it.

There is a tag struct corresponding to each property map category. The `boost::property_traits` class is used to deduce the types associated with the property map types, that is the key and value types as well as the property map category.

16.3.2 Property Map Types

The Boost Property Map Library provides various property map types that can be used in applications:

- `Standard pointers` (the library provides functionality to use standard pointers as a property map).
- `identity_property_map` (the value is the same as the key; it contains no data and the key is returned).
- `iterator_property_map` (this is an adapter that converts a random access iterator to an *lvalue* property map).
- `shared_array_property_map` (this is an adapter that converts a `boost::shard_array` to an lvalue property map).
- `associative_property_map` (this is an adapter that converts a unique and pair associative container to an lvalue property map).
- `const_associative_property_map` (this is an adapter that converts a unique and pair associative container to a constant lvalue property map).
- `vector_property_map` (provides a global function to easily create a vector property map).
- `ref_property_map` (wraps references to an object).

We have already given an example of `associative_property_map`. As second example, we take a function working on a map that implements the lvalue (readable/writeable) map concept. The (key = `int`, value = `double`). The code shows some of the features that we have already discussed:

```
template <typename MapType>
void LvalueMapTestIntDouble(MapType map)
{
    // Make typedefs for the value- and key-types.
    typedef typename boost::property_traits<MapType>::key_type key_type;
    typedef typename boost::property_traits<MapType>::value_type
        value_type;
    typedef typename boost::property_traits<MapType>::reference reference;
    typedef typename boost::property_traits<MapType>::category category;

    // Alternative typedef directly from MapType instead of traits.
    // typedef typename MapType::key_type key_type;
    // typedef typename MapType::value_type value_type;
    // typedef typename MapType::reference reference;
    // typedef typename MapType::category category;

    // Check what the map category is (using typeid)
    if (typeid(category)==typeid(boost::lvalue_property_map_tag))
        cout<<"Map category is lvalue (read/write)."<<endl;
    if (typeid(category)==typeid(boost::read_write_property_map_tag))
        cout<<"Map category is read/write."<<endl;
    if (typeid(category)==typeid(boost::readable_property_map_tag))
        cout<<"Map category is readable."<<endl;
    if (typeid(category)==typeid(boost::writable_property_map_tag))
        cout<<"Map category is writable."<<endl;
    // Check what the map category is (using id enum)
    if (category::id==boost::detail::LVALUE_PA)
        cout<<"Map category is lvalue (read/write)."<<endl;
    if (category::id==boost::detail::READ_WRITE_PA)
```

```
        cout<<"Map category is read/write."<<endl;
    if (category::id==boost::detail::READABLE_PA)
        cout<<"Map category is readable."<<endl;
    if (category::id==boost::detail::WRITABLE_PA)
        cout<<"Map category is writable."<<endl;

    cout<<"Index 1 (get): "<<get(map, 1)<<endl;
    cout<<"Index 1 (operator []): "<<map[1]<<endl;

    put(map, 1, 4.44);
    cout<<"Index 1 (after put): "<<get(map, 1)<<endl;
}
```

An example of use is:

```
double values[]={3.14, 2.790, 8.97};

cout<<endl<<"*** Native pointer ***"<<endl;
LvalueMapTestIntDouble(values);
```

You can run the code and examine the output.

16.4 An Introduction to Data Structures in BGL

We now give a global overview of the most important template classes and data structures in BGL. The underlying theory has been discussed in detail in chapter 15. The classes have quite a few template parameters (many of which have default values, fortunately) and understanding them can be a challenge and can take some time to learn. First, BGL has two main classes for graphs, namely:

1) `adjacency_list`: this is represented by a collection of vertices; corresponding to each vertex is a collection of its out-edges. This class has several template parameters corresponding to the following features:
   - *Edge list*: determines which container to use in order to represent the sequence of out-edges for each vertex (default `std::vector`).
   - *Vertex list*: controls the kind of container to use in order to represent the sequence of vertices (default `std::vector`).
   - *Directed*: determines if the graph is directed, undirected or directed with access to both the in-edges and out-edges (*bi-directional*).
   - *Vertex Properties*: specify internal vertex property storage.
   - *Edge Properties*: specify internal edge property storage.
   - *Graph Properties*: specify internal graph property storage.

The default values for the last three parameters are `no_property`.

The class parameters are:

```
template <class OutEdgeListS = vecS,
          class VertexListS = vecS,
          class DirectedS = directedS,
          class VertexProperty = no_property,
          class EdgeProperty = no_property,
          class GraphProperty = no_property,
          class EdgeListS = listS>
class adjacency_list
{
    //..
};
```

2) `adjacency_matrix`: this class implements the BGL graph interface using the traditional adjacency matrix storage format. It has several template parameters corresponding to the following features:
   - *Directed*: determines if the graph is directed, undirected or directed with access to both the in-edges and out-edges (*bi-directional*).
   - *Vertex Properties*: specify internal vertex property storage.
   - *Edge Properties*: specify internal edge property storage.
   - *Graph Properties*: specify internal graph property storage.

The class parameters are:

```
template <typename Directed = directedS,
          typename VertexProperty = no_property,
          typename EdgeProperty = no_property,
          typename GraphProperty = no_property,
          typename Allocator = std::allocator<bool> >
class adjacency_matrix
{
    //
};
```

We give two simple examples on how to use these classes. First, the BGL header files to include are:

```
#include <boost/graph/adjacency_matrix.hpp>
#include <boost/graph/adjacency_list.hpp>
#include <boost/graph/graph_utility.hpp>

using namespace boost;
```

Next, we take the first graph component in Figure 15.5, chapter 15. It has four vertices called A, B, C and D; the edges are (A,B), (A,D), (B,C), (C,D). We create two undirected graphs based on an adjacency list and an adjacency matrix:

```
enum nodes { A, B, C, D, N};
const char* name("ABCD");

typedef adjacency_list<vecS, vecS, undirectedS> ListGraph;
ListGraph g(N);

// Create the edges (Figure 15.5).
add_edge(A, B, g);
add_edge(A, D, g);
add_edge(B, C, g);
add_edge(C, D, g);
```

and

```
typedef adjacency_matrix<undirectedS> MatrixGraph;
MatrixGraph ug(N);

// Create the edges (Figure 15.5).
add_edge(A, B, ug);
add_edge(A, D, ug);
add_edge(B, C, ug);
add_edge(C, D, ug);
```

We wish to view these graphs in different ways. To this end, we print the graph that uses an adjacency list. Similar code is used to print `ug`:

```
cout << "Undirected graph:\n";
cout << "Vertex set: ";
print_vertices(g, name);
cout << endl;

cout << "Edge set: ";
print_edges(g, name);
cout << endl;

cout << "Print graph: " << endl;
print_graph(g, name);

cout << "Print graph, basic version: " << endl;
print_graph(g); cout << endl;
```

where we have used the following functions to print the vertices, edges and current graph. These print functions are part of BGL:

```
template <class VertexListGraph, class Name>
void print_vertices(const VertexListGraph& G, Name name)
{
    typename graph_traits<VertexListGraph>::vertex_iterator vi,vi_end;
    for (boost::tie(vi,vi_end) = vertices(G); vi != vi_end; ++vi)
    {
        std::cout << get(name,*vi) << " ";
    }
    std::cout << std::endl;
}

template <class EdgeListGraph, class Name>
void print_edges(const EdgeListGraph& G, Name name)
{
    typename graph_traits<EdgeListGraph>::edge_iterator ei, ei_end;
    for (boost::tie(ei, ei_end) = edges(G); ei != ei_end; ++ei)
    {
        std::cout << "(" << get(name, source(*ei, G))
                << "," << get(name, target(*ei, G)) << ") ";
    }
    std::cout << std::endl;
}

template <class IncidenceGraph, class Name>
void print_graph(const IncidenceGraph& G, Name name)
{
    typedef typename graph_traits<IncidenceGraph>::directed_category Cat;
    print_graph_dispatch(G, name, Cat());
}

template <class IncidenceGraph>
void print_graph(const IncidenceGraph& G)
{
    print_graph(G, get(vertex_index, G));
}
```

The output from the code is:

```
Undirected graph:
Vertex set: A B C D

Edge set: (A,B) (A,D) (B,C) (C,D)

Print graph:
A <--> B D
B <--> A C
C <--> B D
```

```
D <--> A C
Print graph, basic version:
0 <--> 1 3
1 <--> 0 2
2 <--> 1 3
3 <--> 0 2

Vertex set: A B C D

Edge set: (B,A) (C,B) (D,A) (D,C)

Print graph:
A <--> B D
B <--> A C
C <--> B D
D <--> A C
Print graph, basic version:
0 <--> 1 3
1 <--> 0 2
2 <--> 1 3
3 <--> 0 2
```

You can check this output by comparing it with the fist component consisting of vertices A, B, C and D in Figure 15.5. Finally, we implement the directed graph of Figure 15.10 as follows:

```
cout << "Directed graph:\n";
typedef adjacency_matrix<directedS> MatrixDirectedGraph;
MatrixDirectedGraph dg(N);

// Create the edges (Figure 15.10).
add_edge(A, B, dg);
add_edge(B, C, dg);
add_edge(B, D, dg);
add_edge(C, A, dg);
add_edge(C, D, dg);
```

When printed the output for dg is:

```
Directed graph:
Vertex set, : A B C D

Edge set: (A,B) (B,C) (B,D) (C,A) (C,D)

Print graph:
A --> B
B --> C D
C --> A D
D -->

Print graph, basic version:
0 --> 1
1 --> 2 3
2 --> 0 3
3 -->
```

The reader may have noticed that we used a number of traits in the above code. We now place them centre-stage as shown in Figure 16.1.

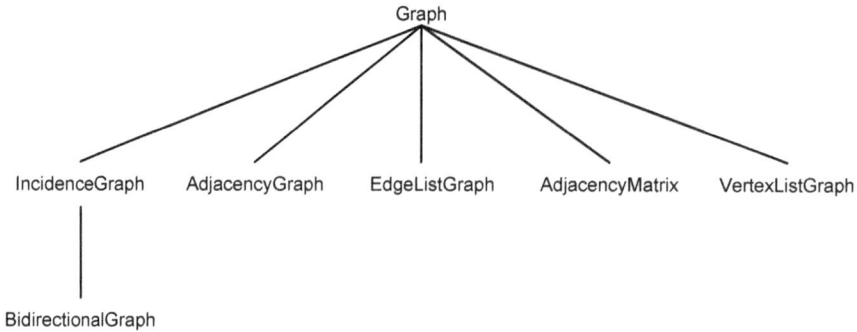

Figure 16.1 Graph Concepts and refinement relationships

16.5 Auxiliary Classes

The `graphs_traits` class allows us to access the associated types of a graph type as defined by the various BGL graph concepts:

```
template <typename G>
struct graph_traits
{
    typedef typename G::vertex_descriptor        vertex_descriptor;
    typedef typename G::edge_descriptor          edge_descriptor;
    typedef typename G::adjacency_iterator        adjacency_iterator;
    typedef typename G::out_edge_iterator        out_edge_iterator;
    typedef typename G::in_edge_iterator          in_edge_iterator;
    typedef typename G::vertex_iterator          vertex_iterator;
    typedef typename G::edge_iterator            edge_iterator;

    typedef typename G::directed_category        directed_category;
    typedef typename G::edge_parallel_category    edge_parallel_category;
    typedef typename G::traversal_category        traversal_category;

    typedef typename G::vertices_size_type        vertices_size_type;
    typedef typename G::edges_size_type          edges_size_type;
    typedef typename G::degree_size_type          degree_size_type;

    static inline vertex_descriptor null_vertex();
};
```

If we wish to use one of the associated types of a graph we need to instantiate `graph_traits` with the graph type and access the appropriate typedef. We note that this class can be specialised on the graph type.

We now describe the concepts in Figure 16.1.
*   *IncidenceGraph*: provides an interface for efficient access to the out-edges of each vertex in a graph. Valid expressions are:
    - `source(e,g)` : return the vertex descriptor for u for the edge e = (u, v).
    - `target(e,g)` : return the vertex descriptor for v for the edge e = (u, v).
    - `out_edges(v,g)` : return an iterator range providing access to the out-edges (for directed graphs) or incident edges (for undirected graphs) of vertex v.
    - `out_degree(v,g)` : return the number of out-edges (for directed graphs) or the number of incident edges (for undirected graphs) of vertex v.
*   *BidirectionalGraph*: this is a refinement of *IncidenceGraph* and it adds the requirement for efficient access to the in-edges of each vertex. This interface provides efficient access to the in-edges of a directed graph. Valid expressions are:

- in_edges(v,g): return an iterator range providing access to the in-edges (for directed graphs) or incident edges (for undirected graphs) of vertex v.
- in_degree(v,g): return the number of in-edges (for directed graphs) or the number of incident edges (for undirected graphs) of vertex v.
- degree(v,g): return the number of in-edges plus out-edges (for directed graphs) or the number of incident edges (for undirected graphs) of vertex v.

- *AdjacencyGraph*: defines the interface for accessing adjacent vertices. We can access these vertices as the target vertex of an out-vertex. Valid expressions are:
  - adjacent_vertices(v,g): return an iterator range providing access to the vertices adjacent to the vertex v.

- *EdgeListGraph*: a refinement of Graph that adds the refinement for efficient access to all the edges in a graph. Valid expressions are:
  - edges(g) : return an iterator range providing access to all the edges in graph g.
  - source(e,g) : return the vertex descriptor for u for the edge e = (u, v).
  - target(e,g) : return the vertex descriptor for v for the edge e = (u, v).
  - num_edges(g) : return the number of edges in graph g.

- *AdjacencyMatrix*: a refinement of Graph that adds the refinement for efficient access to any edge in the graph given the source and target vertices. Valid expressions are:
  - edge(u, v, g) : return a pair consisting of a flag stating whether there is an edge between u and v in graph g; it contains an edge descriptor if the edge was found.

- *VertexListGraph*: a refinement of Graph that adds the refinement for efficient access to all the vertices in a graph. Valid expressions are:
  - vertices(v,g) : return an iterator range providing access to the vertices in graph g.
  - num_vertices(g) : return the number of vertices in graph g.

We take an example to show to access the vertex set and edge sets of the weighted directed graph as shown in Figure 16.2 (we have included the weights because we will discuss shortest-path problems in a later section). The code to create the directed graph is:

```
typedef adjacency_matrix<directedS> MatrixDirectedGraph;

const int N = 9;
MatrixDirectedGraph dg(N);

// Create the edges (Figure 16.2).
add_edge(0, 1, dg); add_edge(0, 2, dg); add_edge(1, 3, dg);
add_edge(1, 4, dg); add_edge(2, 3, dg); add_edge(2,4, dg);

add_edge(3, 4, dg); add_edge(3, 5, dg); add_edge(3, 6, dg);
add_edge(3, 7, dg);

add_edge(4, 6, dg); add_edge(5, 7, dg); add_edge(5, 8, dg);
add_edge(6, 8, dg); add_edge(7, 8, dg);

cout << "Print directed graph: " << endl;
const char* name("012345678");
print_graph(dg, name);   cout << endl;
```

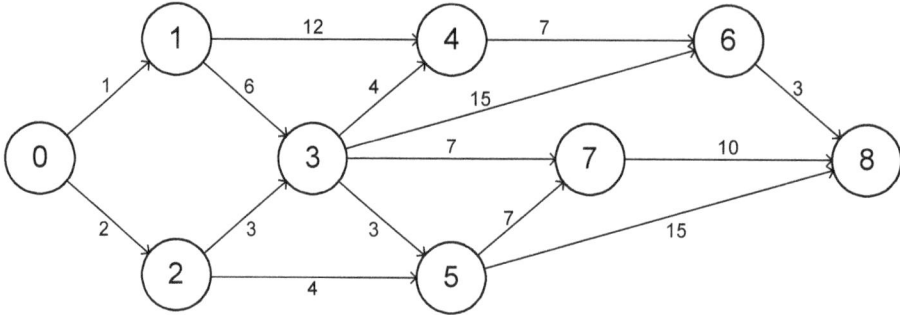

Figure 16.2 Weighted directed graph test of BGL

The output from this code is:

```
Print directed graph:
0 --> 1 2
1 --> 3 4
2 --> 3 4
3 --> 4 5 6 7
4 --> 6
5 --> 7 8
6 --> 8
7 --> 8
8 -->
```

We first use the graph interface to access the vertices of the above directed graph using the `vertices()` function. In particular, we print the index for each vertex in the graph:

```
// Vertex set.
cout << "Vertex information, number of vertices: "
     << num_vertices(dg) << endl;

// Get the property map for vertex indices.
typedef property_map<MatrixDirectedGraph, vertex_index_t>::type IndexMap;
typedef graph_traits<MatrixDirectedGraph>::vertex_iterator VertexIter;
IndexMap index = get(vertex_index, dg);

std::pair<VertexIter, VertexIter> vp;
for (vp = vertices(dg); vp.first != vp.second; ++vp.first)
{
    // Derefence to get a vertex object.
    cout << index[*vp.first] <<  " ";
}
cout << endl;
```

The output from this code is:

```
Vertex information, number of vertices: 9
0 1 2 3 4 5 6 7 8
```

We now produce the code to access the edges in the graph using the `edges()` function (notice we use tuples):

```
// Edge set.
cout << "Edge information, number of edges: " << num_edges(dg) << endl;
graph_traits<MatrixDirectedGraph>::edge_iterator ei, ei_end;
for (tie(ei, ei_end) = edges(dg); ei != ei_end; ++ei)
{
    cout << "(" << index[source(*ei, dg)]
         << "," << index[target(*ei, dg)] << ") ";
```

```
}
cout << std::endl;
```

The output from this code is:

```
Edge information, number of edges: 15
(0,1) (0,2) (1,3) (1,4) (2,3) (2,4) (3,4) (3,5) (3,6) (3,7) (4,6) (5,7)
(5,8) (6,8) (7,8)
```

16.6 Minimum Spanning Tree (MST) Algorithms

We have discussed the MST problem in section 15.5: given an undirected graph G = (V,E) find an acyclic subset T of edges of E that connects all of the vertices in the graph and whose total weight is minimised. An acyclic subset of edges that connects all the vertices in the graph is called a *spanning tree*. A tree T with minimum total weight is a *minimum spanning tree* (MST). Computing the MST is of particular importance in network applications, for example communication networks, transportation networks, energy and water pipelines and VLSI chips, for example. For an undirected graph we are interested in computing the MST (its vertices) and the total weight in the MST. We note that the MST is not unique; there may be several equally valid MSTs for a given undirected graph.

16.6.1 Kruskal Algorithm

The Kruskal algorithm starts with an empty graph (no edges) and it adds edges rather than removing them. The algorithm is described in section 15.5 and the example we take here is from Figure 15.14. We first rename the vertices in the graph to 0, 1, 2, 3 and 4 for convenience. The code to initialise the graph and to define some typedefs is:

```
// Definitions and the ubiquitous typedefs
typedef adjacency_list<vecS, vecS, undirectedS,
                       no_property, property<edge_weight_t, int> > Graph;
typedef graph_traits<Graph>::edge_descriptor Edge;
typedef graph_traits<Graph>::vertex_descriptor Vertex;
typedef std::pair<int, int> E;

// Graph data (Figure 15.14).
const int num_nodes = 4;
E edge_array[] = { E(0, 1), E(1, 2), E(2, 3), E(0, 3), E(0, 2), E(1,3) };
int weights[] = {2, 5, 4, 5, 10, 1};

// Create the graph.
std::size_t num_edges = sizeof(edge_array) / sizeof(E);
cout << "Number of edges: " << num_edges << std::endl;
Graph g(edge_array, edge_array + num_edges, weights, num_nodes);
print_graph(g); cout << endl;
```

Next, we model edge weights and the vertices on the MST as follows:

```
// Edge weights and vertices.
property_map<Graph, edge_weight_t>::type weight = get(edge_weight, g);
std::vector<Edge> spanning_tree;
```

We now call the Kruskal algorithm and we initialise the MST:

```
// Calculate MST using Kruskal Algorithm. (prim_minimum_spanning_tree.hpp)
kruskal_minimum_spanning_tree(g, std::back_inserter(spanning_tree));
```

Finally, we compute the total length of the MST is:

```
// Display MST and calculate total weight.
```

```
long totalWeight = 0;
cout << "Print the edges in the Kruskal MST:" << endl;
for (vector<Edge>::iterator ei = spanning_tree.begin();
     ei != spanning_tree.end(); ++ei)
{
    cout << "(" << source(*ei, g) << "," << target(*ei, g) <<")"
         << " with weight of " << weight[*ei]   << endl;
    totalWeight += weight[*ei];
}
cout << "Total weight, Kruskal: " << totalWeight << endl;
```

You can run the code and check that the MST is {(0,1), (1,3),(3,2)} and that the total length is 7 as shown in Figure 15.15.

16.6.2 Prim Algorithm

The Prim algorithm is a greedy algorithm because we grow the MST steadily from one initial arc. At each stage of the algorithm the arc that is added is the shortest arc remaining that has one vertex in the tree. In other words, the tree is grown one vertex at a time.

We take the same example as in section 16.6.1. In this case we record the MST in the `parent` array. We calculate the total weight by looping through all the vertices in the graph and summing the weight of each edge (parent[j], j). If parent[j] = j then either j is the root of the tree or it was not in the same connected component as the rest of the vertices. In either case (parent[j], j) is not a spanning tree edge and is skipped:

```
// Calculate MST using Prim Algorithm. (prim_minimum_spanning_tree.hpp)
std::vector<Vertex> parent(num_vertices(g));
prim_minimum_spanning_tree(g, &parent[0]);

// Calculate total weight.
long totalWeight = 0;
cout << "Number of vertices: " << num_vertices(g) << endl;
property_map<Graph, edge_weight_t>::type weightMap = get(edge_weight, g);
for (size_t j = 1; j < num_vertices(g); ++j)
{
    if (parent[j] != j)
    {
        totalWeight += get(weightMap, edge(parent[j], j, g).first);
    }
}
cout << "Total weight, Prim: " << totalWeight << endl;
```

Finally, for the example in Figure 16.3 the MST is {(0,1), (2,3), (3,4), (0,2)} and the total length is 23. The C++ code is:

```
// Graph data (Figure 16.3).
const int num_nodes = 5;
E edge_array[] = { E(0, 1), E(0, 2), E(0, 4), E(1, 2), E(2, 3),
                   E(2, 4), E(3,4) };
int weights[] = {5, 8, 10, 10, 4, 7, 6};
```

You can run the code and check the validity of the output.

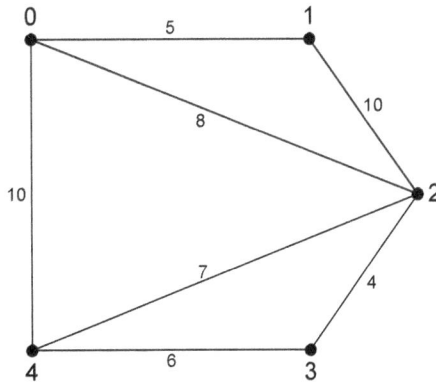

Figure 16.3 Minimum Spanning Tree example

16.7 Shortest Path Algorithms

We have already discussed shortest-path problems in section 15.7. The main scenarios are:
- *Single-pair shortest-path problem*: find the shortest path that connects a given pair of vertices. The output is a chain of vertices.
- *Single source shortest-path problem*: find the shortest path from a source vertex to every other vertex in the graph. The set of shortest paths emanating from the source vertex is called the *shortest-path tree*.
- *All-pairs shortest-path problem*: find the shortest path from every vertex to every other vertex in the graph. The output is a graph.

We first discuss the Dijkstra shortest-path algorithm.

16.7.1 Dijkstra's Algorithm

This algorithm solves the single-source shortest-path problem on a weighted directed or undirected graph for which all edge-weights are *nonnegative*. When all weights are equal to one then we use the breadth-first search algorithm instead of Dijkstra's algorithm. When some edge-weights are negative we use the Bellman-Ford algorithm to compute the shortest path.

The input to the algorithm is:
- The graph object to which we apply the algorithm. It must be a model of `VertexListGraph` and `IncidenceGraph`.
- The source vertex (a `vertex_descriptor` instance). The shortest-path tree is rooted at this vertex and all distances are calculated from it.

The named parameters input are:
- Weight map giving the 'length' of each edge in the graph.
- Vertex index map that maps each vertex to an integer in the closed-open range [0, N) where N is the number of vertices in the graph.

The most important output for our purposes here consists of:
- Predecessor map that records the edges in the minimum spanning tree. It contains the vertices of the MST when the algorithm completes.
- Distance map: this is a property map that records the shortest-path weight from the source vertex to each vertex in the graph.

As initial example, we examine Figure 15.18 of chapter 15. We wish to calculate the shortest path from vertex A to vertex G. By inspection, we see that there are three paths from A to G having lengths 11, 15 and 21. Thus, the shortest paths is $A \rightarrow D \rightarrow E \rightarrow G$ and we would like to produce the same output in software. The graph data structure for the graph in Figure 15.18 is:

```
#include <boost/graph/dijkstra_shortest_paths.hpp>

// Create a weighted directed graph.
typedef adjacency_list<listS, vecS, directedS, no_property,
                      property<edge_weight_t, int> > Graph;
typedef graph_traits<Graph>::vertex_descriptor VertexDescriptor;
typedef graph_traits<Graph>::edge_descriptor EdgeDescriptor;
typedef pair<int, int> Edge;

// Build up the edges (Figure 15.18).
const int num_nodes = 7; enum nodes {A, B, C, D, E, F, G};
char name[] = "ABCDEFG";
Edge edge_array[] = { Edge(A, B), Edge(A, C), Edge(A, D), Edge(B, E),
                      Edge(D, E), Edge(C, F), Edge(E, G), Edge(F, G) };
int weights[] = { 4, 7, 5, 10, 2, 2, 4, 12};
int num_arcs = sizeof(edge_array) / sizeof(Edge);

// Create the graph.
Graph g(edge_array, edge_array + num_arcs, weights, num_nodes);
print_graph(g, name);   cout << endl;
```

We now call the algorithm and produce output statistics:

```
// Now for Dijkstra's algorithm.
vector<VertexDescriptor> parent(num_vertices(g));
vector<int> d(num_vertices(g));
VertexDescriptor s = vertex(A, g);

// Calculate the shortest path using Dijkstra's algorithm.
dijkstra_shortest_paths(g, s,
                        predecessor_map(&parent[0]).distance_map(&d[0]));

// Display the distances.
cout << "Distances and parents:" << endl;
graph_traits<Graph>::vertex_iterator vi, vend;
for (boost::tie(vi, vend) = vertices(g); vi != vend; ++vi)
{
    cout << "Distance(" << name[*vi] << ") = " << d[*vi] << ", ";
    cout << "Parent(" << name[*vi] << ") = " << name[parent[*vi]] << endl;
}
cout << endl;
```

The output from this executable code is:

```
A --> B C D
B --> E
C --> F
D --> E
E --> G
F --> G
G -->

Distances and parents:
Distance(A) = 0, Parent(A) = A
Distance(B) = 4, Parent(B) = A
Distance(C) = 7, Parent(C) = A
Distance(D) = 5, Parent(D) = A
Distance(E) = 7, Parent(E) = D
```

```
Distance(F) = 9, Parent(F) = C
Distance(G) = 11, Parent(G) = E
```

We thus see that the minimum length is 11 and we can trace the path from vertex G back to vertex A. Finally, the shortest path from vertex 0 to vertex 8 in Figure 16.2 is along the arcs $\{(0,2), (2,3),(3,4),(4,6),(6,8)\}$ and has length 19.

16.7.2 Bellman-Ford Algorithm

The Bellman–Ford algorithm computes single-source shortest paths in a weighted digraph. For graphs with only non-negative edge weights, the faster Dijkstra's algorithm also solves the problem. Thus, Bellman–Ford is used primarily for graphs with some negative edge weights. The main step in the algorithm is called *edge relaxation* and it based on *Bellman's equations*:

$$u_1 = 0$$
$$u_j = \max_{k \neq j} \{u_k + a_{kj}\}, \quad j = 2, 3, \ldots, n \tag{16.1}$$

where

$$u_1 = \text{origin of the network with } n \text{ vertices,}$$
$$u_j = \text{distance of the shortest path from the origin to vertex } j,$$
$$a_{kj} = \text{length of the arc } (k, j).$$

We solve the equations (16.1) by successive approximations, in other words by an iterative method. Initially, we set:

$$u_1^{(1)} = 0$$
$$u_j^{(1)} = a_{1j}, j \neq 1. \tag{16.2}$$

We then compute successive approximations as follows:

$$u_j^{(m+1)} = \min \left\{ u_j^{(m)}, \min_{k \neq j} \left\{ u_k^{(m)} + a_{kj} \right\} \right\}, \quad \begin{matrix} j = 1 \\ m \geq 0 \end{matrix}, 2, \ldots, n. \tag{16.3}$$

We can see from equation (16.3) that successive approximations are monotonically decreasing:

$$u_j^{(1)} \geq u_j^{(2)} \geq \ldots \geq u_j^{(m)} \geq u_j^{(m+1)} \geq \ldots \tag{16.4}$$

Equation (16.3) is solved for $m = 1, 2, \ldots, n - 2$. There are n equations to be solved for each value of m.

We note that the performance of the method can be improved by making use of the best information available at each iteration. If a graph contains a *negative cycle*, that is a cycle whose edges sum to a negative value, then walks of arbitrarily low weight can be constructed, that is, there may be no shortest path. Bellman-Ford can detect negative cycles and report their existence but it cannot produce a correct answer if a negative cycle is reachable from the source.

We now discuss the BGL implementation of the Bellman-Ford algorithm and we then proceed to give an example. The function prototypes are:

```
template <class EdgeListGraph, class Size, class P, class T, class R>
bool bellman_ford_shortest_paths(EdgeListGraph& g, Size N,
                        const bgl_named_params<P, T, R>& params)
```

```
template <class EdgeListGraph, class Size>
  bool bellman_ford_shortest_paths(EdgeListGraph& g, Size N);

template <class EdgeListGraph, class Size, class WeightMap,
          class PredecessorMap, class DistanceMap,
          class BinaryFunction, class BinaryPredicate,
          class BellmanFordVisitor>
bool bellman_ford_shortest_paths(EdgeListGraph& g, Size N,
                                 WeightMap weight,
                                 PredecessorMap pred,
                                 DistanceMap distance,
                                 BinaryFunction combine,
                                 BinaryPredicate compare,
                                 BellmanFordVisitor v);
```

In this section we take the example as shown in Figure 16.4 (note the presence of some negative weights). The steps are:
1. Create the digraph corresponding to Figure 16.4.
2. Assign edge weights.
3. Create the property map for the lengths and vertex property storage.
4. Call the Bellman-Ford algorithm.
5. Print shortest-path related information.

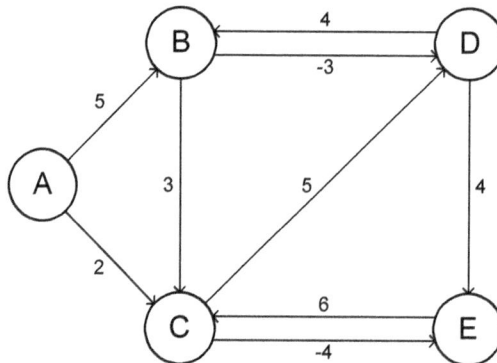

16.4 Network containing negative weights

The code that implements these steps is:

```
#include <boost/graph/edge_list.hpp>
#include <boost/graph/bellman_ford_shortest_paths.hpp>

#include <iostream>

using namespace std;
using namespace boost;

int main()
{
    typedef std::pair<int, int> Edge;

    // Graph data (Figure 16.4).
    const int n_edges = 9;
    const int n_vertices = 5;
    enum nodes {A, B, C, D, E}; char name[] = "ABCDE";
    Edge edges[] = { Edge(A, B), Edge(A, C), Edge(B, C), Edge(B, D),
                     Edge(D,B), Edge(C,D), Edge(C,E), Edge(E, C),
                     Edge(D,E) };
    int delay[] = { 5, 2, 3, 4, -3, 5, -4, 6, 4};
```

```
// Specify the graph type and declare a graph object.
typedef edge_list<Edge*, Edge, std::ptrdiff_t,
        std::random_access_iterator_tag> Graph;
Graph g(edges, edges + n_edges);

// Number th vertices.
int parent[n_vertices];
for (int i = 0; i < n_vertices; ++i) parent[i] = i;

// Create the distance vector.
double distance[n_vertices];
std::fill(distance, distance + n_vertices,
        std::numeric_limits<double>::max());

// Specify A as the source vertex.
distance[A] = 0;

// Calculate the shortest path using Bellman-Ford Algorithm.
bool r = bellman_ford_shortest_paths
(
    g, n_vertices,
    weight_map
    (
        make_iterator_property_map(&delay[0], get(edge_index, g),
                                delay[0])
    ).distance_map(&distance[0]).predecessor_map(&parent[0])
);

if (r)
{
    // Display the distances.
    for (int i = 0; i < n_vertices; ++i)
    {
        cout << "Destination node: " << name[i] << ": " << distance[i]
            << ", predecessor: " << name[parent[i]] << endl;
    }
}
else
{
    cout << "negative cycle" << endl;
}
cout << "\nStatus of algorithm: " << boolalpha << r <<endl;

return 0;
}
```

16.8 Summary and Conclusions

We have given an introduction to some of the most important interfaces and data structures in BGL and we showed how to use them in conjunction with shortest-path and minimum spanning tree algorithms. BGL can be a difficult library to learn and to use and we paid some attention to showing how to use it in a step-by-step manner. In chapter 17 we discuss BGL and its applications in more detail.

17 The Boost Graph Library (BGL) Advanced Algorithms

17.1 Introduction and Objectives

In this chapter we introduce some of the advanced functionality in BGL that has applications to engineering, communication networks, finance, transportation and logistics. We discuss the following topics and we show how they are implemented in BGL:

- Advanced shortest path algorithms.
- Graph connectivity and connected components.
- Network maximum flow algorithms.
- Graph isomorphisms.
- Floyd-Warshall and Johnson shortest-path algorithms.
- Boost Visitor to customise algorithms.
- Basic graph algorithms.
- Sparse matrix ordering algorithms.
- Random graphs.

We describe each of these areas in some detail and we give examples of use.

17.2 More Shortest-Path Algorithms

The main scenarios are:

- *Single-pair shortest-path problem*: find the shortest path that connects a given pair of vertices.
- *Single source shortest-path problem*: find the shortest path from a source vertex to every other vertex in the graph. The set of shortest paths emanating from the source vertex is called the *shortest-path tree*.
- *All-pairs shortest-path problem*: find the shortest path from every vertex to every other vertex in the graph.

17.2.1 Floyd-Warshall Algorithm

This algorithm compares all possible paths between each pair of vertices in a directed graph. The algorithm estimates the shortest path incrementally until an estimate becomes optimal. We first describe the algorithm in mathematical terms. To this end, let W denote the *weight matrix* between vertices i and j defined as:

$$W(i,j) = \begin{cases} 0 \text{ if } i = j, \\ \text{weight } (i,j) \text{ if the graph contains an edge between } i \text{ and } j \ (i \neq j), \\ \infty, \text{ otherwise.} \end{cases} \tag{17.1}$$

For example, the (non symmetric) weight matrix for the directed graph in Figure 17.1 is:

$$W = \begin{pmatrix} 0 & 4 & \infty & 3 & \infty \\ \infty & 0 & 6 & \infty & 2 \\ 1 & \infty & 0 & \infty & \infty \\ 4 & \infty & 2 & 0 & 3 \\ \infty & \infty & 1 & \infty & 0 \end{pmatrix}. \tag{17.2}$$

We introduce some notation. Let $S_k(i,j)$ be the weight of the shortest path P from vertex i to vertex j whose interior vertices (if any) all lie in V_k, where V_k is the subset of vertices $0, 1, 2, \ldots k$. If no such path exists then $S_k(i,j) = \infty$. By definition, $S_0(i,j) = W(i,j)$ is the weight of the shortest path from i to j. Finally, we note that $S_n(i,j)$ is the weight of a shortest path in the digraph from vertex i to vertex j.

The *recurrence relationship* to compute the shortest distance between all vertices is:

$$S_0(i,j) = W(i,j), \quad \forall\, i,j \in V$$

$$S_k(i,j) = \min\left\{ S_{k-1}(i,j), S_{k-1}(i,k) + S_{k-1}(k,j) \right\}. \tag{17.3}$$

The complexity of the Floyd-Warshall algorithm is $O(n^3)$ where n is the number of vertices in the graph. Negative weights are allowed.

17.2.2 Johnson Algorithm

This algorithm computes the shortest paths between all pairs of vertices in a sparse directed graph. As with the Floyd-Warshall algorithm, it allows some of the edge weights to be negative but negative-weight cycles are not allowed. It uses the Bellman-Ford algorithm to compute a transformation of the input graph that removes all negative weights, thus allowing Dijkstra's algorithm to be applied to the transformed graph.

The time complexity of Johnson's algorithm is $O(n^2 \log n + nm)$, where n is the number of vertices and m is the number of edges in the graph, since it uses $O(nm)$ time for the Bellman-Ford stage of the algorithm and $0(n\log n + m)$ for each of the n instantiations of the Dijkstra algorithm.

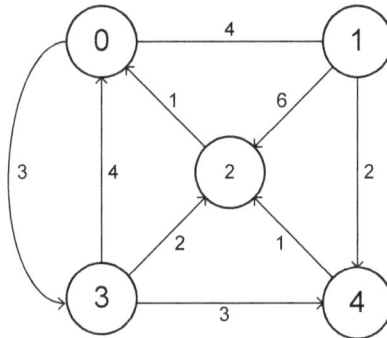

Figure 17.1 Network for Floyd's and Johnson's algorithm

As example, we examine Figure 17.1. We can calculate the shortest paths using the Johnson Algorithm or the Floyd-Warshall algorithm (see section 17.2.1). The code is:

```
#include <iostream>
#include <vector>
#include <iomanip>

#include <boost/property_map/property_map.hpp>
#include <boost/graph/adjacency_list.hpp>
#include <boost/graph/johnson_all_pairs_shortest.hpp>
#include <boost/graph/floyd_warshall_shortest.hpp>

using namespace std;
using namespace boost;
int main()
{
    int choice=0;
    while (choice<1 || choice>2)
```

```cpp
{
    cout<<"1. Floyd Warshall\n2. Johnson\nChoice: ";
    cin>>choice;
}

// Typedef for the graph.
typedef adjacency_list<vecS, vecS, directedS, no_property,
  property<edge_weight_t, int, property<edge_weight2_t, int> > > Graph;

// Graph data (Figure 17.1).
const int V = 5;
typedef std::pair<int, int> Edge;
Edge edge_array[] = { Edge(0,1), Edge(0,3), Edge(1,2),
                      Edge(1,4), Edge(2,0), Edge(3,2),
                      Edge(3,4), Edge(3,0), Edge(4,2) };
const std::size_t E = sizeof(edge_array) / sizeof(Edge);

// Create graph.
Graph g(edge_array, edge_array + E, V);

// Create weight data.
int weights[] = { 4, 3, 6, 2, 1, 2, 3, 4, 1};

// Fill property map with weight data.
property_map<Graph, edge_weight_t>::type w=get(edge_weight, g);
int *wp = weights;
graph_traits<Graph>::edge_iterator e, e_end;
for (boost::tie(e, e_end) = edges(g); e != e_end; ++e)
{
    w[*e] = *wp++;
}

std::vector<int> d(V, std::numeric_limits<int>::max());
int D[V][V];

// Calculate the shortest paths.
if (choice==1)
{
    floyd_warshall_all_pairs_shortest_paths(g, D, distance_map(&d[0]));
}
else
{
    johnson_all_pairs_shortest_paths(g, D, distance_map(&d[0]));
}

// Display header for matrix with shortests paths.
cout << "Shortest path matrix:\n\n";
cout << setw(5) <<" ";
for (int k = 0; k < V; ++k) cout << setw(5) << k ;
cout << endl << endl;

// Display shortest paths.
for (int i = 0; i < V; ++i)
{
    cout << setw(5) <<  i;
    for (int j = 0; j < V; ++j)
    {
        cout << setw(5) << D[i][j] ;
    }
    cout << endl;
}

return 0;
}
```

The output from the shortest-path algorithm is the matrix:

$$S_5 = \begin{pmatrix} 0 & 4 & 5 & 3 & 6 \\ 4 & 0 & 3 & 7 & 2 \\ 1 & 5 & 0 & 4 & 7 \\ 3 & 7 & 2 & 0 & 3 \\ 2 & 6 & 1 & 5 & 0 \end{pmatrix}$$

You can check that this output is correct by manually computing the shortest paths in Figure 17.1 and comparing them with the computer-generated results. For example, note that the shortest path from vertex 3 to vertex 0 is now 3.

17.2.3 Transitive Closure

We are now interested in answering questions concerning *reachability* in graphs. The main question is to determine if we can move from one vertex to another vertex in a graph in one or more *hops*. To this end, we define a *binary relation* R between two vertices u and v by uRv that tells us if u is connected to v. When the *transitive closure* has been constructed we can determine if one node is accessible from another one in $O(1)$ time. As example, let us consider the simple graph in Figure 17.2(a). The code to compute the transitive closure is:

```
#include <iostream>

#include <boost/graph/adjacency_list.hpp>
#include <boost/graph/graph_utility.hpp>
#include <boost/graph/transitive_closure.hpp>

using namespace std;
using namespace boost;

// Typedef for graph.
typedef adjacency_list<> Graph;

int main()
{
    // Create graph.
    Graph gInput(4), gOutput;
    add_edge(1,2,gInput);
    add_edge(2,3,gInput);
    add_edge(3,4,gInput);
    print_graph(gInput); cout << endl;

    // Calculate the transitive closure.
    transitive_closure(gInput, gOutput);

    // Print the edges.
    cout << "Transitive closure: ";
    Graph::edge_iterator i, iend;
    for (tie(i,iend) = edges(gOutput); i!=iend; ++i)
    {
        cout << source(*i,gOutput) << "->" << target(*i,gOutput) << " ";
    }
    cout << endl;

    return 0;
}
```

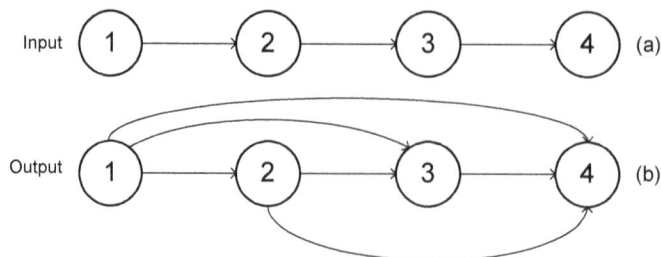

Figure 17.2 Transitive Closure

You can run this code and check that the output is the same as that given in Figure 17.2 (b).

17.3 Connected Component Algorithms

In this section we discuss various aspects of graph and digraph connectivity that we introduced in section 15.2.2.

17.3.1 Connected Components

We are interested in graphs that are not connected, in other words graphs for which it is not possible to connect all vertices with other vertices in the graph. In that case the graph will then have two or more *connected components*, an example of which is given in Figure 15.5 of chapter 15; in this case there are three connected components and the corresponding code to compute these components is:

```
#include <iostream>

#include <boost/graph/adjacency_list.hpp>
#include <boost/graph/graph_utility.hpp>
#include <boost/graph/connected_components.hpp>

using namespace std;
using namespace boost;

int main()
{
    // Typedef for graph and vertex.
    typedef adjacency_list<vecS, vecS, undirectedS> Graph;
    typedef graph_traits<Graph>::vertex_descriptor Vertex;

    // Graph data (Figure 15.5: A B C D E F G H I -> 0 1 2 3 4 5 6 7 8).
    const int N = 9;
    Graph g(N);
    add_edge(0,1,g); add_edge(0,3,g); add_edge(1,2,g); add_edge(2,3,g);
    add_edge(4,5,g); add_edge(4,6,g); add_edge(5,6,g);
    add_edge(7,8,g);
    print_graph(g);

    // Calculate the total number of components by giving the graph and
    // component vector as input.
    vector<int> c(num_vertices(g));
    int num = connected_components(g,
        make_iterator_property_map(c.begin(), get(vertex_index, g), c[0]));
    cout << "Total number of components: " << num << endl;

    // Print vertices and the components in which they reside.
    vector<int>::iterator i;
    for (i = c.begin(); i != c.end(); ++i)
    {
```

```
            cout << "Vertex " << i - c.begin() << " is in component "
                << *i << endl;
    }

    return 0;
}
```

The output from this code is:

```
Total number of components: 3

Vertex 0 is in component 0
Vertex 1 is in component 0
Vertex 2 is in component 0
Vertex 3 is in component 0
Vertex 4 is in component 1
Vertex 5 is in component 1
Vertex 6 is in component 1
Vertex 7 is in component 2
Vertex 8 is in component 2
```

There are thus three components which is in accordance with a visual inspection of Figure 15.5.

We now discuss how to connect these graph components to form one single component. The following code achieves this end:

```
#include <boost/graph/make_connected.hpp>

vector<graph_traits<Graph>::vertices_size_type>
    component(num_vertices(g));

cout << "Before calling make_connected, the graph has "
    << connected_components(g, &component[0])
    << " connected components" << endl;

make_connected(g);

cout << "After calling make_connected, the graph has "
    << connected_components(g, &component[0])
    << " connected components" << endl;

print_graph(g);
```

The output from this code is:

```
Before calling make_connected, the graph has 3 connected components
After calling make_connected, the graph has 1 connected components
0 <--> 1 3
1 <--> 0 2
2 <--> 1 3
3 <--> 0 2 4
4 <--> 5 6 3
5 <--> 4 6
6 <--> 4 5 7
7 <--> 8 6
8 <--> 7
```

The corresponding visual representation of this graph is shown in Figure 17.3.

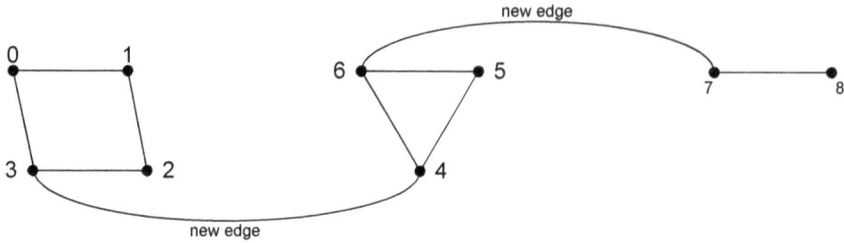

Figure 17.3 Make a connected graph

The *number of connected components* is an important topological invariant in a graph. For example, in topological graph theory it can be interpreted as the *zeroth Betti number* of a graph. The *first Betti number* is the number of two-dimensional or 'circular holes' and is given by the formula:

$$b_1 = m - n + k$$

where

$m =$ number of edges
$n =$ number of vertices
$k =$ number of components.

The first Betti number is used in software engineering when measuring the complexity of programs. This is called the *McCabe complexity* (or *conditional complexity*) and it is a direct measure of the number of linearly independent paths through a program's source code. We can formulate this problems in terms of graph theory; the vertices correspond to indivisible groups of commands of a program. The directed edges connect two vertices if the second command might be executed immediately after the first command. We take an initial example to show how to reformulate a program in graph-theoretic form. A simple test program is:

```
int main()
{
    // Using 6 functions.
    if (ChoiceA())
    {
        F1();
    }
    else
    {
        F2();
    }

    // "join 1"

    if (ChoiceB())
    {
        F3();
    }
    else
    {
        F4();
    }

    // "join 2"

    return 0;
}
```

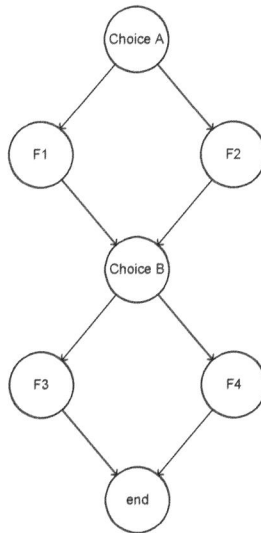

Figure 17.4 Control Flow graph

The corresponding graph is shown in Figure 17.4. We see that the graph has one connected component, seven vertices and eight edges. The cyclomatic complexity of the program is 8 − 7 + 2*1 = 3. In general, the formula for the *cyclomatic complexity* M is:

$$M = m - n + 2k.$$

Many experiments have been done using this metric and there seems to be a strong correlation between cyclomatic complexity and the number of faults in a program. In particular, the number of faults tends to increase dramatically for values of M above 20.

We conclude our discussion of connected components by noting that the first Betti number is equal to the multiplicity of zero as an eigenvalue of the *Laplacian matrix* L with vertices $\{v_j\}$ of a graph:

$$L = (l_{ij}) \text{ for } i, j = 1, \ldots, n$$

$$l_{ij} = \begin{cases} \deg(v_i), & i = j \\ -1, i \neq j \text{ and } v_i \text{ is adjacent to } v_j \\ 0, \text{ otherwise.} \end{cases}$$

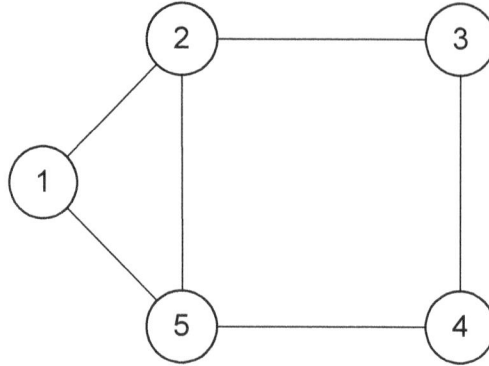

Figure 17.5 Graph for Laplacian matrix

In other words, this matrix is the difference of the degree matrix and the adjacency matrix of the graph. Consider the example in Figure 17.5. Based on the above definition you can check that the Laplacian matrix is the same as the matrix as given in Figure 17.6.

$$
\begin{pmatrix}
2 & -1 & 0 & 0 & -1 \\
-1 & 3 & -1 & 0 & -1 \\
0 & -1 & 2 & -1 & 0 \\
0 & 0 & -1 & 2 & -1 \\
-1 & -1 & 0 & -1 & 3
\end{pmatrix}
$$

Figure 17.6 Computed Laplacian matrix

Next, we wish to compute the number of spanning trees in a graph. This is answered by *Kirchoff's theorem* which is stated as follows:

For a given graph G with n labeled vertices, we let $\lambda_1, \lambda_2, \ldots, \lambda_{n-1}$ be the non-zero eigenvalues of its Laplacian matrix. Then the number of spanning trees of G is given by:

$$
t(G) = \frac{1}{n} \prod_{j=1}^{n-1} \lambda_j. \tag{17.4}
$$

17.3.2 Biconnected Components and Articulation Points

A graph is called *biconnected* if the removal of any single vertex (and edges incident on that vertex) cannot disconnect the graph. In other words, the graph has still one component when any vertex is removed. The graph is said to be connected and *nonseparable*, that is if any vertex is removed then the graph will remain connected. The *biconnected components* (also known as *2-connected components*) of a graph are the maximal subsets of vertices such that the removal of a vertex will not disconnect the components; in other words, a biconnected component is a maximal biconnected subgraph of a graph. For example, the graph in Figure 17.3 is not biconnected (why?). Vertices that belong to more than one biconnected component are called *articulation points* (or *cut vertices*). In other words, articulation points are vertices whose removal will increase the number of components in a graph. For example, the vertices 3, 4, 6 and 7 in Figure 17.3 are articulation points. We thus conclude that a graph without articulation points is biconnected. In general, vertices can be in multiple biconnected components but an edge can only be contained in a single biconnected component. The use of biconnected graphs is important in networking (in particular, network flow) because of *redundancy*; it should be possible for a node in a network to fail without destroying network connectivity. Examples of articulation points are airline hubs, traffic routers, electric circuits and bonds in protein.

BGL has functions to compute the number of biconnected components and articulation points in a graph. The code for a generic graph g is given by:

```cpp
#include <iostream>

#include <boost/graph/adjacency_list.hpp>
#include <boost/graph/graph_utility.hpp>
#include <boost/graph/biconnected_components.hpp>

using namespace std;
using namespace boost;

namespace boost
{
    struct EdgeComponent
    {
        enum { num = 555 };
        typedef edge_property_tag kind;
    }
    edge_component;
}

int main()
{
    typedef adjacency_list<vecS, vecS, undirectedS, no_property,
                        property<EdgeComponent, std::size_t> > Graph;
    typedef graph_traits<Graph>::vertex_descriptor Vertex;

    // Define graph (Figure 17.3).
    Graph g(9);
    add_edge(0,1,g); add_edge(0,3,g); add_edge(1,2,g); add_edge(2,3,g);
    add_edge(4,5,g); add_edge(4,6,g); add_edge(5,6,g);
    add_edge(7,8,g);
    add_edge(3,4,g); add_edge(6,7,g);
    print_graph(g);

    // Determine biconnected components.
    property_map<Graph, EdgeComponent>::type component =
        get(edge_component, g);
    size_t num_comps = biconnected_components(g, component);
    cout << "Found " << num_comps << " biconnected components.\n";

    // Determine articulation points.
    vector<Vertex> art_points;
    articulation_points(g, std::back_inserter(art_points));
    cout << "Found " << art_points.size() << " articulation points.\n";

    return 0;
}
```

Our final remark is that this algorithm can be implemented using Depth-First Search and the time complexity to compute biconnected components and articulation points is $O(n+m)$, where n is the number of vertices and m is the number of edges in the graph.

17.3.3 Incremental Connected Components

We now describe a method to compute the connected components of an undirected graph. The method is useful in situations where the graph is growing (edges being added) and if the information relating to the connected components is repeatedly updated. The method is implemented by a family of functions and classes that are based on fast union-find called *disjoint sets*. The functions use a graph g and a disjoint set ds:

- `initialize_incremental_components(g, ds)`: basic initialisation of the disjoint-sets structures. Each vertex in the graph g is in its own set. This function prepares the disjoint-sets data structure for the incremental connected components algorithm by making each vertex in the graph a member of its own component (or set).
- `incremental_components(g, ds)`: compute the connected components based on the edges in g and the information in ds. The results are embedded in the disjoint-sets data structure.
- `ds.find_set(v)`: extract the component information for vertex v from the disjoint-sets. In general this function returns the representative for the set containing v .
- `ds.union_set(u, v)`: update the disjoint-sets structure when edge (u,v) is added to the graph. In general, this function returns the set that contains both u and v.

We first describe disjoint sets. The class template has three parameters:
- *Rank*: is a model of *ReadWritePropertyMap* with key type equal to the set's element type and an integer value type.
- *Parent*: is a model of *ReadWritePropertyMap* with key type and value types being the same as the set's element type.
- *FindCompress*: is one of the find representative and path compress function objects.

The full syntax is `disjoint_set<Rank, Parent, FindCompress>`.

We now take an example of calculating the connected components of an undirected graph using the current methods. The graph we take again is shown in Figure 15.5. We already know that there are three components named 0, 1 and 2; vertex 1 is the representative for component 0, vertex 5 is the representative for component 1 and vertex 8 is the representative for component 2. The new code is now:

```
#include <iostream>

#include <boost/foreach.hpp>
#include <boost/graph/adjacency_list.hpp>
#include <boost/graph/graph_utility.hpp>
#include <boost/graph/incremental_components.hpp>
#include <boost/pending/disjoint_sets.hpp>

using namespace std;
using namespace boost;

int main()
{
    // Typedefs for graph.
    typedef adjacency_list <vecS, vecS, undirectedS> Graph;
    typedef graph_traits<Graph>::vertex_descriptor Vertex;
    typedef graph_traits<Graph>::vertices_size_type VertexIndex;

    // Create graph.
    const int N = 9;
    Graph g(N);

    // Prepare rank and parent for disjoint set.
    typedef VertexIndex* Rank;
    typedef Vertex* Parent;
    vector<VertexIndex> rank(num_vertices(g));
    vector<Vertex> parent(num_vertices(g));
```

```
    disjoint_sets<Rank, Parent> ds(&rank[0], &parent[0]);
    // Initialise the disjoint-sets.
    initialize_incremental_components(g, ds);

    // Calculate the connect components of the graph.
    incremental_components(g, ds);

    graph_traits<Graph>::edge_descriptor edge;
    bool flag;

    // Set up the edges; this is the example of Figure 15.5
    // Notice that we have THREE components.
    boost::tie(edge, flag) = add_edge(0, 1, g); ds.union_set(0,1);
    boost::tie(edge, flag) = add_edge(0, 3, g); ds.union_set(0,3);
    boost::tie(edge, flag) = add_edge(1, 2, g); ds.union_set(1,2);
    boost::tie(edge, flag) = add_edge(2, 3, g); ds.union_set(2,3);

    boost::tie(edge, flag) = add_edge(4, 5, g); ds.union_set(4,5);
    boost::tie(edge, flag) = add_edge(4, 6, g); ds.union_set(4,6);
    boost::tie(edge, flag) = add_edge(5, 6, g); ds.union_set(5,6);

    boost::tie(edge, flag) = add_edge(7, 8, g); ds.union_set(7,8);

    // Print the graph to check OK.
    cout << "An undirected graph:" << endl;
    print_graph(g, get(boost::vertex_index, g));
    cout << endl;

    // Extract component information regarding a vertex.
    BOOST_FOREACH(Vertex current_vertex, vertices(g))
    {
        cout << "representative[" << current_vertex << "] = "
            << ds.find_set(current_vertex) << endl;
    }
    cout << endl;

    typedef component_index<VertexIndex> Components;
    Components components(parent.begin(), parent.end());

    // Iterate through the component indices.
    BOOST_FOREACH(VertexIndex current_index, components)
    {
        cout << "component " << current_index << " contains: ";

        // Iterate through the child vertex indices for [current_index].
        BOOST_FOREACH(VertexIndex child_index, components[current_index])
        {
            cout << child_index << " ";
        }
        cout << endl;
    }

    return 0;
}
```

Finally, we discuss the function `same_component` to determine if two vertices are in the same component and the class `component_index` that provides an STL container-like view for the components in a graph. Again, we discuss the graph in Figure 15.5. We test if vertices 1 and 2 are in the same component and we repeat the experiment for vertices 0 and 8:

```
// Determine if vertices are in the same component.
cout << "Vertex 0 and 2 in same component?: " << boolalpha
    << same_component(0, 2, ds) << endl;  // true
cout << "Vertex 0 and 8 in same component?: " << boolalpha
```

```
    << same_component(0, 8, ds) << endl;  // false
```

Next, we briefly discuss the class `component_index`. Each component is a container-like object and access is provided using the `[]` operator. We initialise instances of `component_index` with the parent's property in the disjoint-sets calculated from the `incremental_components()` function.

17.3.4 Strong Components

The `strong_components()` functions compute the strongly connected components of a directed graph using Tarjan's algorithm based on DFS. The output of this algorithm is a component property map that contains the component ID assigned to each vertex. The return value of the function is the number of components. A *strongly connected component* of a directed graph $G = (V, E)$ is by definition the maximal set of vertices U which is in V such that there is a path from both u to v and from v to u. We say that u and v are reachable from each other.

The input to `strong_components()` is a directed graph and the output is a component map.

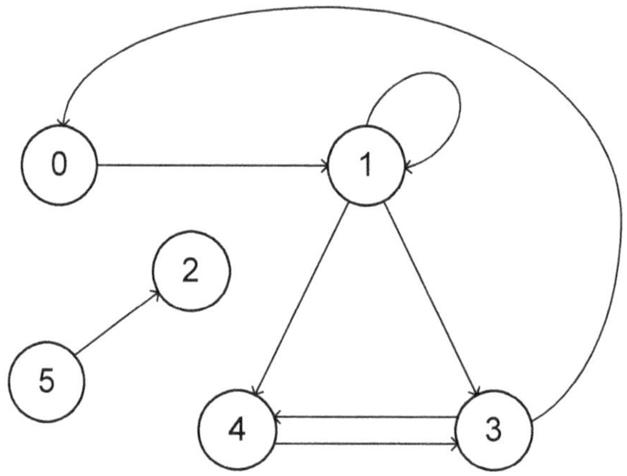

Figure 17.7 Strong Components

We take the example in Figure 17.7. The corresponding code to compute strong components is:

```
#include <iostream>

#include <boost/graph/adjacency_list.hpp>
#include <boost/graph/graph_utility.hpp>
#include <boost/graph/strong_components.hpp>

using namespace std;
using namespace boost;

int main()
{
    // Create the graph (Figure 17.7).
    typedef adjacency_list < vecS, vecS, directedS > Graph;
    const int N = 6;
    Graph g(N);
    add_edge(0,1,g); add_edge(1,1,g); add_edge(1,3,g); add_edge(1,4,g);
    add_edge(3,4,g); add_edge(3,0,g); add_edge(4,3,g); add_edge(5,2,g);
```

```
    // Create the strong components.
    vector<int> c(N);
    int num = strong_components(g,
        make_iterator_property_map(c.begin(), get(vertex_index, g), c[0]));

    // Print vertices and their component.
    cout << "Total number of strong components: " << num << endl;
    vector<int>::iterator i;
    for (i = c.begin(); i != c.end(); ++i)
    {
        cout << "Vertex " << i - c.begin() << " is in component "
            << *i << endl;
    }

    return 0;
}
```

The output is given in Figure 17.8.

Vertex	Component
0, 1, 3, 4	0
2	1
5	2

Figure 17.8 Vertices and Components

17.4 Graph Structure Comparison

We now discuss some algorithms that compare graphs with each other in some way. For example, we can determine if two graphs can be placed in a one-to-one correspondence, finding all the common subgraphs between two graphs and finding maximal common subgraphs. Another problem is called *subgraph isomorphism* that determines if a graph G contains a subgraph that is isomorphic to a graph H.

We first give some definitions. Let G be an arbitrary graph and let $V(G)$ denote its vertices and let $E(G)$ denote its edges. Let u and v be two vertices of the graph and let (u, v) be the edge between u and v.

In general, a *homomorphism* is a structure-preserving map between algebraic data structures (for example, groups, rings and vector spaces). A mapping

$$f : V(G) \rightarrow V(H)$$

is called a *graph homomorphism* if $(u, v) \in E(G) \rightarrow (f(u), f(v)) \in E(H)$.

Now let S and T be discrete sets having the same number of elements. A mapping $f : S \rightarrow T$ is called a *bijection* if the following conditions are satisfied:

- The mapping is *onto*, that is if each element t in T has at least one preimage s in S $\forall t \in T, \quad \exists s \in S$ such $f(s) = t$.
- The mapping is *one-to-one*, that is distinct elements of S are mapped to distinct elements (images) $s_1, s_2 \in S$ ($s_1 \neq s_2 \Rightarrow f(s_1) \neq f(s_2)$).

17.4.1 Isomorphic Graphs

Two undirected, non-labelled, non-weighted graphs G and H are said to be *isomorphic* if there exists a bijection between their vertices and that adjacent vertices in G are mapped to adjacent vertices in H. As an example, let us consider the graphs in Figures 17.9 and 17.10. They do not even resemble each other even though they both have eight vertices and twelve edges. But they are isomorphic, as we prove using the following code:

```
#include <iostream>

#include <boost/graph/adjacency_list.hpp>
#include <boost/graph/graph_utility.hpp>
#include <boost/graph/isomorphism.hpp>

using namespace std;
using namespace boost;

int main()
{
    // Typedef for graphs.
    typedef adjacency_list<vecS, listS, undirectedS,
                           property<vertex_index_t, int> > Graph;

    const int N = 8;
    Graph g1(N), g2(N);

    // Declare vertices.
    property_map<Graph, vertex_index_t>::type v1_index_map =
        get(vertex_index, g1), v2_index_map = get(vertex_index, g2);
    vector<graph_traits<Graph>::vertex_descriptor> v1(N), v2(N);

    // Initialise vertices.
    graph_traits<Graph>::vertex_iterator i, end;
    int id = 0;
    for (boost::tie(i, end) = vertices(g1); i != end; ++i, ++id)
    {
        put(v1_index_map, *i, id); // (map, key, value)
        v1[id] = *i;
    }

    id = 0;
    for (boost::tie(i, end) = vertices(g2); i != end; ++i, ++id)
    {
        put(v2_index_map, *i, id);
        v2[id] = *i;
    }

    // Create edges for graph 1 (Figure 17.8).
    add_edge(v1[0], v1[4], g1); add_edge(v1[0], v1[5], g1);
    add_edge(v1[0], v1[6], g1); add_edge(v1[1], v1[4], g1);
    add_edge(v1[1], v1[5], g1); add_edge(v1[1], v1[7], g1);
    add_edge(v1[2], v1[6], g1); add_edge(v1[2], v1[4], g1);
    add_edge(v1[2], v1[7], g1); add_edge(v1[3], v1[7], g1);
    add_edge(v1[3], v1[6], g1); add_edge(v1[3], v1[5], g1);
    print_graph(g1);  cout << endl;

    // Create edges for graph 2 (Figure 17.9).
    add_edge(v2[0], v2[1], g2); add_edge(v2[0], v2[3], g2);
    add_edge(v2[0], v2[4], g2); add_edge(v2[1], v2[2], g2);
    add_edge(v2[1], v2[5], g2); add_edge(v2[2], v2[6], g2);
    add_edge(v2[2], v2[3], g2); add_edge(v2[3], v2[7], g2);
    add_edge(v2[4], v2[5], g2); add_edge(v2[4], v2[7], g2);
    add_edge(v2[5], v2[6], g2); add_edge(v2[6], v2[7], g2);
    print_graph(g2);  cout << endl;
```

```
// Determine if graphs are isometric.
vector<graph_traits<Graph>::vertex_descriptor> f(N);
bool ret = isomorphism(g1, g2,
    isomorphism_map(make_iterator_property_map(f.begin(),
                                        v1_index_map, f[0])));
cout << "Isomorphic? " << boolalpha << ret << endl;

// Display the isometric mapping.
cout << "Isomorphic mapping f: ";
for (size_t v = 0; v != f.size(); ++v)
{
    cout << get(get(vertex_index, g1), f[v]) << " ";
}
cout << endl;

return 0;
}
```

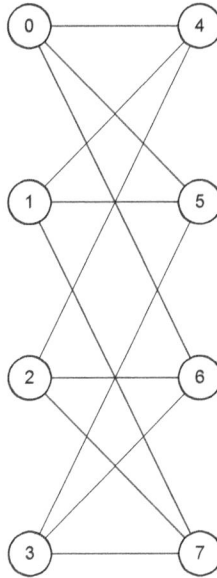

Figure 17.9 First graph

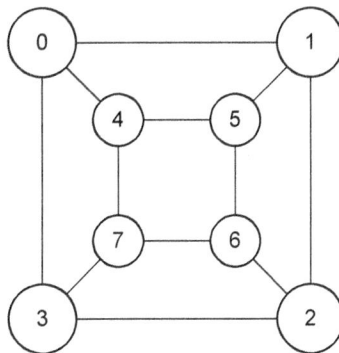

Figure 17.10 Second, Isomorphic Graph

You can run the code and check the output.

17.5 Extending Algorithms with Visitor

BGL allows the developer to customise the behaviour of algorithms to suit a given application by using BGL *visitors*. A BGL visitor is similar to a function object but instead of implementing the function call operator () a BGL visitor creates a class with several member functions that are defined at different locations or *event points*. In this sense BGL visitors are the generic equivalent of the GOF *Template Method Pattern* as described in GOF 1995. In short, this pattern 'describes the skeleton in an operation, deferring some steps to subclasses. *Template Method* lets subclasses redefine certain steps of an algorithm without changing the algorithm's structure'. The *BGL Visitor* is thus the generic version of the GOF *Template Method Pattern* as we shall see in this section. In this sense calling it a visitor is somewhat of a misnomer in our opinion because a *GOF Visitor* is defined as follows: "*represent an operation to be performed on the elements of an object structure. Visitor lets you define a new operation without changing the classes of the elements on which it operates*". We conclude that *Visitor* corresponds to a *service extension pattern* (that is, it adds new methods) while *BGL Visitor* corresponds to a *service variation pattern* (no new methods are defined but we interchange one implementation of a method by another implementation). Summarising, a BGL *Visitor* is like a functor but in contrast to a functor – that has just one *apply* method – a BGL Visitor has several apply methods.

BGL provides default visitors for a number of algorithms. Each visitor class has a number of *hook member functions*, each one containing a default implementation (usually empty). You can define your own derived classes and implement these hook functions to suit your needs.

The default visitor concepts that BGL supports are (more details in Siek 2002):
- *BFSVisitor*: this concept defines the visitor interface for breadth_first_search(). Users can define a class with the *BFSVisitor* interface and pass an instance of the class to breadth_first_search(). In this way we can augment the actions taken during the graph search.
- *DFSVisitor*: this concept defines the visitor interface for depth_first_search(). Users can define a class with the *DFSVisitor* interface and pass an instance of the class to depth_first_search(). In this way we can augment the actions taken during the graph search.
- *Dijkstra Visitor*: this concept defines the visitor interface for dijkstra_shortest_paths() and related algorithms. Users can define a class with the Dijkstra *Visitor* interface and pass an instance of the class to dijkstra_shortest_paths(). In this way we can augment the actions taken during the graph search.
- *BellmanFordVisitor*: this concept defines the visitor interface for bellman_ford_shortest_paths(). Users can define a class with the *BellmanFordVisitor* interface and pass an instance of the class to bellman_ford_shortest_paths(). In this way we can augment the actions taken during the graph search.

An example of how to customise BGL visitors to augment some behaviour in a BFS visitor is given by:

```
// Customise basic BFS algorithm with a Visitor.
template <typename VertexNameMap>
class bfs_name_printer: public default_bfs_visitor
{ // inherit default (empty) event point actions.
```

```
public:
    bfs_name_printer(VertexNameMap n_map): m_name_map(n_map)
    { }

    template <typename Vertex, typename Graph>
    void discover_vertex(Vertex u, const Graph&) const
    {
        cout << get(m_name_map, u) << ' ';
    }

private:
    VertexNameMap m_name_map;
};
```

We shall now use this visitor to customise the BFS algorithm.

17.6 Basic Graph Algorithms

Last but not least, we discuss two fundamental graph search algorithms called *Breadth-First Search (BFS)* and *Depth-First Search (DFS)*. BFS begins at a root vertex and it explores all the neighbouring vertices. DFS also begins at a root node in the graph and it explores as far as possible along each branch before *backtracking*. These algorithms are well-known in the literature and we do not repeat a discussion of them here. However, we do give some examples of how BGL implements these algorithms.

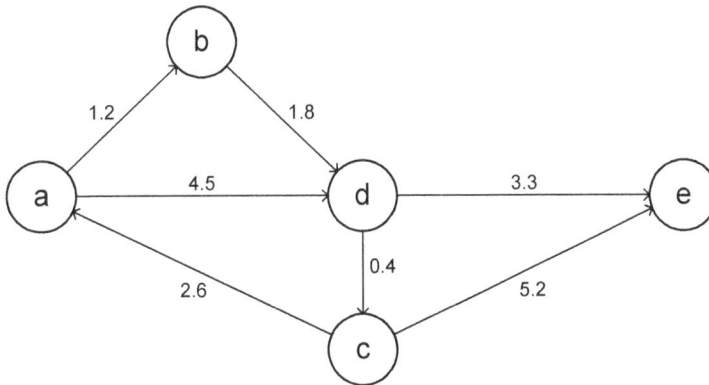

Figure 17.11 BFS for simple router problem

The test case in this section is given in Figure 17.11 (which is taken from Siek 2002, page 12). The objective is to perform a breadth-first search in a network of internet routers. The directed edges signify that one router can send data to another router; the delay time is an edge weight. The source vertex is 'a' while the sink vertex is 'e'. The code for a BFS search is now introduced. First, the code to create the network is:

```
template <typename Graph, typename VertexNameMap, typename TransDelayMap>
void build_router_network(Graph& g, VertexNameMap name_map,
                          TransDelayMap delay_map)
{
    // Create the vertices as a map of vertex descriptors and char values.
    typename graph_traits<Graph>::vertex_descriptor a, b, c, d, e;
    a = add_vertex(g);   name_map[a] = 'a';
    b = add_vertex(g);   name_map[b] = 'b';
    c = add_vertex(g);   name_map[c] = 'c';
    d = add_vertex(g);   name_map[d] = 'd';
    e = add_vertex(g);   name_map[e] = 'e';
```

```
    // Create edges.
    typename graph_traits<Graph>::edge_descriptor ed;
    bool inserted;

    boost::tie(ed, inserted) = add_edge(a, b, g);   delay_map[ed] = 1.2;
    boost::tie(ed, inserted) = add_edge(a, d, g);   delay_map[ed] = 4.5;
    boost::tie(ed, inserted) = add_edge(b, d, g);   delay_map[ed] = 1.8;
    boost::tie(ed, inserted) = add_edge(c, a, g);   delay_map[ed] = 2.6;
    boost::tie(ed, inserted) = add_edge(c, e, g);   delay_map[ed] = 5.2;
    boost::tie(ed, inserted) = add_edge(d, c, g);   delay_map[ed] = 0.4;
    boost::tie(ed, inserted) = add_edge(d, e, g);   delay_map[ed] = 3.3;
}
```

The structures for vertices and edges are:

```
    // Vertices and edges.
    struct VP
    {
        char name;
    };

    struct EP
    {
        double weight;
    };
```

Finally, the test program is:

```
int main()
{
    // Define graph.
    typedef adjacency_list<listS, vecS, directedS, VP, EP> Graph;
    Graph g;

    // Build the graph (Figure 17.10).
    property_map<Graph, char VP::*>::type name_map = get(&VP::name, g);
    property_map<Graph, double EP::*>::type delay_map =
        get(&EP::weight, g);
    build_router_network(g, name_map, delay_map);

    // Use our 'visitor' to print the network using breath first algorithm.
    typedef property_map<Graph, char VP::*>::type VertexNameMap;
    graph_traits<Graph>::vertex_descriptor a = *vertices(g).first;
    bfs_name_printer<VertexNameMap> vis(name_map);
    cout << "BFS vertex discover order: ";
    breadth_first_search(g, a, visitor(vis)); // Output a, b, d, c, e
    cout << endl;

    return 0;
}
```

The output is the path {a, b, d, c, e}.
For more information on more fundamental algorithms, we refer the reader to Siek 2002.

17.7 Other Graph Algorithms in BGL

For completeness, we give a brief description of some families of algorithms in BGL. Due to lack of time, space and practical experience we are unable to discuss them in any great detail but we feel that it is a good idea to mention them. There is much literature on these topics and the BGL online documents also devote some attention to them. Code examples can also be found on the boost distribution media.

17.7.1 Sparse Matrix Ordering Algorithms

We discuss a number of algorithms to reduce the bandwidth of sparse matrices. In particular, the *bandwidth* B of a graph's adjacency matrix is defined by:

$$B = \max_{1 \le i,j \le n} |L(i) - L(j)|$$

where n is the number of vertices in the graph, $L(i)$ is the label of vertex i, $L(j)$ is the label of vertex j and finally where vertices i and j are adjacent. In general terms, the graph bandwidth is the maximum absolute value of the difference of label numbers of adjacent vertices. We take an example in Figure 17.12. By inspection, we see that the bandwidth is 6.

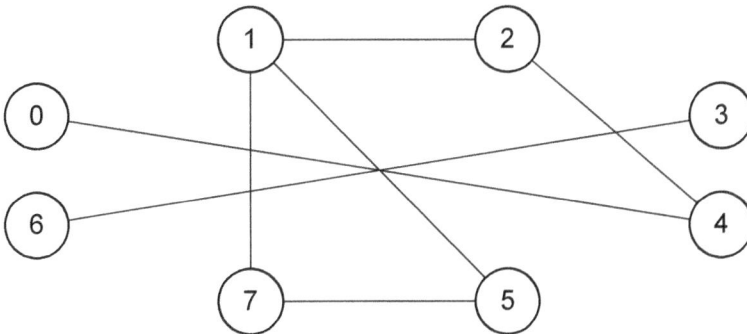

Figure 17.12 Graph with bandwidth = 6

We now discuss the *graph bandwidth problem*: reorder the labels of the vertices of a graph in order to reduce its bandwidth. We discuss three algorithms for reducing the bandwidth:

- *Cuthill-McKee algorithm*: given a symmetric nXn matrix we visualise the matrix as the adjacency matrix of a graph. This algorithm relabels the vertices of the graph to reduce the bandwidth of the adjacency matrix. It uses a local minimisation of the ith bandwidths. The vertices are assigned a BFS order and the adjacent vertices are placed in the queue in order of increasing magnitude at each step.
- *King algorithm*: The goal of the King ordering algorithms to reduce the bandwidth of a graph by reordering the indices assigned to each vertex. The King ordering algorithm works by a local minimisation of the ith bandwidths. The vertices are basically assigned a breadth-first search order except that at each step the adjacent vertices are placed in the queue in order of increasing pseudo-degree, where *pseudo-degree* is defined as the number of outgoing edges with white endpoints (vertices yet to be examined).
- *Sloan algorithm*: The goal of the Sloan ordering algorithm is to reduce the profile and the wavefront of a graph by reordering the indices assigned to each vertex. The Sloan algorithm needs a start and an end vertex.

As an example of a *bandwidth reduction problem*, we again consider Figure 17.12. Applying one of the above algorithms could lead to the result in Figure 17.13. We can see by inspection that its bandwidth is now two.

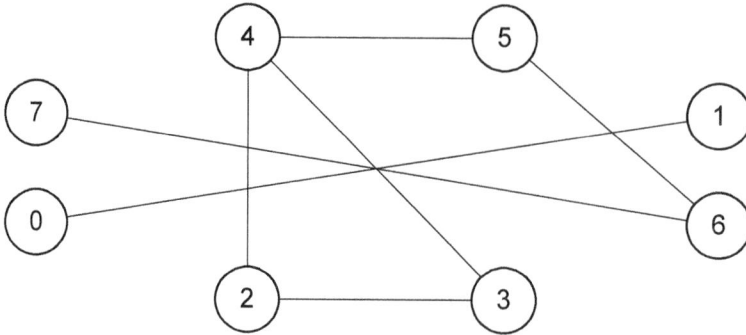

Figure 17.13 Graph with bandwidth = 2

We now discuss the Boost C++ code that implements the Cuthill-McKee algorithm. The other two algorithms' code is similar and can be found on the Boost software distribution medium. We take the example graph in Figure 17.12. First, we create the graph vertices and edges:

```
// Graph and Vertex types.
typedef adjacency_list<vecS, vecS, undirectedS,
    property<vertex_color_t, default_color_type,
             property<vertex_degree_t,int> > > Graph;
typedef graph_traits<Graph>::vertex_descriptor Vertex;

// Handy typedef stuff.
typedef graph_traits<Graph>::vertices_size_type size_type;
typedef std::pair<std::size_t, std::size_t> Pair;

// The edges of the graph (Figure 17.11).
const int NE = 7;
Pair edges[NE] = { Pair(0,4), Pair(1,2), Pair(1,5), Pair(1,7),
                   Pair(2,4), Pair(3,6), Pair(5,7)};

// Define the graph (Figure 17.11).
const int NV = 8;  Graph g(NV);
for (int i = 0; i < NE; ++i) add_edge(edges[i].first, edges[i].second, g);

// Print the vertices and graph.
char* name("01234567");
cout << "Vertices: "; print_vertices(g, name);
print_graph(g);  cout << endl;
cout << "Original bandwidth: " << bandwidth(g) << endl;
```

We now permute the vertices by calling the Cuthill-McKee algorithm:

```
property_map<Graph, vertex_index_t>::type index_map = get(vertex_index, g);

// The graph vertices will be permuted.
vector<Vertex> inv_perm(num_vertices(g));
vector<size_type> perm(num_vertices(g));

Vertex s = vertex(0, g);
// Reverse cuthill_mckee_ordering.
cuthill_mckee_ordering(g, s, inv_perm.rbegin(), get(vertex_color, g),
                       get(vertex_degree, g));

cout << "Reverse Cuthill-McKee ordering starting at: " << s << endl;
cout << "Permuted vertices: ";

for (vector<Vertex>::const_iterator i = inv_perm.begin();
```

```
      i != inv_perm.end(); ++i)
{
    cout << index_map[*i] << " ";
}

for (size_type c = 0; c != inv_perm.size(); ++c)
{
    perm[index_map[inv_perm[c]]] = c;
}

cout << "  Bandwidth: "
     << bandwidth(g, make_iterator_property_map(&perm[0], index_map,
                                                perm[0])) << endl;
```

A typical example of the reordered vertex labels after execution of the algorithm is shown in Figure 17.13.

17.7.2 Random Graphs

A *random graph* is one that is generated by a random process. This theory uses both results from graph theory and probability theory. In order to create a random graph we begin with a set of n vertices and we add edges between them at random. We can define various *graph models*, each one producing different probability distributions on graphs. For example, a common model is the *Gilbert model* G(n,p) in which edges occur with equal probability p. The *Erdös-Renyi model* G(n, M) is similar and it assigns equal probability to all graphs with exactly M edges. This model can also be seen as a snapshot at a particular time M of a *random graph process* that starts with n vertices and no edges; at each step a new edge is added and this edge is chosen uniformly from the set of missing edges.

We now discuss the main functionality and tools for random graphs in BGL:

a) Select a random vertex and random edge from a graph and return them. We can use the random number generators from the Boost Random library, for example using Mersenne Twister in combination with a Uniform random number generator. We can also generate a random graph by randomly selecting source and target vertices.

b) It is possible to set the random property value on all vertices or on all edges, depending on the choice (the *randomize_property* choice).

c) A generator for Erdos-Renyi graphs by initialising their adjacency lists or other graph structures.

d) A class template that implements a generator for scale-free graphs based on the *Power Law Out Degree* (PLOD) algorithm. A *scale-free graph* is a graph whose degree distribution follows a *power law*, that is the fraction P(k) of vertices in a graph having k connections with other vertices, has the representation

$$P(k) \sim ck^{-b}$$

for large k. Here c is a normalisation constant and b is a parameter whose values are typically in the open range (2, 3). An example can be found in the studies of the networks of citations between scientific papers. In this case the number of links to papers (that is, the number of citations that they receive) has a heavy-tailed distribution following a Pareto distribution or power law. Another example is found in the networks that represents the World Wide Web in which some nodes (called *hubs*) have many more connections than other nodes and the network can have power-law distribution of the number of links connecting to a vertex. The most notable characteristic in a scale-free network is the relative commonness of vertices whose degree far exceed the average value.

e) A class template that implements a generator for small-world graph. A *small-world network* is a kind of graph in which most vertices are not neighbours of one another but most vertices can be reached from every other vertex in a small number of hops or steps. In particular, a small-world network is one in which the typical distance L between two randomly chosen vertices grows proportionally to the logarithm of the number of nodes N in the network:

$$L \, \alpha \log(N).$$

An example is a social network in which strangers are linked by mutual acquaintance.

17.8 Summary and Conclusions

We have given an introduction to a number of advanced features and algorithms in BGL. We discussed advanced shortest-path problems, computing transitive closure, finding connected components and graph comparison algorithms. We also gave an introduction to the *Boost Visitor* concept and how its realisations can be used to modify BGL algorithms. It is a useful technique and we see opportunities to use it as a technique to customise algorithms and applications.

18 Interval Container Library

18.1 Introduction and Objectives

In this chapter we introduce the *Interval Container Library* (ICL) that provides a number of classes for intervals, collections of intervals and related computations. Many developers use intervals – either implicitly or by creating user-defined classes – and they have many applications. For this reason we feel that it is useful to discuss ICL because it contains functionality that we can use in applications without having to reinvent the wheel:

- Defining discrete and continuous intervals.
- Associative containers: interval sets and interval maps.
- Adding intervals to, and removing intervals from associative containers.
- Splitting, joining and separating intervals.

The focus in this chapter is on introducing essential functionality in ICL and giving some examples. More examples can be found in the Boost online documentation.

Finally, we note that there is in principle no relationship between ICL and the Interval library (that we discuss in chapter 13), the latter being an implementation of interval arithmetic which is a branch of numerical analysis.

18.2 Overview of the ICL

ICL is a library that supports the creation of one-dimensional intervals as well as sets and maps of intervals. Intervals are ubiquitous in applications. Many developers have probably developed their own interval classes and other related components but since Boost version 1.46 the ICL provides much of the functionality that developers need. We discuss this functionality and we give examples of use.

We mention that ICL and the Boost Interval libraries have similar sounding names and there is a certain amount of overlap in functionality. However, Interval is concerned with applications in numerical analysis (in particular, mathematical operations on intervals and imprecise numbers) while ICL is concerned with sets of intervals and relationships between them. ICL intervals can be 'added' but not in the sense of real number or extended real number arithmetic. We discuss this particular feature in later sections. In particular, ICL has many applications to MIS (*Management Information Systems*). Discussion of MIS and other reference software architectures can be found in Duffy 2004A.

The ICL was originally developed at Cortex Software GmbH to solve problems related to date and time interval computations in the context of a hospital information system. There are very many application areas where ICL can be employed.

18.3 What Kinds of Intervals?

An *interval* represents a continuous or discrete range of values between a *lower value* and an *upper value.* In this sense it can be seen as a one-dimensional data structure. ICL has two template classes:

- `continuous_interval<T>`: intervals whose underlying types are `float`, `double` or Boost `rational`.
- `discrete_interval<T>`: intervals whose underlying types are `int`, `long` or `string`.

Furthermore, we have the issue of whether the interval *borders* (or *boundaries*) belong to the interval. This is a well-known concept in mathematics and there are four possibilities. To this end, let us assume that an interval has borders A and B. Then the four choices for the interval are:

- *closed*: both A and B are contained in the interval. Syntax is [A,B].
- *open*: neither relating to intervals A nor B are contained in the interval. Syntax is (A,B).
- *right_open*: A is contained in the interval but not B. This is the default case in the ICL implementation of intervals. Syntax is [A,B).
- *left_open*: B is contained in the interval but not A. Syntax is (A,B].

Both `continuous_interval<T>` and `discrete_interval<T>` are dynamic types in the sense that their instances can be constructed with any one of the above four options.

We now give some examples:

```
// Dynamically bounded intervals.
#include <boost/icl/continuous_interval.hpp>
using namespace boost::icl;

cout << "*** Continuous intervals of doubles ***" << endl;
{
    double lower = 0.0; double upper = 1.0;
    continuous_interval<double> unitIntervalClosed(lower, upper,
                                    interval_bounds::closed());
    continuous_interval<double> unitIntervalRightOpen(lower, upper);
                                    // right_open() is default.
    continuous_interval<double> unitIntervalLeftOpen(lower, upper,
                                    interval_bounds::left_open());
    continuous_interval<double> unitIntervalOpen(lower, upper,
                                    interval_bounds::open());
    cout << unitIntervalClosed << endl;
    cout << unitIntervalRightOpen << endl;
    cout << unitIntervalLeftOpen << endl;
    cout << unitIntervalOpen << endl;
}
```

The output of the different continuous intervals is:

```
[0,1]
[0,1)
(0,1]
(0,1)
```

Next we create intervals of rational numbers (fraction of two integers) that is also part of ICL:

```
// Rational numbers.
#include <boost/icl/rational.hpp>

cout << "\n*** Continuous intervals of rational numbers ***" << endl;
{
    rational<int> lower(0,1); rational<int> upper(1,3);
    continuous_interval<rational<int> > ratIntervalClosed(lower, upper,
                                    interval_bounds::closed());
    continuous_interval<rational<int> > ratIntervalRightOpen(lower, upper);
                                    // right_open() is default.
    continuous_interval<rational<int> > ratIntervalLeftOpen(lower, upper,
                                    interval_bounds::left_open());
    continuous_interval<rational<int> > ratIntervalOpen(lower, upper,
                                    interval_bounds::open());
    cout << ratIntervalClosed << endl;
    cout << ratIntervalRightOpen << endl;
    cout << ratIntervalLeftOpen << endl;
```

```
        cout << ratIntervalOpen << endl;
    }
```

The output of the different rational number intervals is:

```
[0/1,1/3]
[0/1,1/3)
(0/1,1/3]
(0/1,1/3)
```

Finally, we can create discrete intervals, as the following example shows:

```
#include <boost/icl/discrete_interval.hpp>

cout << "\n*** Discrete intervals of int ***" << endl;
{
    int lower = 0; int upper = 1;
    discrete_interval<int> unitIntervalClosed(lower, upper,
                              interval_bounds::closed());
    discrete_interval<int> unitIntervalRightOpen(lower, upper);
                              // right_open() is default.
    discrete_interval<int> unitIntervalLeftOpen(lower, upper,
                              interval_bounds::left_open());
    discrete_interval<int> unitIntervalOpen(lower, upper,
                              interval_bounds::open());
    cout << unitIntervalClosed << endl;
    cout << unitIntervalRightOpen << endl;
    cout << unitIntervalLeftOpen << endl;
    cout << unitIntervalOpen << endl;
}
```

The output from this code is:

```
[0,1]
[0,1)
(0,1]
()
```

18.3.1 Statically Bound Interval Types

ICL has support for the different kinds of intervals that we introduced in section 18.3. Instead of providing an extra parameter in the constructors of `continuous_interval<T>` or `discrete_interval<T>` we can use specialised classes that directly model right-open, left-open, open and closed intervals. We can use them by including the following header files in our code:

```
// Statically bounded intervals
#include <boost/icl/right_open_interval.hpp>
#include <boost/icl/left_open_interval.hpp>
#include <boost/icl/closed_interval.hpp>
#include <boost/icl/open_interval.hpp>
```

It is easy to construct instances of these classes; we just instantiate the appropriate class and give it lower and upper bounds:

```
// Statically bounded intervals
double lower = 0.0; double upper = 1.0;
closed_interval<double> unitIntervalClosed(lower, upper);
right_open_interval<double> unitIntervalRightOpen(lower, upper);
left_open_interval<double> unitIntervalLeftOpen(lower, upper);
open_interval<double> unitIntervalOpen(lower, upper);
cout << "Statically bound intervals types:" << endl;
cout << unitIntervalClosed << endl;
cout << unitIntervalRightOpen << endl;
```

```
cout << unitIntervalLeftOpen << endl;
cout << unitIntervalOpen << endl;
```

The output from this code is:

```
Statically bound intervals types:
[0,1]
[0,1)
(0,1]
()
```

18.3.2 Modelling Intervals by Parameter Variation

In the previous sections we gave some simple examples on how to create intervals using fixed lower and upper bounds. In many applications however, the bounds can be generated at run-time, for example they may be computed by calling functions that depend on some parameter that represents time or some other physical property. To this end, let us consider two functions that model two time-dependent boundaries:

```
// Two function to model intervals depending on a parameter.
float LowerTimeDependependentBoundary(float t)
{
    return exp(-t);
}

float UpperTimeDependependentBoundary(float t)
{
    return exp(t);
}
```

We now create an ICL interval by calling these functions for a specific value of the input parameter. Instead of the constructor we can use the free `construct()` function:

```
float t = 0.5;
continuous_interval<float> myInterval;
myInterval = construct<continuous_interval<float> >(
    LowerTimeDependependentBoundary(t),
    UpperTimeDependependentBoundary(t));
cout << "Time-dependent interval: " << myInterval << endl;
```

The output from this snippet of code is:

```
Time-dependent interval: [0.606531,1.64872)
```

In applications we are usually interested in computing an array of intervals by varying the input parameter `t`. In this case we construct a discrete set of *mesh-points* and we then construct an interval for each point in the set. Finally, we append each interval to an array of intervals:

```
float T = 5.0; float t = 0.0;
long NT = 4; float step = T/NT;

cout << "Array of time-dependent intervals:" << endl;
vector<continuous_interval<float> > boundaries(NT+1);
for (size_t n = 0; n < boundaries.size(); ++n)
{
    boundaries[n] = construct<continuous_interval<float> >(
        LowerTimeDependependentBoundary(t),
        UpperTimeDependependentBoundary(t), interval_bounds::closed());
    t += step;
    cout << "{" << t << ":" << boundaries[n] << "} ";
}
```

```
cout << endl;
```

The output from this code is given by:

```
Array of time-dependent intervals:
{1.25:[1,1]} {2.5:[0.286505,3.49034]} {3.75:[0.082085,12.1825]}
{5:[0.0235177,42.5211]} {6.25:[0.00673795,148.413]}
```

This example has shown how to use functions to compute the lower and upper bounds of an interval and the principle can be applied to various kinds of applications, for example when modelling initial-boundary value problems for partial differential equations in financial derivatives pricing (see for example, Duffy 2006).

18.3.3 Intervals and Temporal Types

It would seem that one of the motivators for developing ICL was the wish to work with date and time entities in Management Information Systems (MIS). In particular, an important feature is to create intervals whose lower and upper bounds are of type `boost::date`. ICL has wrapper classes that allow developers to create code in the spirit of chapter 4 of this book, for example:

```
#include <boost/icl/gregorian.hpp>
using namespace boost::gregorian;

// Create interval [2011-09-16, 2011-09-24].
discrete_interval<date> vacation(from_string("2011-09-16"),
                                 from_string("2011-09-24"),
                                 interval_bounds::closed());
cout << "Vacation: " << vacation << endl;

// Create three dates.
date d1(day_clock::local_day());  // Today.
date_duration myDuration(10);     // 10 days duration.
date d2 = d1 + myDuration;        // Today + 10 days.
date d3 = d2 + myDuration;        // Today + 20 days.

// Create two intervals [today, today+10), [today+10, today+20).
discrete_interval<date> planningI(d1, d2, interval_bounds::right_open());
discrete_interval<date> planningII(d2, d3, interval_bounds::right_open());
cout << "From d1 to d2: " << planningI << endl;
cout << "From d2 to d3: " << planningII << endl;
```

The output from this code is given by (depending on the current date):

```
[2011-Sep-16,2011-Sep-24]
From d1 to d2: [2011-Aug-15,2011-Aug-25)
From d2 to d3: [2011-Aug-25,2011-Sep-04)
```

Some other example code is given by:

```
// Medium-term planning.
date today = day_clock::local_day();
date nextMonth = today + months(1);
discrete_interval<date> manPowerPeriod =
    discrete_interval<date>::right_open(today, nextMonth);
cout << "Monthly schedule: " <<  manPowerPeriod << endl;

// Longer-term planning.
date fiveYearDate = today + years(5);
discrete_interval<date> fiveYearPlan =
    discrete_interval<date>::right_open(today, fiveYearDate);
cout << "Five year plan: " <<  fiveYearPlan << endl;
```

We shall see more extended examples as we progress in this chapter.

18.4 Interval Sets and Interval Maps

We now come to the central theme of ICL, namely *interval sets* and *interval maps*. An interval set is implemented as a set of intervals while an interval map is implemented as a map of interval-value pairs. There are five template classes that model sets and maps. We discuss two of them in this section; the header files to be included are:

```
#include <boost/icl/interval_set.hpp>
#include <boost/icl/interval_map.hpp>
```

We give simplified UML class diagrams for these classes in Figures 18.1 and 18.2. Paraphrasing, we say that an interval set is a set of either continuous or discrete intervals while an interval maps is a set of pairs. Each pair has an interval as key and the value element V is generic. The classes are implemented by using the CRTP pattern that we discussed in Demming 2010:

```
class interval_set:
    public interval_base_set<interval_set<Domain,Compare,Interval,Alloc>,
                             DomainT,Compare,Interval,Alloc>

class interval_map:
    public interval_base_map<
        interval_map<DomainT,CodomainT,Traits,Compare,Combine,
                     Section,Interval,Alloc>,
            DomainT,CodomainT,Traits,Compare,Combine,Section,Interval,Alloc>
```

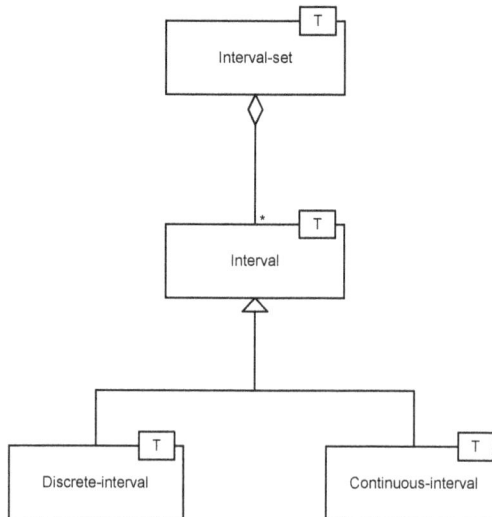

Figure 18.1 UML structure of ICL interval sets

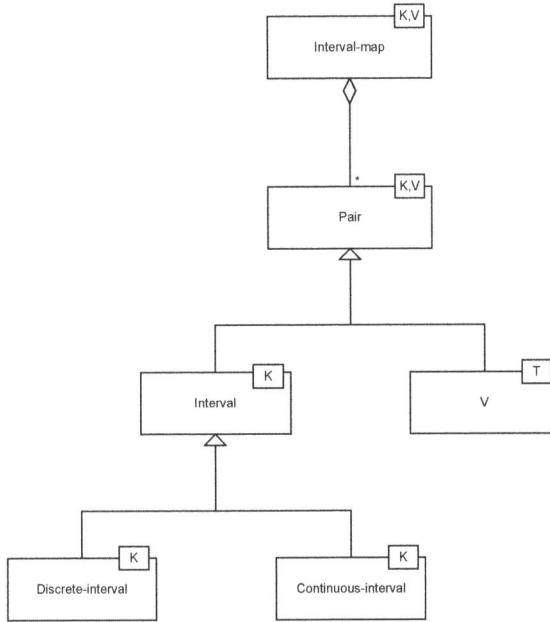

Figure 18.2 UML structure of ICL interval maps

In most examples we shall be satisfied with the default parameters provided by ICL.

We now create instances of interval sets and interval maps (the so-called *abstract aspect*) and we also discuss the *segmental aspect* that relates to the fact that interval sets and maps are clustered in intervals or *segments* that we can iterate over. In this section we take the intervals as shown in Figure 18.3 and these will be added to merge, split and separate styles:

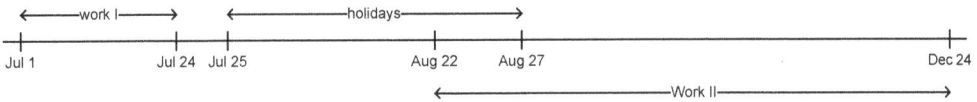

Figure 18.3 Test intervals for date

The first example creates an interval set which will merge the given intervals. Overlapping and adjoining intervals will be merged in one interval:

```
// Create three intervals.
discrete_interval<date> workI(from_string("2011-07-1"),
    from_string("2011-07-24"), interval_bounds::closed());
discrete_interval<date> holidays(from_string("2011-07-25"),
    from_string("2011-08-27"), interval_bounds::closed());
discrete_interval<date> workII(from_string("2011-08-22"),
    from_string("2011-12-24"), interval_bounds::right_open());

// Interval (merge) sets based on discrete intervals and date.
// Combine (merge) the intervals in a set.
interval_set<date> mySchedule;
mySchedule += workI;
mySchedule += holidays;
mySchedule += workII;
cout << "Merged set schedule:" << endl << mySchedule << endl;
```

The output from this code is given by:

```
Merged set schedule:
{[2011-Jul-01,2011-Dec-24)}
```

We now give an example of an interval map (key, value) which also merges the intervals. The values of overlapping sections of intervals will be added (or subtracted when −= is used) and combined in a new interval with the resulting value. Any resulting adjoining intervals will be merged if their value is the same:

```
// Interval (merge) maps based on continuous intervals and date.
// Combine (merge) the intervals in a map.
interval_map<date,int> myMappedSchedule;
myMappedSchedule += make_pair(workI,1);
myMappedSchedule += make_pair(holidays,1);
myMappedSchedule += make_pair(workII,42);
cout << "Merged mapped schedule:" << endl << myMappedSchedule << endl;
```

The output from this code is given by:

```
Merged mapped schedule:
{([2011-Jul-01,2011-Aug-22)->1)
 ([2011-Aug-22,2011-Aug-27]->43)
 ((2011-Aug-27,2011-Dec-24)->42)}
```

We see that the intervals that comprise interval_set<K> and interval_map<K,V> are in a so-called *minimal representation* according to the ICL online documentation at www.boost.org because we ignore the points of intersection of intervals that comprise these. In other words, we ignore interval overlap and we only return the largest intervals that contain other intervals as subsets, as can be seen in both of the above two examples. There are two other ways to represent intervals and how they relate to each other in interval sets and maps. We now discuss this topic.

18.5 Interval Combining Styles

There are three template classes implementing *splitting* and *separating* interval containers. The following files should be included if you wish to use the corresponding functionality:

```
#include <boost/icl/split_interval_set.hpp>
#include <boost/icl/split_interval_map.hpp>
#include <boost/icl/separate_interval_set.hpp>
```

The classes split_interval_set<T> and split_interval_map<K,V> have an *insertion memory* which means that they accumulate interval borders from both additions and subtractions. They are useful when we wish to enrich an interval container with certain time grids, for example. The class implements the *separating style* which preserves borders that are never destroyed by an overlapping interval. In other words, borders are preserved. For example, combining two intervals of which only a part of each interval overlaps will be splitted in three intervals. In case of splitting maps the values of overlapping intervals are combined in one new interval with the combined value.

18.5.1 Splitting Interval Containers

Our first example of the splitting style relates to interval sets of dates as well as interval maps whose keys are date intervals and whose values are integers:

```
// Create three sets.
discrete_interval<date> workI(from_string("2011-07-1"),
    from_string("2011-07-24"), interval_bounds::closed());
```

```
discrete_interval<date> holidays(from_string("2011-07-25"),
    from_string("2011-08-27"), interval_bounds::closed());
discrete_interval<date> workII(from_string("2011-08-22"),
    from_string("2011-12-24"), interval_bounds::right_open());

// Interval (splitted) sets based on discrete intervals and date.
// Create a splitted interval set.
split_interval_set<date> mySchedule;
mySchedule += workI;
mySchedule += holidays;
mySchedule += workII;
cout << "Split set schedule:" << endl << mySchedule << endl;
```

The output is:

```
Split set schedule:
{[2011-Jul-01,2011-Jul-24]
 [2011-Jul-25,2011-Aug-22)
 [2011-Aug-22,2011-Aug-27]
 (2011-Aug-27,2011-Dec-24)}
```

In the case of `split_interval_map<K,V>`:

```
// Interval (split) maps based on continuous intervals and date.
// Create a splitted interval map.
split_interval_map<date,int> myMappedSchedule;
myMappedSchedule += make_pair(workI,1);
myMappedSchedule += make_pair(holidays,1);
myMappedSchedule += make_pair(workII,42);
cout << "Split mapped schedule:" << endl << myMappedSchedule << endl;
```

The output is:

```
Split mapped schedule:
{([2011-Jul-01,2011-Jul-24]->1)
 ([2011-Jul-25,2011-Aug-22)->1)
 ([2011-Aug-22,2011-Aug-27]->43)
 ((2011-Aug-27,2011-Dec-24)->42)}
```

18.5.2 Separating Interval Containers

There is one class in this category, namely `separate_interval_set<T>`. This merges overlapping intervals but leaves adjoining intervals separate. An example of use is:

```
// Create three intervals.
discrete_interval<date> workI(from_string("2011-07-1"),
    from_string("2011-07-24"), interval_bounds::closed());
discrete_interval<date> holidays(from_string("2011-07-25"),
    from_string("2011-08-27"), interval_bounds::closed());
discrete_interval<date> workII(from_string("2011-08-22"),
    from_string("2011-12-24"), interval_bounds::right_open());

// Interval (separate) sets based on discrete intervals and date.
// Create a separated set.
separate_interval_set<date> mySchedule;
mySchedule += workI;
mySchedule += holidays;
mySchedule += workII;
cout << "Separated set schedule: " << mySchedule << endl;
```

The output is:

```
Separated schedule: {[2011-Jul-01,2011-Jul-24][2011-Jul-25,2011-Dec-24)}
```

18.5.3 Iterators for Interval Sets and Maps

Iterators are supported in ICL. For example, here is code to iterate in an interval set:

```
split_interval_set<date> mySchedule;
mySchedule += workI;
mySchedule += holidays;
mySchedule += workII;

// Iterating over interval sets
cout << "Iterating in interval sets:" << endl;
split_interval_set<date>::iterator iter = mySchedule.begin();
while (iter != mySchedule.end())
{
    cout << *iter << endl; iter++;
}
```

The output is:

```
Iterating in interval sets:
[2011-Jul-01,2011-Jul-24]
[2011-Jul-25,2011-Aug-22)
[2011-Aug-22,2011-Aug-27]
(2011-Aug-27,2011-Dec-24)
```

An example of code for iterating in an interval map is:

```
split_interval_map<date,int> myMappedSchedule;
myMappedSchedule += make_pair(workI,1);
myMappedSchedule += make_pair(holidays,1);
myMappedSchedule += make_pair(workII,42);

// Iterating over interval maps.
cout << "Iterating in interval maps:" << endl;
split_interval_map<date,int>::iterator iter = myMappedSchedule.begin();
while (iter != myMappedSchedule.end())
{
    cout << iter->first << " * ";
    cout << "value: " << iter->second << endl;
    iter++;
}
```

The output is:

```
Iterating in interval maps:
[2011-Jul-01,2011-Jul-24] * value: 1
[2011-Jul-25,2011-Aug-22) * value: 1
[2011-Aug-22,2011-Aug-27] * value: 43
(2011-Aug-27,2011-Dec-24) * value: 42
```

The ability to iterate in ICL structures is very useful and has many applications in MIS.

18.6 Some '101' Examples

In section 18.4 and 18.5 we gave a number of examples using dates. In this section we examine the somewhat more illustrative (with less cognitive overload) example as shown in Figure 18.4. In this the underlying data type is int. We now give the code and output without further comment:

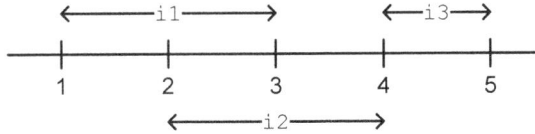

Figure 18.4 Test Intervals for double

```cpp
// Create three intervals.
continuous_interval<double> i1(1.0, 3.0);
continuous_interval<double> i2(2.0, 4.0);
continuous_interval<double> i3(4.0, 5.0);

// Interval (splitted) sets based on continuous variables.
// Output: [1,2) [2,3) [3,4) [4,5)
{
    split_interval_set<double> myRanges;
    myRanges += i1; myRanges += i2; myRanges += i3;
    cout << "Split ranges: " << myRanges << endl;
}

// Interval (merged) sets based on continuous variables.
// Output: [1,5)
{
    interval_set<double> myRanges;
    myRanges += i1; myRanges += i2; myRanges += i3;
    cout << "Merged ranges: " << myRanges << endl;
}

// Interval (separated) sets based on continuous variables.
// Output: [1,4) [4,5)
{
    separate_interval_set<double> myRanges;
    myRanges += i1; myRanges += i2; myRanges += i3;
    cout << "Separated ranges: " << myRanges << endl;
}

// Interval (merged) maps based on continuous variables.
// Output: [1,2)->1 [2,3)->2 [3,5)->1
{
    interval_map<double, int> myRanges;
    myRanges += make_pair(i1,1);
    myRanges += make_pair(i2,1);
    myRanges += make_pair(i3,1);
    cout << "Merged map ranges: " << myRanges << endl;
}

// Interval (split) maps based on continuous variables.
// Output: [1,2)->1 [2,3)->2 [3,4)->1 [4,5)->1
{
    split_interval_map<double, int> myRanges;
    myRanges += make_pair(i1,1);
    myRanges += make_pair(i2,1);
    myRanges += make_pair(i3,1);
    cout << "Split map ranges: " << myRanges << endl;
}
```

The output from this code is:

```
Split ranges: {[1,2)[2,3)[3,4)[4,5)}
Merged ranges: {[1,5)}
Separated ranges: {[1,4)[4,5)}
Merged map ranges: {([1,2)->1)([2,3)->2)([3,5)->1)}
Split map ranges: {([1,2)->1)([2,3)->2)([3,4)->1)([4,5)->1)}
```

As an exercise for the reader, what is the output if we modify the last block of code above by removing an interval?

```
continuous_interval<double> i4(2.5, 3.5);

split_interval_map<double, int> myRanges;
myRanges += make_pair(i1,1);
myRanges += make_pair(i2,1);
myRanges += make_pair(i3,1);
myRanges -= make_pair(i4,1); // Subtract an interval
```

18.7 Applying ICL to Managements Information Systems (MIS)

Perhaps the most suitable application area for ICL is the domain of Management Information Systems (MIS) in which time and dates play an important role. In these applications we may also need to estimate, schedule, monitor and aggregate data at different levels of granularity. For example, in engineering projects we are usually interested in monitoring the project progress (such as hardware usage and manpower) at department, division and project level during the life of a project (see Duffy 1995). Some use cases in this multidimensional problem are:

- Creating monthly reports on used versus scheduled resources for each department for each project in each project period.
- We can aggregate resources to division and project level in each project period.
- Create reports (at different levels of granularity) on project status.

It is not possible to discuss MIS systems in detail in this book. Instead, we create code that gives an impression of some of the issues involved. To this end, we revisit section 15.9.1 in chapter 15. In this case we are first interested in defining project activity (activity duration in days) and then pinning down the estimated activity duration to specific date intervals. In the latter case we use the ICL split_interval_map<date, ActivityDuration> class. The class models a project activity. Its interface is:

```
// Modelling activities in project planning.
struct ActivityDuration
{
    // Description of ActivityDuration.
    string m_description;

    // ActivityDuration time estimates.
    int m_a;   // Most optimistic.
    int m_b;   // Most likely.
    int m_c;   // Most pessimistic.

    // Constructors.
    ActivityDuration(): m_description("empty"), m_a(1), m_b(1), m_c(1) {}
    ActivityDuration(const string& description, int a, int b, int c):
        m_description(description), m_a(a), m_b(b), m_c(c) {}

    // Calculate expected completion time.
    int ExpectedCompletionTime() const
    {
        double d = (m_a + 4.0*m_b + m_c)/6.0;
        return (int)ceil(d);
    }

    // ICL expects '==' and '+=' operators!
    bool operator == (const ActivityDuration& a2) const
    {
        return m_description == a2.m_description;
    }
```

```
    ActivityDuration& operator += (const ActivityDuration& a2)
    {
        return *this;
    }

    // I/O.
    friend ostream& operator << (ostream& os, const ActivityDuration& act)
    {
        os << "ActivityDuration: " << act.m_description << ":[" << act.m_a
           << "," << act.m_b << "," << act.m_c <<";"
           << act.ExpectedCompletionTime() << "]" << endl;
        return os;
    }
};
```

The simple example we take is based on a software development project with three activities for design, coding and review. We estimate the activity duration as follows:

```
// Create a small planning with 3 'software' activities (in days).
ActivityDuration a1("Design", 20, 25, 30);
ActivityDuration a2("Coding", 30, 35, 55);
ActivityDuration a3("Review", 10, 12, 16);
```

We now pin down these floating schedules to points in time. In particular, we compute the start and end dates of each activity as shown in Figure 18.5. To this end, we use the functionality in Boost *date and time* library in combination with ICL discrete intervals:

```
// Compute start and end dates of each ActivityDuration
// and corresponding discrete interval.
date s1(day_clock::local_day());
date e1 = s1 + date_duration(a1.expectedCompletionTime());
discrete_interval<date> design(s1, e1, interval_bounds::right_open());

date s2 = e1;
date e2 = s2 + date_duration(a2.expectedCompletionTime());
discrete_interval<date> coding(s2, e2, interval_bounds::right_open());

date s3 = e2;
date e3 = s3 + date_duration(a3.expectedCompletionTime());
discrete_interval<date> review(s3, e3, interval_bounds::right_open());
```

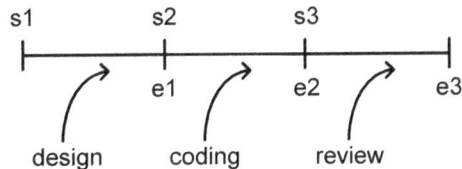

Figure 18.5 Project planning activities

Having created the required dates we are now in a position to construct the required interval map:

```
// Create the interval map containing these plannings
split_interval_map<date, ActivityDuration> schedule;
schedule.add(make_pair(design, a1));
schedule += make_pair(coding, a2);
schedule += make_pair(review, a3);
cout << "Project schedule:" << endl << schedule << endl;
```

The output from this code is now (depends on the current date):

```
Project schedule:
{([2011-Aug-18,2011-Sep-12)->ActivityDuration: Design:[20,25,30;25]
)([2011-Sep-12,2011-Oct-20)->ActivityDuration: Coding:[30,35,55;38]
)([2011-Oct-20,2011-Nov-02)->ActivityDuration: Review:[10,12,16;13]
)}
```

In general, it is possible to write complete applications of this sort using a combination of ICL, *date and time* and BGL. For example, the class ActivityDuration could be used as an edge descriptor if we decided to design the software system using the functionality in BGL.

18.7.1 Daily Planning

As a last example, we show how to use the class ptime from Boost date and time library to schedule the availability of members of a software team. The code is adapted from the ICL online documentation and it is useful because it can be applied in various contexts:

```
#include <iostream>
#include <string>

// Dynamically bounded intervals and time.
#include <boost/icl/ptime.hpp>
#include <boost/icl/interval_map.hpp>

using namespace std;
using namespace boost::icl;
using namespace boost::posix_time;

// Typedef for set of developers.
typedef std::set<string> Developers;

int main()
{
    // Create designers set.
    Developers designers;
    designers.insert("Wilfrid");
    designers.insert("Jan");

    // Create developers set.
    Developers coders;
    coders.insert("Pete");
    coders.insert("Clemens");

    // Create bosses set.
    Developers bosses;
    bosses.insert("Bill");

    // A team is an interval map that maps time intervals
    // to sets of designers.
    interval_map<ptime, Developers> team;

    // Add an element (coders) to the team.
    team.add(make_pair(
        interval<ptime>::right_open(time_from_string("2008-05-20 19:30"),
        time_from_string("2008-05-20 23:00")), coders));

    // Element addition can also be done via operator +=. Add designers.
    team += make_pair(
        interval<ptime>::right_open(time_from_string("2008-05-20 20:10"),
        time_from_string("2008-05-21 00:00")), designers);

    // Add bosses to the team.
```

```
team += make_pair(
    interval<ptime>::right_open(time_from_string("2008-05-20 22:15"),
    time_from_string("2008-05-21 00:30")), bosses);

cout << "----- Availability of design team -----" << endl;
interval_map<ptime, Developers>::iterator it = team.begin();
while (it != team.end())
{
    interval<ptime>::type when = it->first;

    // Who is in the team within the time interval 'when' ?
    Developers who = (*it++).second;
    cout << when << ": " << who << endl;
}

return 0;
}
```

The output from this code is:

```
----- Availability of design team -----
[2008-May-20 19:30:00,2008-May-20 20:10:00): {Clemens Pete }
[2008-May-20 20:10:00,2008-May-20 22:15:00): {Clemens Jan Pete Wilfrid }
[2008-May-20 22:15:00,2008-May-20 23:00:00): {Bill Clemens Jan Pete Wilfrid
}
[2008-May-20 23:00:00,2008-May-21 00:00:00): {Bill Jan Wilfrid }
[2008-May-21 00:00:00,2008-May-21 00:30:00): {Bill }
```

18.8 Summary and Conclusions

We gave a detailed overview of the ICL (Interval Container Library) that supports the creation and manipulation of intervals, interval sets and interval maps. ICL has applications to *Management Information Systems* (MIS) in which use cases such as scheduling and planning play a role. ICL can also be used with other Boost libraries such as BGL, date-time and Rational, for example.

19 Boost Functional Factory

19.1 Introduction and Objectives

In this chapter we introduce the Boost Functional Factory for dynamic and static object creation. This library is in fact the Boost implementation of the Gamma (GOF) *creational patterns* that are based on the object-oriented paradigm (see GOF 1995 for a detailed discussion of object-oriented design patterns). In general, creational patterns abstract the instantiation process. The advantage is that they allow developers to create systems that are independent of how its objects are created, composed and represented. In general, a *class creational pattern* uses inheritance to vary the class that is to be instantiated, while an *object creational pattern* delegates class instantiation to another object. The object creation process is an important part of the process of writing software because in general we need to create objects from a range of data sources. Furthermore, we achieve these ends by avoiding having to write too much boilerplate code. To this end, we compare the two competing approaches, namely the GOF object-oriented approach and the more generic approach as embodied in Boost Functional Factory.

19.2 An Overview of GOF Patterns

The origins of design patterns date back the 1980's and 1970's. It was not until 1995 that they were published by Eric Gamma and co-authors (GOF 1995). This influential book spurred interest in the application of design patterns to software development projects in C++ and Smalltalk.

The motivation for using design patterns originated from the work of the architect Christopher Alexander, who used the following description:

"Each pattern describes a problem which occurs over and over again in our environment, and then describes the core of the solution to that problem, in such a way that you can use this solution a millions times over, without ever doing the same way twice."

The authors have been working with design patterns since 1993 and they have applied them to various kinds of applications such as Computer Aided Design (CAD) and computer graphics, process control, real time and finance. Once you learn how a pattern works in a certain context you will find that it is easy to apply in new situations. The GOF patterns are applicable to objects and to this end they model *object lifecycle*, namely object creation, then the structuring of objects into larger configurations and finally modelling how objects communicate with each other using *message passing*. The main categories are:

- *Creational*: These patterns abstract the instantiation (*object creation*) process. The added-value of these patterns is that they ensure that an application can use objects without having to be concerned with *how* these objects are created, composed or internally represented. To this end, we create dedicated classes whose instances (objects) have the sole responsibility for creating other objects. In other words, instead of creating all our objects in `main()`, for example we can delegate object creation to dedicated *factory objects*. This approach promotes the *single responsibility principle*.

  The specific creational patterns are:
  - *Builder* (for complex objects).
  - *Factory Method* (define an interface for creating an object).
  - *Abstract Factory* (defines an interface for creating hierarchies of objects or families of related objects).
  - *Prototype* (create an object as a copy of some other object).
  - *Singleton* (create a class that has only one instance).

For more details on these and other patterns, we refer the reader to GOF 1995.

- *Structural*: These patterns compose classes and objects to form larger structures. We realise these new relationships by the appropriate application of modelling techniques such as *inheritance, association, aggregation* and *composition*.

  The specific structural patterns are:
  - *Composite* (recursive aggregates and tree structures).
  - *Adapter* (convert the interface of a class into another interface that clients expect).
  - *Facade* (define a unified interface to a system instead of having to access the objects in the system directly).
  - *Bridge* (a class that has multiple implementations).
  - *Decorator* (add additional responsibilities to an object at run-time).
  - *Flyweight* (an object that is shared among other objects).
  - *Proxy* (an object that is a surrogate/placeholder for another object to control access to it).

- *Behavioural*: These are patterns that are concerned with inter-object communication, in particular the implementation of algorithms and sharing of responsibilities between objects. They describe run-time control and data flow in an application. We can further partition these patterns as follows:
  - *Variations*: Patterns that customise the member functions in a class in some way. In general, these patterns externalise the code implementing these member functions. The main patterns are:
    - *Strategy* (families of interchangeable algorithms).
    - *Template Method* (define the skeleton of an algorithm in a base class; some variant steps are delegated to derived classes; common functionality is defined in the base class).
    - *Command* (encapsulate a request as an object; execute the command).
    - *State* (allows an object to change behaviour when its internal state changes). The Boost metastate machine library models state machines and it then subsumes the GOF State pattern.
    - *Iterator* (provide a means to access the elements of an aggregate object in a sequential way, without exposing its internal representation).

  - *Notifications*: These patterns define and maintain dependencies between objects:
    - *Observer* (define one-to-many dependency between a *publisher* object and its dependent *subscribers*).
    - *Mediator* (define an object that allows objects to communicate without being aware of each other; this pattern promotes *loose coupling*).
    - *Chain of Responsibility* (avoid coupling between *sender* and *receiver* objects when sending requests; give more than one object a chance to handle the request).

  - *Extensions*: Patterns that allow us to add new functionality (in the form of member functions) to classes and to classes in a class hierarchy. There is one such pattern in GOF:
    - *Visitor* (define an operation on the classes in a class hierarchy in a non-intrusive way).

There are some other, somewhat less important behavioural patterns in GOF 1995:

- *Memento* (capture and externalise an object's internal state so that it can be restored later).
- *Interpreter* (given a language, define a representation for its grammar and define an interpreter to interpret sentences in the language).

Which GOF patterns are useful when developing applications? An initial answer is that 20% of the patterns are responsible for 80% of developer productivity in our experience.

19.2.1 Strengths and Limitations of GOF Patterns

Design patterns are an essential tool in the software developer's toolbox in our opinion. They are based on the object-oriented paradigm that became popular in the 1990's. The GOF book is based on inheritance, composition and subtype polymorphism that languages such as C++, Java and C# support. The authors use them on a regular basis. However, GOF patterns are not a panacea for all software problems and it is important to know in which situations their use is sub-optimal or in which situations they do not function properly. We give a list of these limitations and we propose how to resolve them:

- GOF patterns are *micro-patterns*; they are not suitable as a tool for architectural or logical design. We resolve this shortcoming by first applying appropriate POSA patterns (for example, *Whole-Part* and *PAC*). The POSA patterns evolve naturally into GOF patterns. This is a process of *elaboration*.
- Support for other software paradigms: many textbooks describe and apply GOF patterns from a pure object-oriented perspective. But it is also possible to describe design patterns by posing them as *generic design patterns*. For example, we have created the following patterns as C++ template classes:
  - *Singleton<T>*.
  - *Composite<T>*.
  - *Command<Receiver, Action>*.

19.3 An Example: Traditional Windows Factories

We discuss the *Abstract Factory* design pattern (GOF 1995) that enables the creation of particular concrete objects depending on the situation at hand. It consists of an abstract base class with a `Create()` function that is implemented in one or more concrete subclasses. An example structure is shown in Figure 19.1 where factories are used to create GUI controls for Windows or HTML depending on the factory chosen.

We discuss an example of a client for the above control factories. Here the user is asked to choose a factory. Then the factory is used to create some controls which are added to a list. Smart pointers are used to ease memory management. First, we decide which factory to use:

```
// Typedef for STL list with controls using shared pointer.
typedef list<shared_ptr<Control> > ControlList;

// Ask for the type of factory to create.
cout<<"1. Windows controls\n2. HTML controls\nChoice: "<<endl;
int choice; cin>>choice;
```

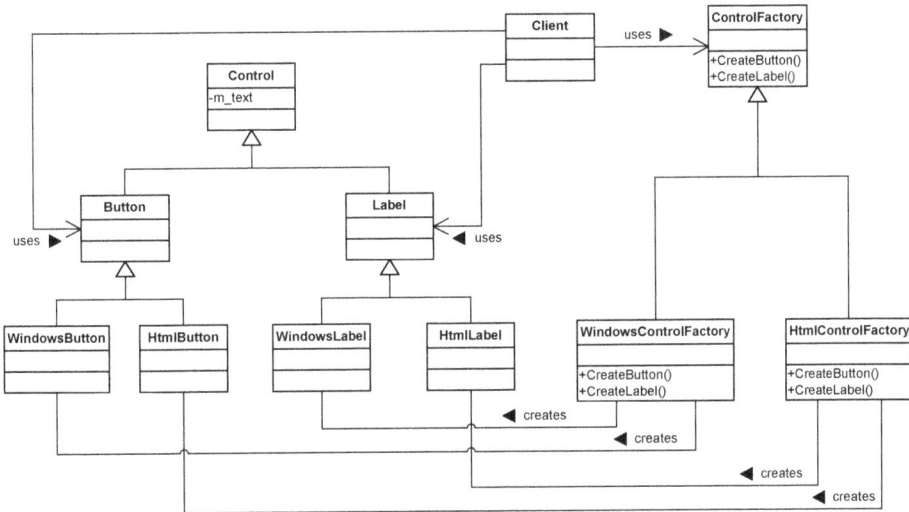

Figure 19.1 Traditional Factory Pattern Implementation

```
// Create a factory for controls depending on the user input.
shared_ptr<ControlFactory> factory;
if (choice==1)
{
    factory=shared_ptr<ControlFactory>(new WindowsControlFactory());
}
else if (choice==2)
{
    factory=shared_ptr<ControlFactory>(new HtmlControlFactory());
}
else return;
```

Now the factory creates some buttons and labels and we add these to a list of controls:

```
// Create a list for storing controls.
ControlList controls;

// Create some controls.
controls.push_back(shared_ptr<Control>(factory->CreateButton()));
controls.push_back(shared_ptr<Control>(factory->CreateLabel()));
controls.push_back(shared_ptr<Control>(factory->CreateLabel()));
controls.push_back(shared_ptr<Control>(factory->CreateButton()));
```

Finally, we display the controls in the list:

```
// Print the controls.
cout<<"Controls created:"<<endl;
for (ControlList::iterator it=controls.begin(); it!=controls.end(); it++)
{
    cout<<"- "<<**it<<endl;
}
```

The factory approach needs much *boiler-plate* code to achieve relatively simple functionality. We create factory subclasses that contain just a few lines of code. In some cases it is not as flexible as we would wish, for example when using several constructors with different arguments, creating objects on the stack instead of the heap and using custom allocators.

Boost Functional Factory provides a simpler alternative, needing just a few lines of code for
a new factory and without the need to create extra classes.
It encapsulates the creation of objects in a templated function object.

19.4 Boost Functional Factory

The `boost::factory` class is a function object to create objects on the heap:

```
#include <boost/functional/factory.hpp>

// Performs: new T(arg1, arg2, ..., argN)
boost::factory<T*>()(arg1, arg2, ..., argN);
```

Using the `boost::factory`, we can remove the factory classes from the example in
section 19.3 by using `boost::factory` instead. Here the constructed `boost::factory`
object is stored in a `boost::function` object so we can determine which factory to use at
runtime. Note that we need separate factory objects for each type of control (button/label) to
create. Thus, every `CreateXXX()` function of the GOF factory, is translated to a
`boost::factory` object, as the following code shows:

```
// Typedef for STL list with controls using shared pointer.
typedef list<shared_ptr<Control> > ControlList;

// Typedef for a boost::function that returns a control.
// Using this we don't need to decide at compile time the type of the
// factory but it can be done at run time.
typedef boost::function<Control*()> Factory;

// Ask for the type of factory to create.
cout<<"1. Windows controls\n2. HTML controls\nChoice: "<<endl;
int choice; cin>>choice;

// Create a factory for controls depending on the user input.
Factory buttonFactory, labelFactory;
if (choice==1)
{
    buttonFactory=boost::factory<WindowsButton*>();
    labelFactory=boost::factory<WindowsLabel*>();
}
else if (choice==2)
{
    buttonFactory=boost::factory<HtmlButton*>();
    labelFactory=boost::factory<HtmlLabel*>();
}
else return;

// Create a list for storing controls.
ControlList controls;

// Create some controls.
// Factories implement the function call operator() and the
// return type is a pointer to the appropriate object to be created.
controls.push_back(shared_ptr<Control>(buttonFactory()));
controls.push_back(shared_ptr<Control>(labelFactory()));
controls.push_back(shared_ptr<Control>(labelFactory()));
controls.push_back(shared_ptr<Control>(buttonFactory()));

// Print the controls.
cout<<"\nControls created (runtime factory):"<<endl;
for (ControlList::iterator it=controls.begin(); it!=controls.end(); it++)
{
    cout<<"- "<<**it<<endl;
```

```
    }
```

If we store the factory in a normal variable instead of a `boost::function` object, then we can only decide at compile-time which factory to use. But the advantage is that we can use all constructors of the control that we create without having to write additional code for the factory. For the GOF factory we would need to write a `Create()` function for each constructor that we wish to use. In this case we create buttons and labels by calling two different types of constructors:

```
// With compile-time decided factory (direct access instead
// via boost::function), we can also use other constructors.
#ifdef HTML_GUI
    boost::factory<HtmlButton*> bf; boost::factory<HtmlLabel*> lf;
#else
    boost::factory<WindowsButton*> bf; boost::factory<WindowsLabel*> lf;
#endif

controls.push_back(shared_ptr<Control>(bf()));
controls.push_back(shared_ptr<Control>(bf("My Button")));
controls.push_back(shared_ptr<Control>(lf()));
controls.push_back(shared_ptr<Control>(lf("My Label")));
```

The Boost factory frees us from having to create a factory class hierarchy. Furthermore, we can use all the constructors of a class to create objects. A disadvantage however, is that we need a `boost::factory` object for each type of object that we wish to create. In this example we have a separate factory for labels and a factory for buttons.

19.5 Function Factory with Smart Pointers

In the previous section we assigned the result of the factory to a smart pointer. However, the function factory can create smart pointers directly. In order to create objects including smart pointers we create the factory object with a smart pointer as template argument:

```
// Typedef for STL list with controls using shared pointer.
typedef list<shared_ptr<Control> > ControlList;

// Typedef for a boost::function that returns a control in a shared
// pointer. Using this we don't need to decide at compile time the type
// of the factory but it can be done at run time.
typedef boost::function<shared_ptr<Control>()> Factory;

// Create a factory for controls.
Factory buttonFactory, labelFactory;
buttonFactory=boost::factory<shared_ptr<WindowsButton> >();
labelFactory=boost::factory<shared_ptr<WindowsLabel> >();

// Create a list for storing controls.
ControlList controls;

// Create some controls.
controls.push_back(buttonFactory());
controls.push_back(labelFactory());
controls.push_back(labelFactory());
controls.push_back(buttonFactory());
```

Thus, when using a smart pointer as template argument the objects created by the factory are returned as smart pointer. Thus the user does not need to wrap the created object in a smart pointer.

19.6 R-Value Arguments

When the constructor of the object that the factory creates accepts a *value type* then the value passed must be an *l-value* (meaning that the lifetime of the argument must be longer than that of the function call). Thus anonymous objects cannot be passed directly and must be encapsulated with `boost::forward_adapter` or `boost::bind`.

We now try to create a button with an `int` as argument using the functional factory. We cannot pass a literal integer since that is an r-value. But we can pass an `int` variable or bind a literal value using `boost::bind`.

```
boost::factory<shared_ptr<WindowsButton> > buttonFactory;

// Error, 10 is r-value (Cannot convert parameter from 'int' to 'int&').
controls.push_back(buttonFactory(10));

// OK, i is l-value.
int i=10;
controls.push_back(buttonFactory(i));

// OK, r-value bound as l-value using bind.
controls.push_back(boost::bind(buttonFactory, _1)(10));
```

To summarise, when the constructor argument is a value type we can only pass l-values. In other words, the argument must then be a variable or bound using `boost::bind`.

19.7 Allocators

An added advantage of the Functional Factory library is that it can use *custom allocators*. Thus the memory for the objects created by the factory can be managed by the `boost::pool` library, for example. We discussed this library in chapter 14.

To use a different allocator we specify the allocator to use as second template argument for the factory. We show how to declare a factory for `WindowsButton` controls that use the `pool_allocator` of the boost Pool library:

```
buttonFactory=boost::factory<shared_ptr<WindowsButton>,
                    boost::pool_allocator<WindowsButton> >();
```

Firthermore, a third template argument can be passed that determines if the allocator is forwarded to the smart pointer:

- `factory_alloc_for_pointee_and_deleter`: The allocator is not forwarded to the smart pointer (default behaviour).
- `factory_passes_alloc_to_smart_pointer`: The allocator is passed to the smart pointer.

When the allocator is forwarded to the smart pointer then the smart pointer can also use the allocator to allocate its internal data such as its internal reference counter.

In the following code we declare two factories with custom allocators. The first factory does not forward the allocator to the smart pointer and the second factory does forward the allocator to the smart pointer:

```
buttonFactory=boost::factory<shared_ptr<HtmlButton>,
                    boost::pool_allocator<HtmlButton>,
                    factory_alloc_for_pointee_and_deleter>();
```

```
labelFactory=boost::factory<shared_ptr<HtmlLabel>,
                 boost::pool_allocator<HtmlLabel>,
                 factory_passes_alloc_to_smart_pointer>();
```

The allocator option allows us to choose the best memory management algorithm in a given context. In this sense we see that the memory management of the Boost Functional Factory is more flexible than that of the standard GOF factory patterns.

19.8 Value Factory

The `boost::factory` creates objects on the heap. In some cases we need to create objects on the stack. In these cases we can use the `boost::value_factory` class:

```
#include <boost/functional/value_factory.hpp>

// Performs: T(arg1, arg2, ..., argN)
boost::value_factory<T>()(arg1, arg2, ..., argN);
```

The `value_factory` has one template argument, namely the type to create. It can be used to decide at compile time which type to create, for example a Windows or HTML control:

```
// Determine at compile time the value factory to use.
#ifdef HTML_GUI
    typedef boost::value_factory<HtmlButton> ButtonFactory;
    typedef boost::value_factory<HtmlLabel> LabelFactory;
#else
    typedef boost::value_factory<WindowsButton> ButtonFactory;
    typedef boost::value_factory<WindowsLabel> LabelFactory;
#endif

// Create the value factories.
ButtonFactory buttonFactory;
LabelFactory labelFactory;

// Create controls on the stack using a value factory and print them.
PrintControl(buttonFactory());
PrintControl(labelFactory());
PrintControl(buttonFactory("My Button"));
PrintControl(labelFactory("My Label"));
```

where the `PrintControl()` function is defined as follows:

```
// Print a control.
void PrintControl(const Control& control)
{
    cout<<"Control: "<<control<<endl;
}
```

In the above example the object created is directly passed to a function that accepts a base class reference. However, it is not necessary to use polymorphic functionality. Both the `factory` and `value_factory` have a nested `result_type` that can be used to declare variables for the created type without the need to know which type is to be created. This enables us to determine the type to create at compile time and use its functionality without the need for polymorphic functions or base classes. This improves run-time performance.
We now use the value factory from the previous example to declare a variable for the created type without having to know if a Windows or HTML control is created.

```
// Using the factory's result type we can declare variables.
ButtonFactory::result_type button=buttonFactory("Test Button");
LabelFactory::result_type label=labelFactory("Test Label");
```

```
button.DialogResult(0);
label.Text("New Label");
```

We saw that by using the `value_factory` we can create the objects on the stack, something that is not possible with the standard GOF factory. Furthermore, when using the `result_type` of the boost functional factory, we can get polymorphic behaviour without the need to have base classes and virtual functions. The disadvantage is that we can only determine at compile-time which factory to use.

19.9 Factory with Algorithms

The functional factory is a function object. This means that it can also be used with algorithms having a function object without input arguments but having a return value. An example of this is the `std::generate()` algorithm.

We give an example that uses the `std::generate()` algorithm with functional factory to fill a vector with default buttons.

```
// Typedef for STL list with controls using shared pointer.
typedef vector<shared_ptr<Control> > ControlVector;

// Typedef for a boost::function that returns a control
// in a shared pointer.
// Using this we don't need to decide at compile time the type of
// the factory but it can be done at run time.
typedef boost::function<shared_ptr<Control>()> Factory;
Factory buttonFactory;

buttonFactory=boost::factory<shared_ptr<WindowsButton> >();

// Create a vector for storing controls.
ControlVector controls(3);

// Fill the vector with default buttons.
generate(controls.begin(), controls.end(), buttonFactory);
```

19.10 Summary and Conclusions

We have seen that Functional Factory can be used to implement the *Factory Pattern* without having to write a factory class hierarchy. In combination with `boost::function` we can decide at run-time which factory to use. An additional benefit is that Functional Factory is easily combined with smart pointers and custom allocators. And it is possible to use the factory as function object to algorithms.

Finally, we saw that when using the nested `result_type` of the factory, we can use the created objects without the need for a base class and virtual functions. Thus we can create flexible software (at compile time) while avoiding the overhead of subtype polymorphism.

Bibliography

Alefeld, G. and Mayer, G. 2000 *Interval analysis: theory and applications Journal of Computational and Applied Mathematics* 121 421 – 464.

Coplien, J. 1992 *Advanced C++ Programming Styles and Idioms* Addison Wesley.

Dahlquist, G. Å. Björck 1974 *Numerical Methods* Prentice Hall, Inc.

Date, C. 1981 *An Introduction to Data-base Systems* Addison Wesley.

Demming, R. and Duffy D.J. 2010 *Introduction to the Boost C++ Libraries; Volume I – Foundations* Datasim Press

Duffy, D.J. 1995 *From Chaos to Classes* McGraw-Hill.

Duffy, D.J. 2004 *Financial instrument pricing using C++* John Wiley & Sons.

Duffy, D.J. 2004A *Domain Architectures; Models and Architectures for UML Applications* John Wiley & Sons.

Duffy, D.J. 2006 *Finite difference methods in financial engineering* John Wiley & Sons.

GOF 1995 Gamma, E., Helm, R., Johnson, R. and Vlissides, J. *Design Patterns: Abstraction and Reuse of Object-Oriented Design* Addison Wesley.

Isaacson, E. and Keller, H.B. 1966 *Analysis of Numerical Methods* Dover.

Josuttis, N. M. 1999 *The C++ Sandard Library* Addison Wesley Boston.

Knuth, D. 1997 *The Art of Computer Programming Volume I* Addison-Wesley.

Krylov, V.I. 2005 *Approximate Calculation of Integrals* Dover.

MacCluer C. R. 2004 *Boundary Value Problems And Fourier Expansions*, Dover Publications.

Mattson, T.G., Sanders, B. A., Massingill, B. L. 2005 *Patterns for Parallel Programming* Addison Wesley.

Moore, R. E. (1966). *Interval Analysis* Englewood Cliffs.

Parmakian, J. 1963 *Waterhammer Analysis* Dover Publications.

POSA 1996 Buschmann, F., Meunier, R., Rohnert, H., Sommerlad, P. and Stal, M. *Pattern-Oriented Software Architecture* John Wiley & Sons.

Press, W. H., Teukolsky, S. A., Vetterling, W. T. and Flannery, B. P. 2002 *Numerical Recipes in C++* Cambridge University Press.

Siek, J.G., Lee, L. and Lumsdaine, A. 2002 *The Boost Graph Library* Addison-Wesley.

Rogerson, D. 1997 *Inside COM* Microsoft Press.

van de Riet, R.P. 1964 *A computational method for the water hammer problem* Mathematisch Centrum Amsterdam.

Index

Book Registration Form – Boost Volume II

In order to receive the source code for this book please fill in the original (**not a copy**) registration form and send it to:

Datasim Education BV
't Veer 1
1832 AK Koedijk
The Netherlands

Do not lose this form as we cannot accept copies.

Name: ....

Title: ....

Company: ....

Address: ....

City: ....

Postal Code: ....

Country: ....

Email-address*: ....

Terms:
I agree that this code is for my own personal use and ownership cannot be transferred. I also accept the user terms of the User Agreement.

☐ Keep me informed on new developments

* We need your e-mail address in order to send you the source code.

User Agreement

The following terms govern use of the book 'An Introduction to the C++ Boost Libraries – Volume II – Advanced Libraries', by Robert Demming and Daniel J. Duffy, ISBN 978-94-91028-02-1 and its accompanied software and code examples (the *product*).

a) The entire contents of the *product* are protected by copyright.

b) You may not copy, distribute, transmit or otherwise reproduce material from the *product* in any form or media other than for your own personal use.
This is not meant to prohibit quotations for purposes of comment, criticism or similar scholarly purposes.

c) The *product* may provide links to third party websites. Where such links exist, Datasim Education BV disclaims all responsibility and liability for the content of such third party websites. Users assume the sole responsibility for the accessing of third party websites and the use of any content appearing on such websites.

d) You may compile, test and run the provided code examples and they may serve as inspiration for software you create. But code examples are provided for educational reasons only and should not used 'as is' in production software. They come without any warranty and usage is on your own risk.

e) The *product* is provided on an 'as is' basis, without warranties of any kind. The use of the material in the *product* is on your own risk. Neither Datasim Education BV nor anyone else involved in creating the *product* shall be liable for any direct or indirect damages arising from using the *product* or the inability to use the *product*.

f) The user accepts and agrees to the terms above and accepts and agrees that the information provided is intended as general information only and does not provide any substitute for advice from a qualified professional.

www.ingramcontent.com/pod-product-compliance
Lightning Source LLC
Chambersburg PA
CBHW081338190326
41458CB00018B/6045